THE POWER OF PROBLEM SOLVING

RELATED TITLES OF INTEREST

Starting Early with Study Skills: A Week-by-Week Guide for Elementary Students
Judith L. Irvin and Elaine O. Rose
Order No. H39431
0-205-13943-4

The New Sourcebook for Teaching Reasoning and Problem Solving in Elementary School
Stephen Krulik and Jesse A. Rudnick
Order No. H48267
0-205-14826-3

Self-Talk for Teachers and Students: Metacognitive Strategies for Personal and Classroom Use
Brenda H. Manning and Beverly D. Payne
Order No. H59488
0-205-15948-6

The Integrated Technology Classroom: Building Self-Reliant Learners
Joan Riedl
Order No. H61575
0-205-16157-X

Cooperative Learning: Theory, Research, and Practice, Second Edition
Robert E. Slavin
Order No. H56302
0-205-15630-4

The Thinking Classroom: Learning and Teaching in a Culture of Thinking
Shari Tishman, David N. Perkins, and Eileen Jay
Order No. H65089
0-205-16508-7

THE POWER OF PROBLEM SOLVING

Practical Ideas and Teaching Strategies for Any K–8 Subject Area

Juanita S. Sorenson
University of Wisconsin–Eau Claire

Lynn R. Buckmaster
Madison, Wisconsin, Metropolitan School District

Mary Kay Francis
Chippewa Falls, Wisconsin, Area Unified School District

Karen M. Knauf
Eden Prairie, Minnesota, Schools

Allyn and Bacon
Boston   London   Toronto   Sydney   Tokyo   Singapore

Copyright © 1996 by Allyn & Bacon
A Simon & Schuster Company
Needham Heights, Massachusetts 02194

All rights reserved. No part of the material protected by this copyright
notice may be reproduced or utilized in any form or by any means, electronic
or mechanical, including photocopying, recording, or by any information
storage and retrieval system, without written permission from the
copyright owner.

Library of Congress Cataloging-in-Publication Data

The power of problem solving : practical ideas and teaching strategies
  for any K–8 subject area / Juanita S. Sorenson . . . [et al.].
     p.   cm.
  Includes bibliographical references and indexes.
  ISBN 0-205-15943-5
  1. Problem solving—Study and teaching.   I. Sorenson, Juanita S.
LB1590.3.P67   1996
370.15′2—dc 20   95-12679
                                                                 CIP

Printed in the United States of America
10 9 8 7 6 5 4 3 2 1   99 98 97 96 95

We dedicate this book to our spouses and children

Douglas Sorenson
Dale Buckmaster
Raymond and Kirsten Francis
Lee, Chelsea, and Bradley Knauf

who helped and encouraged us during the writing process.

Contents

Preface   xv

Chapter 1   Why Solve Problems?   1

Why Is Problem Solving Important?   1
   All Students Must Be Able to Solve Problems   2
   Recommendations for Teaching Problem Solving in the Curriculum   3
   Social, Political, and Economic Influences on Educational Change   3
Problems and Problem Solving   5
   Defining the Parameters   5
   Types of Problems   6
   Problem Solving As a Part of the Curriculum   7
Clues to Success and Failure in Problem Solving   8
   Stumbling Blocks to Problem Solving   8
   Characteristics of Good Problem Solvers   9
   Strategies of Good Teachers of Problem Solving   10
Problem Solving Is a Powerful Learning Tool: An Overview   10
Summary   11
References   11

Chapter 2   Thinking Skills and Problem Solving   13

Content: The Knowledge Base   14
   Selecting Content   15
   Organizing Content   16
   Forming Concepts   16
   Analyzing Concepts   17
   Teaching Concepts   17
Process: Thinking Skills Groups   19
   Inquiry Processes   20
   Creative Thinking Processes   23
   Critical Thinking Skills   26
   Single-Step Problem-Solving Techniques   28
   Bloom's Cognitive Levels   31

Process: Multistep Problem Solving   32
    Guidelines for Problem Solving   32
    Ways to Solve Different Kinds of Problems   34
Products: Applications of Learning   39
    Real Problems   40
    Real Audiences   42
    Real Evaluations   42
Environment: A Support System for Learning   43
    Physical Sites   43
    Human Resources   44
    Teaching Styles   45
    Student Learning Styles   47
    Student Characteristics   48
    Technology   48
Strategies for Teaching and Assessing Problem Solving   50
    Practical Teaching Strategies   50
    Ways to Assess Thinking and Problem Solving   51
Resources for Teaching Thinking Skills and Problem Solving   53
    Kinds of Resources   53
    Sources of Resources   55
Summary   55
References   55

Chapter 3   Challenging Primary-Level Problem Solvers   57

The Problem-Solving Classroom   57
    Students Should Take Risks and Try Different Strategies   58
    Students Need to Challenge Themselves and Not Fear Failure   58
Strategies for Successful Problem Solving   59
    Prepare Your Students to Spend Time on a Problem   59
    Let Students Know That It Is OK to Feel Frustrated or Anxious   59
    Model Metacognition   60
    Make Problem Solving a Join Effort   60
    Let Students Experience the Joy of the "Aha!" Moment   60
Ways to Integrate Problem Solving into Your Classroom   60
    Consider Student Learning Styles   60
    Group Students in Many Ways   61
    Organize Your Curriculum for Interdisciplinary Teaching   61
    Help Students Learn and Master Basic Content   61
Planning for Problem Solving   62
    Revising a Successful Unit   62
    Building a New Unit   65
    Party Planning: An Opportunity to Practice Problem Solving   68
Problem Solving in Action in the Primary Classroom   70
    Focusing on Inference and Deduction   71
    Grouping Things Together   72
    Learning How to Experiment   75
    Blowing Bubbles Goes Beyond Fun and Games   76

Assessment in the Primary Classroom   79
    Teacher Observation   79
    Student Journals   79
    Peer Teaching   80
    Student Portfolios   80
    Paper-and-Pencil Tests   81
    Performance Assessments   82
    Projects   83
Discovering Dinosaurs: An Interdisciplinary Unit for Primary Students   84
    Lesson One: Every Footprint Tells a Story   86
    Lesson Two: Open Up Your Dinofile   87
    Lesson Three: Dinosaur Scavenger Hunt   88
    Lesson Four: I Dig Dinosaurs!   90
    Lesson Five: Bone Up On Dinosaurs   91
    Lesson Six: A Dinosaur By Any Other Name . . .   94
    Lesson Seven: Whatever Happened to My Old Friend, Dino?   95
    Lesson Eight: Debatable Dinosaurs   97
    Lesson Nine: Working in a Dinosaur Museum   98
    Lesson Ten: Extension Activities   99
Summary   100
References   100

Chapter 4   An Interdisciplinary Approach to Problem Solving at the Intermediate Level   101

Students Love Interdisciplinary Learning   101
Preparing for Successful Teaching: Ten Basic Elements   102
    Unit Overview   102
    Instructional Objectives   102
    Resources   103
    Activities for Students   103
    Authentic Products   103
    Learning Environments   104
    Opportunities to Use Thinking Skills and Problem Solving   104
    Instructional Grouping   105
    Timeline and Budget   105
    Assessment Considerations   106
Reaching Beyond the Classroom   106
    There's No Place Like Home   106
    It's a Jungle Out There: A Trip to the Zoo   112
Communicating with People   120
    "And Now A Word from Your Sponsor . . ."   121
    "Sincerely Yours"   128
It's a Mystery to Me   136
    Setting the Stage to Teach Mysteries   136
    Investigating Mysteries: More Than Eighty Activities and Ideas   138
    Looking at Where, What, and How Well   140
Summary   140
References   141

Chapter 5 Problem Solving: The Perfect Match for Middle Schoolers 142

Why Problem Solving and Middle Schoolers Go Together   143
The Problem-Solving Classroom   144
    Teacher Attitudes and Behaviors Set the Stage   144
    Environments to Promote Learning   145
    Creativity Is the Key to Success   146
    Creative Techniques that Work in the Classroom   146
The Future Problem Solving (FPS) Program   149
    FPS: The Six-Step Process   149
    Benefits of FPS   153
    Techniques to Enhance the FPS Process   153
    Teambuilding and Teamwork   156
    Options for Implementation   158
    Additional Components of the FPS Program   158
    Evaluating the Program   160
Interdisciplinary Units Generate Student Interest   161
    Jam and Peas on Rye . . . Hold the Mustard!   161
    U.S. Trip Plan   164
Social Studies Doesn't Have to Be Deadly   167
    Survival of the Fittest   167
    Create a Country   170
The Power of Positive Argumentation   173
    Why Argumentation?   173
    The Argumentation Format   174
    Getting Started Using a Sample Argument   175
    Analyzing the Argument   177
    Exploring the Issues   177
    Planning the Arguments   177
    Presentation of Arguments   179
    Evaluating the Unit   180
Summary   181
References   181

Chapter 6 Model Problem-Solving Programs 182

Creative Problem Solving with an Interdisciplinary Twist   182
    Gulf Gate Elementary School, Sarasota County, Florida, Public Schools   182
    Setting Goals and Getting Started   183
    Staff Communicated with Parents and Community   185
    Action Plans Bring Thinking and Problem Solving to the Students   187
Thinking About Thinking and Problem Solving   189
    Lincoln Elementary School, Community Unit District 205, Elmhurst, Illinois   189
    Supporting the Program with Staff Development   190
    Communicating with Parents and Community   191
    Developing and Teaching Interdisciplinary Units of Instruction   192

Keeping the Program Alive and Well   194
Start Solving Problems at the Primary Level   195
   San Marcos, Texas, Independent School District   195
   Elements of the Program   196
   Foundations of the Program   196
   Kindergarten Level   197
   First-Grade Level   197
   Second-Grade Level   198
   Results of the Program   202
Technology Provides the Base for a Quality Communications School   202
   Eastern Middle School, Montgomery County, Maryland, Public Schools (MCPS)   202
   Teaming Facilitates the Use of Technology   203
   Technology Integrates with Interdisciplinary Curriculum   204
   Technology Supports, Motivates, and Enhances Learning   205
   Staff Development Is Crucial to Program Success   207
   Results of the Program   208
Problem-Based Learning "Turns Kids On"   209
   Merwin Elementary School, West Clermont County, Ohio, Public Schools   209
   Experiences as Producers and Consumers   210
   Invention Convention   212
   More Problem-Solving Projects   213
   Parents and Community Are Vital to Success   215
Summary   215
References   215

Chapter 7   Effective Staff Development   216

Rationale for Staff Development   216
   Why Is Staff Development Important?   216
   Stumbling Blocks to Staff Development   217
   How Can We Improve Staff Development?   218
   Needs of Teachers as Learners   219
   Characteristics of Successful Staff Development Programs   220
Roles in Staff Development   220
   Teachers   221
   Principals   222
   Administrators and Policy Makers   224
   Students   224
   Parents   225
   College and University Personnel and "Expert" Consultants   225
   Service and Community Groups   225
   School Support Staff   226
Staff Development Structures and Strategies   226
   Frameworks and Delivery Systems   226
   What Research Tells Us   227
   Teaching and Learning Strategies   228
   Peer Coaching   228

Successful Staff Development Programs 230
    Relating Teacher Needs to Staff Development 230
    Overview of Models and Programs 231
    The RPTIM Model for Staff Development 232
A Sample Staff Development Program to Infuse Thinking Skills and Problem Solving into the Curriculum 234
    Planning the Program—Stage 1 235
    Training the Staff—Stage 2 236
    Implementing the Program with Students—Stage 3 243
    Maintaining the Program—Stage 4 243
Resources for Staff Development 244
    Print Materials 244
    Videotapes and Packets 244
Summary 245
References 245

Appendix 247
    A Dictionary of Eighty Ideas for Creative Products 249
    Resources for Teaching Thinking Skills and Problem Solving 251
        General References for Teachers 251
        Resources for Student Activities 251
        Catalogues for Thinking Skills and Problem-Solving Materials 252
    Cryptoquotes 253
    Enrichment Opportunities at Your Fingertips 254
        Community Enrichment 254
        School Enrichment 255
        Summer Academic Experiences 255
        Individual or Small-Group Work at Home or in School 255
        References for Information on Enrichment 255
        References for Further Exploration, Catalogues and Directories 258
    U.S. Trip Plan 259
        Instructions 259
        Daily Log 260
        Daily Costs 261
        How to Calculate Gas Costs 262
        Total Costs 262
    Survival Skills 263
        Survival Quiz and Answer Key 263
        Project Instructions Sheet 265
        Survival Kit 266
        Survival Project: Social Studies Challenge 266
        Survival Project: Book Review 267
        Survival Project: Building a Model Shelter 267
    Create a Country 269
        Project Format 269
    Argumentation 270
        Guide 270
        Worksheet 271
        Example Student Argument 1 272

Example Student Argument 2   273

Author Index   275

Subject Index   277

Preface

Awesome! Wow! Cool! Neat! Aha, I've got it! Let's try another one! These exclamations from students are "music" to teachers' ears. They show that students are really involved in learning and relish it at the same time. Giving students opportunities to think and solve problems independently is the best way to help them enjoy learning. These same skills bring personal success in school, in the workplace, and in everyday life.

This book is about how to teach and guide students, grades K–8, to solve problems in all subject matter areas of the curriculum. It is based on the belief that all primary, intermediate, and middle level students can be successful problem solvers if they learn the necessary skills and strategies and have time to practice them. Once they have been successful at solving problems, they will want to do it again.

The authors had two goals in writing this book: (1) sharing practical ideas and strategies they use in their classrooms, and (2) providing background information teachers need "to make thinking and problem solving happen." To meet the first goal, they have described more than 300 hands-on, problem-based activities for students in Chapters 3, 4, 5, and 6. Challenging units for primary-level students are the focus of Chapter 3. Topics that emphasize math and science include focusing on inference and deduction, blowing bubbles, grouping things together, and learning how to experiment. A unique, interdisciplinary unit about dinosaurs is the highlight of this chapter.

Chapter 4 deals with advertising techniques, historical homes, writing different kinds of letters, a trip to the zoo, and a myriad of mystery topics for intermediate students. Language arts and social studies are emphasized, but integrated with art, science, math, and performance. In Chapter 5, middle-level students create a sandwich, design a model country, develop survival skills, vicariously take a trip across the United States, and practice the power of positive argumentation. Elements of the Future Problem Solving (FPS) program are often used in these units.

The role of the teacher as guide and resource person rather than as "teller of information" is illustrated throughout these three chapters. Learning environments such as teaching and learning styles, grouping patterns, learning sites and resources beyond the classroom, and technologies are varied according to the topics and the age and grade level of the students. Thinking skills and problem solving are applied to produce real products for real audiences.

"The proof of the pudding is in the eating." This relates to schools, too. Chapter 6 explores approaches that schools and districts with diverse populations in different parts of the country have used to integrate thinking and problem solving into their curriculums. The discussions focus on units of instruction, staff development strategies, parents and community, and keeping their programs "alive and well."

The second goal of the book is to provide background information. A rationale for teaching problem solving is developed in Chapter 1. Here, educators, politicians, and business and industry leaders cite problem solving as the most important survival skill for the twenty-first century. Reasons why problem solving has been considered difficult for both teachers and students and ways to change that attitude are also discussed.

"We cannot teach well what we do not know and understand." Teachers and other staff need a strong knowledge base about thinking skills and problem solving. In Chapter 2, five groups of thinking skills are explained and illustrated with practical examples. Then, a model to help students solve multistep problems is described and its use is illustrated in three different situations: everyday living, a science experiment for intermediate students, and a social studies dilemma for middle-level students. Thinking skills and problem solving, as process, are related to content, product, and environment. No new terms or strategies are invented. Instead, the emphasis is on ways students can use thinking skills and problem solving in all subject matter areas.

Staff development is the topic of Chapter 7. The discussion accentuates realistic and practical approaches, roles of school personnel, and characteristics of successful programs. A feature of the chapter is an outline of a 60-hour training program to help teachers and other staff infuse thinking skills and problem solving into their curriculum.

This book with its hundreds of practical, hands-on ideas and detailed background information is designed for two main groups of readers: practicing teachers in all subject matter areas, grades K–8; and preservice teachers in college and university programs. Administrators, coordinators, and university instructors will also find it useful. Throughout the book, the authors take a straight forward, no-nonsense approach. They also suggest that teachers can teach thinking skills and problem solving without expensive materials or elaborate equipment.

The four authors bring a variety of educational and personal experiences to their writing. They have taught at the primary, intermediate, middle school, high school, and university levels. They earned graduate degrees in a variety of specialties, and have developed and directed programs for students at all levels. But most of all, they love to teach and interact with "kids of all ages."

J. S. S.

THE POWER OF PROBLEM SOLVING

CHAPTER 1

Why Solve Problems?

Problem solving has been a survival skill for individuals, humans, families, communities, and countries from the time of cave dwellers to the present. Failure to solve important problems successfully has meant death, extinction, war, recession, and mediocrity. Today, we have a global economy that brings a constant array of problems to the workplace and the marketplace. And, technology brings a never-ending stream of new knowledge and change to every individual person, organization, and institution. This increasing demand to solve problems requires our educational system to produce people who are well prepared to deal with their world.

Problem solving is not new to our educational system. We have always dealt with problems in math—structured problems, puzzle problems, and those sometimes-dreaded word problems. Science, in the post-*Sputnik* era, advocated the "process approach," which emphasized thinking skills and problem solving. This approach was also called "discovery learning" or "inquiry learning." Many of these process-oriented programs were well intended and well designed. But too often, their execution was a failure for both the students and the teachers. Problem solving was identified less often in social studies and language arts, but was included in the discussions, assignments, and projects of good teachers.

Many people remember problem solving as an unpleasant school experience where they blindly fought their way through the problems in assignments without much help from the teacher or the textbook. The example problem in the text was usually easy and dealt with only one or two variables. When students tried to work more complex problems, they were "lost." Teachers often provided little guidance. They relied heavily on the solution in the famed "answer book," which they guarded carefully. Many teachers seemed uncomfortable with teaching problem solving. Did they lack in knowledge of ways to solve problems as well as strategies to teach problem solving to their students? Also, since problem solving was not a favorite task of many teachers, class time to carry it out was often cut short or omitted.

Sometimes middle and high school students who were fascinated with solving problems formed their own groups and helped each other—seeking to verify their solutions with those of the teacher's answer book. Here, too much emphasis was placed on the answer rather than on how they arrived at it, but they learned a lot from interacting with each other.

These scenarios have repeated themselves again and again over the past five decades in the United States. Yet enough students had good teachers or somehow taught themselves how to solve problems as they progressed through the educational system to fill the job market for engineers, mathematicians, computer scientists, and other occupations with strong demands for problem-solving skills. Today the world has changed. People in all jobs need to be able to solve problems.

The remainder of this chapter focuses on why problem solving is important in the school curriculum, definitions of problems and problem solving, what determines success and failure in solving problems, and an overview of the topics in this book. Discussions focus on students and teachers at the primary, intermediate, and middle school levels. Practical approaches to problem solving in all subject matter areas and everyday living for all students are emphasized.

WHY IS PROBLEM SOLVING IMPORTANT?

Since the 1970s, the achievement scores of American students have fared poorly in comparisons with students in other industrialized nations of the world, particularly in higher-level thinking and problem solving. Their scores have also lagged behind those of American students of the 1950s and 1960s. Newspaper headlines provide some flavor to these happenings: "Johnny Can't Read!" " Nearly 2000 and Johnny Can't Do Math?" " U.S. Schools Get Failing Marks" "Poorly Educated Workforce" "U.S. Students Can't Solve Problems." The examples go on and on.

Reasons for these negative trends have been explained in many ways: a changing student population now comes from diverse backgrounds; English is a second language for immigrant students; a larger percent of high school students are taking college admission tests than in earlier decades; the curriculum is not as rigorous as it should be; current teaching methods do not meet the needs and personal characteristics of today's students; we are not using technology effectively in our schools. Reasons are endless. But the fact remains that today's students are tomorrow's workers and they will not be prepared to compete in the world unless changes in education are made promptly and effectively.

All Students Must Be Able to Solve Problems

The scores of the upper 10 percent of American students compare favorably with those of other countries, but that is not enough. We need new ways to educate all of our students. Helping them learn how to think and solve problems is one important way to provide individuals with both intellectual and psychological success.

Solving Problems Successfully Is Crucial in a Global Workplace. American workers need problem-solving skills to survive in a world economy. Robert Reich (1993), U.S. secretary of labor, has emphasized that our educational system has been "the best" in preparing students for higher education and "the worst" in providing vocational education. He reiterated the alarming trend that students with a high school diploma are doomed to a future of downward mobility with an increasing earnings gap between those with advanced education and those without. He called bridging this gap a priority for our government in the 1990s and identified four elements as the most important knowledge and skills for the future. They are (1) "learning how to learn; " (2) being able to think creatively; (3) being able to solve problems successfully; and (4) being able to work as a team member.

Solving Problems Is Personally Satisfying. Finding a solution to a difficult problem provides a "mental high" to the person(s) involved. This probably happens because we reach a successful solution when three sets of mental processes—experience factors, affective factors, and cognitive factors—interact with appropriate balance (Charles & Lester, 1982, pp. 10–12). *Experience factors* include age, previous background in the subject matter of the problems (e.g., math, science, social studies, language arts), familiarity with ways to arrive at solutions, and familiarity with the problem context and content. *Affective factors* include tolerance for ambiguity, interest in the problem, levels of motivation, pressure, anxiety, stress, perseverance, and resistance to getting a quick answer. *Cognitive factors* (for example, in solving a math problem) are memory, computational skill, ability in reading, and spatial, analytical, and logical abilities.

Solving Problems Encourages Independent Learning. The ability to solve problems successfully allows individuals to become independent learners. This is important not only in school, but in the workplace where additional training and retraining occurs with considerable frequency over a worker's lifetime. It is important, too, because we are being bombarded with so much new knowledge that people who do not have the ability to learn independently will not be able to adapt to their ever-changing roles.

Solving Problems Enhances Success in School. The ability to solve problems successfully is an underlying factor for success in school, K–university. Problem solving at some difficulty level has traditionally been a part of the mathematics and science curriculum and is rapidly becoming a factor in social studies, language arts, physical education, and the arts. Interdisciplinary curriculum and technology enhance opportunities for teachers to challenge students to solve problems at all levels of difficulty according to their needs and abilities. Learning facts and learning for understanding is enhanced by several factors including "*problem-based learning,* where students study content by seeking out the information they need to solve the problem; *project-based learning,* where students gain content knowledge through complex, often socially meaningful projects; *use of authentic problems* that have real-world significance and a messy open-ended character; and *infusion of critical and creative thinking into subject matter instruction* where students analyze, critique, defend, ask what-if questions, and explore alternative points of view" (Perkins, 1993–1994, p. 84).

Solving Problems Is Vital to a Democratic Society. The ability to think and solve problems is essential for Americans as citizens and as fully functioning individuals. These skills define our very existence as a country and as a world leader. In 1993, Ralph Tyler, one of the most influential American educators of the twentieth century, said, "Schools in America should seek to develop problem-solving citizens who can actively engage in the work of a democratic society" (Hiatt, 1994, p. 786). In addition, people who can solve their personal and everyday problems and interact effectively with others are better prepared to live a meaningful and happy life.

Many reasons for a citizenry that is skilled in thinking and problem solving have been cited. These have also have been brought to the attention of citizens, business leaders, educators, politicians, and others by all avenues of the media. Representatives from these groups will be involved in reforming education at the local, state, and national levels under the *Goals 2000 Educate America Act* of 1994. Details of this legislation are discussed later in this chapter.

Recommendations for Teaching Problem Solving in the Curriculum

National curriculum organizations representing teachers of math, science, language arts, and social studies have reflected the need to develop students who can think and solve problems in their "agendas for the 90s." Their improvement and renewal efforts have emphasized five common elements (O'Neil, 1990, pp. 1, 8):

1. An explosion of information in all disciplines makes it impractical to emphasize content at the expense of process and other indepth learning.
2. Curriculum must become more efficient by cutting down needless review.
3. The emphasis on transmission of facts from teacher to student must be replaced by curriculums that support students' abilities to think critically and creatively to solve problems—to become active learners.
4. Rigid boundaries between the disciplines should be softened and disciplines should be connected together through interdisciplinary learning.
5. It is no longer acceptable to offer worthwhile content to advanced students and a mishmash of endless review to the rest. Overall, we need to offer a solid common core of learning to all students with provision for enrichment, acceleration, and special assistance to those who need it.

The National Council of Teachers of Mathematics (NCTM) led the way among professional organizations by making specific recommendations to improve the *mathematics* curriculum. They developed a set of K–12 standards that called for teachers to emphasize problem solving, mathematical reasoning, real-world applications, communication about mathematics, and the use of manipulatives and technology. These standards were prompted in part by recent data that three-fourths of all students leave school without taking enough math to satisfy college or career prerequisites and that only about 6 percent of American 17-year-olds can solve math problems that require multiple steps or the use of algebra.

NCTM suggested further that students need to experience genuine problems regularly, instruction should persistently emphasize "doing" rather than "knowing," and that experience with real-world problems helps students develop the ability to compute. In addition, all students should have access to computers and a strong core program with some variations for college-bound students (Willis, 1992, p. 3).

Professional organizations in science, language arts, and social studies also emphasized active learning (ASCD Curriculum Update, 1990, pp. 2–7). The National Science Teachers Association (NSTA) stressed "hands on" experiences in science. They also indicated that students are more likely to learn science if they explore natural phenomena directly, pose their own questions, design their own experiments, and discuss their results with others. In *language arts*, the National Council of Teachers of English (NCTE) suggested that students should be "active" learners where they are encouraged to develop and test hypotheses on their own. This includes a process approach to writing. The National Commission on Social Studies in the Schools wants teachers to use geography and history as background subjects in *social studies*. They also suggest that they deal with problems related to these subject areas and other subdisciplines of social studies for products and projects in assignments.

Social, Political, and Economic Influences on Educational Change

American business and industry have traditionally influenced what goes on in the public school curriculum. In the 1990s, that trend has intensified. Today's workplace wants workers—both those entering the work force directly and those seeking higher education—who can think their way through unfamiliar problems, use complex tools and technology, and see their own activity in the larger context of the total workplace. The Secretary's Commission on Achieving Necessary Skills (SCANS) has suggested that "workplace know-how" rests on foundation skills and competencies. Three types of foundation skills (O'Neil, 1991, p. 5) are

1. *Basic skills,* such as reading, writing, math operations, and listening and speaking effectively
2. *Thinking skills,* such as the ability to think creatively, make decisions, solve problems, visualize, and knowing how to learn
3. *Personal qualities,* such as displaying responsibility, self-esteem, sociability, self-management, integrity, and honesty.

Is Our Nation at Risk? Education did not receive much attention at the national level during the 1970s. But, during Ronald Reagan's first term as president, 1981–1985, Secretary of Education Terrel Bell established a National Commission on Excellence in Education to investigate and report on the condition of education in America (Bell, 1993, p. 593). This commission's 1983 report, *A Nation at Risk,* shocked most Americans and thrust education into the national spotlight. Statements in the report such as "The educational foundations of our society are presently being eroded by a rising tide of mediocrity that threatens our very future as a nation and a people" and "If an unfriendly foreign power had attempted to impose on America the mediocre educational performance that exists today, we might well have viewed it as an act of war" were a cause for alarm to both society and the educational establishment (National Commission on Excellence in Education, 1983). Once Americans were alerted to the condition of education in their country, they gave it a higher priority in their everyday thinking and actions and on legislative agendas.

National Education Goals Are Established. President George Bush said, "Excellence in education is crucial to maintaining a strong democracy with a well-informed electorate, to building a competitive economy, and to solving the problems plaguing the poor in our nation's inner cities.... If we want to change the country, we have got to change the schools" (Bush, 1992, p. 130). From 1989–1993, Bush visited over 100 schools, talking to students, teachers, parents, educators, and community leaders. He called a summit conference on education with all the governors in 1989. This meeting resulted in agreement on four points: (1) establish a set of national goals or standards, (2) establish ways to measure those goals, (3) provide greater flexibility to states and localities in how they use federal education funds, and (4) provide that each state would restructure its education system. In 1990, as a follow-up to the summit, governors working with citizens and the president, developed six national education goals to be reached by the year 2000 (Bush, 1992, p. 132).

In 1994, Congress passed, and President Clinton signed, the *Goals 2000 Educate America Act.* It is the most far-reaching education bill of this decade. It focused on eight goals, including the original six, to be reached by the year 2000:

1. All children in America will start school ready to learn.
2. The high school graduation rate will increase to at least 90 percent.
3. American students will leave grades 4, 8, and 12 having demonstrated competency in English, mathematics, science, history, and geography. Every school in America will ensure that all students learn to use their minds well so they will be prepared for responsible citizenship, further learning, and productive employment.
4. American students will be first in the world in science and mathematics.
5. Every adult American will be literate.
6. Every school in America will be free of drugs and violence and offer a safe, disciplined environment.
7. Schools will encourage parental involvement in education.
8. Schools will promote professional training for teachers.

This act also dealt with standards, indicated how progress would be measured, and provided for the formation of oversight committees. States would not be required to adopt the national standards. But, the act offered strong incentives to do so—nearly $5 billion in grants during the next five years for districts that make an effort to reform their educational systems to meet the standards. Legislation is not the complete solution because "politicians can't and won't resolve this (education) problem for you. If we are going to compete and win again, we are all going to have to work harder and work smarter and become learners" (Clinton, 1992, p. 137).

Reform at the State and Local Levels. Reforms have been underway since the *A Nation at Risk* report in 1983. High school graduation standards and college entrance requirements have been overhauled and strengthened. Managerial reforms such as site-based management have been introduced nationwide, and programs to better serve groups of special needs students have been implemented in many schools and districts. "Restructuring" various aspects of curriculum, teaching, administration, and management have reached all 100,000 schools in 15,000 districts in America in one way or another.

Thinking and problem solving as forces in the curriculum will continue to be influenced by society, government, and economics as well as by educators and their professional organizations. In addition, the ability to think and solve problems now takes on an urgent need —survival for our society.

PROBLEMS AND PROBLEM SOLVING

Problem! Problem! What's the problem? A situation that presents itself as a problem to one person may not be a problem to another. Some problems are quickly solved while others take minutes, hours, weeks, or even years. Definitions of problems and problem solving, types of problems, and solving problems in the curriculum are explored here.

Defining the Parameters

Problems and problem solving have been widely discussed in the educational literature. Several definitions for both terms are provided here, along with working definitions that are used in this book.

Problems. "A problem is a task for which the person confronting it wants or needs to find a solution; the person has no readily available procedure for finding the solution; and the person must make an attempt to find a solution" (Charles & Lester, 1982, p. 5). "A problem involves a situation in which a person wants something and does not know immediately what to do to get it" (Reys, Suydam, & Lindquist, 1992, p. 28). "A problem is a situation, quantitative or otherwise, that confronts an individual or group of individuals, that requires resolution, and for which no path to the answer is known " (Krulik & Rudnick, 1993, p. 6). Krulik and Rudnick suggest further that a problem in contrast to a question or exercise is a situation that requires thought and use of knowledge to resolve it. Using these definitions as a base, a working definition for our discussions here is: *a problem is a situation for which the problem solver (1) has no immediate solution, and (2) needs or wants, and is willing to seek a solution.*

Problem Solving. Solving problems is a skill that is not usually easily learned without systematic and continuous exposure to problems, experience in solving them, and identification of the subskills and knowledge used to solve them. Investigating some formal definitions of problem solving will help us to better understand the skill:

- "Problem solving is the process of confronting a novel situation, formulating connections between the given facts, identifying the goal, and exploring possible strategies for reaching the goal" (Szetela & Nicol, 1992, p. 42).

- Problem solving is "the process by which one devises and executes a plan to resolve a question, situation, or condition that needs but does not yet have an answer or solution" (Beyer, 1991, p. 184).

- "Problem solving is broad and refers to a complex of cognitive activities and skills.... To solve a problem is to find a way where no way is known, to find a way out of a difficulty, to find a way around an obstacle, to attain a desired end... not immediately attainable" (Hatfield, Edwards, & Bitter, 1993, p. 54).

- Problem solving is a complex thinking process "to resolve a known or defined difficulty, assemble facts about the difficulty and determine additional information needed; infer or suggest alternate solutions and test them for appropriateness; potentially reduce to simpler levels of explanation and eliminate discrepancies; provide solution checks for generalizable value" (Presseisen in Costa, 1985, p. 45).

A synthesis of these definitions leads to a working definition: *problem solving is a process by which the problem solver, consciously or unconsciously, moves systematically or randomly through a series of operations using thinking skills appropriate to the problem being solved, gathers more information as needed, makes choices, and selects priorities to arrive at one or several solutions.*

Types of Problems

Authors have used a variety of terms to identify different types and difficulty levels of problems. Many terms and the kinds of problems they refer to have initially been associated with mathematics, but they relate to problems in all subject areas. A brief review of common types of problems follows.

Problems Based on Operations. Charles and Lester have defined six types of problems based on the kind of mental operations the solver carries out to reach a solution (1982, pp. 6–10). Types and related operations are

1. *Drill exercises,* which give students practice in using an algorithm and helps them maintain mastery of basic computation facts
2. *Simple translation problems,* where students translate real-world situations into mathematical expressions to reinforce understanding of math concepts
3. *Complex translation problems,* where students translate real-world situations into mathematical expressions with more than one translation and operation
4. *Process problems* that involve thinking and solving a problem and demands that students develop general strategies for understanding, planning, and solving problems as well as evaluating possible solutions
5. *Applied problems,* where students use a variety of math skills, processes, concepts, and facts to solve realistic and everyday problems
6. *Puzzle problems*, in which students engage in thinking and problem solving as well as flexible ways to attack a problem.

Problems Based on Knowns and Unknowns. Another approach to classifying problems is through what the presenter and problem solver know and do not know about (1) the problem, (2) the method used to solve it, and (3) the solution. The problem presenter can be the teacher, the textbook, computer program, and so on. The problem solver is the student or other person. Five types of problems along with a description of each and its knowns and unknowns are described here and summarized graphically in Figure 1-1 (Schiever, 1991, pp. 14–15).

1. *Type I:* The problem and the method of solution are known to the problem presenter and the problem solver; the presenter knows the correct solution. Solving math problems by a known method or algorithm is a Type I problem.
2. *Type II:* The problem is known by the presenter and the solver, but the method of solution and the solution are known only to the presenter. Story problems or answering questions about factual material are Type II problems.
3. *Type III:* The problem is known to the presenter and the solver, more than one method may be used to solve the problem, and the solution or range of solutions is known only to the presenter. Problems that can be solved inductively but have an accepted answer or range of answers are Type III. Solving a geometry problem by using manipulatives is a Type III problem.
4. *Type IV:* The problem is known to the presenter and solver, but the method and solution are unknown to both. Open-ended problems that can be solved in a number of ways and that have more than one correct or acceptable solution are Type IV problems. A question such as "In what ways might you share the results of your survey?" is an example of this type of problem.
5. *Type V:* The problem is unknown or undefined and the method and solution are unknown to both presenter and solver. Problem situations, in which the problem may be defined in more than one way, and real-life problems are Type V. This type of problem includes cafeteria waste, environmental pollution, or student behavior on the playground or campus.

A review of these five problem types indicates that Types I and II are usually emphasized in the traditional curriculum with fewer problems or situations for Types III and IV. And Type V occurs all too rarely in our school curriculum. Types I through IV represent varying degrees of defined or structured problems while Type V could be termed ill defined or ill structured.

FIGURE 1–1 Summary: Problem Types Based on Knowns and Unknowns

	Problem		Method		Solution	
Type	Presenter	Solver	Presenter	Solver	Presenter	Solver
I	K	K	K	K	K	U
II	K	K	K	U	K	U
III	K	K	R	U	R	U
IV	K	K	U	U	U	U
V	U	U	U	U	U	U
	K = Known		U = Unknown		R = Range	

Source: Shirley W. Schiever, *A Comprehensive Approach to Teaching Thinking.* Copyright © 1991 by Allyn and Bacon, pp. 14–15. Adapted with permission.

Other Ways of Labeling Problems. Another way to look at types of problems is to identify them as open-ended, discovery, and guided discovery (Hatfield, Edwards, & Bitter, 1993, p. 55). *Open-ended problems* have several possible solutions and the process of solving the problem is as important as the answer. *Discovery problems* have an answer, but the student may use a variety of methods to reach it. *Guided discovery* problems include clues and sometimes directions for solving them.

Problems are also commonly classified as routine and nonroutine. *Routine* problems involve an application of a procedure in much the same way as it was learned. *Nonroutine* problems require more thought because the choice of procedures to solve them is not as obvious (Reys, Suydam, & Lindquist, 1992, p. 28). Some authors refer to routine problems as defined or structured and nonroutine problems as ill-defined and ill-structured. Problems can also be categorized as simple or complex, concrete or abstract, or varying combinations of these.

A Summary of Problem Difficulty. The terminology of various authors is depicted on a continuum of difficulty in Figure 1–2. Here, problems range from easy (Level 1), which give the solver considerable information about the problem, to difficult (Level 5), which provide the solver only skeletal information.

The important message for teachers in interpreting the kinds and difficulty levels of problems from this chart is to give students opportunities to move from level 1 and 2 problems across the continuum to levels 3, 4, and 5. Problems exist in all subject matter areas and in everyday life. Most of them are not at levels 1 and 2. They usually occur at levels 3, 4, and 5. Likewise, most problems in high school and college academic work and in the workplace also occur at these higher levels. If we don't provide experiences for students to solve higher-level problems consistently during all years of elementary and middle school, we are shortchanging their education. We must reverse the statistics that show American students at all ages perform well in international competition at levels 1 and 2 but not very well at the higher levels.

Discussions about problem solving in this book focus on the three higher levels, with particular emphasis on Level 5 problems. Practical examples are used throughout to illustrate that students of all ages can solve higher-level problems if the material is presented in the context of their experiences, interests, and vocabulary.

Problem Solving as a Part of the Curriculum

Teaching problem-solving strategies in all subject matter areas of the curriculum is the most likely single change we can make in American education to bring about higher student achievement (Wooten, 1992, p. 7). The idea of teachers talking and students listening will not work for schools in the twenty-first century. Students need to identify and set up problems, work with peers, and solve problems in a variety of ways. Teachers should become guides or coaches to provide students with these strategies.

The emphasis in curriculum for the future will be on teaching students to "learn how to learn." This type of curriculum has four main elements: *content, process, product , and environment* (Bechtol & Sorenson, 1993; Schiever, 1991; Maker, 1982).

FIGURE 1–2 A Continuum of Terms Representing Problem Difficulty

Level 1	Level 2	Level 3	Level 4	Level 5
Simple				Complex
Concrete				Abstract
Routine				Nonroutine
Structured				Ill structured
Defined				Ill defined
Type I	Type II	Type III	Type IV	Type V
Guided Discovery		Discovery		Open-ended
Drill	Simple Translation	Complex Translation	Process	Applied

(*Note:* Puzzle problems can exist at all levels)

Content consists of ideas and concepts, facts, principles, and theories that make up our body of knowledge. *Process* is at the heart of a "learning how to learn" curriculum. It includes how information is gathered, how it is presented, the activities that students carry out to learn, and what questions are asked about a subject. Problem solving is the ultimate goal of process learning. *Product* refers to outcomes students are expected to produce as "ends" of learning and *environment* provides the support system for learning. These elements are discussed in detail in Chapter 2.

CLUES TO SUCCESS AND FAILURE IN PROBLEM SOLVING

Why do some people relish the chance to solve problems—in school, in magazines, in video games, on the computer, for recreation as well as in academics—while others dislike the process? Reasons for these behaviors and how they relate to learners and teachers are discussed here.

Stumbling Blocks to Problem Solving

Solving problems has long been considered "difficult" by students and teachers alike. In fact, some students barely try to solve problems because others have told them it is "hard." Some blocks are inherent in the problem and others in the solver.

Problem Conditions. Factors that have a strong influence on our outlook towards the problem include (Charles & Lester, 1982, pp. 13–15):

1. Complexity of the problem statement such as syntax, amount of information given, number of variables and conditions.
2. Manner in which the problem is posed for the individual to form a mental picture of it.
3. Problem requires use of a particular solution or procedure.
4. Manner in which a problem is posed implies a particular solution or solution procedure that is misleading or of no help in solving the problem.
5. Subgoals are difficult to identify because of the way the problem is stated.
6. Information given in the problem is difficult to understand or is arranged in such a manner that it implies a constraint that is not there.
7. Problem is not presented in an interesting manner and causes students to lack interest and motivation to solve it.

Problem Solver Conditions. Another way to view stumbling blocks to problem solving is from perceptual, cultural, and emotional points of view of the solver. *Perceptual* conditions include difficulty in isolating a problem; inability to define terms; failure to use all the senses when observing; difficulty in seeing remote relationships; and failure to investigate the obvious. *Cultural* conditions involve desire to conform to an adopted pattern, being overly practical, judging too quickly, believing that extreme doubting and questioning is impolite, overemphasis on competition, too much faith in statistics, relying too much on reason and logic, overgeneralizing, and believing that indulging in fantasy as worthless. *Emotional* conditions deal with fear of making a mistake or of making a fool of one's self, grabbing the first idea that comes along, rigidity in thinking, desire for security, fear of supervisors and distrust of colleagues and subordinates (e.g., classmates, teachers, parents), and lack of drive to complete a problem.

A review of stumbling blocks to problem solving poses two new questions: What characteristics do students who are successful problems solvers exhibit? What strategies do teachers use to help their students become successful problem solvers?

Characteristics of Good Problem Solvers

Some people are "naturals" at solving problems. Is this "knack" innate or learned or both? We will examine some characteristics and try to find out.

Employ Strategies. These involve both affective and cognitive factors. One set that focuses on affective influences includes (Krulik & Rudnick, 1993, p. 61):

- The desire to solve a problem; persistence—if one method of attacking a problem fails to lead to a satisfactory solution, try another
- A willingness to skip some of the steps in the solution process
- Not being afraid to make "educated guesses"
- Being curious and willing to take risks.

Another list of different strategies good problem solvers use are (Meiring, in Hatfield, Edwards, & Bitter, 1993, pp. 61–62):

- Note likenesses and differences and discard irrelevant details.
- Identify critical and relevant elements.
- Evaluate and select alternative routes to the solution.
- Estimate, approximate, and check for reasonableness.
- Generalize from a few examples and switch methods easily.
- Learn from mistakes.
- Have less anxiety and more confidence.
- Be sure to understand concepts and terms.
- Transfer learning to similar problems.

Good problem solvers practice *metacognition*—that is, they learn how to carry out problem solving by observing their own actions and mental processes as they work on problems. They "talk to themselves." Eight specific ways to help students do this are (Capper, in Hatfield, Edwards, & Bitter, 1993, p. 62):

1. Read and reread the problem to be sure to understand it.
2. Plan and schedule appropriate subskills and goals to solve the problem.
3. Separate important from unimportant information in the problem.
4. Break the problem down into smaller units.
5. Connect information in the problem to what is already known.
6. Organize information listed in the problem in a logical manner.
7. Supply missing or implied information.
8. Keep track of time limits; monitor and evaluate progress toward the solution.

Refer to a "Do" List. Students should use guidelines to keep their thinking "on track." These can be written in simple language for elementary and middle-level problem solvers and take the form of a "Do List." Here is an example:

- Stay in a good mood, be positive.
- Explore, be willing to take risks.
- Read the problem carefully; if you have trouble getting started, make a diagram or picture, and take notes on the information given in the problem.

- Don't rush; some problems take time; sometimes take a break, then try again.
- Try alternative ways to solve the problem if the first one doesn't bring success.
- Be confident, have faith in your own ability.
- Brainstorm and communicate ideas with other students.
- Try to form a visual image of the problem.
- Think about your thinking—metacognition
- Organize data in the problem to help make your thinking as clear as possible.

Strategies of Good Teachers of Problem Solving

Good teachers of problem solving have a confident, enthusiastic, and positive attitude toward the process. They act as a model for the students—thinking with them and asking questions. They don't focus on the answer, but on the different routes that can be taken to reach a solution.

Some other strategies teachers can use to help their students succeed are (Meiring, in Hatfield, Edwards, & Bitter, 1993, p. 62):

- Teach a variety of problem-solving strategies, plus an overall plan; promote the idea that there are many ways to solve the same problem.
- Help students select an appropriate strategy for a particular problem.
- Have students solve some problems in small groups to share ideas.
- Encourage students to use dramatization, manipulatives, models, pictures, diagrams, charts, tables, graphs as aids to solve problems.
- Help students to simplify a problem.
- Present many and varied problems to meet needs of various students.
- Help students see relationships among different kinds of problems.
- Demonstrate to students how they can estimate and test their answers.
- Allow students enough time to solve problems, discuss results, and reflect on the problem-solving process.

PROBLEM SOLVING IS A POWERFUL LEARNING TOOL: AN OVERVIEW

The emphasis of this book is on practical ways to teach problem solving to all students at the primary, intermediate, and middle school levels. Background information on thinking skills and problem solving, strategies for staff development, and more than 300 examples of "how to do it" approaches to problem solving that "work" in the classroom are described.

The discussion in Chapter 1 focused on the importance of problem solving in academic success, the workplace, and everyday living. Problems and problem solving were defined, and the relationships of problem solving to our society and the school curriculum were explored.

Background information about thinking skills and multistep problem solving is the subject of Chapter 2. Five groups of thinking skills—inquiry processes, creative thinking processes, critical thinking skills, single-step problem-solving techniques, and Bloom's cognitive levels—are defined and illustrated with practical examples. Multistep problem solving is explored along with a model to help students do it. Detailed explanations of how to use the model with two different kinds of problems, one at the intermediate level and one at the middle level, are featured.

Teaching problem solving to students, grades 1–4, is the topic of Chapter 3. Practical ways to "fit or infuse" problem solving into regular lessons or units of instruction and strategies to make problem solving exciting and relevant for young children are featured. Motivational techniques, learning and teaching styles to accommodate a diverse population, and a variety of grouping patterns are also discussed. Problem solving is illustrated with activities in science and math and in interdisciplinary units. Specific topics include focusing on inference and deduction, grouping things together, learning how to experiment, and blowing bubbles. A unique, creative, and detailed unit on dinosaurs completes the curricular descriptions.

Chapter 4 deals with helping students in grades 4–6 "grow" as problem solvers. Ways learning and teaching styles, grouping patterns, and technology can be used to furnish students with diverse interests and academic achievements the opportunities to solve problems that are meaningful to them is also described. Interdisciplinary learning is emphasized, but curriculum objectives and activities are also related to traditional subject matter areas. Specific topics deal with historic homes in the community, a field trip to the zoo, advertising, writing letters, and intriguing the imagination through mysteries. Retaining the innate creativity that young students exhibit readily, but often "disappears" at the intermediate level are featured.

In grades 6–8, the target group of Chapter 5, both students and teachers tend to "specialize" in their academic and personal interests. This leads to criticisms that the middle school curriculum focuses on content with little attention to process. Ways to avoid these pitfalls are suggested along with strategies to integrate problem solving into every lesson of a subject area. Procedures to apply the techniques of the Future Problem Solving Program (FPS) in any subject area are highlighted. Specific topics deal with making a creative sandwich, a trip across the United States, survival of the fittest, and creating a country. A unique unit on "the power of positive argumentation" is featured. Assessment strategies that are important at this age level are also explained.

Examples of how schools and districts have developed outstanding programs and approaches to give their students experiences to think and solve real problems in their curriculums is the subject of Chapter 6. These primary, intermediate, and middle-level schools represent urban, suburban, and outer-city schools and districts in different geographical areas of the country. Practical "in the classroom" applications of problem solving along with staff development, communicating with parents and community, and ways to start and maintain their changes are discussed.

Staff development, the "secret to success" in changing the curriculum, is the topic of Chapter 7. Problem solving does not come easily or naturally to most teachers. Yet if hands-on ideas and strategies are proposed to teachers in workshops where they can "get involved," they are willing to teach it and they are very excited about the positive reactions from their students. Objectives, agendas, a time frame, and resources for a series of workshops to introduce problem solving into subject area or interdisciplinary units of instruction are highlighted in the discussion.

SUMMARY

Educational experiences and student skills must improve if the United States is to compete successfully in the global society of the twenty-first century. One important way to bring this about is to focus on a "learning how to learn" approach that emphasizes thinking skills and problem solving in relation to the other three elements of the curriculum—content, product, and environment. Problem solving is often considered difficult by both students and teachers. But it can be taught and learned if practical, meaningful methods that students and teachers understand are used. Students should have experiences that require them to think and solve problems starting in the primary grades and continuing at ever-increasing levels of difficulty through the intermediate and middle-level years of schooling—and beyond.

REFERENCES

Association for Supervision and Curriculum Development. (September 1990). Mathematics, science, social studies, language arts. *ASCD Curriculum Update,* 2–7.

Bechtol, W., & Sorenson, J. (1993). *Restructuring schooling for individual students.* Boston: Allyn and Bacon.

Bell, T. (1993). Reflections one decade after *A Nation at Risk. Phi Delta Kappan,* 74(8): 592–597.

Beyer, B. (1991). *Teaching thinking skills: A handbook for elementary teachers.* Boston: Allyn and Bacon.

Bush, G. (1992). A revolution to achieve excellence in education. *Phi Delta Kappan,* 74(2): 130, 132–133.

Charles, R., & Lester, F. (1982). *Teaching problem solving: What, why and how.* Palo Alto, CA: Dale Seymour.

Clinton, B. (1992). The Clinton plan for excellence in education. *Phi Delta Kappan,* 74(2): 131, 134–138.

Costa, A. (Ed.). (1985). *Developing minds: A reference book for teaching thinking.* Alexandria VA: Association for Supervision and Curriculum Development.

Hatfield, M., Edwards, N., & Bitter, G., (1993). *Mathematics methods for the elementary and middle school.* Boston: Allyn and Bacon.

Hiatt, D. (1994). An interview with Ralph Tyler: No limit to the possibilities. *Phi Delta Kappan,* 75(10): 786–789.

Krulik, S., & Rudnick, J. (1993). *Reasoning and problem solving: A handbook for elementary school teachers.* Boston: Allyn and Bacon.

Maker, C. J. (1982). *Teaching models in education of the gifted.* Rockville, MD: Aspen.

National Commission on Excellence in Education. (1983). *A nation at risk.* Washington, DC: U.S. Government Printing Office.

O'Neil, J. (1991). Building links between schools and the workplace. *ASCD Update,* 33(9): 4–5,8.

O'Neil, J. (September 1990). New curriculum agenda emerges for the '90s. *ASCD Curriculum Update,* 1,8.

Perkins, D. (1993–1994). Thinking-centered learning. *Educational Leadership,* 51 (4): 84–85.

Reich, R. (March 1993). Paper presented to the Annual Conference of the Association for Supervision and Curriculum Development, Washington, DC.

Reys, R., Suydam, M., & Lindquist, M. (1992). *Helping children learn mathematics*. Boston: Allyn and Bacon.

Schiever, S. (1991). A *comprehensive approach to teaching thinking*. Boston: Allyn and Bacon.

Szetela, W., & Nicol, C., (1992). Evaluating problem solving in mathematics. *Educational Leadership,* 49(8): 42–45.

Willis, S. (January 1992). Mathematics education: Standards 'revolution' takes hold. *ASCD Curriculum Update:* 1–8.

Wooten, P. (1992). Issue. *ASCD Update,* 34(1): 7.

CHAPTER 2

Thinking Skills and Problem Solving

The Mystery of the Stained Shirt

Eight-year-old Kevin liked going to the ice cream store with his grandfather, and today it was such a nice summer day that the two of them walked through the park to get their special treat. They sat at an outdoor table enjoying their ice cream. When it was time to leave, Kevin noticed a purple blotch of color on his clean white shirt. "I'll be in trouble with Mom when she sees this!" He exclaimed, "What can I do now?"

"We'll think of something," said his grandfather, "but let's try to figure out where that fresh stain came from." First they felt of the chair. No old or new fruit stains there. Next they checked the nearby tables. Nothing there either. They asked a waitress if she had brought out any fruit sundaes, or if anybody had an accident with their ice cream. There was nothing on the floor, and nobody had bought a fruit sundae or other colored food recently.

"It didn't come from here," said Kevin's grandfather, "so let's trace our steps back home and look for clues." Kevin thought the stain might have come from the bushes that hang over the park path, but on investigation there weren't any ripe berries or rotted leaves to be found. Soon they were back at the house, still without any clue to the source of the mysterious purple stain.

His grandfather said, "Let's try to get the stain out anyway. It would be easier if we knew what it was, but we'll have to experiment with it." Kevin peeled off his shirt, and his grandfather ran cold water on the stain. Nothing happened, so he tried hot water, which only spread the stain out wider. Next he tried soap—and still no results.

"We've tried all the logical solutions. Our last resort is bleach," said the grandfather, and he poured on a little from the big bottle. Kevin watched with interest as the stain became more faint. His grandfather blotted the stain with a paper towel, then poured on more bleach. The spot was disappearing like magic. In a few minutes it was gone and the shirt was spinning in the dryer.

"Well, we didn't find out where the stain came from, but we found out how to get rid of it," said Kevin as he pulled on his shirt. His mother came in the door and asked, "Did you two get along OK while I was gone? The grandfather winked at Kevin as he replied, "No problem."

Most young children want to solve everyday problems. They are curious about how the stain got on Kevin's shirt and how he and his grandfather got it out. They like to solve all kinds of puzzles and are fascinated by strategy games. It is almost as if children like to solve problems when they don't realize they are doing it. When they get older and are asked to solve problems in more formal settings such as the classroom, many of them are not willing or able to do it. *How can we keep this from happening?*

It is a major purpose of this book to address that question. This chapter focuses on background information on thinking skills and problem solving and how they relate to the subject areas the students study. Chapters 3, 4, 5, and 6 illustrate practical ways that teachers keep students "on track" in the classroom so they can think and solve increasingly more complex problems as they progress through school.

Thinking skills and problem solving make up the *process* element of curriculum. Process, content, product, and environment are the four basic elements of curriculum that were defined in Chapter 1. These elements are shown in relation to each other in the houselike diagram in Figure 2–1. Here, the "doors" from each element are open to let information flow freely among them. In process, multistep problem solving, which is the goal of learning in school, the workplace, and everyday life is located at the peak of the "house." Five thinking skills groups—inquiry processes, creative thinking processes, critical thinking skills, single-step problem-solving techniques, and Bloom's cognitive levels—support it. When multistep problem solving is carried out, the problem solver selects and uses those thinking skills and subskills that are most appropriate to solve the problem at hand.

Simultaneously, the problem solver searches for and uses *content* in terms of facts, principles, concepts, and theories that are most useful to solve the problem. Content is shown at the right side of the diagram. A *product* results from the application of content and process. Products should involve real problems, real audiences, and undergo real evaluations. Product is shown at the left side of the diagram. *Environment*, located at the floor level, provides a support system for the other three elements. Definitions and dimensions including subskills and subcategories for the four curriculum elements are presented in Figure 2–2.

These curriculum elements form the framework for discussions in this chapter. First the role of content with an emphasis on concepts is considered. Then, the skills and subskills of five thinking skills groups are defined and their use illustrated with classroom activities. Multistep problem solving and a practical model to help students carry it out is featured. Various ways teachers can use the model to help students solve problems are shown. The roles of product and environment in problem solving are also explored. Practical strategies to teach and assess problem solving and resource materials for teachers conclude the discussion.

CONTENT: THE KNOWLEDGE BASE

Content is the "stuff" we use in thinking. Probably its most common synonym is knowledge. Several definitions of content along with a working definition derived from them are presented in this section. Content can be defined as "knowing" or "that which is to be processed" (Suhor in Brandt, 1988, pp. 31, 42). Curriculum content is made up of ideas, concepts, descriptive information, and facts (Maker, 1982, p. 3).

FIGURE 2–1 Relationships Among the Four Elements of the Curriculum

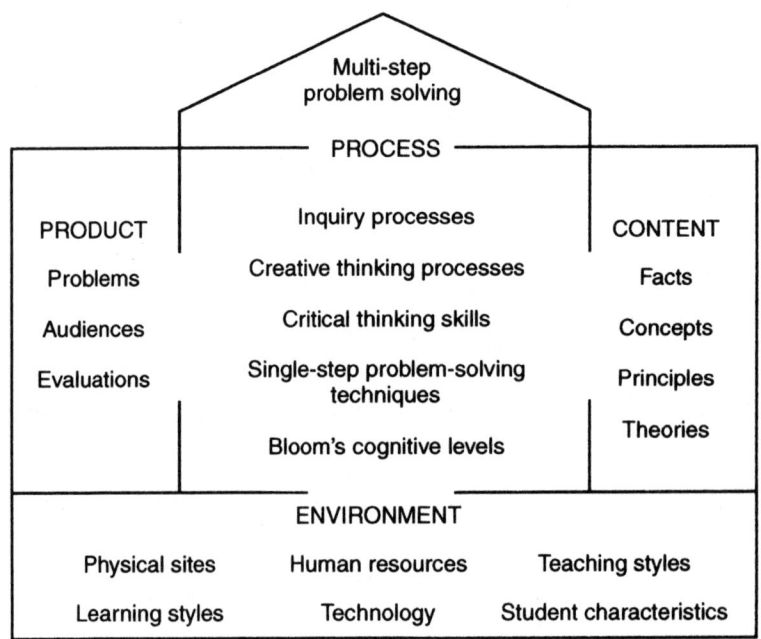

FIGURE 2–2 Definitions and Dimensions of the Curriculum Elements

- *Content* refers to knowledge students learn in terms of facts, principles, concepts, and theories
- *Process* relates to the ways students go about learning in terms of thinking and problem solving:

Thinking Skill Groups

Inquiry Processes	*Creative Processes*	*Single-Step Techniques*
Observing	Comparing and contrasting	Working backward
Classifying	Distinguishing between fact and opinion	Simplifying and reducing
Inferring		Recognizing patterns
Predicting	Distinguishing between relevant and irrelevant information	Organizing lists
Measuring		Guessing and testing
Communicating	Distinguishing between reliable and unreliable sources	Forming analogies
Interpreting data		Making a drawing or figure
Formulating operational definitions	Identifying cause and effect	Making a table or graph
	Sequencing and prioritizing	Making a model
Formulating questions and hypotheses	Identifying bias and stereotype	Acting it out
	Recognizing point of view	
Experimenting	Recognizing consistent and inconsistent reasoning	*Bloom's Cognitive Levels*
Formulating models		Knowledge
	Recognizing assumptions and generalizations	Comprehension
Creative Processes	Analyzing arguments	Application
Fluency	Recognizing induction and deduction	Analysis
Flexibility		Synthesis
Elaboration		Evaluation
Originality		

Multistep Problem Solving

Clarify:	State the problem
Forecast:	Select the best solution(s)
Investigate:	Select and implement the best design to test solution(s)
Evaluate:	Judge the results—Is the problem solved?

- *Product* refers to kinds of outcomes students produce as evidence of learning in terms of real products, real audiences, and real evaluations
- *Environment* provides the support system for learning in terms of physical sites, human resources, teaching styles, learning styles, student personal characteristics, and technology

Source: Adapted from W. Bechtol and J. Sorenson, *Restructuring Schooling for Individual Students* (Boston: Allyn and Bacon, 1993), p. 154. Reprinted with permission.

Content can also be defined as "facts, principles, theories, and concepts and their interrelationships" (Sorenson, J., Engelsgjerd, J., Francis, M., Miller, M., & Schuster, N., 1988, p. 59). A simple working definition is: *content describes the knowledge base of the subject matter areas or disciplines we teach in the curriculum; it has four forms—facts, principles, theories, and concepts*.

Five aspects of content are discussed here—selecting content, organizing content, forming concepts, analyzing concepts, and teaching concepts. Strategies that teachers can use to help students learn content more thoroughly and effectively are also illustrated with practical examples (Bechtol & Sorenson 1993, pp. 153–161).

Selecting Content

Content selection often involves controversy since it brings concerns to teachers, parents, and administrators about "what the children should be taught." Here are some rules to consider when selecting content for the lessons and units of instruction of the curriculum (Kaplan in Renzulli, 1986, p. 183):

- Select content that is related to the organizing theme or topic.
- Identify some sections or subtopics of the theme that are multidisciplinary.
- Identify topics or subtopics of the theme that are mandatory for all students to learn as well as those that meet needs, interests, and abilities of special groups (e.g., special education or academically able students).
- Select topics that provide a time perspective relating past, present, and future.

Organizing Content

Content can take four forms: facts, principles, theories, and concepts. These can be organized in a hierarchy that relates them in any discipline or subject matter area of a curriculum (Bechtol & Sorenson, 1993; Haney & Sorenson, 1977). Here are their definitions and relationships:

Facts. Facts are information based on observable experiences and related to particular objects and events. Examples are "a ball held above the ground falls downward when released" or "2 pens plus 3 pens are 5 pens." Descriptions from observable examples of rocks, animal behaviors, and sports events are also facts.

Principles. Principles are general statements that relate several facts. A basic economic principle is "When a product is in short supply and high demand, the price increases; when the demand is low and there is an adequate or high supply, the price decreases, if other factors remain stable." In science, a commonly learned principle is "The volume of a confined gas varies inversely with the pressure if the temperature remains constant."

Theories. Statements of theory represent the highest level of generality and normally relate several principles. For example, the principles governing the behavior of gases can be explained using the kinetic molecular theory of gases, which contains statements about molecules and their interactions.

Concepts. Concepts appear in statements at all levels of generality—facts, principles, and theories. Concepts are abstractions or ideas based on many encounters with similar objects and events. Math concepts include those of divisor, subtraction, and fraction; social studies concepts include those of government, exchange, and democracy; and language arts concepts include those of noun, consonant, and paragraph.

Relationships among facts, concepts, principles and theories are shown in Figure 2-3 . Here, several facts are shown at the base. Located between the theory and facts are principles; and concepts appear in statements at all three levels. Reasoning deductively, it can be said that theory explains principles, which in turn explain facts, and that a concept(s) at any level can be explained from concepts at a higher level. Conversely, reasoning inductively, several facts can be related to form a principle, and several principles related to form a theory, using individual concepts at all levels.

Forming Concepts

Thinking should not be limited to facts because the type of learning that helps students profit from past experience and cope more readily with new experiences would be lacking. Structured knowledge becomes possible only when people make generalizations from the specifics of their experience and form abstractions. These generalizations and abstractions range from the informal concepts or principles of common sense to precisely defined concepts, principles and sophisticated theories of a discipline such as math, science, language arts, or social studies.

No two experiences are identical. Everything changes, yet people can find commonalities from one experience to another. For example, individuals may never encounter the same robin, apple, or car twice, yet they recognize new robins, apples, and cars when they come in contact with them.

Human beings represent concepts by words, sounds, and other symbols when they communicate. People develop their own private concept of something by the idea a symbol brings to mind as well as by the thing itself. Chair, pencil, house, dog, cloud, melting, dissolving, and bending are all everyday concepts. The first five words represent classes of objects, and the last three represent classes of events. Most people find it easier to think "chair" than to list descriptions of kitchen chairs, folding chairs, upholstered living room chairs, and so on. All these objects have features in common that make up the concept of chair. Likewise, people have a concept of melting that depends on many experiences with substances such as butter, chocolate candies, and ice that may undergo

FIGURE 2–3 A Hierarchical Arrangement of Facts and Principles, Correlated by a Theory That Uses Concepts at All Levels

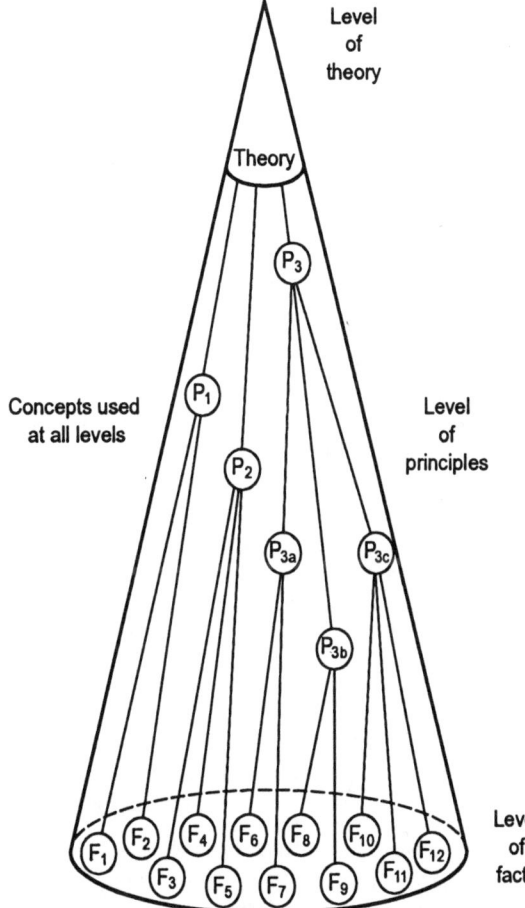

Source: R. Haney and J. Sorenson, *Individually Guided Science* (Reading, MA: Addison-Wesley, 1977) p. 20. Reprinted with permission.

this physical change from a solid to a liquid. The richness of people's concepts depends on their range of experiences with the objects and events that the concepts represent.

Analyzing Concepts

Students can learn concepts in a subject matter area by placing them in a hierarchy that incorporates the following features (Harris & Harris, 1973):

- Criterial, relevant, and irrelevant attributes
- Examples and nonexamples of the concept
- Definition of the concept
- Subordinate, coordinate, and supraordinate concepts to the one under study
- Relationships between the concept of interest and other concepts.

The concept *planet* can be analyzed according to this hierarchy by identifying features that are appropriate for intermediate and middle school students as follows (Sorenson et al., 1988, p. 63; Harris & Harris, 1973):

- Criterial relevant attribute(s): revolves around the sun; shines by reflected light.
- Relevant attributes that related concepts share: is located in space; motion is affected by other heavenly bodies.
- Irrelevant attributes: visibility to the naked eye; surface temperature; apparent color to the earthly observer; may support life.
- Examples: picture or description of a body orbiting the sun.
- Nonexamples: picture or description of a body orbiting the earth.
- Subordinate concept(s): major or minor planet.
- Coordinate concept(s): moon, meteor.
- Supraordinate concepts(s): heavenly body, solar system.
- Definition (includes name of supraordinate concepts and criterial attributes): *A planet is a heavenly body that revolves around the sun and shines by reflected light.*
- Relationships: *Planets* travel in paths called *orbits*.

For teachers, the most important things to help students learn concepts are the relevant, criterial attributes that separate the concept under study from all other concepts. When students have mastered these, the others are easily determined.

Teaching Concepts

The features discussed in the analysis of a concept are presented in diagram form in Figure 2–4. Here they are arranged in an order to use in teaching important and difficult concepts to students at varying age and grade levels. The six sequential steps are illustrated here for two different kinds of concepts, "bird" and "sentence."

The Concept of "Bird." Steps that can be followed here are (Voelker, Sorenson, & Frayer, 1971, pp. 46–47):

1. *Criterial attribute(s).* The criterial attribute is "covered with feathers." The teacher needs to be sure all students can distinguish between covered with feathers and other common animal coverings such as hair, scales, skin.
2. *Examples and nonexamples.* It is often useful to include pictures as well as words in teaching examples and nonexamples and this is possible with the concept of "bird." Students can identify pictures and descriptions of mammals, amphibians, reptiles, and fish along with a variety of birds from robins to chickens to ostriches that can be labeled as "birds and nonbirds."
3. *Attributes.* Bird shares being warm-blooded, female lays eggs, and having a backbone with various other classes of vertebrates. Bird also shares being an animal and a living thing with large numbers of other organisms. Irrelevant attributes for bird include size, coloration, habitat, migration patterns, and types of food.
4. *Classification.* This step has three substeps—identifying supraordinate, coordinate, and subordinate concepts. Supraordinate or higher groups to which bird belongs include vertebrate, animal, living thing. Coordinate or parallel concepts include mammal, amphibian, reptile, and fish. Subordinate concepts include habitat (water, woods, prairie); the food they eat (seeds, insects, or other animals); or specific kinds of birds (blackbirds, flamingos, ducks, and so on).
5. *Definition.* In textbooks, dictionaries, or references, definitions usually include the name of the concept (bird); the supraordinate group to which the concept belongs (vertebrate, animal, living thing); and the criterial attribute(s) separating a given concept from all others (covered with feathers). Therefore, the definition for bird would be that *a bird is a warm-blooded, vertebrate animal covered with feathers; and the female lays eggs.* A definition should be the *result* of understanding a concept, not the starting point of learning as so often occurs in our classrooms.
6. *Relationships with other concepts.* These can be simple or complex according to the age and grade level of the students. Some examples: Many birds migrate from colder to warmer climates during the winter season (bird and migrate), birds and mammals form the two classes of warm-blooded vertebrates (birds and mammals), and birds use a gizzard to help digest food (bird and gizzard).

One of the most important parts of "analyzing" a concept in this fashion is the natural way in which attributes of related concepts—in this case, fish, reptile, amphibian, mammal—come into the discussion to differentiate them from bird.

The Concept of "Sentence." The s*entence* concept is analyzed here (Golub, Frederick, Nelson, & Frayer, 1971):

1. *Criterial attributes*: subject and predicate; begins with a capital letter; ends with a punctuation mark; tells something or asks something.
2. *Examples and nonexamples.* Examples: "We saw a flower. Cats like to chase mice. Why does a deer run so fast? After school, the students played ball." Nonexamples: "Since you went away; at the bottom of the box; across the street; leaning on a locker."
3. *Attributes.* Relevant attribute: groups of words. Irrelevant attributes : type of punctuation (., ?, !); number of words; and position of subject and predicate.
4. *Classification:* three subgroups: supraordinate (a group of words); coordinate (phrase, clause); subordinate (question, command, or statement).
5. *Definition*: *A sentence is a group of words with a subject and predicate that begins with a capital letter and ends with end punctuation.*
6. *Relationships with other concepts:* A paragraph is made up of one or more sentences, and sentences can be made up of several clauses.

When teachers make plans to teach a concept using the "analysis" format, they would probably start with the definition from a reliable source such as a textbook or dictionary. Then they would identify the information for the other five steps. The sequence

FIGURE 2–4 Steps in the Analysis of a Concept

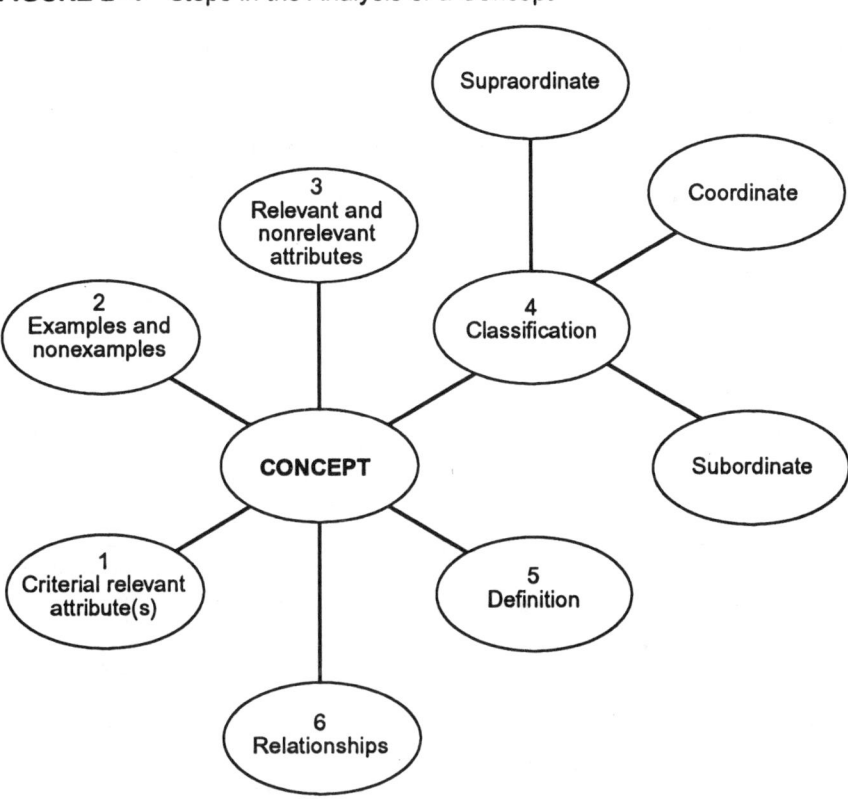

Source: W. Bechtol and J. Sorenson, *Restructuring Schooling for Individual Students* (Boston: Allyn and Bacon, 1993), p. 159. Reprinted with permission.

presented in Figure 2–4 is suggested to help students gain understanding of a concept before they are asked to memorize the definition. In certain situations, the teacher may wish to present the definition to the students and have them share the "analysis" process by asking them to help identify the other five elements of the concept. Also, older students might work alone, with a partner, or as a part of a small group to develop their own "analysis" of important and/or difficult concepts in various subject matter areas.

PROCESS: THINKING SKILLS GROUPS

Thinking skills and problem solving make up the process element of the curriculum. Process has been defined as "ways in which students go about learning including encountering, storing, retrieving, and using information." Five thinking skills groups—inquiry processes, creative thinking processes, critical thinking skills, single-step problem-solving techniques, and Bloom's cognitive levels— which are outlined in Figure 2–2 are discussed here. Several or all of these groups have been identified by various authors (Bechtol & Sorenson, 1993; Beyer, 1988; Marzano, Brandt, Hughes, Jones, Presseisen, Rankin, & Suhor, 1988; Sorenson, Engelsgjerd, Francis, Miller & Schuster, 1988). Problem solving is described in the next section.

Note that the five groups of thinking skills do not come in neat, well-defined, and discrete packages. Subskills from one group overlap into those of another one. For example, observation is not just a subskill of the inquiry processes group, but is basic to carrying out all subskills in all groups. Not all the groups are parallel in construction. Bloom's cognitive levels are guidelines for developing learning objectives and asking questions from low (knowledge) to high (evaluation) levels of thinking to form a hierarchy. Subskills in the inquiry processes group are also in a hierarchy, as are the creative skills to a lesser degree. The subskills of critical thinking and single-step problem-solving techniques do not form a hierarchy. Critical thinking skills are conditions or tests to help evaluate a situation for cause and effect, bias and stereotype, or fact and opinion. Single-step problem-solving techniques such as working backward or making a drawing or graph are methods the problem solver can apply to solve a problem.

Often the margins between subskills in a group are blurred. For example, although measurement is listed as the fifth step from the bottom in the inquiry processes hierarchy, the thinker often carries it out simultaneously with observation in terms of size or quantity. Sometimes the thinker is like a tap dancer going up and down the stairs rather than a systematic climber taking one step at a time from bottom to top.

In addition, some subskills can be used singly or in tandem with another subskill. For example, the problem "How are a baseball and a golf ball alike and different?" can be solved at a simple level by using the subskills of observation and classification from the inquiry processes group. Also, problems can be generated by using the names of the subskills as the heart of a problem statement. For example, "Identify the causes and effects of the Civil War in the United States." This statement has been the subject of numerous books and volume sets.

So, generalities such as "overlap," "used instead of," and "you can't do one without the other" make studying and teaching thinking a complex task. Skills in each group might be taught separately initially. But in real-world thinking, many options and routes are available to the thinker depending on his or her experience, content background, the nature of the situation, and personal characteristics.

Subskills in each of the five groups will be defined and their use illustrated with a variety of classroom activities. Subject matter from language arts, math, science, and social studies will be used in the examples. Relationships of thinking skills to content, product, and environment will be pointed out as appropriate to the discussion.

Inquiry Processes

"Inquiry processes are fun to teach to young children because they just love to work with real, hands-on materials." This comment came from a teacher at the primary grades, but could have come from any teacher, kindergarten through university level. Students of all ages learn best from a combination of reading, discussing, working with visual materials and media, and hands-on examining of objects and situations to draw their own conclusions. Inquiry processes help them to develop their own strategies to seek out and organize information to think and solve problems.

A set of inquiry processes that can be used in all subject areas is shown in the following box (Bechtol & Sorenson, 1993, p. 172; Sorenson et al., 1988. p. 79). Here, observing appears at the bottom of the hierarchy. Each process above observing uses the one or ones below it to carry out the process. For example, when students sort or classify objects into groups, they do it on the basis of their observations. When they predict, they first observe, classify, and infer in order to come up with a reasonable prediction. As students experiment, they use most or all of the processes located below "Experiment" in the box. The order of use is not rigid, however.

Sometimes processes above the one being emphasized are also used to solve a problem. It is most important to remember that no single process except observing is used in isolation. A lesson or situation that focuses on one or two processes also offers opportunities to review, use, and reinforce several others. These eleven processes are defined and illustrated in the discussion that follows (Bechtol & Sorenson, 1993, pp.171–172; Haney & Sorenson, 1977; Wisconsin Department of Public Instruction, 1986); Sorenson et al., 1988, pp. 79–80).

Observing. This process involves gathering information directly using the five human senses and indirectly using instruments and other extensions of the

---

Formulating models
Experimenting
Formulating questions and hypotheses
Making operational definitions
Interpreting data
Communicating
Measuring
Predicting
Inferring
Classifying
Observing

senses. Young students are very good observers and pay attention to detail. They like to see, hear, touch, smell, and taste and are willing to talk about their impressions. Students should be encouraged as they get older to look for patterns and number; listen for pitch, loudness, and order; describe the things they touch as smooth, rough, or patterned; and refine their senses of taste and smell. Indirect observing is done with instruments such as microscopes, telescopes, computers, and magnetic resonance imaging as well as tests such as those for human blood, and industrial tests for metal strength.

Classifying. Grouping together objects, events, or situations based on likenesses and differences in arbitrarily selected attributes or characteristics is a very useful process. Students can sort themselves into groups using characteristics such as hair color, eye color, and what they are wearing—glasses or no glasses, skirts or pants, long- or short-sleeved shirts. Several different kinds of songs can be played on a tape recorder or CD player and students can classify them into categories—rock 'n' roll, opera, blues, swing, and so on. The hobbies of students can be listed on the blackboard or overhead transparency and students can classify them into categories. Initial classification can be started simply with one attribute such as color, then go on to size, shape, and as many characteristics as needed until all members in a group or "class" have the same set of characteristics. All plants and animals have been classified into species, and when we find a new member we can easily relate it to similar members we already know.

Inferring. Identifying patterns and relationships among observable facts and groups of facts, situations, events, and so on involves abstract thinking similar to comprehension in reading or other subject matter areas. Some good ways to introduce students to inferring is to have them look at pictures of different seasons. Then ask them to identify the season and to give as many reasons as they can for their "inferences." Another common exercise would be to look at sets of animal prints and infer as many characteristics as they can about the animal that made the prints—maybe even its name. Do a similar exercise with human foot- or handprints. Inferences are an important part of detective stories about Sherlock Holmes and novels by Agatha Christie. An everyday mystery is "How did that mark get on the classroom floor?" Inferences can be simple or complex, but they are always fascinating and challenging.

Predicting. Guessing what will happen in the future based on what we know happened in the past using as much relevant information as we can gather defines this process. Weather predictions for tomorrow, five days from now, or for the next month are available twenty-four hours a day on television and radio. Students can listen carefully to the broadcasts, perhaps even taping a short segment, to find out the reasons given for the prediction. They might also want to track five days of predictions against five days of actual weather conditions to see how accurate the predictions were. Try to find reasons for accurate or inaccurate predictions. In science, we often predict what will happen in an experiment based on what we know happened in the same situation in an earlier experiment. This is a fairly safe prediction.

Sometimes we are confronted with a new situation where we do not have data since we have not worked with the same situation earlier. In this case, we have to give an "educated guess" based on what we know for sure in cases as similar as we can find to the one at hand. Have students try predicting wins, losses, and scores for school and local team sports events. Outcomes versus predictions are easy to evaluate in this case, but again the emphasis should be on reasons not just scores. Predicting is an important part of our academic and everyday worlds. The financial world is heavily involved in predicting as are outcomes of scientific work and what happens in our global society.

Measuring. Properties and conditions of objects are compared directly or indirectly with arbitrary or standardized units. For young students, we start out the process of measuring using nonstandard units such as a cutout footprint or a length of cardboard. They can measure their desk by counting how many of a unit make up the width and depth. This gives them a "feel" for the real measuring. Then we can move on to varying degrees of detail in measuring—from yards to inches to parts of inches and so on. These are concrete measuring experiences that can be repeated in volume and mass as well as length and can use the metric as well as the English measurement system. Of course, more precise measuring uses instruments from the microscope to emissions from certain elements such as carbon 12.

Communicating. Observations and data are shared so that others can verify and use them. Communicating should be a part of all subject matter areas, not just language arts. Communication can take the form of a report on a science experiment, a videotape about a social studies survey in the community with accompanying script, a radio or television broadcast on how they developed and checked predictions on a sports event, and so on. Students should also communicate about "how" they go about doing things and reasons for successes and failures at every step of their work. By doing this, reading, writing, and speaking become real tools, not just something to complete a language arts assignment.

Interpreting Data. Data that are relevant to a given problem or situation are analyzed and sifted, and interpretations are limited to the data. Students often need help to carry out this process because they don't think through a situation carefully and do jump at the first bits of information they come to. Teachers can ask them to give reasons for their interpretations and help them to see which data are useful to their situation and which are not. Organizing their information into reasonable categories also helps students to start the interpretation process. Students can take data from a science experiment or an historical situation (e.g., a presidential inauguration or some phase of a major piece of legislation such as the Civil Rights Act of 1964) and practice interpreting the data to write a story.

Making Operational Definitions. The physical characteristics of object(s) or phenomena and the conditions under which the descriptions are made as well as intended uses of the object(s) or information are described in this process. For example, to distinguish between two girls' blouses that both share similar physical characteristics of two sleeves and buttons down the front, the writer needs to consider their functions. Is the blouse worn for dress, "roughing it," or for school? Let's look at another example. The description from a lab test using a low-powered microscope might be "10 milliliters of fresh blood from patient number 5 did not contain any irregularities." But if a very powerful microscope was used, a description of the same blood could read: "10 milliliters of fresh blood from patient number 5 contains irregularities that require further tests." These two descriptions are quite different, and their implications would be significant in terms of a doctor's conclusions.

Formulating Questions and Hypotheses. Questions are asked on the basis of observations and data and hypotheses are set based on answers to the questions. Hypotheses should be simple and testable. Teachers need to generate motivation for questioning. One way to do that is to bring objects into the classroom such as rubber bands of different lengths, widths, and colors. Ask the students to pose questions and then hypotheses about these rubber bands. Questions might be, Which rubber band would stretch the greatest distance? Why? After some discussion, hypotheses supported by reasons could be developed.

Experimenting. Experimenting gives students the opportunity to use many processes. It involves testing hypotheses through observing, identifying and controlling variables, and gathering, classifying, and interpreting data. Science experiments can range from simple ones such as "determining which ball—golf, rubber, or pingpong—bounces higher when the three are dropped from the same height" to more complex ones such as "getting a water balloon out of a bottle without breaking the balloon or bottle."

An opportunity to experiment in language arts includes comparing the effectiveness of communicating the same information as a narrative, a poem, or a mystery. Students could (1) hypothesize about which method is most effective, (2) prepare the information in each format, and (3) test their hypotheses by having the students in the class vote on which method was most effective. Students should include reasons for their choices. Although language arts is a very different type of subject from science, the basics of experimenting are the same. We experiment with doing things different ways in daily life, too. An example question is, What is the best route to drive to work in terms the amount of time it takes, cost of gasoline, pressure on the driver? Then test the hypotheses, and evaluate and communicate the results.

Formulating Models. In this process, representations of the states, objects, and events help explain and describe ideas and events in the present and predict future events or phenomena that are not yet explained. Three types of models are

- *Iconic models,* which are large- or small-scale representations of states, objects, or events such as globes, model airplanes, plastic skeletons, and planetary systems
- *Analog models,* where one property is used to represent another such as the color blue to represent water areas on a globe or map or different thicknesses of lines to indicate different types of highways

- *Symbolic models* where the properties of the thing to be represented are expressed symbolically as in a chemical equation. Symbolic models are more abstract than iconic and analog models and are widely used in science, mathematics, and computer science.

To get students involved in inquiry processes, teachers often use one or more of the following techniques: (1) guide the students' thinking with questions without giving answers; (2) ask the students to explain and explore; (3) ask the students to describe; (4) encourage the students to ask questions; (5) encourage learning to occur as an outgrowth of the familiar; and (6) share planning for learning with the students.

Creative Thinking Processes

To be creative is one of the human being's most widely held dreams. All students can participate in creative thinking, and all teachers can provide a classroom or other environment where students feel free to think creatively. Creative thinking calls for recognizing the existence of a problem, generating and testing a variety of ideas to solve it, and communicating possible solutions (Torrance, 1977, p. 6).

During creative thinking, students learn by exploring, trying out, manipulating, experimenting, questioning, and modifying ideas. If teachers expect students to think creatively, they need to allow them the freedom to inquire, search, and speculate without fear of penalties for "wrong" or "crazy" answers. Creative thinking and creative activities should be a planned part of all lessons and instructional activities.

Divergent and convergent thinking play an important role in creative thinking. *Divergent thinking* is "the kind of thinking required to generate many different responses to the same question or problem" (Costa & Presseisen, in Costa, 1985, p. 310). Divergent thinking also helps people express creative, innovative, and nontraditional ideas. Here are some guidelines to encourage divergent thinking (Isaksen, Dorval, & Treffinger, 1994; Davis, 1983): defer judgment, generate many ideas or options, accept all ideas, reach for limits, don't jump to conclusions, take risks, and let one idea lead to another.

Convergent thinking is a way to narrow down ideas to the one or two that are best, correct, or most useful to answer a question or solve a problem. Converging needs criteria against which to make decisions. For example, in purchasing a pair of shoes, several criteria might be cost, quality, durability, fit, and color. Guidelines for convergent thinking include (Isaksen, Dorval, & Treffinger, 1994; Klein, 1982; Costa, 1985): focus on the problem or goal; be clear, concise, and specific about evaluation criteria; be positive; don't overlook difficult or troublesome areas; and be deliberate and reflective. Divergent thinking is necessary to get creative thinking going and convergent thinking is needed to bring it to closure, to apply it to a particular situation, and to keep it practical and realistic.

Four creative processes—fluency, flexibility, elaboration, and originality—are useful in creative thinking (Klein, 1982; Sternberg, 1986). They are listed and defined in the following box.

Fluency is the ability to think quickly and in quantity—to generate a large number of ideas or possibilities, including relevant responses.

Flexibility involves thinking in different modes, ideally using different categories and mind-sets; it is seeing things from another point of view.

Elaboration is to think in detail—to embroider on and extend an idea.

Originality is to think in new, unique, clever, and unusual ways.

Ways to teach the processes along with related activities that are applicable to various subject areas follow. An interdisciplinary activity, built around a central theme, illustrates how the four processes interact with each other. Strategies that students and teachers can use to enhance creativity are also presented.

Fluency. Brainstorming, listing, and collecting activities encourage fluency. Teacher suggestions such as " think of several ways to ....," and "come up with as many ideas as you can for ..." help students become more fluent. There are also specific ways to encourage fluency at primary, intermediate, and middle levels. In science, give students an outline of an animal and ask them to think of many ideas as they can based on what they know about the animal and the images it brings to mind. This same technique could be used for pictures of monuments, statues, and scenes in social studies. In language arts, students could generate ideas in relation to pictures of situations such as joy, danger, and sadness.

Flexibility. Activities that incorporate role playing, decoding, using symbols, and forecasting and predicting help develop flexible thinking. Teacher statements to help students think flexibly include "list many different kinds of ways to . . . , think of different kinds of reasons for..., and what are several different kinds of. . . ." A variety of activities to encourage students to think flexibly are illustrated below.

Elaboration. Designing, editorializing, illustrating, and inventing rely heavily on elaboration skills. Teachers can help students elaborate on their ideas by suggesting they add supplemental ideas to make the basic idea clearer and think of ideas to add to the main idea. There are several other ways to extend and embellish on an idea. For example, by taking any body part such as head, foot, arm, leg, eye, heart, and so on, you can identify as many words as possible where the name of the body part is included. For arm, you could have armchair, armband, strongarm, and so on; for foot, you could have *football, foothill, footer, foot rest;* for heart you could have *heartthrob, heartily, heartless, heart-shaped*. Other ways for teachers to help students elaborate in the classroom would be to take one of these words and use it in a sentence, a paragraph, and perhaps a short story. Once students get started on elaboration, the possibilities are unlimited. They can refer to dictionaries and encyclopedias to get started

---

ACTIVITY • *Flexible Fun*

SCIENCE DING-A-LINGS *(Match phrase to words: Only medium tall-Fahrenheit)*

WORDS TO CHOOSE FROM

A huge, purple, spring flower	geyser	kilogram
What gram hunters hope to do	tide	aquifer
Condition my shoe laces are in	monsoon	eclipse
What does a barber do?	ultraviolet	atmosphere

WORD AND NUMBER JUMBLES *(5 D in a Z C = 5 digits in a ZIP code)*

24 H in a D	90 D in a R A	7 W of the A W
9 I in a B G	360 D in a C	64 S on a C B
4 and 20 B B in a P	88 K on a P	5 F on a H
20 N in a D	36 I in a Y	3 S on a B

I'D RATHER BE *(discuss, write, act out)*

A snake or a skunk	A basketball or a baseball
A knife or a spoon	An elephant or a chipmunk
A robin or a crow	A rose or a violet
A table or a chair	A doctor or an architect
A radio or a television set	A turtle or a dinosaur

COMBINE NAMES TO MAKE NEW ONES *(combining* snake *and* wolf *= swolf)*

Choose from the following words plus those you add to make new names for people, places, animals, things, and so on:

rabbit, canary, dog, nautilus, eagle, beetle, fly, swallow, koala, crocodile, recorder, television, computer, camera, opener, octopus and then let their imaginations and creativity "take off."

Originality. This process is not easy for students to show in a short time. In addition to asking questions, encourage students to come up with unique, "off beat," and unusual ideas. Some suggestions to help students think of *original* ideas are "think of ideas no one else will think of . . and think of unique and unusual ways to . . " True originality is difficult to achieve, but many students display it in a given situation. Students often show originality as a part of a larger project or assignment.

The "Candy Creations" activity illustrates how students can experience all four creative processes in relation to one theme. The emphasis here is on originality. Note how one process overlaps another. Students can work in a class-sized group, in pairs, or small groups on this activity.

Teachers and students often need "quick references" or strategies to help them carry out activities that provide opportunities for creative thinking in all subjects of the curriculum. One such strategy is SCAMPER (Eberle, 1977, pp. 24–27):

"S" means *substitute*— one person, place, or thing can replace another.

"C" is for *combine*, putting two things together in a different way.

"A" is *adapt* from one situation to another.

ACTIVITY • *Candy Creations*

To have the students experience *fluency,* ask them to think of or brainstorm the names of as many candy bars or candies as they can. Write the names on the blackboard or on a transparency so they can refer to them later. In addition, have students bring wrappers, boxes, or bags that candy comes in from home. Make a display of these coverings on the bulletin board. One or two students might list the candy names from the brainstorming and the bulletin board in the computer.

After the students have the names of 20–30 kinds of candy, have them look at some common candy bar names such as Baby Ruth, Heath, Bounty, and Milky Way in a different or *flexible* way. See if you and your students can identify these:

Crowded closely together	Baseball giant
A lonely English field	Mutinous ship
Open to everybody	Heavenly body

When the students have identified the candies from their "new" descriptions, have them write some "different descriptions" of their own for the names on their list. Have students explain how they arrived at their different ways of expressing the name of the candy. Make a list of the student contributions—probably next to the alphabetized list of the names from the computer printout.

Elaboration can take many forms in relation to several subject matter areas. The students can (1) investigate the nutritional values of different kinds of candies according to the calories of energy they provide (science); (2) write to major makers of candies to find out how they got the names for their candies and how they market them; (3) identify the most popular candy in their age or grade group by conducting a well-designed survey and writing up the results (social studies and language arts); and (4) determine which kind of candy gives the best value for the cost (mathematics).

Students can show originality by inventing a new kind of candy. They might start by listing all the kinds of coverings and basic materials they already know are used in candies (e.g., caramel, dark chocolate, white chocolate, sugar). Then, they can make a list of ingredients (e.g., peanuts, raisins, citron, chocolate bits) and flavors (e.g., spearmint, butterscotch, licorice). "Inventing" new kinds of candies includes both combining old ingredients and flavors in new ways and adding new ones.

More originality could be generated by having students design a wrapper for their new product, give it an appropriate name, and design an advertising plan to introduce it to the public. This activity can be expanded for more student originality and relate to several subject areas—art for the wrapper design, social studies and language arts for the advertising campaign, and mathematics for determining how much the new product should cost.

"M" represents three types of manipulations—*modify, magnify,* and *minify* (diminish).

"P" puts something to uses other than its traditional ones.

"E" is for *eliminate*—omit or get rid of something, either a part of it or all of it; and for e*laborate,* which is to add details, embellish, or extend.

"R" is for *reverse* and *rearrange.*

SCAMPER techniques are easy to remember and easy to use. They can help students create almost any new thing or situation—from an animal, to a type of government, to a song or limerick. For example, students can start with something concrete, such as a traditional chair, and end up with something very different with a variety of functions and an interesting decorative appearance. When creativity wanes in a classroom or while working on an assignment, reference to the strategies of SCAMPER helps students and teachers "get going again."

A second strategy is to refer to a list of products for students to create. Products can relate to a subject matter lesson or unit of instruction or to thematic and multidisciplinary work. Products take many different forms from concrete to abstract and simple to complex. A list of eighty-five product ideas in a dictionary format is presented in the Appendix. Many of them bring together several subjects such as science and social studies along with art, music, or physical education. Students as well as teachers can use the "dictionary list" to find ideas. Together they can judge the appropriateness of the product for primary, intermediate, or middle school levels. And, good teachers can adapt almost any idea to any age or grade group with a "creative" touch. Products are discussed in detail later in this chapter.

Critical Thinking Skills

Critical thinking is a general term that has been defined in many ways. "Critical thinking is a sort of cognitive accountability" (Lipman, 1988, p. 40). Critical thinking is "essentially evaluative in nature. It involves precise, persistent, and objective analysis of any claim, source, or belief to judge its accuracy, validity, or worth" (Beyer, 1988, p. 61). Skills to carry out critical thinking are not used in any particular sequence. They are a collection of specific operations that can be used alone or in combination with other skills in any order. Critical thinking skills can be integrated into every subject matter from kindergarten through high school. They are best learned when students have opportunities to practice them until they become a part of their everyday thinking.

Twelve critical thinking skills are listed in the following box. Definitions and examples of practical ways to use them in the classroom follow (Bechtol & Sorenson, 1993, p. 176; Sorenson et al., 1988, pp. 71–72; Beyer, 1988, pp. 60–64).

Comparing and contrasting	Identifying bias and stereotype
Distinguishing between fact and opinion	Recognizing point of view
Distinguishing between relevant and irrelevant information	Recognizing consistent and inconsistent reasoning
Distinguishing between reliable and unreliable sources	Recognizing assumptions and generalizations
Identifying cause and effect	Analyzing arguments
Sequencing and prioritizing	Identifying induction and deduction

Comparing and Contrasting. These processes are carried out by determining similarities and differences about objects, situations, ideas, institutions, and so on. Some examples for students to consider are, How are spiders and ants alike and different? How are baseball and football alike and different? Compare and contrast several religions such as Christianity, Judaism, and Islam.

Distinguishing Between Fact and Opinion. Here, statements that can be verified (facts) are separated from those that can not (opinion). Have students give reasons why some statements are facts and others are opinions in the following scenario:

> The fire started at 2:30 A.M. while the three children and the mother were asleep. No one called the fire department until 2:50 A.M. when the fire was raging out of control.

Distinguishing Between Relevant and Irrelevant Information. Deciding whether something is related (relevant) to the item or situation under discussion or not (irrelevant) is the basis for this process. For the following situation, students can identify which items are relevant and which are irrelevant. They can give reasons for all their decisions.

> In selecting a band instrument for a student, the following items need to be considered: shape of mouth; dental structure; willingness to practice; interest in being in the color guard and/or marching band; the instrument a friend is going to play; cost of the instrument; color of the lining in the instrument case; physique of student.

Distinguishing Between Reliable and Unreliable Sources. The reliability of a source is determined by whether it is believable or not. This is based on the author's expertise and reputation, the reputation of the publisher, the accuracy of the information, and the agreement of the information under discussion with that of other sources. For example, an auto manufacturer advertised that its Alpha model got more miles per gallon than its competitor, Beta. *Consumer Reports* magazine ranked Alpha's mileage lower than that of Beta. Which source is probably more reliable? Why?

Identifying Cause and Effect. This process involves both identifying the causes, reasons, or motives for a condition or action and the effects, results or outcomes of the cause. Some examples are: What were the main causes and effects of these three wars—World War II, Vietnam War, and the Gulf War? What were the major causes and effects of the stock market crashes of 1929 and 1987?

Sequencing and Prioritizing. These are organizational skills. Sequencing involves determining the logical order of tasks or events to produce a product or attain a goal. Prioritizing involves ranking each item or step according to its importance in the situation at hand. For example, determine the steps an individual needs to take to get a job. Then, put the steps in order from least important to most important.

Identifying Bias and Stereotype. Personal feelings are involved in these processes. Bias is recognized as a view slanted in favor or against something or someone, a view often formed unfairly. Stereotype is a form of bias where certain characteristics are considered common to a group without respect or consideration for individuals and their differences. Examples are (1) in settling playground disputes, one female teacher always takes the side of the girls (bias); (2) third world countries are unable to maintain a democratic form of government for more than a few years (stereotype).

Recognizing Point of View. This involves identifying the position or situation from which something is observed, presented, or considered. Possible elements of bias may also enter in. For example, the Democrats considered the Supreme Court candidate a moderate while the Republicans considered the candidate to be liberal. The boy thought the tennis shoes were a "bargain"; his mother thought they were "expensive."

Recognizing Consistent and Inconsistent Reasoning. Decide whether the line of reasoning is logical (consistent) or contradictory (inconsistent). Example: The family had always said one of its ancestors came to the United States from England in 1852. His naturalization papers indicated he came in 1854. These two sets of data are inconsistent, and more information is needed to decide which date is correct.

Recognizing Assumptions and Generalizations. Both processes demand keen judgments. Assumptions involve identifying and exploring the validity of the beliefs or ideas we take for granted or tend to accept as true. Generalizations are statements, laws, or principles drawn from specific verifiable situations or information. For example, " a 3.5 grade point out of a possible 4.0 ensures a student's acceptance at a highly-rated college or university" is an assumption that may or may not be valid depending on other characteristics of the student and qualifications of the school. In contrast, "when the pressure of a confined gas increases, the volume of the gas decreases if the temperature is held constant" is a generalization that can be verified by scientific experiment.

Analyzing Arguments. Identify the elements of an argument and then determine the strength or weakness of each element. For example, a teenager tells her parents, "Everyone else in my class gets to buy a T-shirt with the school's new logo on it. You are not being fair when you won't let me buy one." What are the elements of this argument? Which ones are strong, and which are weak?

Identifying Induction and Deduction. These are very general ways of thinking. *Induction* is often called "bottoms-up" thinking because conclusions are drawn from specific instances—one building on another until the conclusion is reached (Clarke, 1990, pp. 61, 158). Deduction is often referred to as "top-down" thinking because the conclusion or result is known and the search is for specific instances that led to that particular conclusion (Albrecht, 1980). For example, an inductive approach follows:

> You are given four different shapes and sizes of triangles—right-angled, obtuse, isosceles, equilateral. You measure the angles in each one and add them up. The sum for each triangle is 180 degrees. You therefore reason that "the sum of the angles of any triangle is 180 degrees."

Reasoning *deductively*, you can make the following decision. The small creature you found in the grass has six legs. Since you know the generalization that "insects have six legs and mites and spiders have eight legs," you reason that the creature is an insect. Solving "mysteries" of all kinds involves deductive reasoning because you are confronted with the conclusion and solving involves identifying the specific instances that led to it. For example, "How did that hole get in my sweater?" In an attempt to identify specifics, one would look at the size, location, and kind of hole—rip, burn, large, small, and so on. Then one would recount where the sweater had been worn, when it was last seen without a hole, and what kind of activities the wearer had been doing between when the sweater was noted without the hole and when the hole was identified. All kinds of mysteries can be "solved" in this same manner.

Single-Step Problem-Solving Techniques

Some or all of these skills are often presented in math teaching materials. But they are useful in all subject areas and in everyday living. These skills are easy for students to understand and use and have self-explanatory titles. They can be introduced in the primary grades and expanded in complexity and difficulty for a variety of situations as students progress through the intermediate and middle grades.

Ten techniques are listed in the following box. The first six—working backward, simplifying and reducing, recognizing patterns, organizing lists, guessing and testing, and forming analogies—are fairly precise in nature. The other four—making a drawing or figure, making a table or graph, making a model, and acting it out—give students more opportunities for open-ended thinking and exploration. Definitions, along with examples and suggestions of appropriate situations in which to teach and use the techniques in various subject areas, are discussed below (Bechtol & Sorenson, 1993, pp. 177–182; Sorenson et al., 1988, pp. 74–76; Reys, Suydam & Lindquist, 1992, pp. 34–37).

Working Backward	Forming analogies
Simplifying and reducing	Making a drawing or figure
Recognizing patterns	Making a table or graph
Organizing lists	Making a model
Guessing and testing	Acting it out

Working Backward. This technique is used when the answer or situation is known. For example, Sean has to catch the school bus at 7:50 A.M. In order to determine the correct time to set his alarm, he can work backward from 7:50. He needs to estimate how much time it takes him to get up and dressed, eat breakfast, gather together his books and other school materials, get to the bus stop, and to do any other chores. By adding up the total times and subtracting them from 7:50, he has a good idea of what time he should set the alarm. This skill is used in planning situations whenever the limits of cost, time, distance, and so on are known. When problems become more complex, students should write down the amounts or situations so they can be accounted for in an orderly fashion and so they do not become frustrated or lost in the process of working from the general to the specific.

Simplifying and Reducing. This skill is useful in any situation involving numbers. Often large numbers distract students, but if they reduce the size of the numbers to a smaller or "round" amount, they can see the process more clearly and get a good estimate of what the result or answer will be. An example of simplification would be, If you needed 9 rose bushes at $1.89 each, how much would they cost? By simplifying $1.89 to $2, you can come up with an estimate of $18 (9 times $2) which is pretty close to the exact amount of $17.01 (9 times $1.89). For another example, assume that a saleswoman took a 2,100-mile business trip. Her average mileage was 28 miles per gallon, and the average price of a gallon of gasoline was $1.29. How many miles did she travel, and how much did she spend for gasoline? This is how the technique works: Reduce the trip size to 100 miles, change the miles per gallon to 10, and assume the cost of gas is $1 per gallon to simplify the process as follows. The saleswoman used 10 gallons of gas (100 divided by 10) and paid $10 (10 times $1). Once the process is clear, the student can plug in the exact numbers. For this example, the saleswoman used 75 gallons of gas (2,100 miles divided by 28 miles/gallon) and the cost was $96.75 (75 gallons times $1.29/gallon).

Recognizing Patterns. This technique is applicable in a variety of situations—numbers, words, letters, shapes, and forms. Try extending the patterns for each of the following:

- 3, 6, 9, 12 . . . **15, 18, 21, 24** . . .

  Pattern rule: **Counting by 3's**

- A, B, A, C, A, D, ___, ___, ___,

  Pattern rule: _____

- Barbara, David, Frank, ___, ___

  Pattern rule: _____

Another type of pattern can be found in "puzzles" such as cryptoquotes. Look at the well-known quote and its author below and see if you can "translate" it into English.

LVSVM OWN CBB NAEE NCTCMMCQ QIZN
   PCW DZL
FC NCFZP. — NICTZG HVBBVMGCL

Some of the patterns that you can look for are word length, common letters such as *r, s, t, l, n, e*; parts of speech such as *the, to, an*; location of words in a sentence, and single letters such as *I* and *a*. How did you do? The correct translation of the quote is "Never put off till tomorrow what you can do today" (Thomas Jefferson).

These quotes are motivating for students as well as good practice in identifying patterns. More cryptoquotes are found in the Appendix. After students become good at working these, have them design their own codes for quotes using a random number table for the alphabet and working on the computer. Quotes can be related to work in social studies, science, math, and language arts. Patterns can be found in animal and human footprints, geological formations on the earth's surface, cloud arrangements in the sky, outer coverings of many living things, and many other places.

Organizing Lists. This process involves arranging information into categories and/or sequences to make it easier to see relationships and interpret data. For example, if the problem was to "(1) estimate and (2) find out how many jelly beans there were of each color in the jar," information for both operations could be listed under the following headings:

Color of Jelly Beans	Number Estimated	Number Counted
Green		
Black		
Orange		
Yellow		
White		
Pink		
Red		

This technique helps students learn how to organize by selecting categories that are relevant to the problem and then recording data under them. It can also be used to order data in difficult problems and as a tool to classify information.

Guessing and Testing. Students can use this technique to make approximations for an answer, then test the approximation to see if it works. Wild or random guessing is not very effective and teachers should discourage it. Here is an example:

Nine *X*'s are shown in the square. Can you draw two more squares on the diagram so that each *X* has its own area or pen?

```
X  X  X
X  X  X
X  X  X
```

Other examples are the cryptoquotes shown in the Appendix. Users combine guessing and testing with recognizing patterns techniques to solve them.

Forming Analogies. This an extension of recognizing patterns. To solve analogies, students must recognize relationships in which one thing is compared to another. In the following example, (A) is to (B) as (C) is to (D). D is usually the unknown quantity in the analogy comparison.

(A) wheel : (B) bicycle :: (C) leg : (D)? (body)

This example is a "part compared to whole" analogy. Other kinds of analogies include cause compared to effect; user compared to tool; comparing of opposites; object compared to use; specific member compared to a general group; and comparing synonyms. See if you can identify some of the following different types:

(A) human : (B) mammal :: (C) clam : (D)? (mollusk)

(A) hammer : carpenter :: (C) compass : (D)? (sailor)

(A) cold : (B) hot :: (C) black : (D)? (white)

(A) rain : (B) flood :: (C) iceberg : (D)? (shipwreck)

Two basic steps have been suggested to help solve analogies (Sternberg, 1986, pp. 112–122; Beyer, 1988, p. 133). They are (1) look at the A and B side of the analogy to identify or translate the key terms or elements, then recall knowledge associated with each of these key terms and infer the appropriate relationship between them; and (2) look at the C and D side of the analogy to map and apply the inferred relationship between C and D, remembering that D is usually the unknown. Then complete the analogy based on your inferences and decisions. The analogies just shown are verbal, but analogies may also be made with numbers, symbols, figures, and so on.

Making a Drawing or Figure. Drawing comes naturally to young children, and we often ask them to draw what they see and feel. But we use this technique too seldom with older students. For example, if you want to tell someone who is not familiar with your town how to get to your house, you can write down the streets and turns he or she should take from the starting point or a main highway to your house. However, adding a simple map that shows the relationships of the streets with arrows to shows the person where to turn, makes finding your house a lot easier.

Making a Table or Graph. This technique helps us organize and summarize both numerical and verbal data so we can draw inferences and make evaluations of past situations or projections for future actions. An example of a simple table or chart was presented in this section under "organized listing." Students can make tables and charts from stories in newspapers and magazines. A comparison of these tables or charts with the narrative illustrates how much easier the reader can recognize relationships in an organized format compared to only reading it in sentences.

Making a Model. Designing an original model is considered one of the human's highest levels of intellectual performance. Yet young children often make a kind of model when they "show us how it is or was." Students need to gain practice in using models and then make their own. Models help us visualize a situation, explain complex and abstract situations, relate to hands-on activities, and illustrate relationships in information. Three kinds of models—iconic, analog, and symbolic—were discussed in the inquiry processes section of this chapter.

Acting it Out. Many of today's students learn best if they are personally involved. Acting isn't just for plays and skits. It can be achieved in all subject matter areas and usually can be done right in the classroom. For example, two terms that students often confuse or fail to understand are *rotation* and *revolution* as they relate to the bodies of the solar system. To make these terms meaningful, students can *rotate* by putting one leg on the floor and moving their body around on it like a spinning top. *Revolution* can be illustrated by having each student move around a globe, or other object at a set distance to form a path around the object. Math is often considered an "individual" subject, but acting out and getting involved helps many students understand concepts and operations. Basic division, for example, can be illustrated by starting with a group of 26 students on one side of the room. Ask students to leave the group five at a time. Then count how many groups of five left and how many students remain. This is a concrete way of illustrating that 26 divided by 5 equals 5 plus a remainder of 1. Acting out can also be used with fractions, decimals, multiplication, addition, and so on.

Bloom's Cognitive Levels

This taxonomy deals with levels of thinking rather than skills themselves such as those found in the four groups just discussed. But in lesson planning and class discussions, teachers can use them in the same manner—to move student thinking from lower to higher levels. The following diagram illustrates the hierarchical arrangement of this taxonomy (Bloom, 1959; Bechtol & Sorenson, 1993, p. 162). Students need to learn the information on the lower steps or levels before proceeding to the higher ones. This hierarchical arrangement also suggests that lessons should allow for students to progress from the lower levels of knowledge and comprehension to the higher levels of application, analysis, synthesis and evaluation.

Brief definitions, sample verbs, and activities for each of the levels are discussed here (Bechtol & Sorenson, 1993 pp. 162–165; Sorenson et al., 1988, pp. 5–6).

Knowledge. This is the lowest level of learning. It includes recall and memory where learners recall specifics with concrete references. Knowledge includes specific facts, dates, events, persons, places, and so on. Verbs include *define, recall, identify, label, collect,* and *observe.* General activities are defining terminology and symbols; recalling facts, names, examples, rules, and categories; recognizing trends, causes, and relationships; and acquiring procedures, implications, and principles.

Comprehension. Learners can use materials or ideas without relating them to other ideas or materials. Verbs include *infer, paraphrase, explain, give examples, summarize,* and *extrapolate.* General activities are rephrasing definitions, illustrating meanings, interpreting relationships, drawing conclusions, demonstrating methods, inferring implications, and predicting consequences.

Application. Learners use information in specific situations. The information may be in the form of general ideas or concepts, facts, principles, or theories that students remember and apply. Verbs include *demonstrate, modify, change, use,* and *rearrange.* General activities are applying principles, rules, and theories; organizing procedures, conclusions, and effects; choosing situations and methods; restructuring processes, generalizations, and phenomena.

Analysis. At this level, learners take apart information to make new relationships. Learners clarify information by discovering hidden meaning and basic structure. Verbs include *interpret, solve, discriminate, break down,* and *sequence.* General activities are recognizing assumptions and patterns; deducing conclusions, hypotheses, and points of view; analyzing relationships, themes and evidence, causes and effects; and contrasting ideas, parts, and arguments.

Synthesis. Students reassemble or synthesize the component parts of an idea to develop new or creative ideas or structures that were not previously apparent. Verbs include *create, compose, design, construct,* and *propose.* General activities are producing products and compositions; proposing objectives, means, and solutions; designing plans and operations; organizing taxonomies, concepts, schemes, and theories; and deriving relationships, abstractions, and generalizations.

Evaluation. This is the highest level of cognition. It calls for judging materials, information, or methods

A Brief Overview of Bloom's Cognitive Taxonomy

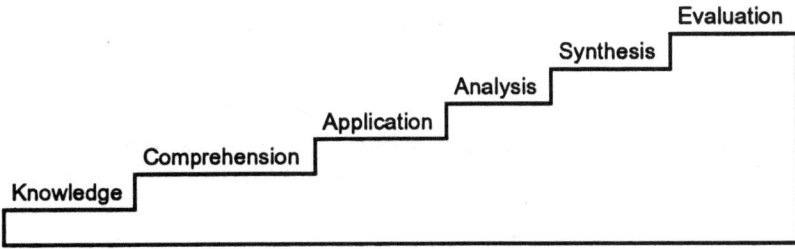

Source: W. Bechtol and J. Sorenson, *Restructuring Schooling for Individual Students* (Boston: Allyn and Bacon, 1993), p. 162. Reprinted with permission.

for specific purposes, and using criteria to make a decision. It relates to the problem-solving process of selecting one of several proposed alternatives for action. Verbs include *appraise, judge, evaluate, justify, criticize*. General activities are judging accuracy, consistency, and reliability; assessing errors, fallacies, predictions, and means and ends; considering efficiency, utility, and standards; and contrasting alternatives and courses of action.

Bloom's cognitive levels are useful in planning, teaching, and questioning for all students in any classroom starting in kindergarten. They provide a vehicle to move from simple recall to indepth probing of information as a lesson or unit of instruction develops. They also provide ways to meet needs of individual students. Some students will need more practice at lower levels while others who have already mastered this information, should spend more time on higher-level tasks and activities. Also, many students can learn to use the levels of the taxonomy in their own writing and questioning in lessons and assignments. Sample writing tasks for intermediate and middle-level students that are appropriate to each of Bloom's levels are presented here (Hollingsworth & Eastman, 1988, p. 14; Sorenson et al., 1988, p. 99).

It should be noted that a task listed at any one level of the taxonomy naturally builds on familiarity with handling information at the level or levels below it. Many of the skills from the other four thinking skills groups are used while manipulating information at various levels of the taxonomy.

Knowledge of the meaning and ways to use more than 40 subskills in five thinking skills groups—inquiry processes, creative thinking processes, critical thinking skills, single-step problem-solving techniques, and Bloom's cognitive levels—have been presented in this section. Mastery of these skills provides the tools and "know-how" to carry out multistep problem solving.

PROCESS: MULTISTEP PROBLEM SOLVING

Solving problems is the highest form of learning. It is a process by which the problem solver, consciously or unconsciously, moves systematically or randomly through a series of operations, gathering more data as needed, making choices and selections to arrive at one or several solutions. Then these solutions need to be tested and the results from them verified and evaluated to determine whether or not they have solved the problem. A series of guidelines to help students carry out multistep problem solving using thinking skills appropriate to the problem situation along with examples to illustrate ways to solve problems are the focus of this section. Relationships of thinking and problem solving to content, product, and environment are also discussed.

Guidelines for Problem Solving

Multistep problem solving can be a complex operation with many thought processes going on at the same time. Students need direction to get started and to keep on task. One way to help them is to provide a set of strategies in the form of a model. The steps of a model are usually shown in sequence, but in reality problem solving can start at any step. Information that influenced the model as well as the model itself are discussed here.

Background to the Model. Education literature provides many sequences and models for solving problems. Four of these that provide the background for the model in Figure 2-5 are summarized here. Wallas (in Davis and Rimm, 1994, p. 191) suggests a simple model with four stages: (1) *preparation,* where the

Writing Tasks Appropriate to Levels of Bloom's Cognitive Taxonomy

Bloom Level	Writing Tasks
Knowledge	Lists, definitions, notes, labels, announcements, autobiographies
Comprehension	Reports, descriptions, explanations, memos, summaries, agendas
Application	Letters, interviews, journals, maps, posters, directions, biographical sketches
Analysis	Opinions, questionnaires, reports, charts, graphs, diagnoses, proposals, comparisons
Synthesis	Advertisements, plays, essays, stories, poems, scripts, lyrics, cartoons, myths, tales
Evaluation	Book reports, research reports, editorials, reviews, debates, decisions, recommendations, weather reports

FIGURE 2–5 Practical Problem-Solving Model

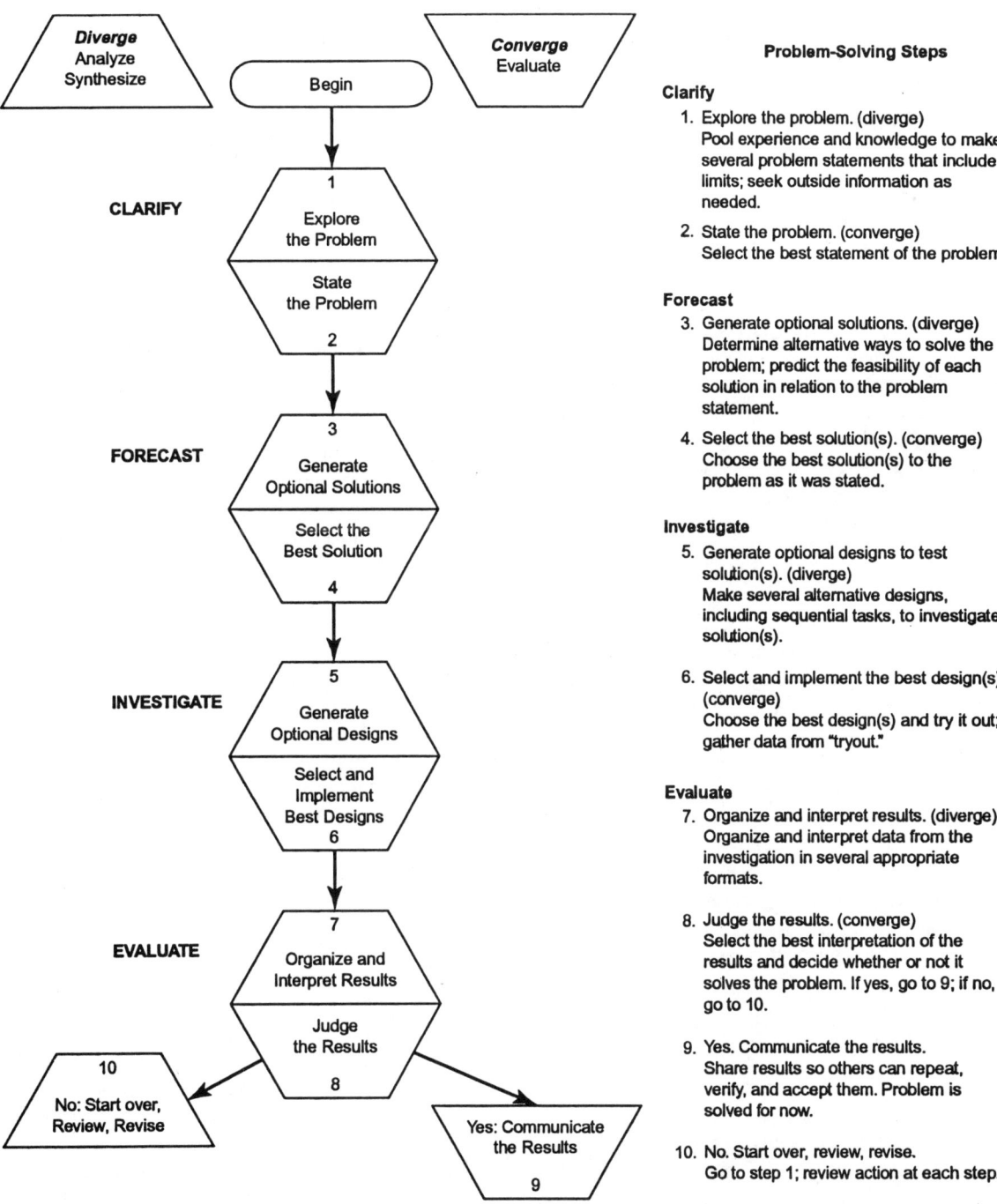

Source: Modified from W. Bechtol and J. Sorenson, *Restructuring Schooling for Individual Students* (Boston: Allyn and Bacon, 1993), p. 185. Reprinted with permission.

elements of the problem are reviewed and clarified and the problem is defined; (2) *incubation,* where the problem solver reflects on the problem, "sleeps" on it, and may be "solving" it unconsciously; (3) *inspiration,* where a solution appears and a sense of excitement exists; and (4) *verification,* where the inspired solution is checked for workability, feasibility, and/or acceptability.

Wales, Nardi, and Stager (1986, p. 38) present a decision-making process with four steps. The titles of these steps are self-explanatory. Step 1 is *state the goal;* step 2, *generate ideas;* step 3, *prepare a plan;* and step 4, *take action.* Each step has three considerations—analysis to identify problems, synthesis to create options, and evaluation to carry out selections.

Isaksen and Treffinger (1985, p. two-4) present a series of six steps for the "creative problem-solving" process. These are (1) *mess finding,* (2) *data finding,* (3) *problem finding,* (4) *idea finding,* (5) *solution finding,* and (6) *acceptance finding.* There is a diverge and converge operation at each step.

Haney and Sorenson (1977, p. 20) and Sorenson et al. (1988, p. 81) suggest seven steps for solving a problem: (1) *sense and define the problem;* (2) *form hypotheses* or tentative solutions; (3) *predict the consequences* of the hypotheses and choose the most plausible one(s); (4) *design and carry out investigations* to test the hypotheses; (5) *gather data;* (6) *interpret data and evaluate data* to determine whether or not it supports the hypotheses; and (7) *communicate the results* of the investigation to others to repeat and verify.

Practical Problem-Solving Model. The sequence shown in Figure 2–5 is simplified to four basic steps—clarify, forecast, investigate, and evaluate—and ten substeps. There is a divergent and a convergent operation at each of the four steps plus a final evaluation to determine whether or not the procedure that was carried out solved the problem. The model can be used to solve problems in all subject matter areas as well as those in daily life. It can be used by students at all age and grade levels with appropriate adjustments for language difficulty, teacher input, student input, and content of the problem.

This model incorporates both words and pictures. The shape of the blocks numbered 1, 3, 5, 7 indicates that the problem solver is *diverging*—starting with an idea and generating a large number of possibilities that can flow to the companion block. In the companion blocks numbered 2, 4, 6, 8, the solver is *converging*—selecting the best possibility or possibilities from the large number of ideas that flowed into the block. Divergence allows for fluent, free, brainstorming and asks students to consider a wide range of ideas; convergence requires students to prioritize and select the "best" of the ideas generated to solve the problem. The four basic steps of this model along with related substeps are summarized here.

- **Clarify:** Explore and state the problem (substeps 1, 2)
- **Forecast:** Generate many solutions and select best one(s) (substeps 3, 4)
- **Investigate:** Select best design and try it out; gather data (substeps 5, 6)
- **Evaluate:** Judge the data from the investigation (substeps 7, 8); and determine whether or not the problem is solved (substeps 9, 10).

The multistep problem-solving process, using the guidelines of the model in Figure 2–5 is illustrated in the next section with two different kinds of problems. A worksheet to help students follow along with the problem-solving process is shown in Figure 2–6.

Ways to Solve Different Kinds of Problems

Two problems are described in detail in this section. The first one is titled "Egg or Water Balloon in a Bottle" and is appropriate for intermediate-level science students (Bechtol & Sorenson, 1993, pp. 184–188). "Too Much Trash" is the second problem and could be part of a middle-level social studies curriculum (Bechtol & Sorenson, 1993, pp. 188–191). The discussion of these two problems illustrates how the teacher and a group of students might proceed through the steps and substeps of the model in Figure 2–5.

Note that an everyday problem, "The Mystery of the Stained Shirt," acted as the introduction to this chapter. It is more open-ended than the two problems discussed here and can be adapted to any level, K–8. The steps are not identified in the discussion. This task is left to the students and the teacher. Teachers might want to work through the "Mystery" problem with their students before they tackle the more formal ones described here. Note how one problem led to another in this situation.

FIGURE 2–6 Student Problem-Solving Worksheet

CLARIFY

1. Explore the problem and make several problem statements; include limits. (diverge)

   _____

   _____

2. State the problem by selecting the best statement from step 1. (converge)

   _____

   _____

FORECAST

3. Generate optional solutions. (diverge) _____

   _____

4. Select the best solution. (converge) _____

INVESTIGATE

5. Generate optional designs to test solutions. (diverge) _____

   _____

6. Select and try out best designs. (converge) _____

   _____

EVALUATE

7. Organize and interpret results. (diverge) _____

   _____

8. Judge the results. (converge)   Yes: Results solve problem; go to step 9.
   Select best interpretation.   No: Results do NOT solve problem; go to step 10.

9. Yes: Communicate the results.   Share results so others can repeat, verify, and accept them; problem is solved for now.

10. No: Start over, review, revise.   Return to step 1; review action at each step. Revise as necessary to solve the problem.

Source: Modified from W. Bechtol and J. Sorenson, *Restructuring Schooling for Individual Students* (Boston: Allyn and Bacon, 1993), p. 390. Reprinted with permission.

Problem 1: "Egg or Water Balloon in a Bottle."
The teacher brought a 2-quart corn syrup bottle (or other wide-mouthed glass bottle) with a peeled, hard-boiled egg (or water balloon) inside it to a science class of intermediate-level students. She turned the bottle upside down. The egg did not come out of the bottle. It appeared to be larger than the mouth opening of the bottle. Now, she asked the students, "How can we solve the problem?" Using the four basic steps and the ten related substeps of the model in Figure 2–5, they carried out the process. Numbers in the text refer to those of the ten substeps.

CLARIFY

1. They *explored the problem* situation, set basic limits such as not breaking the bottle or egg, and arrived at these possible ways to state the problem:

   a. Get the egg out of the bottle.

   b. How can we get the egg out of the bottle without breaking the egg or the bottle?

   c. List ways to get the egg out of the bottle.

2. After discussing the three statements, they selected problem statement b as the best *problem statement* because it clearly stated the situation and included limits that needed to be considered in forming solutions. (This could have been written as a statement such as "Getting the egg out of the bottle without breaking it or the bottle," instead of as a question.)

FORECAST

3. *Generating optional solutions* or ways to solve the problem is probably the part of the process the students liked best. Some of their solutions were

   a. Fill the bottle with water.

   b. Shake the egg very hard against the neck of the bottle.

   c. Add more air molecules to the bottle so there will be more molecules inside the bottle than outside the bottle.

   d. Warm the molecules of air inside the bottle with the egg "sealed" against the neck of the bottle.

   e. While holding the bottle vertically with the egg "sealed" against the neck of the bottle, blow very hard directly under the bottle neck.

4. *Selecting the best solution(s)* offers the most exciting teaching opportunities. Here students need to accept or reject each solution from substep 3 on the basis of what they already know. Or they need to gather new information and use it. They must give reasons for their answers. This part of the problem-solving process uses a variety of thinking skills such as analysis, synthesis, and evaluation from Bloom's cognitive levels, inferring and predicting skills from inquiry processes, and combinations of several creative thinking, critical thinking, and single-step problem solving techniques. The students decided to investigate all five solutions since they seemed possible and did not require elaborate equipment.

INVESTIGATE

For this problem, the students eliminated solution 3a because they tried it and the egg did not come out. They accepted solution 3b because the egg did come out. And, they decided to consider solutions c, d, and e further, but needed to gather more information and set up designs to carry them out.

5. For solution 3c, the students *generated optional designs* to put more molecules into the bottle. These designs included using a tire pump, blowing very hard into the bottle, and blowing air into the bottle with a straw. For solution 3d, they figured they could warm the air molecules inside the bottle by heating the outside of the bottle or by dropping burning paper into the bottle. For solution 3e, they decided to try blowing very hard under the neck of the bottle while holding their hands on one side to direct the molecules under the bottle neck.

6. *Selecting and implementing the best design* held high interest for the students. For solution 3c, they blew very hard directly into the neck of the bottle with the lips in a "trumpet-blowing formation," let the egg slide down into the neck, and then suddenly moved the lips away. The egg came out of the bottle. For solution 3d, they warmed the bottle with hot water from the faucet while holding it at a downward angle with the egg "sealed" in the neck. The egg came out of the bottle. And for solution 3e, they blew very hard under the neck of the bottle. Here, the egg started down the neck, but did not come all of the way out of the bottle. They needed to pursue this further. In summary, implementation of designs for solutions 3b, c, d, and e provided possible ways to solve the problem.

EVALUATE

7. The students *organized the results* in both narrative and chart form, using diagrams as appropriate.

Then, drawing information from both formats, they interpreted the results as follows:

a. Filling the bottle with water does not work since the egg did not come out when they tried it. They need to find reasons for why it did not come out.

b. Shaking will get the egg out of the bottle, but it is a matter of using physical force and gravity.

c. Blowing hard into the neck of the bottle to add more molecules brought the egg out of the bottle. This worked because when the greater number of molecules inside the bottle tried to reach "equilibrium," they pushed the egg out of ahead of them. Molecules move from areas of greater to those of lesser concentrations.

d. Warming air molecules inside the bottle by warming the bottle itself, gave the air molecules more energy causing them to move faster and to exert greater pressure to "push" the egg out of the bottle.

e. Blowing very hard underneath the neck of the bottle was only a partial success, but investigations at the library indicated the idea was feasible. Reducing the number of air molecules under the neck by blowing hard leaves a greater concentration of molecules inside the bottle. When the air molecules try to reach equilibrium by moving from areas of greater to lesser pressure, they push the egg out ahead of them. The students needed to blow harder to reduce the air pressure a bit more. Further experimentation was needed here.

8. In judging the results, they selected "blowing very hard directly into the bottle" and "heating the air molecules in the bottle by running hot water from the faucet over the bottle" as equally effective methods to solve the problem.

9. They decided they had solved the problem successfully, at least for now. Therefore, they communicated *their results* to another class and asked them to try their solutions and verify them. They did not need to proceed to substep 10.

The "egg in the bottle" problem was solved with rather precise results. The strategy the teacher used was to present a stimulus—the egg in the bottle— to the students and then use the inquiry teaching style to guide the entire class-sized group through the steps of solving the problem. They used many of the inquiry thinking skills, along with several critical thinking skills such as identifying cause and effect, identifying relevant and irrelevant data, and identifying inductive and deductive thinking. The teacher also encouraged creative thinking by using fluency in all steps of the model and flexibility in generating solutions. Several single-step problem solving techniques such as guessing and testing, recognizing patterns, and forming analogies as well as thinking at Bloom's higher cognitive levels were used frequently.

A most interesting elaborative feature of this problem was that it automatically led to a second problem: "How did the egg get into the bottle?" To solve this problem, the students could work in small, cooperative, or other groups. Now the teaching style would change to cooperative and/or student-centered rather than inquiry. This situation presents a good example of using teaching styles appropriately—starting students out with guidance in the inquiry style, then moving to more student responsibility in the cooperative and student-centered styles. Of course, the teacher can provide assistance and guidance to the groups if they run into difficulty in keeping the multistep problem-solving process moving along.

Problem 2: "Too Much Trash." The floors in the hallways and cafeteria of the Washington Middle School were littered with candy wrappers, lunch papers, parts of old assignments, occasional bits of food, and other waste materials, to the point where they were nearly unsafe to walk on. Repeated announcements by the principal, student council members, and others reminding students to put their trash in the containers provided for it had not solved the problem.

Finally, the students and a teacher of one of the social studies classes decided to try to solve this problem using the guidelines of the practical problem-solving model in Figure 2–5. First the teacher decided to work on the problem with the students in a class-sized group. Then, he broke them into cooperative groups of four to five students to deal with the more specific aspects of the problem. The narrative below summarizes their work. The titles refer to the steps and the numbers to the substeps of the model in Figure 2–5.

CLARIFY

1. After exploring the main conditions of the problem, the students agreed on four ways to *state the problem:*

a. Ways to keep litter off the floors.

b. Ways to persuade students to put their litter in the cans provided.

c. Putting trash in containers.

d. A strategy to encourage students to put their trash in containers instead of on the floor.

2. They eliminated problem statements a, b, and c as too weak, too mild, or too negative, and agreed to use d as the *problem statement*.

FORECAST

3. They *generated several solutions* to the problem:

   a. Reposition trash cans in areas where they found the most trash.

   b. Identify students who were doing the most littering and fine them.

   c. Station "trash detectives" near stairways and other areas of heavy littering to remind students who littered to put their trash in containers.

   d. Identify the heavy litterers and make them pick up the trash each day.

4. In *selecting the best solution*, they decided to eliminate solution 3b because they didn't want to identify peers if they had to pay money, and fines had not worked very well to get students to return their library books on time. Likewise, they eliminated solution 3d because they thought it would take too much effort to get these students to do the pickup effectively. They couldn't decide between solutions 3a and 3c, so they combined the best elements of each into the solution they would implement.

INVESTIGATE

5. Before they could *generate designs*, they needed to form subgroups from the class to do several preliminary tasks, such as

   a. Identify the areas where most of the trash was deposited. They got a map of the school and collected data for one week. They used "items of trash regardless of size" as their criteria for counting.

   b. Explore ways and locations for stationing "trash detectives." They decided to use the other group's survey data on the "heaviest trash locations" to help find the best locations for the detectives. And they visited the counselor to ask for ways to word "reprimands" from the detectives to trash droppers in a positive, yet firm manner.

   c. Identify ways to select "trash detectives" and reposition the containers. They went to the principal, who met with them and the custodians to be sure everyone would agree on moving containers to the heavy use areas. They conferred with their teacher on the "detective selection" process. She suggested they use leadership inventories and/or data from the sociogram they had completed earlier in the year. One of the students suggested starting with students from the class who were identified as leaders by their peers. They also thought an equal number of boys and girls should be detectives. If the detective idea was successful, they could develop a pool of students to select from.

   d. Determine length of shifts of detectives. The initial survey group had gathered data for one week to determine high-discard areas using 15-minute shifts—one shift before school, two shifts at noon, and one shift after school. This seemed to work well and allowed the detectives time for lunch, so they decided to try it again.

6. From the information they gathered from conversations with peers and others, new ideas they generated, and data from the survey group on discard areas, they went ahead and *implemented the design* as follows:

   a. Trash containers with glow-in-the-dark "TRASH" signs were moved to the ten heaviest discard areas.

   b. Twenty students, who were identified as leaders, were stationed about 3 feet from a trash container for two 15-minute shifts—one group of ten before school and at noon, and the other group of ten at noon and after school. Detectives did not wear any signs or "uniforms."

   c. The plan was outlined and explained to the student council by the chair of the subcommittee that identified heavy use areas along with comments from chairs of the four subcommittees that indicated how they had arrived at their decisions. The council endorsed the plan wholeheartedly. This information was shared with the entire student body and faculty during the announcements over the loud speaker on Friday morning before they planned to start the program on Monday. This information was also repeated each morning during the first week.

EVALUATE

7. *Results were organized and interpreted* from the data of the first "two-week" try-out as follows:

   a. The amount of trash on the floors decreased about 60 percent. This was determined by the same committee that had completed the initial survey, using a map to identify "heavy discard areas."

   b. The "detectives" found the job tolerable and a good opportunity to develop positive leadership in a peer–peer situation. These attitudes were determined through interviews with all twenty detectives.

   c. Although most students reacted positively to more strategically placed containers and a gentle reminder to pick up what they dropped and use the cans next time—there were a few chronic "trashers" who seemed untouched by the campaign. They were mostly "older" boys and a few girls who sometimes mocked what the detectives told them and did exactly as they pleased.

8, 9, 10. *Judging the results* indicated that generally, the problem was on the way to being solved, but reducing trash by 60 percent was not enough. They wanted:

   a. More cooperation from the entire student body

   b. Ways to change the attitude and/or habits of "chronic trashers"

   c. Ways to make the detective job more satisfying

   d. Strategies to sustain the program after the "newness wears off."

As is often the case, working on the solution to one problem leads to the finding of other problems. These new problems can be solved by using the same guidelines as were used to solve the initial problem. In a second attempt, more information is already available to the students and they can probably work much more efficiently and effectively. Also, they can learn from their earlier mistakes or misjudgments—which is a useful skill for us all to learn.

Remember that "repositioning trash containers" and having students act as "trash detectives" is only one way to solve this problem. The characteristics of the student body and school community, size of school, ages of students, and so on, might lead to other ways to better solve the problem.

In this section, guidelines for systematic problem solving have been identified. Two types of problems—a science problem for intermediate-level students, and a social studies problem for middle-level students—have been presented to illustrate the problem-solving process and how thinking skills are used to help carry it out. In addition, dozens of problems and how teachers use them with primary, intermediate, and middle students are described in Chapters 3, 4, and 5.

PRODUCTS: APPLICATIONS OF LEARNING

One of the most important aspects of teaching students to think and solve problems is to provide them opportunities to apply their skills in increasingly challenging situations. Products provide these opportunities better than any other learning outcomes. They not only let students use their skills but also motivate them to learn in an area of their own interest, work in several subject areas as they develop the product, and experience interaction in a variety of group sizes. Students have individual input into their learning because they can take initiative to investigate the background and literature of their topic, manipulate real materials, and report results to a real audience for evaluations of their work. Products let teachers guide the progress of their students and to help them "learn how to learn" new information. Teachers get to know and understand each student better in this situation, too. Products are often called the "ends" of instruction. They can range from simple to complex and concrete to abstract according to the subject matter to be covered, the age/grade levels, abilities, interests, and needs of the students. The difficulty level of a product can fall into any quadrant of the following chart.

	Concrete	Abstract
Simple	A	B
Complex	C	D

Here, an A product would be appropriate for young students and those just getting started on a more sophisticated topic; a B product could introduce students to dealing with abstract ideas; a C product could help students learn to deal with more variables in several settings, yet keep the work at a concrete level; and, a D product would challenge students to deal concurrently with abstract and complex ideas.

Products provide many other positive experiences for students, such as

- Students can work on a product alone, with a partner, in a small group, or as part of a class-sized group.

- Products can be short term (a few hours at a learning station), intermediate term (during a unit of instruction), or long term (semester, year).

- Products motivate students to learn because they can usually select topics that relate to their own interests and expertise according to learning goals.

- Product development encourages interdisciplinary learning.

- Products give students opportunities to practice many basic skills (reading, writing, math, speaking) as well as to think and solve problems.

- Product development often reaches out to parents and community members for problems and projects, resources, and audiences.

- Products promote affective as well as cognitive development when they are selected, developed, displayed, and explained by the students.

- Product development naturally encourages students to use higher levels of thinking and problem-solving strategies.

- Products can relate to units of study such as astronomy, World War II, a Shakespearean play, or to general topics or problems that are not usually a part of any one subject area, such as "How can we educate the growing population of elementary school pupils in our community at the lowest cost?"

Interdisciplinary projects where students develop a wide variety of products give them opportunities to use several of Gardner's intelligences—spatial, bodily kinesthetic, musical, linguistic, logical-mathematical, interpersonal, and intrapersonal (Willis, 1994, pp. 5–6). For example, seventh graders in an integrated unit on genetics had science and math as the main focus, but other disciplines such as music and art were also included. Students observed a simulation where strands of DNA pull apart, wrote essays and poems on "nature and nurture," and created murals to help express their identities. They explored probability when they examined inherited traits and reacted to questions such as "What are the chances of having a dimple in your chin?"

Student products should relate to real problems, be shared with real audiences, and undergo real evaluation by peers, teachers, community members, experts. Their development should encourage students to interact with and manipulate or "transform" ideas and information. Students also need to understand the implications of information in terms of expectations, anticipations, and predictions (Guilford, 1967, p. 104). "Real" aspects of products are explored in the following discussion (Bechtol & Sorenson, 1993, pp. 192–197).

Real Problems

Students often need help from teachers and others to select and investigate problems from authentic situations. Real classwide problems can include first-grade subjects such as a circus. Here, the students read books about circuses, learned words about circuses, and wrote stories involving some facet of them. As a culminating activity, parents were invited to the classroom circus where children dressed as circus performers—working in three rings. They read while on a "high wire," told circus stories on a flying trapeze, juggled while calling out numbers, and counted elephants and horseback riders around the room. The students were not only highly motivated, but they also practiced reading, writing, speaking, number recognition, and counting (Sprague, 1993, pp. 68–70).

Members of a fourth-grade classroom decided to investigate the rain forest. They had greens sprouting from the walls and hanging from the ceiling. For their final activity, they organized a tour of the rain forest, where the students acted as costumed guides. They explained the "layers" of the rain forest for parents and others. They described its plants and animals and the role each played, introduced the people who lived in the forest, and identified the products that non-rain forest people use from the forest. Two university researchers spoke to the audience after the tours were complete and encouraged them to join organizations to help save the rain forest. Learning in this unit ran over into several subject areas—facts about the rain forest, literature, history, science, environmental concerns, geography, and how to conduct an event that instructed their audience (Sprague, 1993, pp. 68–70).

Some essential questions that teachers can ask to determine the realness of an activity in any subject matter area are (Myers, 1993, pp. 71–72): (1) Does this activity provide opportunities for students to achieve something they perceive as real or genuine? (2) Does this activity, challenge, inspire, and empower the learner to take risks and exceed personal limitations? and (3) Are the students and the teacher committed to having this activity make some difference in their lives? If students are to consider an activity real, they must be able to apply it to what they are learning in their lives at the present time and they must have some goal or something at stake that is worth the risk to carry it out. This necessity for "realness" increases as students get older. Four strategies to help students and teachers find and deal with real problems are discussed below.

"W" Questions. The questions "Who?" "What?" "Where?" "When?" and "Why important?" can be used to investigate a historical or current topic, a personality, or a situation (Sorenson et al., 1988, p. 90; Maker, 1982). The "where" narrows the focus to local, state, regional, national, or world physical site and/or geographical location. The "who" is biographical and helps students limit the person(s) of interest within the "where." The "when" is chronological and relates the person, event, or situation to a period of the past, present, or future (e.g., the nineteenth century, this year, or 2010). The "what" is functional and helps students focus on an area such as economics, literature, sports, or government. The "why important" helps students relate the significance of the topic to world events within the period of study as well as its impact on future time periods.

Meaningful Knowledge. Problems can be related to five categories—decision making, investigation, experimental inquiry, problem solving, and invention (Marzano, 1992, pp. 106–130). *Decision making* answers such questions as "What is the best way to . . . ?" or "Which of these is most suitable, or useful, or feasible . . . ?" More decision-making activities are

- Who was the most influential person of the 1960s? There are many answers to this, but seeking the "whys" to this question and justifying their decisions motivated the students and gave them endless opportunities to explore.

- Should the United States continue to get involved in so-called civil conflicts such as those in Somalia, Bosnia, Haiti, the Middle East? Africa?

- How should schools be financed? Property tax, income tax, sales tax? Other?

Investigation provides a framework for forming problems. "What are the defining characteristics of?" " What are the important features of?" "Why did this happen?" "What would happen if?" Practical applications include answering such questions as

- Why did the dinosaurs disappear?
- What would happen if the greenhouse effect became a reality?
- Why did Hemingway commit suicide?
- Will humans live in space?

These general questions lead to many subquestions and a variety of investigations. This type of investigation is applicable to the past, the present, and the future.

Experimental inquiry answers questions such as "How can I explain this?" and "Based on my explanation, what can I predict?" In classroom questions, these could become, "Where should we place plants in the room for maximum growth?" and "Why are students often confused by Faulkner's writing?"

Problem solving as used here answers such questions as "How will I overcome this obstacle?" or "How will I reach my goal but still meet these conditions?" Some classroom activities might include (Marzano, 1992, p. 120):

- Present the Gettysburg address in a new artificial language without using any English words, and explain the words and rules of the new language.

- Build as complex a structure as possible inside a clear plastic, 2-liter container without cutting or altering the container; entry only through mouth.

Here, the students need to go through sequential steps. One such sequence, the practical problem-solving model, was shown in Figure 2–5 and explained earlier.

Invention, a fifth category, produces something that fills an unmet need or desire and is one of the most open-ended and creative tasks students can experience. Questions to guide invention are "Is there a situation that can or should be improved on?" and "Is there something that should be created?" Inventions can be carried out for everyday living, technical situations, and related to any subject area.

Competitions. These can occur at the local, regional, state, and national levels. They involve intermediate- and middle-level students in developing a product. A wide variety of these competitions in all subject areas are available. Many provide teachers and facilitators with topics, resource ideas, and problems. Some examples are Odyssey of the Mind, Future Problem Solving, Invent America, Young Astronauts, Math Pentathlon, and Academic Decathlon. Descriptions of several enrichment programs along with the address, age and grade group for which the program is intended, cost, and requirements are presented in the Appendix. Information on such programs is also available from school counselors, specialists, and subject matter publications.

General Categories of Products. To get ideas for real products, look at lists of products that other students have created. Two sources for such ideas are shown in the Appendix. One is a "dictionary list" describing eighty-five kinds of creative products and the other is a list of resources that teachers can use to identify ideas for student activities. In addition, dozens of ideas are presented at a variety of age and grade levels in Chapters 3, 4, and 5. Some general verbs and projects that relate to products for any subject matter area for any age and grade level are listed here:

- *Write*—letter, poem, song, play, story, article, book, newspaper
- *Create*—puppet show, collage, origami, sculpture, picture, bulletin board
- *Design*—costumes, puzzles, games, a new way to . . . , computer program
- *Give*—speech, television, or radio broadcast, interview, musical performance
- *Make*—collection, chart, videotape, simulation, model, timeline, poster
- *Do*—survey, interview, experiment, activity, puzzle, project
- *Build*—model, object, invention, diorama, instrument
- *Draw*—picture, map, diagram, illustration, graph, chart, floor plans

Although many of these general verbs overlap, each presents some fine distinctions, particularly as they relate to specific subject areas. These verbs and sample products are just "beginners." Students can brainstorm to add to the list in each category depending on their interests and the objectives of the lessons or unit of instruction.

Real Audiences

Students need authentic audiences with which to share their products. One way to seek out audiences is to ask the question "What do professionals such as scientists, writers, and artists do with the products they create?" Some answers might include the following (Sorenson et al., 1988, pp. 91–92):

- They use their products to influence the general public through the media and local, state, and national legislative bodies.
- Artists, writers, and composers create products to bring enjoyment into people's lives or to send a message to promote understanding.
- Scientists might investigate to find a cure for life-threatening diseases such as cancer or AIDS or they might seek additions to the body of knowledge.

Audiences besides classroom teachers who can help students to evaluate their products are peers, teachers with special expertise, parents, professional groups (e.g., engineers, artists, writers, businesspeople), social service groups (e.g., Lions, Rotary, Elks, Shriners, Eagles), government groups (e.g., committees from or entire city councils, county boards, or special interest groups such as the Environmental Protection Agency), media representatives (e.g., radio, television, newspapers, magazines, newsletters), club groups (e.g., Scouts, 4-H, sports groups and teams), and religious groups.

Real Evaluations

Student products need to be evaluated by a real audience. Various kinds of audiences can act in this capacity. But both students and teachers should be aware that the viewpoint of the audience may influence its evaluation. For example, in the case of "seeking a way to solve the problem of overpopulation in elementary schools at the lowest cost to the taxpayer," the school board may be most interested in providing quality education and keeping the teacher–student ratio low. The taxpayer may focus on keeping costs low; and the state might emphasize the safety of the children in terms of space and facilities.

Since students are not professionals at presenting, they need to recognize, develop, and practice a variety of communication skills to relate to any audience. They should also practice sharing information about their products to a "simulated" audience of their peers and/or teacher(s) before they present it to outside groups. Students should be encouraged to self-evaluate their product as well as to receive feedback from the "simulated" audience. Evaluators of products should (Sorenson et al., 1988, p. 93): (1) develop criteria as the basis for judgments and apply them consistently; and (2) develop methods to assist in the evaluation such as checklists and scales and assign values to each item on them when appropriate.

Students can develop products in many formats and receive appropriate evaluation of them. Products can be related to (1) class projects and assignments; (2) local, regional, and state competitions; (3) internships and other experiences with organizations, businesses, and industries in the community; (4) jobs as assistants at television or radio stations, newspapers and other media; or (5) as guides or helpers at museums, libraries, hospitals, government offices, or other sites. Regardless of where students experience developing a product and receive an evaluation on their work, the evaluation should be done in a positive manner that deals with both the strength and weaknesses of the students' product(s) and/or its presentation. Opportunities for students to reach out into the real world convey a partnership between school and community that the students learn from and want to repeat.

ENVIRONMENT: A SUPPORT SYSTEM FOR LEARNING

As we prepare students to live, learn, and work in the twenty-first century, one of the things we need to do in schools is to get students out of that unnatural and limited setting—the classroom. Problem solving in the curriculum requires teachers to find possibilities within their school, district, and community to offer varied learning environments for their students at the primary, intermediate, and middle school levels.

Environment in a modern learning program has several facets. These are (1) physical sites and conditions where instruction and learning take place; (2) a variety of human resources or "teachers," specialists, and facilitators to guide learning; (3) styles of teaching that convey learning to students or develop situations to help students meet learning goals; (4) learning styles of students appropriate to their needs and preferences and to the material to be learned; (5) personal characteristics of the students; and (6) technologies to facilitate learning. These facets of environment along with suggested ways to infuse them into curriculum are discussed next (Bechtol & Sorenson, 1993, pp. 197–201).

Physical Sites

Learning takes place in locations inside and outside the school. Physical sites in the school besides the classroom include media or instructional materials centers, classrooms at other grade levels and in other buildings, resource rooms, special purpose rooms such as those for art, music, physical education, and computer and other laboratories. Specialized sites in the district are also available. Out in the community, learning sites include businesses, industries, libraries, cultural facilities such as museums and theaters, medical facilities, and the facilities of other education institutions such as technical schools, colleges, and universities. Student involvement with specialized sites might be as casual as a field trip or as involved as a mentorship. Regardless of the complexity of the involvement, variety and appropriateness of the learning site increases student interest and motivation and provides "real" learning opportunities.

Designs for New Buildings. Design of a building and the campus area around it should reflect the activities that will take place there, allowing flexibility wherever possible. For example, the traditional egg crate room arrangement, where rows of chairs face the front of the room, is designed for the teacher to "tell" students information and for students to "recite" answers or passages in return. Such an arrangement is not conducive to science or small-group work that requires two to four students to work together using common equipment or for small groups of three to four students to solve problems in social studies, language arts, or math.

An "ideal" set of architectural and environmental requirements for schools being built or remodeled extensively today include the following (Taylor, 1993, p. 39):

- Furniture should be flexible, movable, and changeable for many uses; it should be on pulley systems so the ceiling can be used as a storage area.
- Horizontal and vertical work surfaces should be designed for individual or group work.
- Partitions should be light and movable to allow for adjustable space.
- Water should be available for science and other courses that need it.
- Plants should be growing in the schools for study as well as beauty.
- Schools should have history, art, and science museums with students curators.
- Teachers should have space for dialogue and planning with a professional library close to their work area.
- Systems should be simple, designed to be operated and maintained as much as possible by the users.
- Playgrounds and other space and facilities around the building such as the sports track, football and baseball fields, and tennis courts should be places to learn science, math, social studies, language arts, art, and so on as well as for recreation and sports.

Updating Old Buildings. Although the features just listed are desirable for all schools, many are not available to schools built in previous eras. We must adapt the buildings and campuses we have in the best way possible to meet present and future needs. Some things that can be included in any kind of remodeling are

- Movable furniture and tables so students can work with hands-on materials and in small groups
- Student work areas and storage areas for equipment and materials
- Water as appropriate for science and other classes
- Plants inside and outside the school for students to study and enjoy
- Displays of student work in hallways, on walls, or other areas
- Media and instructional materials centers should be student work areas as well as storage for books and other learning materials
- Some kind of easily movable partitions to make instructional and study areas more flexible
- Appropriate space for computers and other technological equipment so it can be used properly
- Informal "get-away" space for individual students in carpeted corners of a room, study carrels, or other structures
- Work areas for teachers with access to professional materials to use in planning, implementing, and evaluating learning.

Human Resources

In addition to contact with the classroom teacher in elementary schools and specialized class teachers in middle schools, students need contact with other adults with special expertise. In other school sites, they can interact with the media director and other teachers at the media or instructional materials center, and with teachers who have specialties of interest to them when they are working on a product. When they move into the community, they can learn from people with a wide variety of expertise in business, industry, medicine, cultural organizations, institutions, and other fields. These experiences, casual or intensive, can enrich the student's learning environment and also provide them with career education opportunities.

Field trips provide community experiences for a large number of students. Many art and cultural museums and government sites such as county courthouses, city halls, and state capitols have specially trained personnel to guide the students through the site and explain its use and personalities, past and present. Many places also have educational materials for teachers to use with their students to prepare them for the trip and as followup activities to the trip. Mentorships and internships provide intensive experiences with specialized community resource people, but the number of students who can participate is limited. Also, teachers can bring people with special expertise, experiences, or talents into the classroom to interact with the students. The school staff can develop lists of such resource people by surveying parents and community personnel about their interests and expertise as well as working with community agencies such as the chamber of commerce, community organizations, and colleges and universities. Many of these groups have names of people who want to work with students.

Teaching Styles

The ways in which teaching is carried out plays a vital role in providing a motivating learning environment. Teaching style has been defined in various ways as "a set of attitudes and actions that open a formal and informal world of learning to students" (Butler, 1984, pp. 51–52); as a set of decision patterns made by both the teacher and the learner (Mosston & Ashworth, 1990, pp. 2–3); or as elements which the teacher and learner control in the teaching and learning process (Bechtol & Sorenson, 1993, p. 228). While authors have classified these styles in many ways, most of them suggest a continuum from more teacher control to more student control.

Teaching styles need to be appropriate to the material to be learned and to the needs and characteristics of the students who are doing the learning. Five styles—teacher centered, self-instructional, inquiry, cooperative, and student centered—along with appropriate teaching situations in which to use them will be discussed here. Variables that are controlled by the student or teacher or both are goals and objectives, materials and activities, time and space, presentation method, and how evaluation is determined.

Teacher-Centered Style. Here the teacher makes most of the decisions, and the student mainly executes the directions given for all variables. This style is applicable to all subject matter areas at all age and grade levels. It is the most traditional style of teaching and focuses on an active teacher and a passive learner. This style is useful for giving students necessary information and directions, but it has many shortcomings. Many of today's students "tune out" when taught in this style. And it is probably not an effective style to teach students to function in a technological society since the learner is not actively involved in the learning process.

Self-Instructional Style. The student would work on a computer program, or with programmed printed or video material, or on other preplanned sequences of learning activities. While the goals and objectives are set by the materials in the software or other programs, the teacher and student can work together to select the learning material most appropriate to the student's needs. The student has many options and much involvement in all the other variables. A unique characteristic of this style is the immediate feedback the student gets in the evaluation variable. Generally the teacher acts as a resource person. The greatest advantage of this style is that materials can be easily matched to the individual student's needs in any age and grade level for a variety of purposes—remediation, regular ongoing instruction, enrichment, or acceleration. Once selections for the variables have been made by the student and teacher, the teacher need not be immediately available to the student. This allows the student to become an independent learner.

Inquiry Style. The teacher forms a partnership with the students as individuals, pairs, or in small groups. Here, the teacher presents materials to motivate the student to think and learn. A lesson is often started in a class-sized group where the teacher encourages students to find answers to questions by asking yet more questions to help them "discover" the best conclusions on their own. Then students work in pairs or small groups to investigate and find answers to their questions through manipulation, experimentation, survey, or other active means. Students are actively involved in the variables of media, materials and activities, time and space, and evaluation. When students work in small inquiry groups, each person has a specific task such as leader, scribe, information organizer, presenter to total group, and so on. All students are involved in gathering information and discussion.

Cooperative Style. This style can be thought of as an extension of the inquiry style. Some of its major qualities are students working together in small groups on a cooperative, not competitive basis; groups are usually structured in a heterogeneous manner, but groups of students with homogeneous abilities have worked out well in some gifted programs; and, the development of social skills and other affective qualities such as self-esteem and independence as well as cognitive achievement are expected outcomes. These learning groups also provide a structure for group work based on "positive independence"—the success of the group depends on the efforts of all its members—and "individual accountability" where students are individually accountable for mastering skills and concepts.

As in inquiry groups, each student has an assigned responsibility.

Student-Centered Style. The ultimate goal of every teacher is the development of lifelong, self-motivated, independent learners. This style promotes this development because the student takes the major initiative in all five instructional variables. The teacher acts as a resource and provides direction and support to the students' learning. Students may learn alone, in pairs, small groups, or on occasion in class-sized or large groups. As all experienced teachers know, not all students have the motivation, academic skills, and personal discipline to function successfully in this style. But many do, and all students should have the opportunity to move toward independence in situations such as developing products of various kinds as they progress through our educational system.

Every classroom in every school has students that function well with teachers who use one, two, or all five teaching styles. All instruction a teacher plans should provide opportunities for students to learn in more than one style—preferable two or three different styles. The chart in Figure 2–7 will help teachers plan for a variety of styles in their teaching in relation to the five variables and student–teacher input.

FIGURE 2–7 Practical Teaching Styles Patterns Assessment

Who Controls the Learning Variables

LEARNING VARIABLE	Student	Student with Input from Teacher	Student and Teacher Cooperatively	Teacher with Input from Student	Teacher
Who should determine or select goals and objectives for instruction?					
Who should determine media, materials, and activities for instruction?					
Who should determine the time schedule and space for instruction in the classroom, school, and community?					
Who should determine the method of presentation—from structured to unstructured—for instruction?					
Who should determine the method of evaluation of what the student learned from the instruction?					
Other:					

Source: W. Bechtol and J. Sorenson, *Restructuring Schooling for Individual Students* (Boston: Allyn and Bacon, 1993), p. 233. Reprinted with permission.

Student Learning Styles

"When students cannot learn the way we teach them, we must teach them the way they learn" (Dunn, 1990, p. 18). Attention to student learning style is one way to try to help students learn more successfully. Learning style has been defined in many ways such as (1) "stimuli that affect a person's ability to absorb and retain information, values, facts, or concepts" (Dunn and Dunn, 1975, p. 74); (2) "those factors that ease and facilitate learning for an individual student in a given situation" (Bechtol, 1973, p. 46); and (3) as a composite of "cognitive, affective, and psychological factors that serve as relatively reliable indicators of how learners perceive, interact, and respond to the learning environment" (Keefe, 1988, p. 3).

An Overview of Learning Styles. Recognizing that individuals learn differently is not new. An old Confucian proverb states, "I hear, I forget; I see, I understand; I do, I remember." The work of several authors suggests learning has these modalities—auditory, visual, and kinesthetic or hands on (Guild and Garger, 1985, pp. 63–66). *Auditory learners* use their ears and voices as their primary mode for learning. They want to hear to remember and also to discuss what they are learning with others. *Visual learners* like to see things written down as well as look at pictures and diagrams to help them better understand the materials to be learned. *Kinesthetic learners* prefer and actually learn better when they get involved in the learning through some kind of physical activity. They like to act out a situation, handle as many things related to it as possible, and make a product where appropriate. They also like to experiment and be a part of simulations. About 20–30 percent of students learn best from what they hear (auditory); another 40 percent learn best by seeing things (visual); and the remaining 30–40 percent learn best by being actively involved (kinesthetic).

If teachers are to give all students the chance they need to succeed, they should (1) include a variety of learning modes in their lessons; (2) be aware of their own learning styles and how they affect their teaching styles; and (3) help students move from one preferred style to several so they can benefit from a variety of teaching styles (Sorenson et al., 1988).

Research and Programs. Learning style is a complex subject that encompasses the psychological, sociological, philosophical, neurological, emotional, and physical areas and their interaction with the environment. Research on learning style has been difficult because (1) there is confusion in definitions, which vary widely in scale and scope of learning, school achievement, and other behaviors predicted by learning style concepts; (2) research instruments tend to be weak in reliability and validity; and (3) relevant characteristics in learners and instructional settings and their relationships have varied widely and have often been checked out on only small groups of students (Curry, 1990).

Nonetheless, during the past decade research has intensified as a part of U.S. efforts to produce students who can compete successfully in an increasingly complex world. The work of several researchers will interest teachers. Rita Dunn and Kenneth Dunn have worked with four basic stimuli—environmental, emotional, sociological, and physical—and eighteen elements of learning style. Bernice McCarthy developed the 4MAT system, which is based on the major dimensions of processing and perceiving. Anthony Gregorc developed learner styles related to four patterns—concrete sequential, abstract sequential, concrete random, and abstract random. Books and magazine articles by these authors are readily available at any education library. Other references are *Marching to Different Drummers* by Guild and Garger, 1985, and "Learning and Teaching Styles" in *Restructuring Schooling for Individual Students,* by Bechtol and Sorenson, 1993. These provide the reader with a more detailed discussion on teaching and learning styles and lead them to yet more authors and information on both subjects.

Matching Learning and Teaching Styles. Teachers should be concerned about matching their teaching styles to the learning styles of their students. Here are some guidelines to help carry this out (Hunt, 1979; Joyce, 1981):

- Each class of students will have a wide range of learning styles. Thus, the teacher must provide a variety of options and choices for the students with different learning styles to meet the same objectives in academic work.

- Student learning styles and teachers' styles are most easily matched in a team setting. When they are part of a multigraded team, the students with structured, unstructured, or any combination of learning styles can be assigned to teachers with compatible teaching styles—at least part of the time.

- Students should be encouraged to learn in other styles than their dominant one(s). Teachers should try to accommodate a student's preferred style, particularly when learning new or difficult material, but students should also try to stretch to become more comfortable and efficient in learning in more than one style. In careers and life, students must be able to meet changes.

- Nature of the subject matter to be learned should be related to teaching and learning styles. Some students might have a strong preference for learning in a small group, but some tasks such as giving instructions, safety directions, daily schedules, announcements are best presented in a teacher-directed manner. Likewise, some material is best learned alone or with a partner.

Student Characteristics

Student characteristics enter into the student's learning process. These include intrinsic motivation, sensitivity, curiosity, initiative, self-confidence, tolerance, creativity, persistence, flexibility, responsibility, attention span, self-directedness, locus of control, and self-evaluation (Edmund, 1992, p. 35; Bechtol & Sorenson, 1993, p. 200). An investigation of these characteristics by major authors in the learning style field indicates that students who score in the 90th percentile and above show consistent patterns of independence, self-motivation, persistence, and strong perceptual strengths (Dunn, Bruno, & Gardiner, 1984). In the 1990s, these American students continue to compete successfully with the highest achieving students in other developed countries. But we need to encourage all our students to develop a positive sense of these characteristics.

Technology

Technology encompasses two components in its definition: (1) the tools that embody the technology; and (2) the information base of the technology. As such, technology has the capabilities to bring authentic information and experiences into the classroom that students and teachers could have only dreamed of in the past. Today's "technological tools can foster students' abilities, revolutionize the way they work and think, and give them new access to the world" (Peck & Dorricott, 1994, p. 11). Reasons to use technology, strategies to use both commonly available and advanced technology with students, and the reluctance of the educational establishment to incorporate technology into the learning process are discussed.

Reasons to Use Technology. Here are ten rational reasons for using technology in the schools (Peck & Dorricott, 1994, pp. 12–13):

1. Students learn and develop at different rates.
2. Graduates must be proficient at accessing, evaluating, and communicating information.
3. Technology can foster an increase in the quantity and quality of students' thinking and writing.
4. Graduates must solve complex problems.
5. Technology can nurture artistic expression.
6. Graduates must be globally aware and able to use resources that exist outside the school.
7. Technology creates opportunities for students to do meaningful work.
8. All students need access to high-level and high-interest courses.
9. Students must feel comfortable with the tools of the Information Age.
10. Schools must increase their productivity and efficiency.

Commonly Available Technologies. Computer software programs for drill and practice, specific topics, and general processes such as those related to problem solving in all subject areas, videotapes, word processing, and transparencies are used to some extent in nearly all schools. *Drill and practice* activities help both students who need extra work to learn the ongoing curriculum and those who need remediation in specific areas. *Programs on specific topics* can provide situations to encourage all students to learn in correlation with or as enrichment to learning in the ongoing curriculum. They can also provide enrichment for students with high interest in a specific topic. *General process programs* such as those related to thinking and problem solving can help all students practice the process as well as challenge highly able students.

Videotapes provide opportunities to "illustrate with action" those situations we could only read about in the past. Some of these include explanations of phenomena in science such as cell division, atomic reactions, atomic structure, pictures of the surface of the moon, and photos of planets and other space objects. In language arts, videos can bring plays from Shakespeare to Neil Simon, fairytales, and nearly all kinds of stories and poems to life in the classroom. Famous people from films of the past ninety years and those "staged" from earlier times can enter our classrooms. They might deliver their most famous speeches or we might witness wars, constitutional conventions, treaty signings, and so on. Students can make their own videotapes for instructional games or segments to share with a group, for evaluating their own presentations in speaking, plays, reading poems or other literature, or as a vehicle to explain a project on almost any topic.

Word processing can help students in every subject matter area: writing and editing in language arts; math problems with graphics that are more motivating and understandable than the textbook alone; illustrations of science principles and concepts in all text materials; and in social studies, the possibilities for simulations, re-enactments, and graphic displays that make the past come alive, the present more understandable, and the future more realistic. They can use computers to develop their lessons and to produce products such as newsletters or newspapers, announcements, and other things that need to be printed as part of individual, group or schoolwide projects. *Transparencies,* which are easily developed in sophisticated form on any computer, can be used on an overhead projector. Or they can be projected directly from the computer screen onto the classroom wall using a LCD projection panel. Information can also be projected as it is typed in from an ongoing discussion using this panel. Such "on the spot" projection will probably make blackboards, traditional transparencies, and opaque projectors obsolete.

More Advanced Technologies. Laser disks and CD-Roms give students access to thousands of images at the touch of a key. Distance education technology can bring expert doctors, authors, politicians, astronomers, and others "live" into any classroom, even those in remote geographical areas. On the horizon we are researching new technologies for their use in learning. These include *computerized adaptive testing (CAT),* where test questions are presented according to the level of correct student responses; *interactive media,* which deal with linking information from multiple sources and typically include text, line drawings, maps and graphs, animated graphics, voice narration, music, and full-color and full-motion video clips; and *multiuser dimensions (MUDs),* where individuals play out roles in an imaginary context. The user can go back in time to the Revolutionary War or into the future on a space station. Technologies that are already being used in business and industry, but have not yet found applications in schools dazzle the mind. Some examples are broadband networks, groupware, knowbots, pen-based computing, virtual reality, and wireless connectivity (Hancock & Betts, 1994, pp. 24–29). Widespread use of technologies at Eastern Middle School, Silver Spring, Maryland, is described in Chapter 6.

Education Has Been Reluctant to Use Technologies. In industry, business, medicine, and every other facet of modern life, technologies are considered essential to save labor costs and improve productivity, working conditions, and morale. Hundreds of examples show that technologies pay for themselves and return a profit. Technologies also change the relationships in communications, work patterns, work pace, rewards and penalties, and expose the strengths and weaknesses of the workers, managers, and executives within an organization.

Education has generally not been a part of this "revolution." Even when schools use twentieth-century technologies such as computers or videotape, they tend to be "add-ons" rather than an integral part of the instruction" (Mecklenburger, 1990, pp. 106–107). Schools seem to resist the idea that effective use of technology will totally transform what a school accomplishes (Doyle, 1993, p. 519).

Cost has been both an excuse for and a real obstacle to using technology in the schools. Technologies are not widely used in many schools that have them in place, or not used properly to relate learning to technologies. In eight model schools—many of them National Excellence in Education Award winners—reviewed by Bechtol & Sorenson (1993), only three had widespread use of technology. The situation today is not "can we afford to" but "can we afford *not* to" use technologies in educating our students.

Whatever the financial and attitudinal barriers to technology in the schools, one fact remains clear: We are approaching the twenty-first century, and we cannot prepare our students to live and compete in a global society if we let our schools operate in a nineteenth-century manner. Change is inevitable. Effective use of technologies is a challenge that all schools and their staffs at all age and grade levels must meet. Most important of all, students should not only learn from these technologies, but they should learn how to use them to think and solve problems in practical and sophisticated ways.

STRATEGIES FOR TEACHING AND ASSESSING PROBLEM SOLVING

Thinking skills and problem solving can be taught in every subject matter area, starting in kindergarten. The teacher is the most important factor in how they are taught and how the students' learning is evaluated. These topics are explored next.

Practical Teaching Strategies

To think and solve problems successfully, students need a classroom atmosphere that "works with the brain's natural functions," not against them. Some things we already know about this process are (Beamon, 1992, p. 3):

- Students learn by building on what they already know. When the brain encounters new information, it very rapidly tries to match or compare it to what it thinks is similar information stored in its memory. If a match is made, new or expanded learning occurs.

- The brain tends to "resist" instruction when it cannot relate to or find traces of a match or reference point. Teachers need to help students make matches by making information more real and relating it to things they already know. If no relationships are formed, students just store unrelated data—usually in their short-term memory.

- Under stressful conditions such as fear of failure or anxiety, the cerebrum of the brain starts to "shut down" its thought-processing ability. These conditions limit higher and more complex learning.

- Lessons fail to stimulate or encourage learning if they are threatening, offer too little challenge and do not contain connections to what students already know. Students need to feel safe to express ideas or ask questions to be "active" learners.

Teacher Questions. Questioning by the teacher is probably the most important aspect of creating a thinking and problem-solving atmosphere. This not only applies to the teacher–student relationship, but also carries over into small group work where the students pose questions for each other as they think and solve problems. Some of them take a little more time than "telling," but the impact they leave with the students is well worth it. A checklist of positive questioning techniques in the format of questions teachers can ask themselves about their teaching is presented here (Beamon, 1992, p. 5; McTighe & Lyman, 1988, p. 21):

1. Do I ask a few broad, thought-provoking questions rather than many, narrow and inconsequential ones?

2. Do I ask questions that guide students without controlling their thinking and leading them to a set answer? Do I ask for alternative answers?

3. Do I help students use many levels of thinking? Do my questions relate to my students' life experiences? Are they relevant to contemporary issues?

4. What about the way I ask my questions?

    Do I ask the entire class before I invite one student to answer?

    Do I call on students randomly—not just on those with raised hands?

    Do I avoid repeating questions and answers?

    Do I let students ask their own questions?

    Do I ask students to "think aloud"—describe how they arrive at answers?

    Do I ask "follow-ups"—Why? Do you agree, disagree? Give an example?

5. How do I treat student answers?

    Do I follow up incorrect answers and take advantage of them to teach?

    Do I promote interaction by referring students' questions and answers to others?

    Do I allow "wait times" after a question and after a student response?

    Do I respond to student answers in a non-evaluative way?

6. What are the outcomes of my questions?

    Do my questions encourage thought and reason?

Do my questions elicit concepts and generalizations as well as facts?

Do my questions stimulate creative thought and discussion?

Do my questions achieve the objectives of the lesson?

7. Do I use varied groupings such as pairs, small cooperative groups to encourage individual thinking time and share information in discussions?

Teacher Responses. These are perhaps even more important than the questions they ask. They have an affective as well as a cognitive dimension. Teacher responses can extend student thinking, stimulate thinking at a low level, or inhibit it. Some specific teacher responses that extend student thinking and require students to accept responsibility for their ideas and remarks include (Beamon, 1992, p. 6):

1. Clarifies or reflects back the central idea of the student answer.
2. Asks students to tell their points of view, express opinions, give own ideas.
3. Asks students to elaborate on their ideas.
4. Invites additional responses or contributions from other students.
5. Asks for an analysis of the idea—that is, examine all or part of the answer.
6. Asks students to raise a new idea or open up a new line of inquiry.
7. Accepts ideas of the students.
8. Invites students to ask questions.

Teacher responses that stimulate low-level thought include requiring students to recall information, leading students to the right answer, directing the students' thinking; and talking too much. Responses that inhibit student thinking include putting down and judging student ideas and intimidating students. In other words, "Don't tell what you can ask. Don't ask what the student should be asking" (Worsham, 1988, p. 57).

Three current books that will give teachers step-by-step processes for teaching thinking skills and ideas for many classroom activities for elementary and middle-level students are (1) B. Beyer, *Teaching Thinking Skills: A Handbook for Elementary School Teachers* (Allyn and Bacon, 1991); (2) B. Beyer, *Teaching Thinking Skills: A Handbook for Secondary School Teachers* (Allyn and Bacon, 1991); and (3) I. Tiedt, J. Carlson, B. Howard, and K. Watanabe, *Teaching Thinking in K–12 Classrooms: Ideas, Activities, and Resources* (Allyn and Bacon, 1989).

Ways to Assess Thinking and Problem Solving

Assessing student progress in thinking skills and problem solving is one of the most difficult tasks for teachers. To get a fair and valid assessment, multiple strategies and methods need to be used.

Traditional Assessment Strategies. Observations, interviews, checklists and inventories, paper-and-pencil tests, and letter grades are commonly used to assess student performance and progress. Also, since it takes a long time for students to develop problem-solving skills, assessment must be continuous over the school year and from year to year. Let's explore ways to use these different methods.

Teachers can make *observations* as they walk around the room while students are working individually or in small groups. They can listen as students talk among themselves, ask questions, and offer suggestions. Here are some questions to consider:

- Did the students read the problem carefully?
- Do they employ a problem-solving strategy; do they try a second strategy if the first one they use fails?
- Do they use appropriate thinking skills to develop the problem within the strategy they have selected?
- Are they concentrating on their tasks, and do they keep working on them?
- Do they incorporate manipulative materials in their strategy?
- Do they ask for help when they need it?
- Do their behaviors, attitudes, and facial expressions indicate their interest and involvement in the task?

In *interviews,* the teacher (1) presents the students with a problem; (2) lets the students find a solution, describing what they are doing; and (3) challenges them on what they are doing. The teacher may take notes or tape-record the interview conversation for use with the student and parents and for a permanent record.

On *checklists and inventories,* the teacher can check off different categories to indicate what strategies the student has used as well as their work habits, attitudes, and interests. There should always be spaces for observations and information that might not appear on the checklist.

Paper-and-pencil tests should focus on the procedures the students use rather than the answer. The problems selected should be good ones that are interesting and challenging and the student should be allowed enough time to complete the procedure. Whatever methods of assessment are used, they should indicate not only what progress the students have made, but their results should also be used to help the teacher improve ways to teach.

Letter grades have been the standard for assessment over many generations, but today they are losing some of their appropriateness (Willis, 1993). Many educators feel letter grades are not keyed to any common standard. Letter grades also don't tell us much about a student's strengths and weaknesses, don't give teachers and parents much insight on how to help students improve, and tend to label and demoralize slower students.

Alternative Assessment Strategies. Authentic assessment has been addressed by many authors. Criteria for judging the authenticity of a test include the following (Wiggins, 1993, pp. 206–207):

- Engaging and worthy problems or important questions in which students need to use knowledge to give effective and creative performances
- Faithful representations of the contexts found in a field of study or in real-life "tests" of adult life
- Nonroutine and multistage tasks—real problems
- Tasks that require a study to produce a quality product or performance
- Clearly stated criteria and standards
- Interactions between the assessor and assessee; students should justify answers or choices and respond to follow-up or probing questions
- Process and product performance should determine the quality of the result
- Trained assessor judgment in reference to clear and appropriate criteria
- Search for patterns of response in diverse settings.

Alternative assessments include profiles, nontraditional problems, and products. An *assessment profile* is one way to evaluate student work on tasks. It might include weightings to help the teacher quantify assessment. Sample items related to the "experimental inquiry" task discussed previously in this chapter are shown next. Evaluation values run from "1," (low) to "4," (high); weightings are 1, 3, or 5 (Marzano et al., 1992, pp. 172–175).

Selected Items from an Assessment Profile

Meaningful Use Task	Evaluation 1 2 3 4	Weight 1 3 5	Score
Completeness of student's use of strategy of experimental inquiry:			
Did the student provide an explanation of what he or she observed?	3	1	3
Accuracy and effectiveness of student's thinking during experimental inquiry task			
Was the student's explanation accurate?	3	3	9
Was the student's explanation of the phenomena appropriate and accurate?	4	5	20
To what extent did the explanation of the outcome of the experiment adequately relate to the student's initial explanation?	3	5	15

This tally sheet of selected items from an assessment profile provides a pattern of student ratings in the evaluation column as well as a score. The teacher can share this information with the students, and the students can also rate themselves individually, or as a group on their progress towards a goal. Also, both a total score for meaningful use tasks or two subscores—one for completeness and one for accuracy and effectiveness—are available.

Nontraditional problems encourage students to communicate their thinking while they are solving problems. Some ways to get this started include (Szetela & Nicol, 1992, pp. 43–44):

- Present a problem with all the facts and condition, but have the students write appropriate questions, solve the completed problem, and write their explanations about how adequately they solved the problem.

- Present a problem and a partial solution. Have students complete solution.

- Present a problem with facts unrelated to the questions. Have students revise the problem to remove the incongruity.

- Have students explain how they would solve a problem using only words, then solve the problem and construct a similar problem.

- After students solve a problem, have them write a new problem with a different context but preserving the original problem structure.

- Present a problem without numerals. Have students supply appropriate numerals, estimate answers, and solve the problem.

Teachers can assess the quality of each response by using a simple scale such as (1) no response or simplistic or irrelevant response, (2) a relevant response but of minor importance with respect to the problem, (3) a reflective and significant response but with an important omission or misconception, and (4) a comprehensive, logical, and correct response to the problem.

Products as solutions to problems, simple to complex, in elementary and middle school take a variety of forms. Portfolios, journals, logs, plays, simulations and monologues become language arts assignments. Projects, experiments, and simulations are part of the science scene. Surveys, re-enactments, dioramas, and impersonations make social studies interesting. And math incorporates projects, illustrations, and performances in its learning cycle. Elements of artistic and physical performance combine with many of these products to make learning more authentic. "Instead of just collecting and sharing factual information with their classmates, students needed to synthesize what they had learned, integrate it into the form of a decision (or *product*), and justify that decision to others" (Schnitzer, 1993, p. 32). Product development and assessment are discussed in detail in the previous section of this chapter and in Chapters 3, 4, and 5.

RESOURCES FOR TEACHING THINKING SKILLS AND PROBLEM SOLVING

Teachers need a variety of resources to use with their students to teach thinking skills and problem solving effectively. These resources need to be easy for the teacher to access and use in the everyday teaching situation. They need to be designed for or easily adapted to a variety of subjects and if possible, should include more than one subject area. They need to offer students opportunities to practice basic reading, writing, listening, speaking, and math skills. And, they need to allow students to work in a variety of groupings—alone, with a partner, or in a small group—and when possible give students the chance to work on a topic of interest to them.

Kinds of Resources

Six kinds of resources that teachers can use to make their teaching and students' learning more effective are described here. Note that each group of resources offers a variety of possibilities to meet the individual differences of students.

Textbooks and Related Materials. Perhaps the most available resources for teachers are textbooks and teacher guides, activity listings, and problem books that accompany the textbook series. Teachers should review these materials in each subject to find activities and problems that provide opportunities for the students to think and solve problems. They should keep in mind that students need (1) variety in the complexity and abstractness of their thinking and problem solving, and (2) opportunities to move from where they are to more challenging activities regardless of their age or grade levels. These materials are usually designed for a particular grade level, so teachers need to branch out on both sides of any one level to meet the needs of their students.

Teacher Resource File. Within a building or district, teachers could start a "resource file" of thinking skills and problem-solving materials and resources that would be available for all teachers to use. They could start this file by having two or three teachers at a grade level survey the texts, teacher guides, and other materials related to their texts and put them into the file. File headings could be arranged using the titles in Figure 2–2. The main headings could be *the names of the five thinking skills groups along with problems.* Subheads could be the skills and subskills listed under each of the skill groups and three levels of problem difficulty such as starters, challenging, mind twisters. Once the file was in place, teachers could add activities they have used successfully with students over the years as well as new materials they identify into these categories. References to audiovideo and computer software materials as well as print should be included in the file.

Hands-On Materials. Activity books for students and commercial catalogues are resources for print, hands-on, audiovideo, and computer software materials. Some specialize in materials for teaching thinking skills and problem solving or they might be general catalogues that provide materials mainly for subject matter areas. In the general catalogues, the index often has listings such as "thinking skills" or "problem solving" that will lead the teacher directly to the materials. The descriptions of the materials usually indicates the range of grade levels the materials are designed for, along with the content of the activity. These references can also be added to the file.

Teacher Magazines. These might be general magazines such as *Instructor, Teacher,* or *Challenge.* These magazines contain many teaching ideas and also have listings of references as well as advertisements listing more sources of activities. Magazines for teachers related to teaching the content areas are also good sources. Some of these are *Science and Children* at the elementary level and *Science Scope* at the middle school level for science; *Teaching Children Mathematics* (formerly *The Arithmetic Teacher*) for elementary and *The Mathematics Teacher* for secondary mathematics; *Language Arts* for elementary and the *English Journal* for secondary language arts; and *Social Education* for K–12 in social studies. These magazines which are published by their respective subject area professional organizations have articles written by teachers about what works for them in their classrooms and contain many ideas on thinking skills and problem solving as well as sources of more ideas. The magazines also have articles by experts in the field and their articles are also sources of ideas and teaching resources. Resource ideas from these magazines can also be added to the file.

Gifted and Talented Materials. The great majority of the activities in high-quality materials targeted for gifted and talented students and their teachers deal with thinking skills and problem solving. These activities are appropriate for all students with adaptation to age and grade level, abilities, maturity, and other needs and interests of students. In many cases, these materials involve several disciplines in the activities as well as stressing thinking and problem solving. Check general supply catalogues and activity books under "gifted education" and "creativity" as well as under thinking skills and problem solving for these materials.

Specialty Books, Audiovideos, and Computer Software. These materials often focus on thinking skills and problem solving. Global education materials include opportunities for thinking and solving problems—usually on an interdisciplinary basis. Competitions in general or specialized areas such as Future Problem Solving (FPS) and Odyssey of the Mind publish materials related to their programs. Most of these activities are interdisciplinary. Lists of materials available from these resources can be obtained by writing to the addresses for the programs given in the Appendix. Environmental education materials feature many interdisciplinary activities that involve thinking and problem solving.

There are also series of simulation and interaction materials that offer many opportunities to solve problems. These include materials from companies such as Interact, Tom Snyder Productions, and Computer Curriculum Corporation. Teachers should work closely with media or instructional materials center directors and personnel to find print, audiovideo, simulations, computer software and other materials to help them teach thinking and problem solving. These materials should be noted in the file, along with their call numbers so they can be accessed easily when needed.

Sources of Resources

Resources are endless and only a few have been mentioned in this discussion. Three categories of resources are given in the Appendix. They are (1) general resources to help teachers learn more about teaching thinking and problem solving; (2) resources for activities and materials to use with students; and (3) catalogues that contain thinking skills and problem-solving materials to use with students. Teachers could photocopy these lists and include them in their central resource file.

SUMMARY

"Education isn't just a social concern, it's a major economic issue. If our students can't compete today, how will they compete tomorrow" (Akers, 1991). As we prepare for the twenty-first century, American teachers, parents, and students all seek answers to a better education for our children. One of the weakest areas of student accomplishment in both national and international comparisons is problem solving. In this book, thinking skills and problem solving as the process element of the curriculum have been related to the other elements—content, product, and environment.

Content was discussed with an emphasis on forming and teaching concepts. Then, thinking skills in five groups—inquiry processes, creative thinking, critical thinking skills, single-step problem-solving techniques, and Bloom's cognitive levels—were identified and illustrated with examples. A model with sequential steps to help students solve multistep problems was presented, and ways to solve problems using it as a guide were described. Roles of products and environment, along with strategies for assessing problem solving as well as resources for teaching it were discussed.

REFERENCES

Akers, J. (April 21, 1991). *Time.*
Albrecht, K. (1980). *Brain power: Learn to improve your thinking skills.* Englewood Cliffs, NJ: Prentice Hall.
Beamon, G. (1992). *Making classrooms "safe" for thinking.* Paper presented at the Annual Meeting of the National Association for Gifted Children, Los Angeles, CA, November 1992.
Bechtol, W., & Sorenson, J. (1993). *Restructuring schooling for individual students.* Boston: Allyn and Bacon.
Bechtol, W. (1973). *Individualizing instruction and keeping your sanity.* Chicago: Follett.
Beyer, B. (1988). *Developing a thinking skills program.* Boston: Allyn and Bacon.
Bloom, B. S. (1959). *Taxonomy of educational objectives.* New York: David McKay.
Brandt, R. (Ed.). (1988). *Content of the curriculum.* (1988 ASCD Yearbook). Alexandria, VA: Association for Supervision and Curriculum Development.
Butler, K. (1984). *Learning and teaching style in theory and practice.* Columbia, CT: The Learner's Dimension.
Clarke, J. (1990). *Patterns of thinking: Integrating learning skills in content learning.* Boston: Allyn and Bacon.
Costa, A. (Ed.). (1985). *Developing minds: A reference book for teaching thinking.* Alexandria, VA: Association for Supervision and Curriculum Development.
Curry, L. (1990). A critique of the research on learning styles. *Educational Leadership,* 48(2): 50–56.
Davis, G., & Rimm, S. (1994). *Education of the gifted and talented.* Boston: Allyn and Bacon.
Davis, G. (1983). *Creativity is forever.* Dubuque, IA: Kendall/Hunt.
Doyle, D. (1992). *The challenge, the opportunity.* Phi Delta Kappan, 73(7): 512–520.
Dunn, R. (1990). Rita Dunn answers questions on learning style. *Educational Leadership,* 48(2): 15–19.
Dunn, R., Bruno, A., & Gardiner, B. (1984). Put a cap on your gifted program. *Gifted Child Quarterly,* 28(2): 70–72.
Dunn, R., & Dunn, K. (1975). *Educator's self-teaching guide to individualizing instructional programs.* West Nyack, NY: Parker.
Eberle, R. (1977). *SCAMPER; Games for imaginative development.* Buffalo, NY: D.O.K. Publisher.
Edmund, N. (1992). *The general pattern of the scientific method.* Fort Lauderdale, FL: Norman W. Edmund.
Golub, L., Frederick, W., Nelson, N., & Frayer, D. (1971). *Selected analysis of language arts concepts.* Madison, WI: Wisconsin Research and Development Center for Cognitive Learning, The University of Wisconsin.
Guild, P., & Garger, S. (1985). *Marching to different drummers.* Alexandria, VA: Association for Supervision and Curriculum Development.
Guilford, J. P. (1967). *The nature of human intelligence.* New York: McGraw-Hill.
Hancock, V., & Betts, F. (1994). From the lagging to the leading edge. *Educational Leadership,* 51(7): 24–29.

Haney, R., & Sorenson, J. (1977). *Individually guided science*. Reading, MA: Addison–Wesley.

Harris, M., & Harris, C. (1973). *A structure of concept attainment abilities*. Madison, WI: Wisconsin Research and Development Center for Cognitive Learning, The University of Wisconsin.

Hollingsworth, H., & Eastman, S. (1988). *Teaching writing in every class: A guide for grades 6–12*. Boston: Allyn and Bacon.

Hunt, D. (1979). *Student learning system: Diagnosing and prescribing programs*. Reston, VA: National Association of Secondary School Principals.

Isaksen, S., Dorval, K., & Treffinger, D. (1994). *Creative approaches to problem solving*. Dubuque, IA: Kendall/Hunt.

Isaksen, S., & Treffinger, D. (1985). *Creative problem solving: The basic course*. Buffalo, NY: Bearly Limited.

Joyce, B. (1981). *Flexibility in teaching*. New York: Longman.

Keefe, J. (1988). *Profiling and utilizing learning style*. Reston, VA: National Association of Secondary School Principals.

Klein, R. (1982). An inquiry into the factors related to creativity. *Elementary School Journal*, 82(3): 264–265.

Lipman, M. (1988). Critical thinking—what can it be? *Educational Leadership*, 46(1): 38–43.

Maker, C. J. (1982). *Teaching models in education of the gifted*. Rockville, MD: Aspen.

Marzano, R. (1992). *A different kind of classroom*. Alexandria, VA: Association for Supervision and Curriculum Development.

Marzano, R., Brandt, R., Hughes, S., Jones, B. F., Presseisen, B., Rankin, S., & Suhor, C. (1988). *Dimensions of thinking: A framework for curriculum and instruction*. Alexandria, VA: Association for Supervision and Curriculum Development.

McTighe, J., & Lyman, F. (1988). Cueing thinking in the classroom: The promise of theory-embedded tools. *Educational Leadership*, 45(3): 18–24.

Mecklenburger, J. (1990). Educational technology is not enough. *Phi Delta Kappan*, 72(2): 104–108.

Mosston, M., & Ashworth, S. (1990). *The spectrum of teaching styles: From command to discovery*. New York: Longman.

Myers, S. (1993). A trial for Dmitri Karamazov. *Educational Leadership*, 50(7): 71–72.

Peck, K., & Dorricott, D. (1994). Why use technology? *Educational Leadership*, 51(7): 11–14.

Renzulli, J. (Ed.). (1986). *Systems and models for developing programs for the gifted*. Mansfield Center, CT: Creative Learning Press.

Reys, R., Suydam, M., & Lindquist, M. (1992). *Helping children learn mathematics*. Boston: Allyn and Bacon.

Schnitzer, S. (1993). Designing an authentic assessment. *Educational Leadership*, 50(7): 32–35.

Sorenson, J., Engelsgjerd, J., Francis, M., Miller, M., & Schuster, N. (1988). *The gifted program handbook*. Palo Alto, CA: Dale Seymour.

Sprague, M. (1993). From newspapers to circuses—the benefits of production-driven learning. *Educational Leadership*, 50(7): 68–70.

Sternberg, R. (1986). *Intelligence applied: Understanding and increasing your intellectual skills*. Chicago: Harcourt Brace Jovanovich.

Szetela, W., & Nicol, C. (1992). Evaluating problem solving in mathematics. *Educational Leadership*, 49(8): 42–45.

Taylor, A. (1993). How schools are redesigning their space. *Educational Leadership*, 51(1): 36–41.

Torrance, E. P. (1977). *Creativity in the classroom*. Washington, DC: National Educational Association.

Voelker, A., Sorenson, J., & Frayer, D. (1971). *An analysis of selected classificatory science concepts*. Madison, WI: Wisconsin Research and Development Center for Cognitive Learning, The University of Wisconsin.

Wales, C., Nardi, A., & Stager, R. (1986). Decision-making: New paradigm for education. *Educational Leadership*, 45(8): 37–41.

Wiggins, G. (1993). Assessment: Authenticity, content, and validity. *Phi Delta Kappan*, 75(3): 200–214.

Willis, S. (1994). The well-rounded classroom: Applying the theory of multiple intelligences. *ASCD Update*, 36(8): 1, 5–6, 8.

Willis, S. (1993). Are letter grades obsolete? *ASCD Update*, 35(7): 1–2, 8.

Wisconsin Department of Public Instruction. (1986). *A guide to science development*. Madison, WI.

Worsham, A. (1988). A "grow as you go" thinking skills model. *Educational Leadership*, 45(7): 56–57.

CHAPTER 3

Challenging Primary-Level Problem Solvers

As Ms. Kraft's students return from recess, she directs them to sit in a circle around her. They are curious about the large, folded poster she is holding. They wait expectantly for her instructions. She says, "If you look very carefully at this poster, you will see clues in the picture that will tell you a story. Look at this picture for one minute without talking and then we will listen to everyone's ideas." They sit quietly as she opens the poster and gaze intently at it (see Figure 3–1). Before the minute is up, many of them eagerly wave their hands. At the end of one minute, she says simply, "Tell me what you see." One by one, the children share their ideas, and the class is soon engaged in a lively discussion.

Who made the footprints? After several students mention dinosaurs, she asks whether it was dinosaurs, or could other animals have made the footprints? How many dinosaurs are making the footprints? Why did the bigger dinosaur start running and why did the little one not? What is the relationship between the two—could it be a mother and baby? The students give their opinions and point out clues on the poster to back them up. Ms. Kraft says little, speaking only to ask students to explain their hypotheses. The students challenge each other's ideas and present alternative explanations for the clues. By the end of 30 minutes, many stories have been proposed about the footprints. Finally, one of the students asks Ms. Kraft, "Who is right?" She responds that there is no right or wrong answer. Any story that makes sense and fits the clues is correct. The majority of the children believe that the footprints show a big dinosaur catching and eating a little dinosaur, but admit that other stories are plausible as well. At the end of the discussion, the students return to their seats and start to write a story explaining what they saw in the footprints.

Ms. Kraft is a teacher who incorporates problem solving into all aspects of her primary classroom. She used the lesson just outlined as an introduction to a unit on dinosaurs. The lesson was simple, yet it provided the students with the opportunity to think creatively, analyze, compare and contrast, predict or forecast, evaluate, use prior knowledge, make inferences, and synthesize ideas. That's a lot of higher-level thinking for a 30-minute lesson! The students, however, were not drained and exhausted at the end of the lesson. They were energized and excited! Some teachers might feel more comfortable using such an activity at the end of a unit, when students are familiar with a topic, but Ms. Kraft wanted to set the tone for the whole unit by doing it at the start. Throughout the rest of the unit, her students see themselves as amateur paleontologists, actively engaged in learning about dinosaurs.

Problem solving is a natural thing for a primary classroom. From toddlerhood on, young children are engaged in figuring out things in their world. They come to school with a lot of prior experience in problem solving along with the curiosity and the intense desire to learn that all young children possess. Throughout this chapter, ways that primary teachers can effectively infuse problem solving into their classrooms will be presented. Real examples will show ways to plan, implement, and evaluate problem-solving activities.

THE PROBLEM-SOLVING CLASSROOM

There are several "secrets" to using problem solving successfully as an integral part of your primary classroom. Overall, you need to create an atmosphere where students will feel comfortable solving problems. Several characteristics of this kind of atmosphere are described next.

FIGURE 3–1 Dinosaur Footprints

Students Should Take Risks and Try Different Strategies

Students can be successful problem solvers only if they feel safe enough to *take risks*. This can happen in a classroom where the teacher lets students know that learning and perseverance, not just getting the right answer, are valued . Make it a habit to always ask students to tell you how they solved a problem, before asking them to tell you what answer they have for a problem. Praise their efforts and their willingness to keep trying. Let students know that you have problems too, and model how you solve them. (For example, the copy machine broke down that morning. Tell the students how you adjusted your plans.)

Positively reinforce students' attempts to be flexible and *try different strategies*, even if they are not on the right track! It is usually apparent to an adult that a certain strategy won't work, and it is tempting to save the students' time and frustration by stepping in and telling them their idea won't work. Often, however, it's best to let students pursue their strategy until they discover that it won't work. If a student is really confused, then you should step in, but remember that students can learn from their mistakes. Also, students will feel hesitant to take risks and try new ways of doing things if they feel the teacher is watching over their shoulders, waiting to catch them doing something wrong.

Students Need to Challenge Themselves and Not Fear Failure

What student behaviors do you as a teacher need to encourage if you want your students to be successful problem solvers? We can answer that question by examining the behavior of preschoolers. Preschoolers are constantly challenged to master new skills and solve problems. Who challenges them? They challenge themselves. A parent does not need to say to a 3-year-old, "You need to learn how to get dressed. I will teach you how." Instead, the child constantly says to the parent, "Let me do it!" Preschool children will struggle with a task, whether it's getting a jacket zipped or opening a container, until they are successful. Their joy and pride when they finally accomplish a task knows no bounds! They build self-confidence by succeeding at difficult tasks, and sometimes vehemently resist adults' efforts to interfere.

Primary-aged children, in contrast, may be hesitant to try something if they think they will be unsuccessful. Sadly, by the time many children have been in formal schooling only a year or two, they have come to equate success with speed and answers. They believe that being the first one done is something special and that the quicker you can answer a question the smarter you are. Can you recapture in your primary-aged children the stubborn determination that characterized them as preschoolers? Yes! It may not happen overnight, but by using the following strategies to prepare children to be successful problem solvers you can gradually help them rediscover their natural ability to solve problems.

STRATEGIES FOR SUCCESSFUL PROBLEM SOLVING

Preparing children to be successful problem solvers is not difficult to do, but it is important. Just as a runner needs to warm up and train to perform well in a race, children need to have some preparation before they are asked to solve problems. These practical, easy-to-do strategies will help you "warm up" your students for problem solving.

Prepare Your Students to Spend Time on a Problem

When children are used to answering most questions asked of them very quickly, they get nervous if they spend several minutes and an answer is not yet apparent. Cue your students right from the start that they may need to spend quite a while working on the problem and that you have set aside lots of time for them to work. Some people do their best work under time pressure, but you cannot expect this of young children. However, do not make the amount of time required seem threatening. Don't tell your students that the problem is so hard it will take them a long time to solve! Instead, tell them that most people need at least "X" amount of time to think through ways to solve this problem.

Let Students Know That It Is OK to Feel Frustrated or Anxious

Obviously, you as a teacher don't want to present students with problems that are way too difficult for them to solve. Conversely, though, you don't want to present only easy problems that require little thinking or effort to solve. Toddlers and preschoolers are often frustrated. It does them no long-term harm; in fact, it is almost essential to their development! Robert Walrath (in Abarbanel, 1994, p. 36) states that "In many ways, frustration is a prerequisite for growth." Parents who step in often to help a preschooler perform a task are not really helping at all, for they are communicating the message to their child that he or she is incapable of doing it alone. The child is also not learning how to solve problems on his or her own. Dr. Daniel Graybill (in Abarbanel, 1994, p. 37) cautions parents that "You're not doing your children a favor by not allowing them to feel frustration. The more they learn to cope, the happier they will be." A little frustration actually motivates toddlers and preschoolers to keep trying. By school age, however, many children, along with their teachers, have begun to see frustration only as a negative emotion.

Yet "patience and persistence are teachable virtues," (Abarbanel, 1994, p. 34). You as a teacher need to let your students know that they might feel frustrated and that this is not their cue to give up! "If you can make a child feel understood, frustration often evaporates" (Graybill in Abarbanel, 1994, p. 36). To let students know that you understand their feelings, say something like "You may try many ways to solve this problem, and you will feel frustrated if they don't work. You might even start to worry that you won't be able to solve it, and maybe you will feel like giving up. That is usually a good sign, because it means that you have really thought through the problem and have tried many different ways of solving it. You will probably be close to solving the problem at that point, so try again. Or leave the problem for a little while, and come back to it." The author has observed countless times that young students often solve a problem within minutes of saying, "I'll never get this" or "This is impossible." Consider the following story from a new teacher:

> I found a brainteaser problem-solving exercise that I thought would be good to do with my second graders. I put the students into groups to work on it. After about 10 minutes, not a single group had solved it and they were complaining that it was hard. I thought I had made a huge mistake and had picked a problem that was too difficult for them. I was thinking of a way to gracefully say "never mind" and stop the lesson, when I heard a cheer from one of the groups. They had solved the problem and were just thrilled! Within 10 minutes, all the groups had solved it. The students asked if they could do another problem the next day! It turned out to be a great activity, and I had almost ended it due to my discomfort with seeing the students really challenged.

Model Metacognition

Discuss with your students how you are thinking as you work through problems. Demonstrate to students how you vary your strategies as you attempt to solve a problem. Encourage students to discuss their thought processes as they work on a problem. After any problem-solving exercise, always spend more time discussing how students worked through the problem than discussing the actual answer(s).

Make Problem Solving a Joint Effort

If it appears to students that you always know the correct answer and that they are just trying to figure out what you already know, it will diminish their motivation. You should figure out a problem with the students, without first looking up the answer. If you don't feel comfortable doing that, then figure it out yourself before class. Students love it when you let them know that you don't know the answer to a problem. It's the best problem-solving motivator!

Let Students Experience the Joy of the "Aha!" Moment

When students work on simple exercises such as addition facts, they may feel some satisfaction when they are done, but it doesn't begin to compare to how they will feel if they solve something that really made them think. Problem solving can boost students' self-esteem. They will feel very proud of themselves if they solve something that they weren't sure they could. In many instances, the solution to a problem literally comes to a student in a moment of inspiration, and they will say, "I've got it!" or "Aha!" Be prepared for huge grins! Once students have experienced an "Aha!" moment, they will approach the next problem with more confidence and eagerness.

WAYS TO INTEGRATE PROBLEM SOLVING INTO YOUR CLASSROOM

How often have you heard a fellow teacher say, " I'm being asked to include so many things in my teaching these days. Every inservice session introduces some new technique that's a "must" in a good classroom, but nobody tells me how to fit it all together and how to have time to do it all. How am I supposed to develop a "problem-solving" classroom, when I'm already trying to incorporate learning styles, cooperative grouping, interdisciplinary units, and so on into my curriculum? Plus, I still have to cover all the basic curriculum! Help! Help!"

Good news! Problem solving is not something you must "add on" in addition to other learning methods you use in your classroom. In fact, it will enhance them! Yes, you will need to think about and plan your lessons differently, especially at first. But you will find that problem solving helps you to meet different learning styles, provides for truly valuable cooperative learning and other group experiences, fits naturally with interdisciplinary teaching, and helps students learn content.

Consider Student Learning Styles

Problem-solving activities are appropriate for all learning styles. If a problem is open-ended, each child can approach it through his or her own learning style. Some children approach a problem in a very methodical way, organizing the information and taking notes. Other children excel at coming up with creative, offbeat solutions to problems. Still other children solve a problem intuitively and may not be able to explain any process that led them to a solution. Yet all may come up with a satisfactory solution to a problem, especially if the problem doesn't limit itself to only one "right" answer. When a problem does have only one correct solution, as is often the case with math problems, children can benefit from learning skills, such as making a chart or working backward, that are not a strength of their preferred learning style. Whatever their learning styles, children learn best when doing meaningful activities that actively engage their thinking. Doing problem-solving activities is one of the best and easiest ways that a teacher can ensure that children of all learning styles will have the opportunity to learn and succeed in the classroom.

Group Students in Many Ways

Cooperative learning experiences are enhanced by problem solving. When children work on a challenging problem as a group, they truly need to collaborate and cooperate, much more so than if they are working on a more routine assignment. The children will come to see the value of having several minds thinking about a problem. This technique will also benefit them in the workplace as adults.

Students can be grouped in many ways. Teachers can carefully arrange the groups, randomly draw names, or let the students choose their own groups. All strategies can be used successfully, but keep in mind that great differences in ability among members of the group can sometimes cause problems. For example, if the highest-achieving child in the class is in a group with the lowest achiever, both may be frustrated. For problem-solving activities, an arrangement where one cooperative group consists of average and low-achieving students and another includes high- and average-achieving students will be more successful. Completely heterogeneous groups can often be used for social studies, art, science, and other activities. To be successful problem solvers, children need to feel comfortable. Try setting up cooperative groups at the start of the year. If the groups seem to function successfully, these core groups can remain throughout the year. By the end of the year, these groups may have developed into efficiently working teams. At times, children will like and benefit from the opportunity to work with other temporary groups, but they will always have their core group.

Problem solving, however, doesn't have to be done in small groups. Children will also benefit from doing problem-solving activities alone, with a partner, and as a whole class. With young children, it's a good idea to present the first experiences at problem solving as teacher-led, whole-class activities. This gives the teacher the chance to provide some direction to students' efforts and to model metacognition and problem-solving strategies. Until they are quite experienced at problem solving, primary children will probably feel more comfortable working with a partner or in a group. However, some children do prefer to work alone, and that option should be available to them when appropriate.

Organize Your Curriculum for Interdisciplinary Teaching

Many teachers find it difficult to organize their classrooms for interdisciplinary teaching, especially when many texts and curriculum materials are not organized that way. Interdisciplinary activities can seem like a "forced" fit. But they can become more natural and meaningful when a problem is used as the basis for the activities. For example, activities in a classroom could be based on the theme "Water, Water, Everywhere." A local topic related to water, such as water pollution, water conservation, or wetlands maintenance, could serve as a basis for activities in all subject areas. Once a problem related to the topic, such as people wasting water, is identified, students could conduct research about the problem, conduct or design experiments to learn more about the problem and test solutions, graph or chart their results, develop solutions, and communicate their findings to others. A true integration of all subject areas could be achieved. Problems that relate to a school or local problem may be the most relevant to students, but problems of a wider scope, such as rain forest depletion or endangered animals, can also work very well.

Help Students Learn and Master Basic Content

Problem-solving activities do not only need to be reserved for *after* students have learned basic content.

Yes, students will need to know some basic content in order to be effective problem solvers. However, recent research reports that "computational skills do not exist as lower-order prerequisites for higher-order mathematical problem solving, but rather are learned in relation to *and as a part of* problem solving" (Carpenter, Fennema, & Peterson, 1988, p. 42). In fact, when given the chance, many students can figure out their own strategies to solve problems that are much more difficult than would normally be a part of the curriculum for their grade level, even though it would appear that they have not mastered the basic skills necessary to solve the problems. Students can actually learn basic content, such as addition and subtraction facts, while solving challenging, interesting problems. For example, students can figure out how many bean seeds each group of four students will need if each student is to plant six seeds.

No teacher need hesitate to use problem solving in a classroom or fear that it will interfere with other teaching methods or make instruction unmanageable. In fact, for a teacher who truly wants all students to learn to their fullest potential, making problem solving a regular part of his or her instructional strategies will help to reach that goal.

PLANNING FOR PROBLEM SOLVING

Any teacher knows that lessons do not always go exactly as planned, yet planning is still vitally important because it sets the framework for the success of classroom activities. Successful problem-solving experiences rarely happen by accident! Like most classroom activities, they require planning and preparation. Examples of ways to plan units in three different situations—revising a unit that has been taught before, planning a new unit with only skeletal materials from the curriculum, and problem solving in informal situations—are presented here.

Revising a Successful Unit

Ms. Carter, a primary teacher, is working on developing a problem-solving classroom. She is preparing to teach a unit on weather and thinks the present unit is a good one. She likes the way it emphasizes hands-on activities. Students do simple weather experiments, chart the daily weather, learn weather terms, and learn about safety in weather. As she plans the unit, she's not quite sure how to incorporate problem-solving activities and will not be able to spend any more time on the unit than she usually does. Where does she begin?

Problem-solving activities can help turn a good unit into a great one! The most worthwhile problem-solving activities are those that are woven into your regular curriculum. They should be based on the content you are teaching and should incorporate real-life problems whenever possible. Let's take a look at the topic of weather and see how we can plan a unit that incorporates problem solving.

How Does the Topic Affect the Lives of Students? First, we need to look at how the weather affects our everyday lives. Weather can cause many problems, as in the case of droughts, floods, tornadoes, blizzards, and hurricanes. Weather also benefits us in many ways. It helps crops grow, is responsible for our water cycle, and provides sunny weather for picnics. Weather is one topic that lends itself very well to problem solving using real-life situations, since it affects everyone's life daily. Ms. Carter ponders how weather affects her students and develops the following problem to pose to them: "What if we could control the weather? Should we control it?" This activity could be done in many ways. If the students are new to problem solving, she may want to do this as a teacher-led activity. If they are more experienced, she may ask them to think about the problem in groups and follow up with a whole-class discussion of each group's ideas.

Use Webbing as an Organizing Technique. Let's see how this would work as a teacher-led activity. Ms. Carter poses the question "What would happen if we could control the weather?" to her students and tells them to think about it for one minute. She has decided to use a web to record and organize the students' ideas. She places her question on the board and students' ideas are recorded on boxes connected to "spokes" radiating out from the question. (See Figure 3–2.) Webbing is one useful method to use to record forecasting ideas, especially when the problem is abstract rather than hands-on. Students are encouraged to expand on ideas and think about how one thing might lead to another. One line is used to connect ideas to the original question in the box, and ideas that lead off of those ideas are connected by two lines. One more line can be added for every step away from

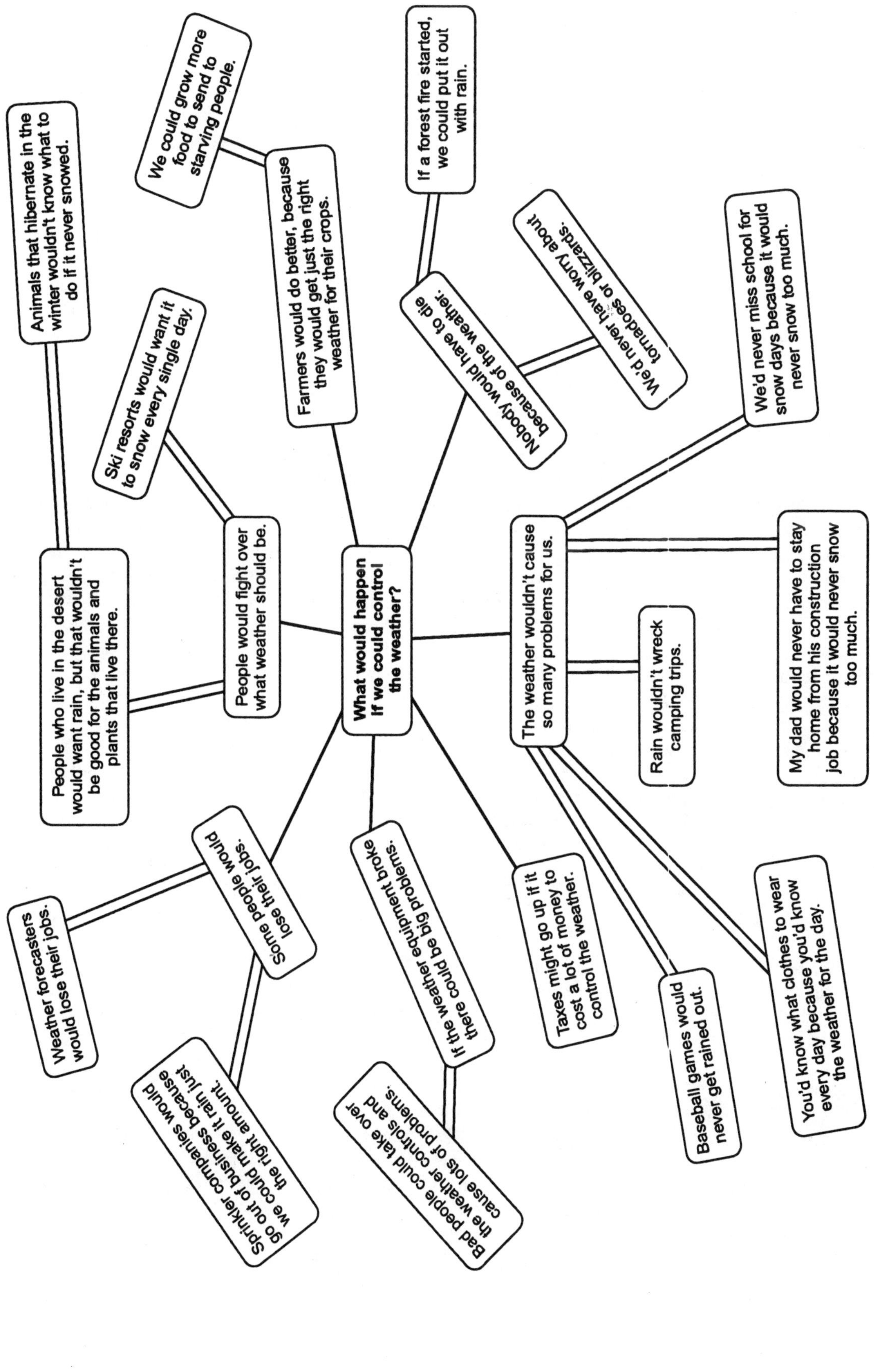

Planning for Problem Solving 63

FIGURE 3–2 Weather Web

the original idea. This can really stretch the students' thinking. They can see how one situation can affect many things in a domino-like effect. To start the discussion, Ms. Carter writes down an idea in one of the boxes, as shown.

> Sprinkler companies would go out of business because we could make it rain just the right amount.

One of the students thinks about the statement and quickly raises her hand. "We'd never miss school for snow days because it would never snow too much!" "My dad would never have to stay home from work at his construction job because of bad weather." One by one students share their ideas, which are recorded on the web.

As Ms. Carter sees that most of the students' responses list positive results of weather control, she poses the question, "Can you think of any bad things that could happen from controlling the weather?" A student responds, "I think people might fight over what the weather should be. Some people like really hot weather so they can go to the beach, and other people want it cooler." Another student says, "I bet some people might never want snow, but animals that hibernate in the winter wouldn't know what to do if it never snowed. "

By the time this lesson was finished, the students had filled the web with many ideas related to controlling the weather, almost all of them the students' own ideas. They had considered how one event affects another. In just one lesson, Ms. Carter met or addressed many of the objectives from her normal weather unit. The students were thinking about how weather affects people and were using weather terminology in a meaningful context.

Allow Students to Conduct Their Own Research. When students collect and analyze their own information, the learning becomes much more meaningful to them. To follow up on this lesson, Ms. Carter might have her students conduct a survey to find out what people consider "perfect" weather. The students could predict what people would say, conduct the survey, and graph the results during a math lesson. Or they could survey to see how many people would like to see the weather controlled. During a geography lesson, they could find places on earth where "perfect" weather can be found. Problem solving easily leads to interdisciplinary activities!

Add a Problem-Solving "Twist" to the Activities. Ms. Carter can continue to do many of her normal unit activities. By changing them slightly, she can add a problem-solving "twist" to them. For example, the students measure and chart the weather every day during the unit. To add some problem solving to the activity, the students could record what the radio or television weather forecast is for each day. When they are measuring and charting the weather, they can compare their findings to the official forecast to find out about forecast accuracy. If they live in an area with more than one television or radio station, they could compare the forecasts to see if one is more accurate than another. They could then consider what affects the accuracy of weather forecasts. Could ancient people predict the weather without using the sophisticated equipment that is used today? Can we predict the weather without using any equipment? How?

One of the objectives for Ms. Carter's weather unit is that students learn that weather changes throughout the year and is different around the world. She teaches the students how weather changes through the year as the earth rotates and revolves around the sun and how a state's or country's climate is affected by its position on the earth. One way that she can see if the students really understand the concepts, and add some problem solving to the activity is to say, "Think about what would happen if the earth turned upside down and stayed that way. What would the weather where we live be like? Would it be the same or different? How about a country on the equator? Would their weather be any different?" This discussion may only add 10 extra minutes to her normal lesson, but the thinking and problem-solving dimension it adds is well worth the time spent.

Use the Daily Newspaper as a Resource. Weather is one topic that is mentioned often in local news, especially when the weather is affecting people negatively. The information provided in a local paper can provide material for problem-solving activities. For example, a flood may devastate a community, a blizzard may block roads, a tornado may cause extensive damage, and so on. Whether it's a local, national, or world event, students can discuss the problems involved and propose solutions. The students can consider what they can do to help solve a problem, such as collecting toys and books to send to children who have lost everything in a flood or tornado. How can they save water during a drought? What can they do to prepare for an approaching blizzard? The problem-solving process becomes more relevant to children when they apply it to real-life problems.

The newspaper can also be used as a basis for developing problem-solving activities for students who need extra challenges or are interested in pursuing the topic of weather in more depth. For example, most newspapers provide detailed information on local weather, along with a national weather map and basic temperature information on weather in major cities around the world. Using this wealth of information, students can find the major city with the highest temperature and the one with the lowest temperature in the country or world on any given day. Students can locate these cities on a map and plot the information. After several days or weeks of doing this, they can draw conclusions by analyzing the maps they have created. What can this information tell us about climate around the world? Are high and low temperatures consistently in the same areas every day, or do weather fronts move around? The newspaper is a very valuable resource for problem-solving activities.

Include Hands-On Activities. A quality science curriculum should provide many opportunities for involving students in hands-on learning. Ms. Carter likes the fact that the weather unit does provide hands-on learning activities for the students. However, keep in mind that not all hands-on activities are problem-solving activities. The best of them are, but many experiments and other hands-on activities are really simple "follow the directions" experiences. Students are told exactly how to do an "experiment" and often know what will happen. The students themselves are not given the chance to propose a hypothesis or design an experiment to test their idea. Yes, students do need to learn careful scientific procedure and replicating an experiment is one way to do that, but to think like scientists they need to do more than that.

Add the "What If?" Step. Ms. Carter needs to add one simple step to each of her weather experiments to make them problem-solving activities: the "What If?" step. After students have completed the "basic" experiment, they get the chance to explore other ideas. For example, if they did an experiment where they measured temperatures in different places outside, they can suggest ways to modify the experiment. What if they hold the thermometer upside down? What if they dip the thermometer in cold water before they set it in the sun? What if they walk around with the thermometer instead of keeping it in one place? The important thing is that the students get to generate the ideas, predict what will happen, and conduct their own experiment. Because they are young children, their ideas may be very simple, illogical, or even silly. Unless safety is an issue, let them test their ideas out anyway! They may or may not discover any additional scientific principles, but they will be gaining valuable experience in problem solving. They are getting the chance to synthesize what they learned with other things they know, analyze their data, and draw conclusions. Also, they will be highly motivated because they have ownership of the idea. They will come to see the excitement of scientific exploration and discovery. A follow-up discussion about all the "What if?" experiments will usually spark even more ideas as students piggy-back off others' ideas.

One note of caution: once students have had some experience with designing their own "What if?" experiments, they may have little patience with doing the basic experiments first! They will be overflowing with ideas the minute they hear the topic of the new experiment. There is nothing wrong with insisting they do the basic experiment correctly first, as long as it is a worthwhile experiment and will serve as a springboard for their own ideas. Eventually, students can be given a question, such as "How can we find out whether salt water or fresh water evaporates sooner?" and they will be able to design their own experiment to answer it.

By using the strategies just discussed, Ms. Carter has changed the focus of her weather unit slightly and improved it greatly. Her students are still learning lots about weather, but they are now applying what they know to think about and solve problems.

Building a New Unit

What do you do if you are planning a brand-new unit? The first thing you need to do is *consider the content and objectives that students need to master*. Students need to have some basic knowledge about a topic before they can become problem solvers. Keep in mind, however, that problem-solving activities can be used to teach content. Decide on the content students need to learn, and start by planning a framework of worthwhile activities that ensures students learn that content.

You will also need to *consider what thinking skills you would like to emphasize in the unit*. For example, if you have emphasized comparing and contrasting or forecasting and predicting heavily in other units, you would want to make sure that you include other thinking skills or problem-solving strategies, such as classifying, experimenting, evaluation, or analysis, in the unit you are planning. Often, the content of the unit easily lends itself to emphasizing particular thinking skills. Don't try to "force fit" a thinking skill if it truly doesn't match the content. However, it is helpful to keep a running list of the thinking skills and strategies that were emphasized in each unit that you have taught so that you can see at a glance if there is a balance of thinking skills. Do not feel pressured, though, to cover all thinking skills and problem-solving strategies yourself in one school year's time! Primary students are just learning these strategies. They will have many more years to practice them and tackle more challenging activities.

Relate the Unit to the General Curriculum. Mr. Douglas will soon be teaching a unit on money, which is part of his upper primary math curriculum. The present unit consists primarily of worksheets. The students count, add, and subtract money on the worksheets. If students have extra time when they finish their worksheets, they can go to the mock store in the back of the classroom and pretend to shop for groceries. Mr. Douglas wants to throw out the math workbook and plan a unit that emphasizes hands-on problem solving while still accomplishing the objectives of the unit. He likes the idea of a mock store, but wants to make it more real-life and an integral part of the unit, rather than a spare-time activity.

Mr. Douglas first needs to consider the objectives of the unit:

1. The student will be able to identify and state the value of a penny, nickel, dime, quarter, half-dollar, and a one-dollar bill.

2. The student will be able to count out the value of a group of similar coins.

3. The student will be able to add up the value of various groupings of coins.

4. The student will be able to add up the total cost of a group of items and express it in dollars and cents notation.

5. The student will be able to calculate the change due from one dollar by subtracting the value of one or more items.

Find Out What the Students Already Know. Mr. Douglas also needs to determine how much of the basic content his students already know, so he can decide how much of the unit needs to be spent on basic content and how much on problem-solving activities where the students can apply what they know. So he gives a pretest to the students, and finds that almost all of them can identify coins, count out the value of similar coins, and add up the value of various groupings of coins, which was covered in the previous grade level. Some of the students show some proficiency with the other objectives of the unit, but it is clear that the majority of them have yet to master these objectives.

Use Problem-Solving Activities to Teach Content. Even basic content can be taught or reviewed through problem-solving activities. To do this, Mr. Douglas has the students practice one of the objectives of the unit, adding up the value of different coins, with the following problem-solving activity.

ACTIVITY • *How Many Ways Can You Make 25¢?*

Mr. Douglas grouped the students into partners. He gave each set of partners a bag of plastic coins and told them that they are going to buy a pack of gum at the store. The four basic steps of the problem-solving model outlined in Figure 2–5, modified for use with primary-age children, were used to solve this problem. The numbers after each heading refer to the steps of this model.

Clarify

1. They *explored the problem* situation, set the rule that only whole coins could be used, and came up with three possible ways to state the problem:

   a. Ways to pay 25¢ for gum

   b. How to find 25¢ in coins to pay for gum

   c. How many different arrangements of coins totaling 25¢ can we make to give to a clerk to buy gum?

2. After discussing the three statements, the class decided that problem statement c was the best *problem statement* because it clearly stated the problem that needed to be solved.

Forecast/Investigate

3-6. For young children, the steps of *generating optional solutions* and *investigating* often overlap. A major value of the problem-solving experience for them is the opportunity to brainstorm ways to solve a problem and try out their ideas. Many young children are unable to solve problems abstractly, and do need "hands-on" materials to help them work through the problems. Mr. Douglas verbally had the children predict how many ways they could arrange the coins before they started working on the problem. Their responses ranged from 3 to 100. He also told them that they needed to record the different ways they found. The different pairs of students approached this problem in many different ways. Most children started by randomly counting out 25¢ using their plastic coins. Some used 25 pennies, some used two dimes and a nickel, some used five nickels, and so on. At first, their methods were rather haphazard, but most gradually started to be more systematic as they worked through the problem. A few of the children were able to figure out a system for solving the problem and didn't even need to use the coins to solve it. *It is important that the teacher let the students solve the problem in their own way. If they are told how to go about it, they are no longer problem solving. They are following directions.* Remember, the important thing is that children learn how to approach and solve problems, and feel confident doing it. Getting the right answer should be a secondary concern at this point. As they gain experience with solving problems, children will gain more specific skills that will help them to become more proficient.

Evaluate

7-10. The students *organized and communicated their results* in various ways. Some of the students drew pictures of the ways to group the coins, some made up simple charts, and some chose to actually demonstrate the different ways to make 25¢. Mr. Douglas asked each group to explain how they had solved the problem before they discussed the answer. Many of the groups reported that they had to develop some sort of system to find out for sure if they had found all the possibilities. It was much more beneficial for them to discover this on their own than if their teacher had set up a system for them beforehand. Almost all of the groups were able to find all of the thirteen ways to make 25¢ out of coins. (See Figure 3–3.)

FIGURE 3–3 How Many Ways Can You Make 25¢?

	Quarters	Dimes	Nickels	Pennies
1.	1	0	0	0
2.	0	2	1	0
3.	0	0	5	0
4.	0	2	0	5
5.	0	0	4	5
6.	0	1	3	0
7.	0	1	0	15
8.	0	1	1	10
9.	0	1	2	5
10.	0	0	3	10
11.	0	0	2	15
12.	0	0	1	20
13.	0	0	0	25

Involve Students in Real Situations. Mr. Douglas chose to continue using his mock grocery store, but in a very different way. He made it the focus of several lessons. All the students got the chance to be shoppers and clerks. They learned how to add up the total costs of purchases and how to make change. Previously, these activities had been done using worksheets. Mr. Douglas did these activities to prepare students to run an actual store in their classroom. The students made products, set prices, and sold them to other students and teachers at the school.

Because it was close to the holiday season, Mr. Douglas and the class decided to make and sell ornaments. He was able to find patterns for several simple, easy-to-make ornaments that used inexpensive supplies such as pipe cleaners, popsicle sticks, and candy canes. He did the division to figure out the cost of each popsicle stick or other item of raw material, but once the students starting making the ornaments they had to figure out the actual cost of each ornament, including any raw materials that were damaged. They then set a price for each kind of ornament, allowing for a small profit. They made posters advertising their sale. On the day of the sale, the students worked in teams selling the ornaments. They were responsible for adding up the cost of purchases and figuring out any change due. Two students at a time did the figuring to ensure accuracy. After the sale, the students made proposals on how to spend their profits and discussed the merits of each idea, finally deciding to use the money to buy groceries to donate to a local food shelf.

This activity allowed Mr. Douglas to meet all the objectives of his math unit, plus it accomplished much more. The students were actively involved and used their skills in a real-life situation. They were solving problems and making decisions in cooperative groups. The unit also provided many opportunities for interdisciplinary learning as the students wrote about their experiences, discussed economic principles such as profit and loss, and designed advertising posters.

Party Planning: An Opportunity to Practice Problem Solving

When planning curriculum units or activities, such as a class play or a classroom party, try to find ways to involve the students in the planning process. Some of the best thinking and problem solving occurs as students plan an activity. If a teacher plans an activity, it will probably go more smoothly, but when students are involved in the planning they are benefiting greatly from the experience, whether or not the actual activity goes as smoothly as planned!

Provide Opportunities for Students to be Involved in Planning. Students need to learn how to consider criteria or limitations, anticipate what problems may occur and how they may prevent or solve them, figure out what supplies and materials will be needed, and plan a sequence of events. Ms. Smith uses her classroom parties as learning activities. Instead of having parents bring treats for parties, she asked parents to contribute money (usually a dollar or two) at the start of the year. Then a certain amount of money is budgeted for students to use for each party. The students do all the planning, most of the preparations, and all the cleanup. The teacher's role is to facilitate the process. Yes, it does take a lot of class time, but students gain valuable experiences in planning and problem solving. Plus, they enjoy the activities and food more when they have been actively involved in planning the party.

Evaluate Options Before Making Choices. A few weeks before the party, Ms. Smith tells the students how much money they have to spend and how long the party will last. Then, she and the students discuss what they want to do at their party. The first thing they do is decide on how the time will be spent during the party. They brainstorm a list of possible activities, such as play whole-class games, play board games, watch a video, play outside, and so on. Of course, each party must include some time to munch snacks! The students discuss the good and bad things about each idea. For example, they may decide that watching a video will take too much time, plus finding a video that many students haven't seen is difficult. Generally, the list gets narrowed down to just a few activities, and the students vote on which ones they want to do. They also make a list of what must be done before the party to prepare for that activity. For example, if the students decide to play whole-class games, they must decide on the games and what supplies they need to gather.

Next, they decide on the food. Once again, they brainstorm possibilities, such as ordering pizza, buying snacks like potato chips and soda pop, buying a cake, making a cake or cookies at school, making healthy snacks such as carrot sticks, and so on. Keeping in mind the money available, the students discuss the choices and vote on the "menu" for the party. Ms. Smith usually does the shopping for the party, and insists that the students be very specific in what they want. If they want soda pop, they must tell her the flavor and the exact brand. The same goes for potato chips, cookies, and so on. This usually leads to a lively discussion as students all have different favorite brands that they prefer. As they prepare for the first party of the year, Ms. Smith does the following problem-solving activity, which prepares students to make educated choices when making purchases.

EXPERIMENT • Choosing the Best Potato Chip

The students work with four different brands of potato chips: two leading national brands, one generic brand, and an unknown brand. Before the experiment, the chips are poured into four bowls, labeled A, B, C, and D. The students are asked to find out which brand of potato chips is the very best. Again, the steps follow the problem solving format of Figure 2–5.

Clarify

1. The students first *explore the problem situation* by discussing their task. Students have suggested these possible ways to state the problem:

   a. How to choose the very best potato chip.

   b. Finding the best brand of potato chip.

   c. How can we choose the overall best brand of potato chip?

2. The students chose one problem statement as the best *problem statement* because it most clearly states the situation. In this instance, they chose problem statement c.

Forecast

3. The students brainstorm to think of ways to solve the problem (*generating optional solutions*). Some of their ideas have been:

   a. Have each student taste each kind of potato chip and vote.

   b. Find the lowest-priced brand of potato chip.

   c. Look to see which brand of potato chip has the fewest broken or burnt chips.

   d. Measure which potato chips are the crunchiest using a machine.

   e. Weigh the potato chips to see which are the lightest.

   f. Check the packages to see which kind of potato chip has the healthiest ingredients.

   g. Rub the different kinds of potato chips between your fingers to see which one is the least greasy.

   h. Taste each kind of potato chip to tell which is the saltiest.

   i. Have each student score each kind of potato chip, like they score skaters at the Olympics.

4. After much discussion, the students *select the best solutions,* which are usually combinations of several of the ideas. The students think that greasiness is an important thing to consider, but decide that they really couldn't tell just by rubbing which chip is the least greasy. They propose that setting the potato chips on brown paper towels for a set amount of time and examining the grease spots would work better. They also choose to eliminate some ideas. They do not have a machine that can measure crunch, and they decide that the weight of the chip wouldn't make much of a difference in selecting the best potato chip. To select the overall best chip, students realize that they must consider several factors besides taste. They also figure out that each student may like something different. For example, one student may like very salty chips, while another prefers a stronger potato flavor. How then can they choose one overall best potato chip? The students realize that voting or rating is the only way to come up with one winner. Like judges at the Olympics, each student needs to rate each chip and give it a score. Typically, students will choose these categories to rate:

- Taste of potato chip
- Amount of grease
- Condition of potato chips (number of burnt and broken chips, size of chips)
- Cost of potato chips
- Quality of ingredients (fresh or dried potatoes, whether it has preservatives).

Once the students have decided which categories they will use to rate each brand of potato chip, they need to decide how the rating system will work. Do they want to rate each potato chip on a scale of *excellent* to *poor*, or do they want to rate them *first place, second place*, and so on? Ms. Smith lets the students discuss and decide which would give them the best information. They usually choose to rank the potato chips from first place to last place. Finally, together Ms. Smith and the students set up a simple chart on graph paper and each student prepares one so that he or she can keep track of the results. The investigation is about to begin.

Investigate

5. Working in small groups, the students conduct their investigation. Ms. Smith starts to hand out the first brand of potato chips, and immediately the students realize there will be a problem. How will they be able to tell one brand of potato chip from another? She asks for their solutions. They quickly decide that each different brand of potato chips needs to be on a separate paper towel, and that each towel needs to be labeled A, B, C, and D. Until the experiment is over, only the teacher will know which brands of potato chips they are rating.

Ms. Smith puts the price of each brand of potato chips on the chalkboard, and together the class figures out which chip deserves first place and on down the line. They all agree that the lowest cost should be first place! Ms. Smith also reads aloud the ingredients for each brand of potato chip (without revealing the brand) and they discuss the differences. The students are usually amazed by the differences. Some of the chips are made from real potatoes, while others are made from dried potatoes. Preservatives are present in some of the chips, but not in others. The students decide that the potato chip with the most natural ingredients should be the first-place chip. They then evaluate the condition of each brand of potato chips, conduct the grease test, and finally taste each brand.

6. Each student figures out a total score for each chip. Then, each small group adds up the scores to find the overall winner for their group. One by one, each group *communicates their results* to the rest of the class, and the class discusses the similarities and differences.

Evaluate

7. The students *organized their results* in chart form and draw these conclusions:

   a. The results for the categories of condition of chips, cost, ingredients, and amount of grease were the same across all groups.

   b. Results from the taste test differed much more, although the majority of the class preferred the taste of the same brand of potato chip.

   c. The students decided that some categories should be more important than others. A brand of potato chip could possibly be chosen the best overall chip even though most of the students didn't like its taste. This leads to a discussion of weighted scores.

Although this activity is primarily teacher-led, the students still design the investigation and conduct it in cooperative groups. The activity naturally leads them through the steps of problem solving. Yet even young primary students can understand and enjoy the process because it is relevant to them. They are using higher-level thinking skills such as comparing and contrasting, analysis, evaluation, and identifying relevant and irrelevant factors. They are learning how scientists conduct investigations using empirical data, and learning how to record information precisely on a chart. Most importantly, most students regard this as a fun activity! They are motivated and engaged during the entire process, and this enables them to do their best thinking. They are not threatened by the higher-level thinking skills or advanced tasks such as chart making, because they are such a natural part of solving the problem.

Any classroom can become a problem-solving classroom with a little planning. Even small changes in how a teacher teaches and organizes learning experiences can make a huge difference. The benefits to students of problem solving are great, and they are cumulative. The more students experience problem solving, the more proficient they become at solving problems. Young children who are given opportunities often to solve problems become capable of doing much more advanced work than are students who are inexperienced with problem solving. Time is always at a premium in a primary classroom, but remember that a well-designed problem-solving activity is one of the best uses of time that a teacher can make. It affords students the opportunity to learn and use higher-level thinking skills, creative thinking skills, and specific academic skills—all at the same time!

PROBLEM SOLVING IN ACTION IN THE PRIMARY CLASSROOM

Because every student and teacher is unique, each classroom is different. However, in classrooms where problem solving is an integral part of the school day, there are common characteristics. Students are actively participating and engaged in their learning. They are discussing and debating ideas and exploring the world around them. They are free to make mistakes and think of alternative ways to do things. Higher-level thinking skills are as familiar to them as basic facts drills are to students in more traditional classroom settings.

The following section describes a variety of problem-solving activities that are suitable for primary students. They are all teacher-tested activities that have been successfully used in heterogeneous primary classrooms. Some of them may fit nicely into your own curriculum, while others may need to be adapted for use in your classroom. But all activities will illustrate the many ways that problem solving can be implemented in the primary classroom and may serve as springboards for further ideas.

Although the activities themselves vary greatly, they all roughly follow the problem-solving model presented in Figure 2–5—*clarifying, forecasting, investigating, a*nd *evaluating.* When doing problem solving activities with young children, the steps in the model may overlap and may not be as clearly defined as they are with older children. Four activities are presented here in a format that teachers can use in the classroom. These activities use easy-to-obtain materials, generate high interest among the students, and focus hands-on involvement for them.

Focusing on Inference and Deduction

Any teacher who wants to guarantee that all students will be paying attention and motivated to learn just needs to bring out a bag of garbage! The novelty of such an event is a great motivator! Some teachers are afraid to do a lesson like this for fear that their students will get too "wound up" and out of control. Usually, that is not a problem. Students who are excited about learning are concentrating on the lesson, not on misbehaving.

ACTIVITY • Every Bag of Garbage Tells A Story

Subject Areas. Science (environment); social studies (archaeology, families)

Grade Level. All primary grades

Thinking Skills. Inferring, predicting, deductive reasoning, analysis, observing, hypothesizing

Materials Needed. Any items may be used for the activity. The following list of items is just a suggestion. However, I have found that a group of items that has been carefully chosen elicits the best thinking from the students, and over time I have settled on this group of items to use for the lesson.

Suggested List of Items for Activity

- A large opaque plastic garbage bag containing items of garbage (not food remains—you will be handling these items!)
- One empty box of baby cereal
- An empty box of adult cold medicine
- A large cardboard paper tube from a roll of wrapping paper
- One pink paper bow
- An empty pie tin or pie box from a bakery
- Several paper streamers-pink and white
- One empty pizza delivery box
- One empty pink envelope with the name "Kelly" on it
- One empty baby wipes container
- A large number of crumpled facial tissues
- One crumpled sheet of multicolored birthday wrapping paper
- Eight crumpled grocery coupons (expired)
- An empty container of dog or cat treats
- One disposable diaper—size large, with tab broken off (not used!)
- One small birthday candle—broken, not burned
- Three small birthday candles—burned

Description of Activity. This activity works very well as a large group, teacher-led activity. The teacher introduces the activity by holding up a bag of garbage and telling the students that it contains one day's garbage from a family. Their job is to be detectives and try to figure out as much as they can about the family by examining the items in the bag.

The teacher pulls out one item at a time from the bag. On the suggested list, items are listed in the order they should be pulled from the bag, since the order can be significant. The goal is to have the students learn a little more from each item, so it is important to pull out the most ambiguous items first so that students consider many different ideas. They can gradually narrow down their hypotheses as more clues are revealed. Each item should be discussed by the class and its relationship to previous items considered. Divergent ideas should be encouraged as well as the most logical explanation for each item. The teacher's role is to facilitate the discussion and make sure that the students fully consider the possibilities of each item.

For a teacher using the suggested list of items, the following questions could be used to guide the discussion:

1. How many people seem to be in the family? What can we learn about them?
(There appears to be at least two people—an adult with a cold and a young baby. There is no specific evidence of a second adult, but that doesn't necessarily prove that there isn't one. The evidence for the adult is the adult cold medicine. The presence of a box of baby cereal, baby wipes container, and the diaper indicate that there is a baby in the household. The family also includes a pet.)

2. What did the family do on this day?
(They celebrated the birthday of someone named Kelly. The evidence for this is the wrapping paper roll, pink bow, crumpled wrapping paper, streamers, pink envelope, candles, and the pie. The first few items could indicate many different celebrations, such as baby shower or bridal shower. However, as the items are revealed one by one they will definitely indicate a birthday celebration. If students only think of birthday from the start, the teacher should encourage them to think of other possibilities. Kelly turned either 3 or 30 on this birthday, which means it is either the mother or the toddler. A baby wearing diapers and eating cereal would not be 3 years old, so there must be two different children. The fact that a pie tin was found but not a cake could mean many things: a cake could be stored somewhere if it was not totally eaten, the mother could have preferred pie over cake, or someone could be allergic to cake. There is evidence of one meal—the pizza and the pie—but nothing to indicate they ate any other meals.)

3. Why is there only one diaper in the garbage bag?
(Anybody who has been around babies knows that they use more than one diaper a day! The presence of only one diaper, plus the absence of baby wipes, could mean that they were not home most of the day, used cloth diapers except for one disposable at night, usually put diapers in a diaper pail, or the baby was just visiting for a short time. The fact that this diaper is broken explains why it was thrown away, but doesn't explain where the other diapers are.)

4. Can we learn anything about this family by what is not in their garbage?
(The fact that there is only one meal could mean that they were not home most of the day and ate elsewhere, or they cleaned their plates at other meals and didn't have any items to throw away. They could be recyclers, since no recyclable items like soda pop cans were in their garbage. They could have put food scraps in a compost pile, or their refrigerator could be filled with leftovers.)

After examining all the garbage and discussing their ideas, the students will come to realize that more than one day's worth of garbage would have to be examined in order to answer all their questions and come up with a more accurate profile of the family.

Extension Ideas

- Students could write a story of the family and their day's activities.
- Students could examine their classroom garbage, or garbage from their own home and analyze it.
- Students could examine items in an old trunk, boxes of old photographs, or other old items and make hypotheses, based on their analysis, about the people represented by the items.
- The teacher could show the students an unfamiliar item, such as an antique utensil that is no longer used, and the students could try to determine its purpose and function.
- Students could sort through garbage at home or school and think of ways to reuse as many items as possible.

Grouping Things Together

A standard part of the primary science curriculum in most schools is a unit on kinds of animals. Students learn about the five major groups of vertebrates—mammals, birds, fish, reptiles, and amphibians—and the characteristics of the animals in each group. In this shoe activity, students learn *how* scientists arrange animals or other things into groups using a taxonomy, which is a classification system based on criteria.

ACTIVITY • Shoe Taxonomy

Subject Areas. Science (animal classification); math (grouping)

Grade Level. Lower primary

Thinking Skills. Classification, comparing and contrasting, analysis, synthesis, observing

Materials Needed. A large number of shoes. These items can be the students' own, or you could collect a large number by shopping at thrift sales or cleaning out your closets. An advantage of supplying your own is that you can keep them in your classroom and students can experiment with them on their own after you have done the activity as a whole class. You should have at least 20 to 30 different items. You will use only one shoe of each pair. (If you can't work with shoes, you might try buttons.)

Description of Activity. To get started, students should take off a shoe, unless the teacher is providing them. Any teacher will definitely have students "hooked" for the entire lesson by telling them to "take off one shoe and put it in the pile!" The students should gather around the pile in as large a circle as space permits. If possible, this activity should be done outside or in a gym or cafeteria, since it requires a lot of space.

1. First, the large pile must be split into two separate groups based on the most obvious, important difference between items. Students should discuss and debate what the first "split" and all subsequent splits should be. For example, a pile of shoes could be split into two groups according to use: dress shoes and tennis shoes.

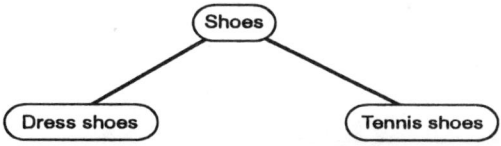

It is *very important* that students make the first split based upon the most important difference between items. Some students may suggest that the pile of shoes be split into two groups based on a characteristic such as color or size. If they are confused about how to determine the most important characteristic, have them consider animal classification. Horses come in many different colors, but they are all still classified as horses. Some horses are the same color as moose, but they do not belong in the same group with moose because of their different body characteristics, which are more important than the color of their coats. Size, although it sometimes differentiates animals into groups (i.e., dwarf rabbits and regular rabbits), is not an important characteristic, because animals of the same species can be different in size. Also, baby animals are smaller than adult animals of the same species.

2. Once the first split has been made, the two different groups should be dealt with separately. It is too confusing for students to go back and forth between groups. Let's consider the pile of shoes, which has been split into the two groups—dress shoes and tennis shoes. It is now time to take one of the groups, the tennis shoes, and split it into two groups. Then, each of these two groups are split into two groups, again using one characteristic for each split, until each shoe stands in a group by itself. (Unless you have two shoes that are identical.) Figure 3-4 illustrates the step-by-step process that is used to arrange items in a taxonomy. However, when doing this activity with students, it is not necessary to write out the taxonomy. They will be actually arranging the shoes into a taxonomy as they physically move the shoes around on the floor.

3. Every subsequent split should be based on smaller and smaller differences. For example, a group of shoes with laces may be split into two new groups: shoes with laces that are solid colored, and shoes with laces that have more than one color. There may be much debate about some of the splits, since there could be many possible ways to do each one. There is no one "right" way to do a taxonomy. However, the students should be able to explain and defend their choices, and they should make logical sense.

Once students have had the opportunity to arrange shoes into a taxonomy, it should make a lot more sense to them how scientists have grouped animals. In fact, this lesson can be extended by creating a pile of cards with a variety of animal names on them which the students can arrange into a taxonomy. They will most likely find that they naturally group robins with seagulls and goldfish with trout. They may also come to see how large groups of animals can be further split into individual species.

This activity could also work well using buttons, although due to their small size they are more suited to individual and small-group work at desks or tables. They can be used very well as a follow-up to a whole class lesson using the shoes. Mittens and gloves can also be used as a substitute for shoes.

FIGURE 3–4 Shoe Taxonomy

Step One:

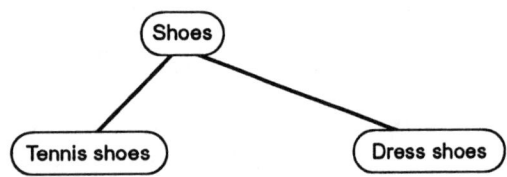

Step Two:

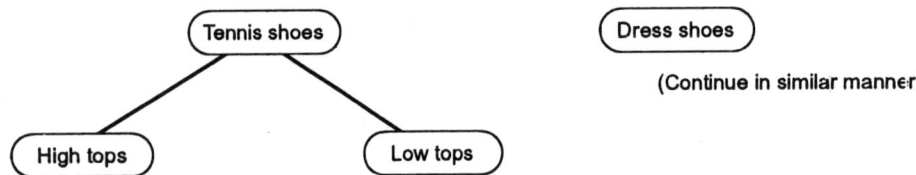

Step Three:

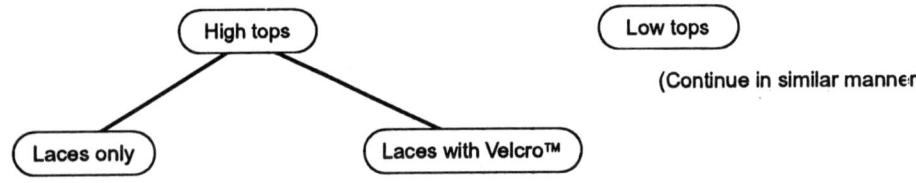

Step Four:

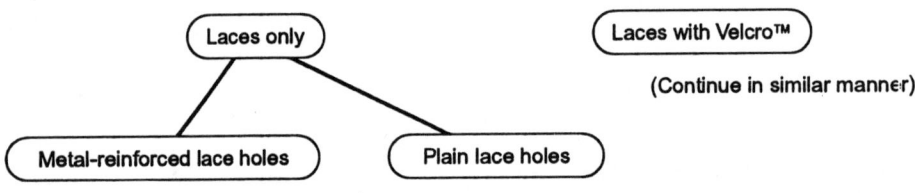

Step Five:

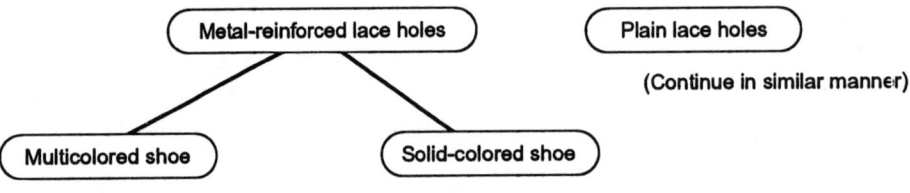

FIGURE 3-4 *(Continued)*

Step Six:

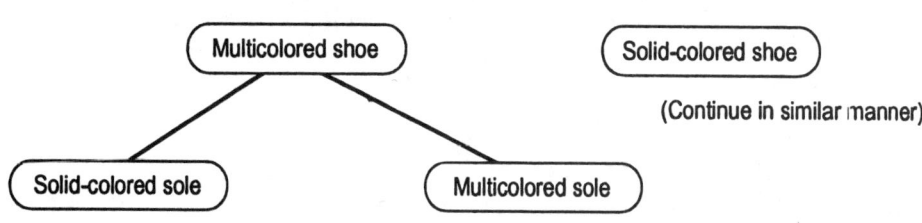

Step Seven:

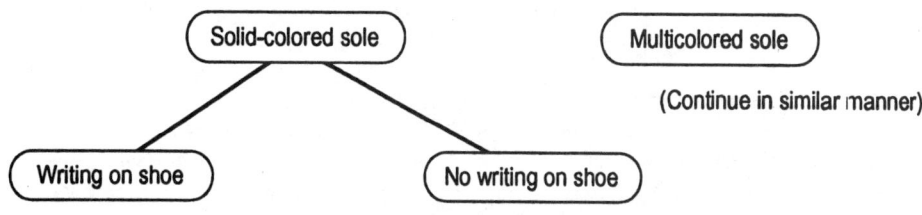

Step Eight:

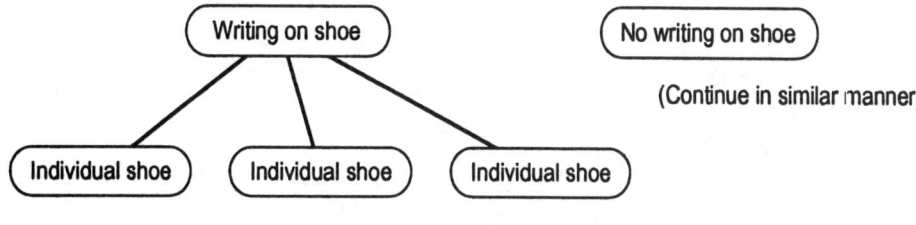

Extension Ideas

- Students can arrange piles of "junk," toys, or other items into a taxonomy. This goes one step further than simply classifying and grouping items.

- Students can do research to find out about animal oddities, such as the duckbill platypus, an animal that has unusual traits that make it difficult to classify.

- Students can create their own animals and develop a taxonomy to classify them.

Learning How to Experiment

Children of today take space travel for granted. Like many other modern technological marvels, such as computers and microwave ovens, space travel has been around all their lives and seems a part of ordinary life. Space shuttle launches are routine and receive little of the media coverage that the first space flights merited. Photographs of far-off planets and stars are present even in books for very young children, with no mention of the space probes that journeyed through space to make the photographs possible. The following activity captures some of the excitement and challenge of the early attempts at designing rockets that could fly in space.

EXPERIMENT • Up, Up, and Away

Subject Areas. Science (space travel, chemical reactions)

Grade Level. Upper primary

Thinking Skills. Predicting, analysis, experimenting and controlling variables, deductive reasoning

Materials Needed. Vinegar (large bottle), box of baking soda, small box of facial tissues, several empty 1-liter and 2-liter plastic bottles, 8–12 corks—size 9 and 10, funnels and measuring spoons and cups (optional)

Description of Activity. Older students can do this activity in small groups, but the teacher should lead the activity for younger students. (A larger quantity of materials would be needed if students work in small groups.) The students' task is to try to launch a cork into the air by doing the following steps:

1. Pour vinegar into an empty plastic bottle. (Use funnel if desired.)

2. Pour baking soda into small piece of tissue, and roll into the shape of a small cigar.

3. Quickly push the baking soda packet into the bottle.

4. Immediately put a cork into the mouth of the bottle, and stand back! (When the baking soda reacts with the vinegar and creates a gas, the pressure of the gas shoots the cork into the air with quite a bit of force. Students should stand at least 10 feet away during a launch.)

5. Rinse out the bottle before attempting another launch.

This activity would be a "following the directions" experiment rather than a problem-solving activity, except for one thing: The amounts of vinegar and baking soda, the size of the tissue, and the size of the cork are not specified in the directions! The problem-solving challenge for the students is to find out the correct quantity of each, otherwise the experiment will not work.

The students may need to try many times before they successfully launch the cork into the air. They need to observe carefully each time and then try to deduce what variable(s) need changing. Before they start experimenting, the teacher should emphasize the importance of changing only one variable at a time. For example, if the first launch is unsuccessful, they may decide that the cork was too loose and try another cork. The amounts of vinegar, baking soda, and tissue should remain the same. Or, students may think that too little baking soda was used, and will increase the amount for the next launch. If students try to change two variables at once, they won't be able to tell which one worked or didn't work. Older students can measure and record the amounts of each variable carefully each time just like real scientists.

Students gain a new appreciation for the NASA scientists who designed space rockets when they see how difficult it is to simply launch a cork from a bottle. They are only dealing with a few variables that can be wrong. NASA scientists were dealing with thousands of parts and variables, all of which had to work perfectly together in order for a rocket to work. However, I've found that, rather than being frustrated, students are inspired by this experiment. They learn how carefully controlled scientific experimentation can solve problems. Things do not work because of magic; they work because scientists carefully design, test, and modify until they are successful. It is sometimes tedious work, but this experiment gives students a taste of the fun and excitement of the successful completion of a challenge.

Blowing Bubbles Goes Beyond Fun and Games

Few people of any age dislike blowing bubbles! Bubble blowing is just plain fun. However, bubble blowing doesn't need to be reserved for bathtub play or backyard picnics. Teachers sometimes feel hesitant about doing things in school that are so blatantly fun, but there is no reason to feel guilty about bubble-blowing activities. Blowing bubbles affords students an excellent opportunity to explore many science and math concepts, and it is a wonderful springboard to problem solving. The following experiment illustrates the learning potential of blowing bubbles.

EXPERIMENT • Bubblemania

Subject Areas. Science (bubbles; solids, liquids, and gases); math (geometry; measurement)

Grade Level. All primary grades

Thinking Skills. Analysis, drawing conclusions, observing, measuring, recording data, experimenting and controlling variables, synthesis

Materials Needed

- 1 gallon of water (distilled water or soft water is preferable if water supply is very hard)
- 1 cupful liquid dish soap (Joy, Dawn, or Ivory are often recommended for best results)
- 2 tablespoons glycerin (optional but helps bubbles last longer)
- Bucket for mixing bubble solution
- Newspaper or plastic to cover tables if working indoors
- Two or three boxes of straws
- A ruler for each student
- Shallow pans for each group or pair of students (pie tin, cake pan, etc.)
- A large variety of bubble-making tools—such as coat hangers, strawberry baskets, scissors, strainers, tin cans with bottoms removed, paper towel rolls, protractors, loops of string, funnels, disposable cups with bottoms removed, rubber bands, tubing, paper clips, or anything else that students find to test
- If possible, do any bubble activities on humid days. Bubbles love humidity. Very dry conditions may make bubble blowing difficult.

Description of Activity

1. It is important to provide students some time to simply explore and play when you start your bubble-blowing activities. They need some time to adjust to the novelty of blowing bubbles before they are ready to engage in any deep thinking! The exploration time also helps students become more proficient at blowing bubbles, which will help them in later activities. Students should work in groups of two or three during the exploration period. Each group needs a pan with some bubble solution (stir water, dishwashing liquid, and glycerin very gently together in large bucket before distributing to each group), along with straws and access to other bubble making tools. Students then explore blowing bubbles. They can experiment with the different bubble making tools to see how they work and can try making different sizes of bubbles. However, this warm-up period shouldn't be considered "wasted" time. Before they start experimenting, students should be instructed to be ready to share with the whole class what they have learned about blowing bubbles during the warm-up period. They should also be encouraged to think of questions they have about bubbles.

2. Once the warm-up period is complete, each group of students should discuss among themselves what they have learned about bubbles. If they are able to write, they should record their findings on paper. Each small group can then share with the whole class what they have learned while the teacher records their responses. For example, students may discover these facts during their "playing" time:

- If you touch a bubble when your hands are dry, it will pop. If your hands are wet, it won't pop.
- You need to blow gently and slowly to make a big bubble.
- If you blow really hard, the bubble will pop right away.
- You can blow a bubble using your bare hands if you dunk them in bubble solution.
- Things with lots of holes, like strawberry baskets, make lots of bubbles.
- If the bubble solution gets too many suds in it, it doesn't work very well.
- You can make a huge bubble by dipping a coat hanger in bubble solution and slowly waving it through the air.

Through their observations, students have already started to discover important concepts about bubbles and are ready to explore further. They have probably generated a lot of "why?" and "what if?" questions. These should be recorded so they can be referred to and discussed throughout their bubble-blowing activities.

3. Students are now ready for more formal bubble-blowing activities. To prepare for the next

activity, the students' tables or desktops need to be cleared of plastic or newspaper. The teacher should start the activity by pouring some bubble solution directly onto a tabletop. Using a straw, the teacher can then demonstrate how to blow a bubble by inserting a straw into the puddle and blowing very gently. The bubble that is formed will not be a round sphere like other bubbles students have made. Instead, it will be shaped like a dome rising from the table. The teacher next asks the students this question: "How can we measure the size of this bubble?" Since they have already had some experience with bubbles, students will probably realize they must think of ways that can be done quickly and that won't pop the bubble. They will be applying what they already know and synthesizing new ideas on how to measure a bubble.

4. After students have been given time to brainstorm, their ideas can be recorded and they can test the ideas to see which ones work. The students will soon discover that the key to measuring a bubble is to never touch it with anything dry, which will cause the bubble to pop instantly. As long as that rule is adhered to, a bubble can be measured in many different ways. The class will need to agree, however, on one best way to measure bubbles to conduct the second half of the experiment. I have found that using a ruler is a quick, accurate, one-step way to measure bubbles. A wet ruler can be slowly inserted right into a bubble without popping the bubble, and the height or diameter of the bubble can be read directly from the ruler.

5. Using their new-found knowledge on how to measure bubbles, students will be blowing several bubbles, measuring their heights and diameters, and recording the information on a chart. They are to find out if there is a relationship between the height of a bubble and the diameter. (Make sure that students understand the terms *height* and *diameter* and, if necessary, review with students how to read a ruler.) A simple chart like the following one should work well, which students can set up for themselves using graph paper with 1-inch squares.

	Height	Diameter
Bubble 1		
Bubble 2		
Bubble 3		
Bubble 4		

6. After they have completed their measurements, students should analyze their findings. They may notice a relationship even before they are done measuring all of their bubbles! The diameter of the bubble will be twice the measure of the height. For example, if the diameter of a bubble is 8 inches, the height will be 4 inches. Younger students may have some difficulty verifying this rule if they have measured bubbles in fractions of an inch. If they have measured a bubble with a 3 1/2-inch height, they may be unable to double this to see if the rule is true. This presents a perfect "teachable moment" to teach students how to round up a fraction to the nearest whole number or how to add two halves to make one whole. However, if any students blew a bubble with a diameter of 16 inches or greater, they will find that the relationship isn't exactly right. This mystery provides an excellent topic for discussion. Why isn't the rule true with big bubbles? The answer is that the weight of the soap causes big bubbles to sag in the middle, much the same way that a tent will sag. Obviously, a bubble can't be supported with poles and stakes!

Many years into the future, these students will learn in geometry class that the diameter of a circle is equal to the radius squared—something they learned as young children while blowing bubbles! Obviously, as young children they aren't expected to make the connection between blowing bubbles and measuring circles, but by doing hands-on problem-solving experiments they gain a solid foundation for future learning.

Extension Ideas

- Have a "Bubble Challenge Day" where students can try to make the biggest bubble, the longest-lasting bubble, the most bubbles in a chain, a bubble inside a bubble, and so on. This could be competitive, or each student could try to achieve a certain standard (such as a bubble that lasts 30 seconds) or a personal best.

- Allow students time to answer some of their "What if?" questions. For example, a student who wonders whether cold or hot water makes better bubbles can set up an experiment to find out.

- Students can conduct an experiment to find out whether certain brands of dishwashing liquid make better bubble solutions than others. Or they can experiment to see if glycerin really does make bubbles last longer. They can experiment with the ratio of water to dishwashing liquid, or with the amount of glycerin to add to the solution.

- Students can experiment to see how the weather affects bubbles. Temperature, wind, and especially humidity can all have an effect on bubbles.

ASSESSMENT IN THE PRIMARY CLASSROOM

Most of us teaching today can sum up our own childhood experiences with assessment with one word: *tests*. We took timed tests, multiple-choice tests, essay tests, true–false tests, standardized achievement tests—the list goes on and on. While the different kinds of tests may have varied in format, they were all basically paper-and-pencil tests. They were given to us to measure what we had learned. We would receive a grade or a score on the test, and then more often than not would go on to learn something else.

Assessment methods have changed greatly since that time, and are still changing. There are many more tools and methods available that teachers can use for student assessment. Rather than simply measuring what a student does or doesn't know, assessments today are being designed to be an integral part of instruction and learning. They are no longer simply synonymous with grading. Teachers are using information gained from student assessments to make decisions about teaching in order to facilitate student learning.

Depending on a teacher's purpose, problem-solving activities can be assessed in several ways. Whatever the method used, it is important to keep in mind that problem solving is not a specific skill or body of knowledge that can be measured definitively at one point in time. Students gradually develop skills as problem solvers over time. In the following section, different methods that can be used to assess problem solving will be presented, along with specific assessment examples from primary classrooms.

Teacher Observation

Teachers have always used observations of students to make decisions about teaching and grading. Some very useful information about students can be gained only through classroom observations. However, teachers may feel hesitant to use observation as an "official" assessment method. They fear that it is too subjective and lacks the reliability of "hard" data such as tests. However, teacher observation, if used effectively, is a valid assessment method that is appropriate for occasional use.

Focus is the key to using observation effectively as an assessment tool. It is difficult if not impossible for a teacher to observe all aspects of all students' performance at the same time. Instead, the teacher should focus on one or two important aspects of a lesson. For example, during a brainstorming session a teacher may want to assess students' ability to generate lots of ideas to solve a problem. During the lesson, the teacher can walk around and observe the quantity of ideas being generated. On a clipboard, the teacher could record a rating after each student's name. A student or group could receive a "+" for generating a high number of ideas, a "√" for an average number, or a "–" for a low number of ideas. Or, comments could be recorded, such as "thought of ideas faster than she could write them down," "thought of only a couple of ideas, but they were original," or "stared at paper, unable to generate even common responses."

Teachers *may* interact with students while observing them. In fact, a teacher may want to ask a clarifying question or two of each student or group of students. For the experiment on measuring the size of bubbles, a teacher could walk around the classroom and ask the students, "What would be the height of a bubble if its diameter is 4 inches?" Their response would indicate whether they truly understood the lesson and can transfer their learning and think more abstractly. An appropriate question to ask students working on the vinegar and baking soda rocket launch is "Why did you use more baking soda this time?" Students' responses to clarifying questions may tell a teacher a lot about how they are thinking and feeling during problem-solving activities.

Student Journals

Another way to learn how students are thinking or feeling is to have them keep a problem-solving journal. In it, they can record how they solved a problem or how they reacted to a frustrating problem. Again, focus is the key. Instead of just telling them to write in their journals about a lesson, the teacher should provide a clarifying question to start them thinking. For example, a useful question to ask for many problems would be "Describe the ways you tried to solve the problem." A student's journal entry can tell a teacher whether a student even understood the problem or help assess a student's comfort with the problem-solving process. Journal entries can help a teacher see growth over time in problem strategies used by a student.

Journals also provide a way for students to assess themselves. (Younger primary students can respond verbally to journal questions.) Students can respond to a question or list of questions provided by the teacher, such as

- Describe the first way you tried to solve the problem. Why did you choose that way?
- What was the hardest thing about solving this problem?
- Did you learn anything from other problems that you've solved that helped you to solve this one?
- How did you feel while your were working on this problem?
- Would you do anything different if you could start over and solve this problem again?
- What would have helped you solve the problem more easily?
- Were you able to think of another way to solve the problem if the first way didn't work?
- How could you tell that you were done solving the problem?

The opportunity for self-assessment is important for students. Students need to learn to be responsible for their own learning, and developing the ability to assess themselves and their own learning progress will help them learn to take charge of their own learning. Students need guidance and practice to learn how to learn from their own mistakes or to identify their own strengths and weaknesses. Problem-solving activities can provide excellent opportunities for this kind of self-assessment, especially when the problems are open-ended or nonthreatening problems that don't confine students to finding the one "right" answer.

Peer Teaching

Although seldom used in this way by most teachers, peer teaching can be used as a form of assessment. Technically it is a form of teacher observation, because the teacher generally observes a student teaching another student. The student being taught can also provide some peer assessment by providing feedback, either verbally or by filling out a questionnaire or checklist, on how well their "teacher" taught the lesson. A student must thoroughly understand something in order to teach it well to someone else, so watching a student teach another student can be very enlightening. Students can teach younger students, or the teacher could have half of the students in a class teach something to the other half of the class. A checklist or narrative comments can be used to record the teacher's impression of each student's performance.

Measuring how well a student understands a concept or a process can be accomplished quite well through a peer teaching assessment. For example, a teacher could assess how well students understand the principles of bubble making by having students teach other students how to successfully blow bubbles. Or, after doing the shoe taxonomy lesson, students could teach other students how a taxonomy works using mittens, buttons, or other similar objects. Does the student understand the principles well enough to answer other students' questions or assist if problems arise? Most students will definitely be actively engaged while interacting with another student, and they may be able to think more clearly and demonstrate their learning better than they would be able to doing other assessment methods such as tests. However, a particularly shy child may be very uncomfortable in the role of teacher, even with a child he or she knows well, and the teacher should consider allowing that child the opportunity to do another form of assessment.

Student Portfolios

Portfolios are becoming the assessment method of choice for teachers who want to use a comprehensive assessment method that "reveals a range of skills and understandings, supports instructional goals, values student and teacher reflection, shows changes and growth over a period of time, and provides for continuity in education" (Vavrus, 1990, p. 48). In the past, many teachers kept folders full of student work samples. However, a student portfolio is much more than a collection of work samples. The contents of a student portfolio are not randomly chosen; a teacher or teachers should decide in advance what the portfolio will contain and how and when it will be evaluated, keeping in mind the purposes of portfolios:

- Allows students the opportunity for reflection and self-assessment
- Showcases a student's accomplishments rather than failures
- Documents a student's growth over time, both academically and affectively
- Helps students and teachers set instructional goals
- Provides a more comprehensive picture of a student's learning than is possible using single test scores.

The contents of a student portfolio, all of which should be dated before inclusion in the portfolio, could consist of one or more of the following items:

- Audio or video tapes that document student performance in a particular area
- Items that a student has chosen as representing his or her best work
- Work samples from important assignments in given areas—with or without student comments or explanations
- Student journals and reflections on their work
- Projects that the student has completed—these can take any form. If they don't fit into a folder, a note should be included that indicates where the project is stored
- A list of topics a student would like to explore or a list of questions a student would like to investigate
- Lab reports from science experiments
- Teacher observation notes
- A complete record of an assignment or project, from the first ideas and drafts to the completed project
- Records of work that a student has completed, such as a list of books read
- Writing samples.

"Portfolios can be evaluated in terms of standards of excellence or on growth demonstrated within an individual's portfolio, rather than on comparisons made among different students' work" (Vavrus, 1990, p. 53). A team of teachers may devise a checklist of skills progression or criteria for standards of excellence, which teachers and students can use as a guideline for assessing the portfolio. For example, if a goal for students is to learn how to use a variety of strategies while solving problems, a checklist such as the following may be used to assess a student's level of performance:

Level One: Student is unable to think of a strategy to use to begin to solve problems.

Level Two: Student chooses unsuccessful strategies and is unable to think of alternative ways to solve problems.

Level Three: Student is able to think of several ways to try to solve problems, but does not seem to consider results of previous attempts when modifying strategies.

Level Four: Student analyzes problems carefully before choosing strategies to use, but chooses inappropriate strategies.

Level Five: Student analyzes problems carefully before choosing strategies, and is able to consider results of previous attempts when modifying strategies.

Level Six: Student analyzes problems carefully and is able to choose successful strategies for solving problems.

After reviewing a student's portfolio, the teacher would decide which level most accurately reflects the student's level of performance. Over time, the portfolio can reveal whether a student is progressing through the levels.

Teachers unfamiliar with student portfolios may feel most comfortable initially using portfolios for a single subject area or for problem solving only. More intensive use of portfolios should be preceded by inservice training. Although the use of student portfolios is time consuming and requires a different philosophy of assessment than most teachers are used to, they offer a valuable way to comprehensively assess student learning.

Paper-and-Pencil Tests

Paper-and-paper tests do have many shortcomings, but are not totally unsuitable for assessing problem solving. When used along with other methods, they can provide valuable information. Their primary use in problem solving is to assess whether a student has learned specific problem-solving strategies, such as working backward, making a chart, drawing a picture, or guessing and testing, that they have been taught previously. The students can be tested using a new problem that is similar to one that they have already solved. The teacher can see whether the strategy was indeed learned and can be transferred to use for a new problem. For example, the following problem could be used to test whether students who did the "How many ways can you make 25¢?" problem have learned how to use a chart to organize information and solve a problem: *How many different ways can you arrange 10 pennies between two piggy banks?* Students can be given 10 pennies to use to help them solve the problem, but they will still need to use some kind of organized record keeping, such as a simple chart, to keep track of they ways they have found. (There are eleven ways to arrange the 10 pennies between the two piggy banks.)

The following problem can be used to test whether students have learned how to use the guess-and-test method of solving problems:

> A grandma and grandpa are waiting for their newest grandchild to be born. If it is a boy, they will have an equal number of boy and girl grandchildren. If it is a girl, they will have twice as many girl grandchildren as boy grandchildren. Right now they have fewer than eight grandchildren. How many of their grandchildren are boys, and how many are girls?

The most effective way to attack a problem with unknowns like this one is to simply start with a guess, see if works, and work from there if it doesn't. Other strategies, such as drawing a picture or making a chart, may also be useful. By analyzing a student's response, the teacher can tell whether he or she can apply previously learned strategies, or whether more practice is needed. (Grandma and grandpa presently have five grandchildren—two boys and three girls. If the new baby is a girl, they will have four girls and two boys. If the new baby is a boy, they will have three boys and three girls.)

Paper-and-pencil tests are unsuitable to use to assess problems that require creative thinking or many other higher-level thinking skills such as synthesis, forecasting, and so on. Before using a paper-and-pencil test, as with any method of assessment, the teacher should consider whether it will indeed accurately measure what is being assessed and whether another method would be more effective.

Performance Assessments

Performance assessments allow students to demonstrate their learning by actually performing an assigned task, which usually involves manipulative, hands-on items. Both the process students use to complete the task and the completed task itself are assessed. Problem-solving and process skills are particularly suited to assessment by practical tests. However, performance assessments aren't well suited for assessing facts or rote knowledge learned by a student.

There are many advantages to using performance assessments. Teachers can see if students are able to actually apply the skills and knowledge they have learned. They work particularly well for students whose reading skills are poor, who often do not do well on written tests. Performance assessments are also more realistic than paper-and-pencil tests. They sometimes allow the students to work in groups, which reflects how tasks are often accomplished in the adult world. Students are actually using their skills and knowledge to accomplish something; they are not just simply choosing or filling in answers. Performance assessments are usually not timed, which makes them more accurate for students who perform poorly on tests with time limits.

However, performance assessments are time consuming and generally only assess one or two objectives at a time. It can be difficult to assess the whole class at the same time, although the task can become more manageable if the assessments are done in groups. Performance assessments also can require lots of prior setup and cleanup. Despite the drawbacks, performance assessments are often the best method to use to assess problem-solving or science skills.

Performance assessments can consist of simple or elaborate tasks, depending on the objective(s) being assessed and the age of the students. The following list gives examples of 10 tasks that would be appropriate to use as performance assessments:

1. Students demonstrate proficiency and understanding of patterning or grouping by arranging pattern blocks into original designs or groupings based on predetermined criteria.

2. As an assessment for the "Shoe Taxonomy" lesson (see p. 73), students group buttons or other

items to demonstrate their understanding of taxonomies.

3. As an assessment for "Choosing the Best Potato Chip" (see p. 69), students devise their own consumer test to evaluate different brands of a product.

4. After a unit on graphing in math, students sort items made of various materials, such as metal, wood, plastic, and so on, and design a simple graph to illustrate the number of items in each group.

5. After a unit on measurement, students measure items in a group and match items to a list of measurements.

6. To demonstrate their ability to set up an experiment to solve a problem, students design an experiment to determine which brand of paper towels is the most absorbent, strongest, and so on.

7. To demonstrate their understanding of mass or volume, students weigh or measure the volume of items and arrange them from heaviest to lightest or smallest volume to largest volume.

8. After a unit on kinds of animals, students look at picture cards and read (or listen to) descriptions of unfamiliar animals. Using the information they've learned about characteristics of animals, they group the cards by kind of animal.

9. To demonstrate their understanding of weather, students measure weather conditions, such as temperature, barometric pressure, types of clouds, and so on, and prepare and videotape a weather report.

10. Given a handful of plastic coins, students make a minimum of three or a maximum of five purchases from a group of priced items. To demonstrate their knowledge of money, they must add up how much money they have, decide what to buy and add up the total cost, make their purchases, count out the proper payment for each purchase, and make sure they still have at least 15¢ left over after making their choices.

After performance assessments are completed (or during them if teachers choose to observe each assessment), teachers can use a criteria checklist of skills appropriate to the task to measure students' performance. Students receive full or partial credit for every skill they demonstrate. They are not simply marked right or wrong.

Performance assessments are a must in the problem-solving classroom. The higher-level thinking skills that problem solving requires are difficult to assess accurately in any other way. Performance assessments are a natural part of the learning process; students get to demonstrate what they've learned in a way similar to how they learned it. And even more importantly, they allow students to apply what they know in the way that they will actually *use* it. Just as a surgeon can only demonstrate surgical skills by doing surgery, students can best demonstrate their problem solving and process skills by actually using them.

Projects

Students can demonstrate their learning in other ways besides "test" situations. They can apply their knowledge and skills to the completion of a project. Students have always done projects, but they were often not considered as an assessment tool. Instead, students took a test and made a project at the end of the unit. However, it is usually unnecessary to do both. If students are given clear criteria in advance of doing a project, it is just as valid a measure of their learning as any test. In fact, it often is more so since doing a project provides the opportunity for students to apply what they know, synthesize new ideas, plan the project, conduct research, and so on—all of which can provide a very comprehensive picture of a student's skills and knowledge!

Any teacher who has ever had students do projects knows that the quality can range from sloppily made, crude projects to sophisticated, beautifully-crafted projects obviously beyond the capabilities of elementary students. Teachers are hesitant to assess students' projects, for they don't want to discriminate unfairly against students who tried very hard to do their best and didn't receive any help.

The key to using projects as an assessment tool is *preparation*. Children, especially young ones, do not instinctively know how to pull all their learning together in a quality project. Teachers need to spell out clearly what makes a quality project and what steps are necessary to make one. Students need to know in advance what the criteria for assessing the project will be. Examples of prior projects should be shown to students so they get an idea of what high-quality projects look like. The planning and making of the project should be a learning process in itself, and teachers of primary-age children need to provide guidance throughout the process. As they grow older and gain experience with making projects, students will become more independent and will possess the knowledge and skills on their own to make a quality project.

The assignment sheet below outlines the requirements for a game-making project assigned by an upper-primary teacher as the culminating activity for a unit on predator and prey animals.

Project Assignment Sheet

Your task is to design and make a game. You need to remember the following guidelines as you work on your project:

1. The game needs to be based on the theme of predator and prey.

2. The game can be any kind of game, such as a board game, card game, ball game, and so on. You can even combine different kinds of games!

3. The game must come with written rules that explain clearly how to play the game. The rules should be easy to understand and neatly written or typed.

4. The game itself should be attractive and neatly made.

5. The game should be interesting and fun to play. You can design it to be played by players of any age. The age range of players the game is designed for needs to be stated in the rules. You should test your game with family or friends before you turn it in.

Depending on the age of the students and the complexity of the project, the teacher may want to set deadlines for completing certain portions of the project. This will alleviate the "night before" problems that can plague long-term projects. Teachers should also devote class time for the projects so that the student has guidance throughout the process. The teacher can meet with each student periodically to review progress. Students can also meet in small groups to discuss their projects. However, feedback groups are usually more effective with older students than with younger students.

Students need to understand how their projects will be assessed before they turn them in. Teachers can share this information with them at the time the assignment is given, or slightly later in the process after the students have had the chance to make a good start on their projects. If the project is a major one, it may be wise to wait to share the assessment criteria with the students. Otherwise they may be overwhelmed by the criteria. However, general guidelines for the project should *always* be discussed at the time the project is assigned. If the guidelines and criteria are clear enough, and if guidance is provided throughout the project, all students should be capable of doing a quality project that reflects their best effort.

It is much more informative for students, teachers, and parents if a student is assessed on how well they met the criteria for the project. A single grade, such as a letter grade, doesn't communicate much information about the strengths and weaknesses of the project. A single grade also forces a teacher to compare students to one another. A criteria checklist allows the teacher to use specific standards and criteria as a basis for assessment, not another student's efforts. Figure 3–5 shows an assessment form for the predator-and-prey game project. Students can also evaluate their own projects using the same form. Notice that the form makes very clear how well the student completed each component of the project.

Students are often enthusiastic about doing projects, especially if the guidelines are open-ended or allow students a choice of projects. They will also feel most enthusiastic if they receive enough guidance and are confident that they can succeed. Project ideas can range from simple to complex. The teacher needs to determine how much time is available, appropriate, and worthwhile to devote to the project. Teachers should keep in mind, however, that projects generally require a large investment of time, and should be used sparingly throughout the school year. If students must complete a major project at the end of every unit, they may soon feel overwhelmed and lose enthusiasm. However, making a quality project does help students develop valuable skills and is a worthwhile assessment tool.

DISCOVERING DINOSAURS: AN INTERDISCIPLINARY UNIT FOR PRIMARY STUDENTS

I first became interested in dinosaurs when I taught a unit on them to my second-grade class. To me, it was just another unit of the many I would teach that year.

FIGURE 3–5 Assessment Form—Predator and Prey Game

Name _____
Teacher _____
Date _____

I. Theme of the game:

    4 = The game is clearly based on the relationship between predator and prey.
    3 = The game contains a predator-and-prey element, but it is not the major theme of the game.
    2 = The game is based on an unclear relationship between predator and prey.
    1 = The game does not relate in any way to predator and prey.
    Rating: _____

II. Originality:

    3 = The game is creative and unique.
    2 = Some elements of the game are creative and unique.
    1 = The game is very similar to another game or games.
    Rating: _____

III. Directions and Rules:

    4 = The directions and rules are thorough, clearly written, and easy to understand.
    3 = The directions and rules are mainly thorough, clearly written, and easy to understand, but do require additional explanation.
    2 = The directions and rules contain several confusing parts.
    1 = The directions and rules are confusing and cannot be understood.
    Rating: _____

IV. Game Construction:

    3 = All parts of the game are attractive, neatly done, and well made.
    2 = The game construction is of generally good quality, but there is room for improvement.
    1 = The game is unattractive, messy, and poorly made.
    Rating: _____

V. Playing the game:

    3 = Most people would enjoy playing this game.
    2 = Some people might enjoy playing this game.
    1 = Few people would enjoy playing this game.
    Rating: _____

VI. Overall quality:

    4 = The quality of the game exceeds the criteria for the project.
    3 = The quality of the game meets the criteria for the project.
    2 = The quality of the game partially meets the criteria for the project.
    1 = The quality of the game does not meet the criteria for the project.
    Rating: _____

Comments:

However, for many of my students it was *the* unit. They were very excited and motivated, and to my chagrin, many of them knew more about dinosaurs than I did! Our roles were soon reversed, as I became the student and the students became the teachers. I was amazed at how sophisticated their knowledge level was when it came to dinosaurs. Students who had difficulty counting to one hundred could tell me how many millions of years ago dinosaurs lived, and students who were still saying "aminal" for *animal* could say *Triceratops* with ease. My pronunciation of dinosaur names was often corrected by these pint-sized dinosaur experts. I soon realized the possibilities of the topic of dinosaurs. Here was a unit I could really put some "meat" into and challenge my students. They already had a knowledge base, they were motivated by the topic, and they loved impressing others with all of the impressive-sounding names and statistics. I started to change the unit from "Let's draw your favorite dinosaur" types of activities to those based on problem solving.

Finding a topic such as dinosaurs about which the majority of the students can become enthusiastic is an important first step in writing an interdisciplinary unit. If a large amount of time is going to be centered around one topic, both the teacher and the students must enjoy learning about it. This immersion in one topic is actually a more efficient use of time than skimming many topics while studying many subjects, since such depth is necessary if students are to learn how to use and apply information and solve problems. Learning facts without learning how to use them is a waste of students' time, especially in today's world when the "facts" and the amount of new information available are constantly changing. Students need to learn how to think and acquire information.

The following dinosaur unit puts students in the role of paleontologists who are analyzing clues to learn about dinosaurs. They even conduct their own dig! As in a traditional unit, some time is spent on the very necessary step of expanding on the students' knowledge base. It is difficult for students to do problem solving without some content knowledge. However, rather than passively absorbing information through lecture or filmstrips, the students are researching and seeking information through a scavenger hunt and conducting surveys. The unit is rich in academic skills, such as measuring, graphing, and creative writing, but they are not isolated skills. They are an integral part of learning about dinosaurs as the students measure things that are the same size as dinosaurs, graph data they've gathered by conducting a survey on why dinosaurs became extinct, and write about the clues in dinosaur fossil footprints. Students have the opportunity to practice a myriad of thinking skills as they plan and create a dinosaur museum, analyze dinosaur items for accuracy, identify a dinosaur skeleton through skeletal clues, and debate a proposed dinosaur dig. Their creative thinking skills are used as they learn about dinosaur names and create and name their own dinosaur, flesh out and color dinosaur skeletons, and brainstorm answers to warm-up questions about dinosaurs.

The unit as presented here is most appropriate for students in grades 2–4. Even younger primary students are able to do the higher-level thinking activities, but the reading level of the activities would need to be modified. The unit is intended as a comprehensive unit on dinosaurs, but obviously other activities could be included. For example, inviting an expert speaker on dinosaurs would be an excellent activity. If available, other media such as CD-ROMs, computer software programs, and video tapes could be included. Art and music activities would be a wonderful addition. A variety of assessment options are included for the activities so that the assessment methods can be can tailored to go along with the focus of the unit. For example, if the academic skills such as measuring, graphing, and writing are to be emphasized, the assessments can be centered around those activities. Or if the problem-solving activities are to be the focus of the unit, they can be the focus of the assessment as well.

Enjoy learning about dinosaurs along with your students!

Lesson One: Every Footprint Tells a Story

Purposes. The purpose of this introductory lesson is to get students excited and curious about dinosaurs and to encourage them to become active thinkers and amateur paleontologists.

Thinking Skills. Creative thinking, analyzing, comparing and contrasting, predicting or forecasting, evaluating, using prior knowledge, making inferences, synthesizing.

Length. 60 minutes

Materials Needed
- A poster of dinosaur footprints (see Figure 3–1)
- Pencils and paper

Procedures

1. Seat students in a semicircle facing you. Hold up the poster of the dinosaur footprints. Say, "If you look very carefully, you will see clues in this picture that will tell you a story. Look at this picture for one minute without talking, and then we will listen to everyone's ideas."

2. At the end of one minute say, "Tell me what you see." Allow students to share their ideas, encouraging them to point to the poster to illustrate their ideas. Let the students do the majority of the talking, but do ask students to explain their hypotheses and encourage divergent ideas. If students are not thinking of many different possibilities or explanations, suggest some. Could the set of small footprints have been made two hours before the other set? Could this be a mother looking for her naughty baby who wandered away? Could the two dinosaurs be dancing? After several students have shared their thoughts, go over the clues in the poster one by one. What can you tell about the bigger footprints? Why might they stop? Why might they start to run? Why didn't the little footprints start running? Ask a few students to summarize what the footprint clues tell us by telling a story about what happened when the footprints were made. Discuss with the students which story seems the most believable based on the clues and what we know about animal behavior.

3. Discuss how we know about dinosaurs. We have never seen a live one, but we know how big they were, what they ate, and so on. Fossils, such as fossil footprints and bones, are the only clues we have about dinosaurs, yet scientists have been able to learn a lot from them by analyzing them the same way the students just analyzed the footprints. Do we know that all our facts about dinosaurs are accurate? No, but scientists try to come up with the explanations that make the most sense. For example, dinosaurs with smooth teeth could have used food processors to grind up their meat before they ate it, but that is highly unlikely. It makes much more sense that they ate plants rather than meat.

4. Each student should now write a story explaining what he or she thinks happened the day the fossil footprints were made.

Assessment Options

- The creative writing sample may be saved for a dinosaur unit portfolio.

- If the dinosaur footprints creative writing activity is expanded and students are given time to edit their stories, a checklist of writing skills can be generated and used to assess specific language arts skills.

- As students share ideas about the dinosaur footprints, or after the lesson, you may unobtrusively write comments or mark pluses, checks, and minuses after students' names to reflect the quality of their ideas. For example, if a student shared an idea that seemed to be totally unrelated to the clues, you would record a minus after that name. If a student's response was particularly original, you would record a plus.

Lesson Two: Open Up Your Dinofile

Purposes. This lesson accesses students' prior knowledge about dinosaurs, which prepares them for new learning and gives the teacher information about the knowledge level of the students. It also prepares them for learning by having them think of what they want to learn about dinosaurs. Often, students focus upon what they already know about a topic, instead of questioning and wanting to learn more.

Thinking Skills. Fluency, originality, flexibility, generating questions.

Length. 30–45 minutes.

Materials Needed

- Pencils and blank file folders
- Large sheet of chart paper

Procedures

1. Five minute warm-up activity. With the whole group, brainstorm a list of things we know a lot about without ever having actually seen them. For example, we know about dinosaurs, atoms, air, Pilgrims, the ocean floor, and so on. Review (or introduce if it's new to them) the idea of piggy-backing or hitchhiking off of another person's idea. They may see it as copying, but encourage them by telling them that piggy-backing is a sign of a good thinker. Good thinkers are good listeners; they listen to other people's ideas because they know that may give them a similar idea.

2. Group the students into groups of three and give each group one blank file folder. Say something like this: "Your brain is a little like a file cabinet. It contains a lot of information about many different things. Your brain organizes all that information in order to keep things straight, the same way that we put similar papers into a file folder so they don't get all mixed up. In a way, you have "file folders" in your brain about all the things you know. Some of them may be very thick and full of lots of information, while others may be almost empty. For example, if you know a lot about baseball, your "file" on baseball is very thick. Maybe all you know about the sport of lacrosse is that it's a sport. The "file" in your brain on that topic is very thin, but you still have one. If you've never heard of it, you don't even have a file and your brain needs to create one. You can't put new information into a file folder unless it's open, so today we are going to open your "file" on dinosaurs by thinking about what you already know about dinosaurs." Allow the groups ten minutes to discuss what they know. A recorder for each group should write down inside the empty file folder key words or brief sentences telling what members in that group already know about dinosaurs.

3. At the end of the time, tell the groups to close their files. On the outside of the folders they should now write as many questions as they can about dinosaurs. (If necessary, review the difference between a question and a telling statement.) Allow five minutes for generating and writing questions. They can always add more questions as they think of them throughout the unit. Emphasize that telling what they already know doesn't add any new information to their files. They add new information by questioning and listening to others.

4. Reassemble as a large group. One by one, have a speaker from each group share three things that they knew about dinosaurs. You can make a web of dinosaur facts on the board or overhead projector as the groups share.

5. Now, each group should choose and share three of their questions that they would most like to be answered. These questions can be recorded on a large piece of chart paper and crossed off throughout the unit as they are answered. At the end of the unit, the questions that aren't answered can be discussed. Why wasn't the answer found? Is more research necessary, or are their some questions about dinosaurs that are unanswerable?

Assessment Options. Assessing this lesson is not necessary, although you may want to note students who generate a large number of questions or especially original or advanced questions.

Lesson Three: Dinosaur Scavenger Hunt

Purposes. This lesson expands students' knowledge base about dinosaurs and provides for practice in using research skills.

Thinking Skills. Analysis, research skills, comparing and contrasting, classification.

Length. 90–120 minutes (may be split into two sessions).

Materials Needed

- Large sheets of chart paper
- Dinosaur Scavenger Hunt sheet (see Figure 3–6)
- A large number of books about dinosaurs
- A few items that depict dinosaurs, such as posters, models, videotapes, and so on
- Pencils

Procedures

1. Five-minute warm-up activity. On the chalkboard, write the question "In what ways are dinosaurs and people alike and different?" Before students start sharing responses, draw a large Venn diagram on the board. As students share their responses, record them in the appropriate circles and show students how a Venn diagram can be used to organize information when comparing and contrasting two things (see p. 59).

2. Introduction of ongoing dinosaur memorabilia project. Show students two or three dinosaur items, such as posters and models, that are scientifically inaccurate. It is easy to find dinosaur inaccuracies! Some are caused by being out of date due to recent discoveries. Others are caused by sloppy research, confusing or misleading presentation of information, or lack of respect for scientific accuracy. (For example, some dinosaur toys show *Stegosaurus* and other plant-eating dinosaurs with big sharp teeth. Some posters show dinosaurs together with woolly mammoths, who did not live anywhere near the same time. There are dinosaur books that label flying or swimming reptiles as dinosaurs, even though scientists don't classify

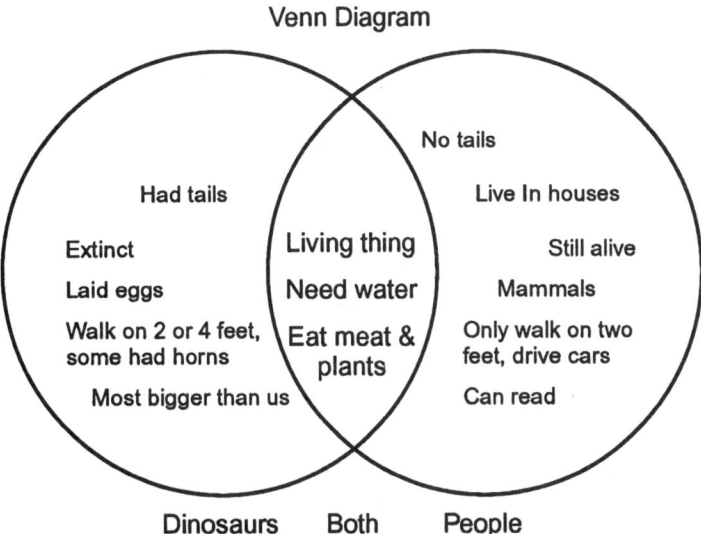

them as such. *Brontosaurus* is still pictured in some books, even though paleontologists have now discovered that it really was *Apatosaurus*.) It is important that students learn how to sort fact from fiction, whether the topic is dinosaurs or something else. Educators have a responsibility to pass along accurate information to students.

Discuss with students how prevalent "mistakes," inaccuracies, and false information are in dinosaur items. Invite them to bring in items that they have at home that depict dinosaurs. Each day, spend a few minutes looking at the items brought in to determine whether they should be placed on the "Right" or "Wrong" table. As they learn more about dinosaurs, your students will become very critical when examining items for accuracy! At the end of the unit, compare the two tables to see which one contains the most items.

3. *Dinosaur Scavenger Hunt* (see Figure 3–6). Using the books on dinosaurs that have been gathered, students should work in partners to complete the dinosaur scavenger hunt activity. If necessary,

FIGURE 3–6 Dinosaur Scavenger Hunt

Names _____

_____

1. Which dinosaur was taller, *Brachiosaurus* or *Tyrannosaurus rex*?
2. Which dinosaur was longer, *Diplodocus* or *Apatosaurus*?
3. Which dinosaur was smaller, *Compsognathus* or *Stegosaurus*?
4. Name a meat-eating dinosaur: _____
5. Name a plant-eating dinosaur: _____
6. Which of these dinosaurs lived at the same time as *Tyrannosaurus rex*, *Triceratops* or *Stegosaurus*?
7. What kind of dinosaur fossil skeleton was found by Dr. Gideon Mantell in 1820? _____
8. Name a lizard-hipped (saurischians) dinosaur: _____
9. Name a bird-hipped (ornithiscians) dinosaur: _____
10. Tell something about dinosaurs that you learned that you did not know before: _____

review how to use an index or table of contents, read picture captions, and other research skills. Set a time limit for the activity, considering the age and research skills of your students. After the time is up, discuss the answers that the students found. If there are disagreements, attempt to find the correct answers by consulting another book, looking to see which book has the most recent copyright, and so on.

> *Answers to scavenger hunt questions:* (1) *Brachiosaurus;* (2) *Diplodocus;* (3) *Compsognathus;* (4) answers will vary; (5) answers will vary; (6) *Triceratops;* (7) *Iguanadon;* (8) answers will vary-examples are *T. rex,* all carnivores, *Allosaurus, Coelophysis, Diplodocus, Apatosaurus, Brachiosaurus, Compsognathus.;* (9) answers will vary—examples are *Stegosaurus, Iguanadon, Triceratops, Ankylosaurus;* (10) answers will vary.)

Assessment Options

- As students work on the scavenger hunt, comments or marks can be recorded indicating their proficiency in research skills.
- A paper-and-pencil test can be given to measure if students have learned basic information about dinosaurs.

Lesson Four: I Dig Dinosaurs!

Purposes. This lesson allows students to assume the roles of paleontologists and learn some of the painstaking techniques of paleontology as they actually conduct their own dig.

Thinking Skills. Mapping, observation, describing, comparing and contrasting, analogies

Length. 60–90 minutes.

Materials Needed

Each group of three students will need the following items:

- One storage bin (or similar item such as a sweater box)
- Bags of sandbox sand (amount necessary will depend on number and size of bins)
- Large tarp or sheet of plastic to protect floor (if working indoors)
- One old toothbrush
- String
- One pair of scissors
- Masking tape
- One ruler
- One bucket or pail
- One garden trowel or small toy shovel
- One small paintbrush—one- or two-inch size
- One or two raw chicken eggs
- A variety of kinds of uncooked pasta (dinosaur skeleton kits may be used if available)
- A small box, such as a shoebox
- Fossil-mapping sheet (see Figure 3–7)

Procedures

1. Five-minute warm-up activity. Pose the question "How is a fossil like a telephone?" to the students. At first, they may be unable to see any similarities at all. You can start them out by suggesting a few, such as they both allow us to learn about things we can't see, they are both hard, or both of them are useless unless you understand what they are. When doing forced analogies, fluency isn't important. The students shouldn't be expected to generate lots of ideas. The idea is that they think creatively and think of ideas that require them to really stretch their thinking and look at two objects in a new way.

2. Classroom dig. Prior to the lesson, you should set up one classroom dig site for every three students. If weather permits, this is best done outside. Each bin should be filled with sand up to approximately six inches from the top. (Large bins will weigh a lot when filled! You should fill them where you want them to use them.) In each bin, bury either one or two eggs and several pieces of pasta. The number of eggs should vary from bin to bin so that the students will not know how many eggs their particular bin contains. Each dig site should also contain a "dig kit" containing all of the other items, which can be stored in their bucket.

3. Introduce the lesson to the students by explaining that they are paleontologists who are exploring a site to see if it contains any fossils. The first thing

they will need to do is split their dig into sections. They should do this by stretching one piece of string across the middle of their bin lengthwise, and two more pieces of string across their bin crosswise to split the bin into thirds. Using pieces of masking tape, they should then label each section as follows:

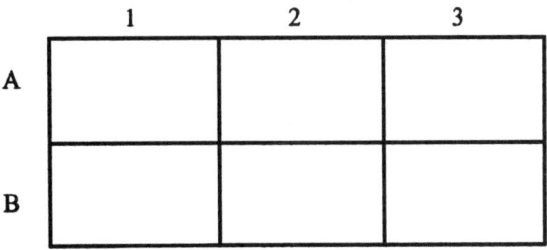

Explain that sectioning needs to be done so that they can keep track of where each "fossil" is found by recording its position in a notebook. The position of a fossil can be important. For example, the position of a fossil may tell paleontologists whether a bone belongs to a particular skeleton or a different one. The students should record their "fossil" finds on a fossil-mapping sheet (see Figure 3–7) by sketching a picture of the object in its approximate position in the bin.

FIGURE 3–7 Fossil-mapping sheet

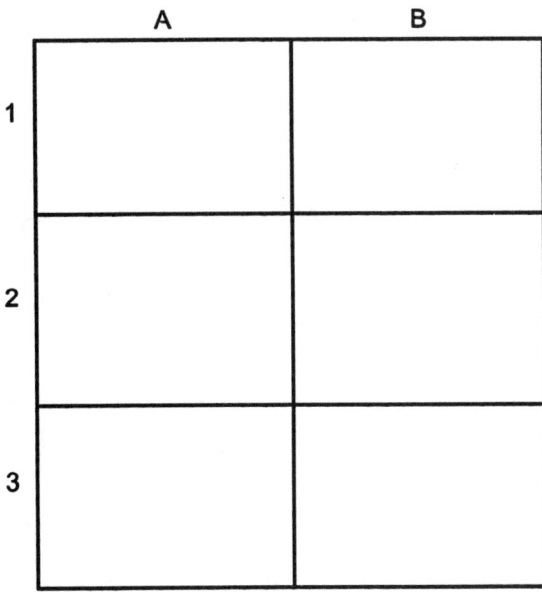

4. The students are now ready to start digging! Warn them to be very careful by hinting that there just might be something breakable in their bin! Careless digging can lead to broken items and overlooked items. As they use the trowel and paintbrushes to move sand, they can deposit any excess sand in their bucket. Caution the students that they must leave an item in its position when they find it. Only after they have sketched it on their fossil-mapping sheet can they remove it and examine it more closely. All "fossils" should be given a number, which can be attached to it with a piece of masking tape, and deposited in their box.

5. Once the students are confident that they have found every item in their bins, tell them to examine all the "fossils" in their box. What do they think they have found? Do the items make a skeleton? Have they found one or more than one? The students will probably be unable to construct anything from their pieces of pasta! Tell them that when paleontologists find a skeleton, it is usually incomplete and all the pieces are mixed together. After the dig is when the hard work of figuring out how the pieces fit together starts!

Assessment Options. Assessment of this lesson is not strictly necessary, as students are learning a brand new skill—digging for fossils—which they are not expected to master. However, students could receive a plus, check, or minus based on how carefully they dug and sketched during their dig. Students could write a journal entry about their feelings about the dig for their portfolios. Does paleontology seem like a career they would enjoy?

Lesson Five: Bone Up on Dinosaurs

Purposes. In this lesson, students get the chance to learn how paleontologists use clues to figure out what species a dinosaur skeleton is and how a skeleton is "fleshed out" so that it looks like a real dinosaur. They also add to their knowledge base about dinosaurs and practice measurement skills by comparing dinosaur lengths to other items.

Thinking Skills. Analogies, comparing and contrasting, inference, analysis, elaboration, originality.

Length. 60–90 minutes (may be split into three sessions).

Materials Needed

- One plastic dinosaur skeleton model kit
- One box of modeling clay
- One pie tin or small cake pan
- Five different dinosaur models representing different body types, such as long necked, heavily armored, and so on. One of the models should be the same kind as the plastic dinosaur skeleton model kit.
- Dinosaur skeleton sheets (see Figures 3-8, 3-9, and 3-10)
- Crayons
- String or rope cut into lengths representing the lengths of various kinds of dinosaurs. Each length should be labeled with the name of the dinosaur it represents. Suggestions:

    Tyrannosaurus rex = 43 feet (13 m)

    Diplodocus = 88 feet (26 m)

    Compsognathus = 2 feet (60 cm)

    Coelophysis = 10 feet (3 m)

    Triceratops = 30 feet (9 m)

    Stegosaurus = 30 feet (9 m)

- Spools or dowels to wrap the string or rope around
- Several meter sticks, yardsticks, or tape measures
- Calculators (optional)

Procedures

1. Five minute warm-up activity. As a group, think of dinosaur analogies. Here are some possibilities:

- _____ is as long as *Diplodocus's* tail.
- _____ is as big as *Ultrasaurus*.
- _____ is as scary as *Tyrannosaurus rex*.

This is a good time to model divergent thinking for the students. If they are thinking of long things, mention an idea such as "My sweater if it was unraveled would be as long as *Diplodocus's* tail." Or, "The walk to the principal's office when I'm in trouble is as long as *Diplodocus's* tail."

2. There are three stations to set up for this lesson. Students will rotate through them in small groups, after the task at each station has been explained to them. A time limit of 20–30 minutes can be set for each station. The stations are

a. "What dinosaur is this skeleton?" For this station, pat and mold a box of modeling clay to fit inside a pie tin or small cake pan. Press in dinosaur bones from a dinosaur skeleton kit. Arrange them so that the bones are laid out roughly head to tail and not all mixed up. To the students, even a skeleton that is neatly laid out will look confusing! Next to this skeleton dig, set up the five dinosaur models.

At this station, students will attempt to identify what kind of dinosaur skeleton is in the dig. Tell them that one of the five model dinosaurs is the same kind as the skeleton. Do not give them any hints at how they are to figure it out. When they first look at the skeleton laid out in the dig, it may look like a mess to them. As they look, however, they will start to recognize features such as the skull, neck, tail, and arms and legs. By the process of elimination they should figure out which dinosaur skeleton is in the dig. If they are having difficulty, you can point out features such as the skull to them and show them how to compare them to the model dinosaurs. Once they have identified the skeleton, the students should write a short press release announcing their discovery.

b. "Fleshing out" dinosaur skeletons. For this station, set up a table with crayons and copies of the dinosaur skeleton sheets. (See Figures 3-8, 3-9, 3-10) Students will be turning the skeleton drawings into dinosaur drawings by adding flesh to the dinosaurs, much the same way as paleontologists make a model of what a certain dinosaur really looked like by adding fat, muscle, and skin on top of a skeleton. Students should not simply outline the skeleton! Tell them that, just like their bodies, dinosaurs had fat and muscle, so they need to estimate how much there was and leave space between the skeleton and their outline of the skin.

The second thing they should do is color the dinosaur. They should decide what color(s) to use, since we don't know for sure what colors dinosaurs were. After they have colored their dinosaur and added features such as eyes, they should write a sentence or two explaining why they chose the color(s) that they did. For example, a student may explain that he or she colored a dinosaur camouflage colors since so many animals today are camouflage colors. Or another student may choose bright colors, because dinosaurs may be the ancestors of birds and many of them are

FIGURE 3–8 Dinosaur Skeleton

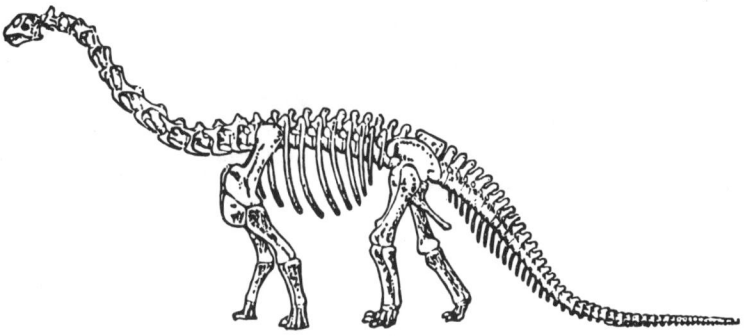

FIGURE 3–9 Dinosaur Skeleton

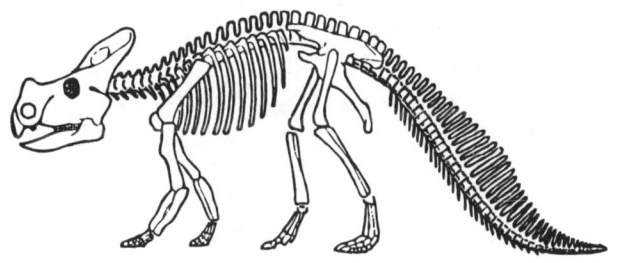

FIGURE 3–10 Dinosaur Skeleton

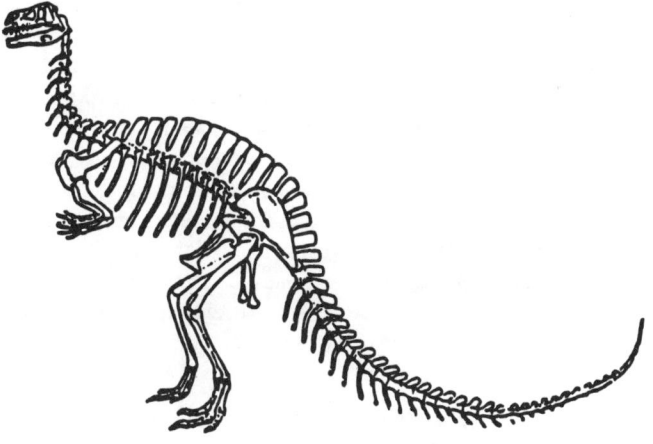

brightly colored. Emphasize to students that there are no right or wrong answers, since nobody has ever seen a real dinosaur. However, they should have an explanation for their color choices that makes sense.

c. "As long as a dinosaur.." At this station, students will be unrolling the rope or string lengths, which represent the lengths of various dinosaurs. Many people think that all dinosaurs were huge, but the lengths will show them that some were small. Just like people, most dinosaurs were of average size; a few were very large or very small, but most were middle-sized. After they have finished unrolling and rolling the dinosaur lengths, each student or pair of students should choose one of them and find as many equivalent measures as they can. For example, if they choose *Coelophysis,* they should measure things in the classroom and make a list of other things that are ten feet long. Perhaps the chalkboard is ten feet long. If they cannot find items that are exactly 10 feet long, they can figure out how many of an item would be 10 feet, such as two teacher's desks. For longer dinosaurs, such as *Diplodocus,* a calculator may be needed to help them figure out how many sinks it takes to equal 88 feet!

Assessment Options

- One station can be the focus of the assessment. For example, you could observe the students and assess them on their accuracy in measuring at the "As long as a dinosaur.." station. Or you could observe the students as they figure out the dinosaur skeleton dig and write comments and rate them on their ability to use their thinking skills to figure out the problem.
- Students could write a response to each station in their journals. They could explain which they found hardest to do and why or which activity they found the most enjoyable.
- Each student could choose the work from one of their stations to include in a portfolio to be reviewed at the end of the unit.

Lesson Six: A Dinosaur by Any Other Name . . .

Purposes. Children love saying all those impressive-sounding dinosaur names! In this lesson, they learn how dinosaurs are classified and named. They will also learn how many scientific words are constructed from Greek and Latin prefixes and suffixes. They will use their creative thinking skills to create and name their own make-believe dinosaur.

Thinking Skills. Originality, elaboration, classification.

Length. 45–60 minutes.

Materials Needed

- "What do you call a terrible lizard?" dinosaur names sheet (see Figure 3–11)
- Paper
- Crayons
- Pencils

Procedures

1. Five-minute warm-up activity. This activity forces students to look at something in a new way. Ask the students to pretend they are *Tyrannosaurus rex,* the most feared of all of the dinosaurs. *T. rex* has a very bad reputation, which they would like to change. They must convince you by telling you about *T. rex's* good features.

2. Ask each student to tell you the name of their favorite dinosaurs. As you write each different name on a chart or the chalkboard, ask that student to describe that dinosaur to you by telling you what makes that dinosaur different from all of the others. After all the students have named a favorite dinosaur, explain that just as they chose one or two major distinguishing characteristics to describe their dinosaur, so do scientists when they name a newly discovered dinosaur species. Those long dinosaur names are actually made up of smaller parts, prefixes and suffixes, that describe that dinosaur in some way. It could be what it eats, what it looks like, where it lived, or even its personality. The prefixes and suffixes come from the Greek or Latin languages, the language of science. A dinosaur name is the same in any language, since scientists around the world use the same Greek and Latin prefixes and suffixes. Many of the same prefixes and suffixes are also used for the scientific names of other plants and animals.

3. Hand out the "What do you call a terrible lizard?" sheet. (See Figure 3–11.) Look at some of the names of dinosaurs written on the board and see if

FIGURE 3–11 Dinosaur Names

What Do You Call a "Terrible Lizard"?

Those long, complicated dinosaur names are made up of smaller parts called *prefixes*, which come before a word, and *suffixes*, which come after. Each dinosaur name usually tells something about that dinosaur. For example, *Triceratops* is made up of three parts: "tri" means three, "cera" means horns, and "tops" means face—a good name for a dinosaur with three horns on its face! Remember, the word *dinosaur* is made up of *dino*, which means "terrible," and *saur*, which means lizard. Here are some more meanings for dinosaur names:

Prefixes

allo = leaping	dodeca = twelve	platy = flat
anato = goose	ennea = nine	poly = many
auri = ear	herb = plant	pter = wing
ankyl = curved	ichthy = fish	retro = backward
apato = goose	iguano = iguana	rex = king
archeo = ancient	labio = lips	rhino = nose
brachio = arms	lepto = small, weak	saur = lizard
bronto = thunder	mani = hand	scolo = crooked
carn = meat	megalo = large	stego = plated
cera = horns	micro = small	stomato = mouth
coelur = hollow	mono = one	struthio = ostrich
compso = elegant	noto = back	tenui = thin
cory = helmet	octo = eight	tetra = four
dactyl = finger, toe	oculo = eye	thero = beast
dasy = hairy	odon = tooth	titano = gigantic
deino = terrible	onycho = claw	tops = face
derma = skin	ornith = bird	trach = duck
di = two	oto = ear	tri = three
dino = terrible	naso = nose	tricho = hair
diplo = double	penta = five	tyranno = tyrant

Suffixes

cephalic = head
cheirus = hand
chus = claw
don = tooth
dont = tooth, bill
ischian = hipped
lestes = stealer
nathus = jaw
pod = foot
pteryx = wing
raptor = thief
saurus = lizard
spinax = spine

---

any parts of their names appear on the list, such as *Stegosaurus*, "plated lizard," or *Tyrannosaurus rex*, "tyrant king." Tell the students that they are going to get the chance to name a brand-new dinosaur species. It's so new it doesn't even exist yet, for they are going to design it using their imagination! Using the list of prefixes and suffixes, they should combine them to come up with a new dinosaur name. The more unusual the better! On a sheet of paper, they should then draw that dinosaur and write a few sentences describing it.

4. After all the students have finished, each one should present his or her dinosaur creation to the class.

Assessment Options

- Each student can receive a grade or plus, check, or minus based on their originality and the match between their dinosaur's name and description.

- Each student should save his or her creation for inclusion in the dinosaur portfolio.

Lesson Seven: Whatever Happened to My Old Friend Dino?

Purposes. This lesson gives students the opportunity to do their own research by conducting a survey to learn what people think caused the extinction of dinosaurs. They also learn how to analyze and graph their data. This is much more time consuming than simply gathering the information from books or other media, but students need the opportunity to learn how to actively gain information for themselves, rather than passively receiving it. Students also gain experience in evaluating differing explanations about a problem with no known answer as they discuss the different theories about how dinosa*urs* became extinct.

Thinking Skills. Forecasting, fluency, flexibility, graphing, surveying, analysis, evaluation.

Length. 60–90 minutes (plus time for surveying).

Materials Needed

- One-inch quadrille (graph) paper
- Paper
- Pencils
- Crayons or colored pencils
- Several books on dinosaurs that cover the question of dinosaur extinction

Procedures

1. Five-minute warm-up activity. Write the question "What would our world be like today if dinosaurs were still alive?" on the chalkboard. Use a web to record the students' ideas. Encourage them to think of as many aspects of our lives as they can. For example, would buildings be designed any differently? Would there be any different jobs, such as dinosaur trainers? Would our transportation methods be any different?

2. After students have considered the idea of dinosaurs still being alive, ask for a show of hands of students who would like to live with dinosaurs. The majority of students will probably agree that we are lucky that dinosaurs are gone! However, it's a mystery why they all became extinct. Explain to the students that they are going to do some research to find out some theories or ideas about what caused the dinosaurs' extinction. Working with partners, they are going to conduct a survey that asks the simple question "What do you think caused the extinction of the dinosaurs?" (For younger students, the wording could be "What do you think caused all the dinosaurs to disappear?") Each pair of students can survey the students in a different classroom, providing that other teachers are willing to participate in the research effort. Another option would be to have students conduct the survey at home with family and friends.

Discuss with students how they might conduct their survey. For example, if they survey younger students they probably would have to record verbal responses to the question and ask the question to one student at a time. With other students, they would have the option of having the students write their opinions on a pieces of paper. They need to keep track of the "I don't know" responses along with all the other responses. Discuss the protocol about conducting a survey, such as "Be polite, explain the question clearly, don't comment on someone's response, don't tell someone what to say, and record responses accurately."

After the students understand what they are to do, they can conduct the surveys at prearranged times. Once they have collected their data, each pair of students needs to analyze and make a bar graph showing the different responses. A lesson on graphing or a review on how to make a bar graph may be necessary, depending on the students' experience with graphs.

3. After each pair of students has graphed their data, all the data needs to be collected to make one large classroom graph. This can be done as a whole-class project, or a few students needing enrichment can work on the graph. The large pool of data can be analyzed to see if there are any differences in opinions between grade levels. Are older or younger students more likely to say, "I don't know," to the question? Why?

Once all the data have been gathered and graphed, they can be discussed and compared to the theories that paleontologists have about dinosaur extinction. Using books about dinosaurs, a list of the scientific theories about dinosaur extinction can be made. This can be done by the students working in partners or small groups, or the teacher can read selections about dinosaur extinctions from the books. Questions for discussion can include the following:

- Did the students who were surveyed know about most of the current theories about dinosaur extinction?
- Was one theory more popular than others? Why?
- Did the students suggest any new theories?
- Why don't we know for sure what caused the dinosaurs' extinction?

After a thorough discussion of the different theories and their merits, a vote can be taken to see if students were convinced by any particular theory, or if they feel the question is still unanswered.

Assessment Options

- Prior to making their graphs, students can be given a checklist on what makes an excellent graph so that they are aware of the guidelines they are expected to meet. For example, they would know that they need to label their graphs, color them neatly, record information accurately, and so on. Their completed graphs would be evaluated against the set of guidelines.

- A performance assessment could be used to see how well students can analyze and graph data. The teacher can provide the results of a survey, either real or contrived, which the students need to analyze and graph. Students could also gather the data by conducting another survey.

- Students could write in their portfolio journals about the question of dinosaur extinction and whether they have changed their opinion or believe in a certain theory based on the information they have learned.

- Students could prepare a short lesson on their findings, using guidelines prepared by the teacher, about dinosaur extinction and return to the classrooms that they surveyed and teach the students what they have learned. Using the set of guidelines as a standard, the teacher can evaluate the lesson the students prepared by observing their final practice session before they do their classroom lesson.

Lesson Eight: Debatable Dinosaurs

Purposes. In this lesson, students learn how to consider an issue from many angles and present their viewpoint without arguing as they debate a proposed dinosaur dig in a nature reserve. They learn how to organize their thoughts and present them concisely. Listening skills will be emphasized, for they need to listen carefully to what others are saying in order to respond. They will also learn how to go beyond simply debating an issue as they practice using their problem-solving skills to attempt to solve the problems involved.

Thinking Skills. Evaluation, analysis, flexibility, synthesis, debating, generating solutions, comparing and contrasting.

Length. 60–90 minutes (may be split into two sessions).

Materials Needed

- Paper
- Pencils
- Timer

Procedures

1. Five-minute warm-up activity. Ask the students the question "Who would you vote for if the dinosaurs were to hold a presidential election?" Discuss their responses and the reasons why they think a certain kind of dinosaur would be the best leader. Would they vote for their favorite dinosaur or for one they think the other dinosaurs would obey, even if it is because of fear? Which dinosaur would be the wisest?

2. The students are going to gather information, debate, and attempt to solve the problems related to the following scenario:

A paleontologist wants to dig up a nature reserve to look for dinosaur skeletons. She believes that there is a good chance of finding skeletons, for a few bones have already been seen in exposed rocks. However, the reserve is home to rare species of plants and animals. Think about how each of the following would feel about it: paleontologists, the director of the reserve, park visitors, animals in the park, and the director of a dinosaur museum.

a. Assemble the students into five different groups, randomly assigning each group to represent one of the five affected groups. Instruct the groups to consider the scenario only from their groups' point of view. Allow them to discuss the issue as a group for 10 minutes. During that time, they should write down reasons why that group would be for or against digging for dinosaur fossils in the park reserve.

b. In a simplified version, explain to the students about debating. They are going to be presenting their viewpoint and trying to convince the others to agree with that viewpoint. In order to do well at debating, they need to think about what points the other sides will be arguing. Give them 20 more minutes to think about how each of the other groups will feel about the scenario. If possible, they should think of arguments against what they think the other groups will be saying.

c. Explain the rules of the modified five-way debate. Each group will have 2 minutes to present their opinion about the proposed dig. A spokesperson for each group should present their arguments. During that time, all the other groups must listen without speaking. After all the groups have presented, the debate is opened up for 10 minutes of comments and counterarguments. However, only one student may speak at a time, and must be called on by the teacher, the moderator of the debate. Two students from the same team may not speak one right after another, unless no other students are waiting to speak. After the open period, each group will have 1 minute to sum up their arguments.

d. After the debate, discuss with the students how it went. Were their arguments convincing? Was it hard to argue a point that wasn't how they really felt? Did they change their minds as they heard different arguments? Did anyone present an argument that hadn't occurred to them? Did they feel comfortable explaining why they didn't agree with another group's arguments? Was it difficult to "think on their feet" and respond to what the other groups were saying?

e. Explain to students that debating is a good way to discuss all the sides of an issue without resorting to arguing. However, if a problem is involved, debating doesn't necessarily solve the problem. As a class, brainstorm ways to solve the problem of the proposed dinosaur dig. Is there a way that everyone could be happy? Is there a way to compromise so that a dinosaur dig could happen without disturbing the rare plants or animals? After several ideas have been brainstormed, discuss the merits of each one and try to reach consensus on the best way to solve the problem of the proposed dinosaur dig.

Assessment Options

- An observation checklist or comment sheet can be used to record information about individual students' performance during the preparation discussions before and during the debate. Students who were able to concisely state their views and respond articulately to others should be noted. Conversely, students who were unable to articulate their thoughts well should also be noted, for they may need extra work on expressing themselves verbally.

- Groups or individual students can be awarded points for every valid argument they present, as well as for refuting another groups' arguments.

- Students can write in their dinosaur journals about how they felt about their performance in the debate and during the problem-solving session.

Lesson Nine: Working in a Dinosaur Museum

Purposes. This student-centered project serves as the culmination to all that the students have learned about dinosaurs. They are going to plan and create a dinosaur museum in their classroom. All the details of the museum project will be the students' responsibility. The teacher's role is to facilitate and offer guidance when necessary. The students will be able to use all their thinking skills, as well as their artistic talents, writing skills, leadership skills, and so on.

Thinking Skills. Synthesis, evaluation, forecasting, skills from all previous lessons.

Length. 4–6 sessions of one hour each.

Materials Needed

- Supplies for making exhibits for classroom dinosaur museum, as determined by students

Procedures

1. Explain to the students that they will be planning and creating a dinosaur museum in their classroom. They will be totally responsible for all aspects of the museum, including planning it, creating it, inviting visitors, staffing it, and even cleaning it up! They will work in groups. Each group will be responsible for its exhibit, plus an organizing committee will be responsible for other aspects such as publicity. The students will decide on the exhibits, but exhibits based on the lessons they have done during the unit are one possibility. Those exhibits would be

   a. Dinosaur footprints and creative stories
   b. "Did you know?" dinosaur facts
   c. Dinosaur memorabilia accuracy
   d. Dinosaur dig
   e. "What dinosaur is this skeleton?"
   f. Fleshing out dinosaur skeletons
   g. "As long as this dinosaur . . ."
   h. "A dinosaur by any other name . . ."

Start the project by having all the students discuss what exhibits they want in their museum. Six to eight exhibits would be the most manageable. After a list of exhibits has been decided on, each exhibit needs to be "staffed" with volunteers, plus a separate organizing committee needs to be formed to oversee the entire project. The number of students staffing each exhibit will depend on the number of students in the class, but two to four students for each exhibit should be sufficient. The organizing committee should have three to five members. In addition, you as the teacher can also be a member of the organizing committee. If some exhibits are more popular than others, the students will need to devise a system for staffing the exhibits. The teacher's role is to facilitate if needed, but otherwise to step back and allow the students to handle things. Remember, they need to learn by experience and even making mistakes can be a learning experience!

2. Explain to the students the guidelines for an exhibit. It must be educational, neat, attractive, easy to understand, accurate, and interesting. The students can be as creative as they want to be, as long as they meet those criteria! The students in each group should meet to brainstorm ideas and plan their exhibits. The organizing committee should also meet to make a list of everything else that needs to be done, including the overall arrangements of the exhibit in the room. Before they start working on their exhibit, each group will need to submit a plan for their exhibit, including a list of materials that they will be needing and the amount of space their exhibit will require, to the organizing committee. The organizing committee will approve plans and help to procure needed materials.

3. Once the planning stage is complete, the students should be free to prepare their exhibits. An opening day deadline should be set, and other classes of students and parents invited. A full "dress rehearsal" run-through may be advisable, with you the teacher as the first visitor.

Assessment Options

- A criteria checklist can be used to rate a student's performance during the project. The students could be evaluated on all aspects of the project, such as planning, working in a group, quality of the exhibit, and so on. Or just the finished product of the exhibit could be evaluated. As always, prior to starting the project students should be made aware of the criteria they will be evaluated on.

- If students have been keeping a portfolio throughout the unit, the portfolio can be evaluated using a criteria checklist, or the portfolio can be given a rating for overall quality. Student self-evaluation should be a part of the portfolio assessment.

- The students could evaluate their own efforts during the dinosaur museum project by writing in their journals and answering questions about their performance.

- Visitors to the dinosaur museum can be asked to fill out comment cards. The cards could ask specific questions, or just ask for written comments on what visitors liked about the museum and how it could be improved.

Lesson Ten: Extension Activities

These activities are included to use during the unit for students who need extra challenge, or after the unit for those students who would like to continue learning about dinosaurs by doing an independent project. The students should be allowed to choose which one of the projects they would like to do.

1. *Evaluating Dinosaur Books:* Your library has several books on dinosaurs. Your teacher wants to use the best one as a resource for students during a dinosaur unit. Your task is to evaluate the books and recommend the best one to your teacher. You need to set up criteria before you can evaluate the books. Think about what makes a good dinosaur book. For example, are the facts accurate? Is the information presented in an easy-to-understand format? Is the book readable? Are the pictures misleading? For example, are dinosaurs shown with woolly mammoths? Make a list of at least five criteria and rate each book on a scale of 1 to 4 for each criteria, with 4 being excellent, 3 good, 2 fair, and 1 poor. The book with the highest total score should be the best one.

2. *The Last Dinosaur:* We are not sure why dinosaurs became extinct, but we do know that at some point the last dinosaur died and there were no more dinosaurs. Pretend that you are that last dinosaur. Write

a biography, the story of your life, telling all about your life, and about your feelings about being the last dinosaur.

3. *Dinosaur Logic Puzzles:* Write dinosaur logic puzzles using facts about dinosaurs as clues. Use the following examples as a guide:

- Which dinosaur is the mystery dinosaur? Is it *Tyrannosaurus rex, Diplodocus, Triceratops,* or *Stegosaurus?*

Clues:

a. The mystery dinosaur was a plant eater.

b. The mystery dinosaur did not have horns.

c. The longest dinosaur is not the mystery dinosaur.

(Answer: *Stegosaurus*)

- Put the dinosaurs in order from first to fifth. The dinosaurs are *Allosaurus, Brachiosaurus, Iguanadon, Compsognathus,* and *Apatosaurus.*

1 _____ 2 _____ 3 _____
4 _____ 5 _____

Clues:

a. The smallest dinosaur is in the middle.

b. *Brachiosaurus* is either first or last.

c. A meat eater is second.

d. *Iguanadon* is before *Allosaurus.*

(Answer: (1) *Iguanadon,* (2) *Allosaurus,* (3) *Compsognathus,* (4) *Apatosaurus,* (5) *Brachiosaurus.*)

Assessment Options. Since these projects are independent, the method of assessment should be decided with each individual student. A contract can be set up that stipulates when the project will be done and the criteria the student agrees to meet.

SUMMARY

Children's experiences during their early years of education are crucially important, for they serve as the foundation for all that is to follow. In a rapidly changing world, we may not know for sure exactly what children will need to know to be successful in the future, but we can be absolutely certain of one thing: children who have the skills and attitudes necessary for solving problems will be able to adapt and succeed in any situation.

Children need to be exposed to problem solving from the first day of their formal schooling, in both formal and informal ways, so that problem solving becomes second nature to them. The classroom needs to be a place where risk taking and perseverance is valued, and higher-level thinking activities are routine. This represents a major shift from the traditional classroom that requires new methods of teaching, writing curriculum, and assessing students.

In relation to this philosophy, guidelines for creating a classroom atmosphere conducive to problem solving were outlined. Ways to integrate problem-solving activities throughout the curriculum were presented, for both writing new curriculum and revising existing units. Model lessons illustrated how to implement problem-solving activities. A variety of assessment methods were presented, along with guidelines explaining their suitability in different situations. A comprehensive, interdisciplinary unit on dinosaurs was included, that pulls all the techniques and strategies of using problem solving in the primary classroom together in one challenging, motivating unit.

REFERENCES

Abarbanel, S. (1994). The feeling kids hate the most. *Sesame Street Parents,* March: 34–37.

Carpenter, T., Fennema, E., & Peterson, P. (1988). Using knowledge of how students think about mathematics. *Educational Leadership,* 46(4): 42–46.

Vavrus, L. (1990). Put portfolios to the test. *Instructor,* August: 48–53.

CHAPTER 4

An Interdisciplinary Approach to Problem Solving at the Intermediate Level

A scan of any intermediate classroom reveals an assortment of "full speed aheads," "for you . . . I'll do anythings," "fumblers," "fretters," and "forget-its." The "full speed ahead" students are capable and curious, ready and anxious to accept challenges. "For you . . . I'll do anything" students want to please and succeed. They make up for any lack of experience or skill with full cooperation and participation. "Fumblers" often seem unable to make connections between school learning and life. The "fretters" perpetually worry about details and outcomes—often missing the big picture altogether. And the "forget-its" lack motivation, confidence, or skills to reach the goals before them or have the attitude, even at a young age, that they have done and learned it all. As a teacher of intermediate students, grades 4–6, I am challenged by the myriad of curricular, social-emotional, and motivational requirements necessary to help mold these diverse types of learners into independent, self-initiated learners for middle school, high school, higher education, and employment success.

STUDENTS LOVE INTER-DISCIPLINARY LEARNING

In my teaching experience, one way I have found to raise the personal involvement, comfort, and learning levels of students is the use of project-based, interdisciplinary units of study that are centered around real problems and authentic products. Employing this method, I feel it is important to communicate a strong sense of purpose and direction, highlight the connections among disciplines or subject matter areas, provide opportunities for student self-selection, and allow time for students to assimilate new knowledge in order to draw conclusions, speculate, and predict outcomes.

There is much in the current literature to validate the use of integrated or interdisciplinary curriculum. The Association for Supervision and Curriculum Development (ASCD) has devoted space almost monthly to this subject in its *Curriculum Update* and other publications as well as publishing numerous paperback books on the topic. Susan Drake suggests that "integration by reducing duplication of both skills and content begins to allow us to teach more. It also gives us new perspective on what constitutes basic skills" (1993, p. 2). David Ackerman and Daniel Perkins (in Jacobs, 1989, p. 90) echo the idea that "skills and content may be loosely coupled;" however "by contrast, when skills teaching and content are tightly coupled the skills are taught with particular content in mind." Benefits of integrating the curriculum can be summed up as follows: "The most obvious payoff is a gain in students' mastery of meta-curriculum—improvement in thinking and learning skills. . . . Just as important are likely gains in the mastery of subjects (where) we expect at least equal, and often better content retention. . . . Students are likely to become more autonomous and proactive in their conduct as thinkers and learners" (Ackerman & Perkins, in Jacobs, 1989, p. 94). Also, since reality is not packaged in separate and unrelated parcels, why should curriculum be? In trying to explain why interdisciplinary instruction appeals to so many educators,

101

Willis (1992, p. 2) states, "first and foremost, it mirrors the real world better than traditional, discipline-based instruction."

I have found that thorough planning, identifying real problems and authentic products, and remaining true to objectives and subject matter areas are crucial to success in a problem-solving approach to curriculum. In this chapter, I will "walk through" the planning, implementation, and assessment aspects of units centered on five topics: historical homes, a class trip to the zoo, advertising, ways to motivate students to write letters, and the intrigue of mysteries. Language arts and social studies are usually the curricular base, but art, music, science, and math are also interwoven.

PREPARING FOR SUCCESSFUL TEACHING: TEN BASIC ELEMENTS

Good planning is basic to successful instruction and learning. For some teachers, the teacher's manual plays the role of planner. Topics, objectives, activities, and assessment tools, usually paper-and-pencil tests, are provided. The teacher follows the plan while the text provides the main resource for information. But to create problem-solving, product-based, interdisciplinary units, the teacher's manual and the student's text become merely one resource in a broader, more encompassing look at curriculum and learning. Although different units will require more or less emphasis on each aspect of traditional planning, implementation, and evaluation, all instructional units should consider the following ten elements:

- Overview of the unit
- Instructional objectives
- Resources: print, audiovisual, human, and real property
- Activities for students to meet objectives
- Authentic products for students to develop
- Learning environments
- Opportunities to use thinking skills and problem solving
- Instructional groupings: independent study, small groups, class size groups, large groups, and mentorships
- Timeline and budget
- Assessment considerations for both student performance and unit design.

Unit Overview

This overview communicates a narrative account of the intent and philosophy of the unit in relation to its content, process, product, and environment. It sets the tone for unit activities and outcomes. It should be shared with students and parents to provide a sense of direction and general enthusiasm. This is especially true for a long-term, multifaceted unit of more than three to four weeks. Often, once parents are aware of an upcoming unit and its components, they can provide otherwise unknown resources and services to improve the quality of the unit and perhaps get involved with the learning program of the school.

Instructional Objectives

These form the framework and structure for the unit. They are a "map" that provides direction and indicates which skills and information in which subject matter areas will be learned as well as differentiation according to grade levels and student academic needs. Traditionally, instructional objectives are identified first with resources to help communicate the objectives, then activities for students to practice the learning related to the objectives are developed, and, third, assessment tools or products to evaluate whether or not the students met the objectives are designed. In planning project-based, interdisciplinary units, I often alter that process. For example, when using a complex product such as an advertisement, informational video, schoolwide campaign and so on, I find working backward to break down the skills and activities necessary to produce a successful product provides better results. By using this planning strategy, I am frequently amazed at the skill level required in a seemingly simple product. The sequence for this latter method would be *product to activities to resources to objectives*.

Since most school districts and textbooks arrange objectives by skill or topic, you may find in using product-based, interdisciplinary units that only certain objectives will be met in any one unit at any one time. For example, in a letter-writing chapter of a language arts text, maybe only the business letter section and objectives will be used in a historical homes unit. But friendly letter format and objectives may be satisfied through a different unit during the same school year. Being familiar with all aspects of your grade level's curriculum and systematically checking off and being accountable to subject area objectives is important to assure there are no gaps or holes in the students' learning.

Resources

Listing resources as *print, audiovisual, human, and real property* serves a variety of needs. First, the categories help the teacher meet learning styles and preferences of students in today's world. Second, they provide an opportunity for the teacher to identify what is already available, then add to that list by going out from the classroom, to the building and district media centers, then to the community. It is often a resource that sparks this author's interest and creativity in relation to how to incorporate an idea and related learning into the established curriculum. As discussed in the previous section on instructional objectives, a resource may be the starting point to generate activities and products. The sequence here would look like this: *resource to activities to products to objectives.*

Except for current events, most print and audiovisual resources will continue to provide information and variety for particular units year after year. Some human and real property resources such as people in business or government positions, and at museums and historical sites are also reusable resources. Being aware of changing resources such as traveling and changing museum exhibits, omnitheater productions, community events, nature preserve activities, and so on provides opportunities for student involvement and curriculum enhancement on a more spontaneous basis. Most community opportunities are publicized enough in advance to use an event in a problem-solving unit.

Activities for Students

A variety of activities to meet objectives make up the "heart" of any unit and student learning. Here, the subject matter areas can be integrated into the topic of the unit and the difficulty levels can vary from simple to complex and concrete to abstract to meet student needs. Activities can also vary according to the amount of time they will take—from a class period to days, weeks, even a year in the case of writing a play or novel. Activities provide real, hands-on experiences and motivate students to get involved. They can also introduce a student to some more unusual facet of subject matter such as oceanography or anthropology or provide an indepth exposure to any topic. Activities, of course, promote active learning and provide opportunities for students to think and solve problems in a natural and meaningful way.

Both required and student self-selected activities should be included in unit planning. In this way, there is an accountability to basic or grade-level objectives plus opportunities for individuals or small groups of students to pursue an interest, work within an area of strength, or enrich their understanding of a topic. Individual learning style and preference options can be accommodated by including oral, written, construction, manipulative, creative, design, and dramatic activities.

When activities are closely tied to products, it is often helpful to select or allow the student to select a particular product such as a brochure, persuasive speech, skit, public announcement, and so on. Then the student and teacher jointly determine activities that would build skills or provide information necessary for a successful product. When product quality is poor, it is often due to a lack of preparation.

Authentic Products

Products provide the perfect vehicle to help students think and solve problems. A product can be as simple as a poem or short story or as complicated as a novel or musical composition. Most products are the result of a series of tasks and activities leading to an end. Many products in final form follow a standardized format. Thus, it is important to break down each product into its small parts, define tasks, and address strategies at each step. A similar final format will probably need to be studied, modeled, and practiced before a quality product will be produced. Knowing what is expected and having the skills to make it happen sets students and their teachers up for success. But after students have had experience in making several products, they should be encouraged to create their own unique and original product in relation to objectives that they and the teacher establish. A dictionary list of more than eighty creative products that can be related to any subject matter area is presented in the Appendix. Many kinds of products were also discussed in Chapter 2.

Learning Environments

Students need to experience learning in sites and with people and materials beyond the classroom. Within a school, other places to learn include the media center, all-purpose room, cafeteria or gymnasium, computer room or other specialized area, and the playground or campus area surrounding the school. Not all schools have all these options, but they do have some of them as well as others that are unique to their building. In a district, there are specialized rooms and laboratories, media centers, outdoor learning classrooms or areas, perhaps even an arboretum or park. And, the community offers an endless list of sites in the fields of medicine, business, finance, environmental concerns, and so on depending on the size and location of the community. Museums of some kind as well as historical buildings and town histories are a part of every town or city. Beyond the local community, a myriad of facilities in the state capitol and nearby cities and towns, as well as rural recreation and environmental education areas await the students.

Another aspect of learning environments is student interaction with nonpeers. Pairing primary and intermediate students to work cooperatively toward a goal is easily accomplished in the school day with no transportation concerns. This pairing may be limited to a specific unit of study or ongoing throughout the school year on a variety of topics. Intergenerational relationships formed with retired school neighbors, grandparents, and/or retirement facility residents also often give a different point of view to many topics and activities. Younger and older groups may play the role of resource people at some times and audience or receiver of a service at others. By working on a task or problem with a nonpeer, the student often gains insights that otherwise would have been missed.

Opportunities to Use Thinking Skills and Problem Solving

These opportunities need to be built into the teacher's outline plans for a unit of instruction. Five clusters of thinking skills—inquiry processes, creative thinking processes, critical thinking skills, single-step problem solving techniques, and Bloom's cognitive levels—and their relationship to multistep problem solving were illustrated in Figure 2–1 and discussed at length in Chapter 2. Although it is possible to teach the skills from any of these groups in any subject area, some lend themselves more naturally to one subject than another. For example, we often think of teaching creative skills in language arts and the arts and critical thinking skills in social studies. Likewise, the inquiry processes are often associated with science and single-step problem-solving techniques with mathematics.

Perhaps Bloom's cognitive levels and the creative skills relate most easily to all subject areas. And, of course, students should have opportunities to carry out multi-step problems at all times. A listing of the skills and subskills in each thinking skills group is presented in Figure 2–2 and an example of a problem-solving model is shown in Figure 2–5. These references could be used by teachers as they plan and develop units of instruction to ensure they include activities that enable students to experience a variety of skills from different groups as well as authentic problem solving.

Creative thinking processes—fluency, flexibility, elaboration, and originality—lend themselves well to all curriculum areas and topics. In order to "speak the same language" throughout the academic year, it is helpful to familiarize students with each creative thinking process and its application to problem solving early in the term. Chapter 2 of this book gives activities which highlight each process and the "Candy Creations" activity presented there illustrates all four processes on a common topic. Once students are familiar with the terminology and strategies, the techniques may be applied to regular curriculum objectives, activities, and products.

Fluency activities of brainstorming and listing possibilities, flexibility tasks involving points of view and bias, and elaboration involving embellishment and detail are emphasized in the interdisciplinary units presented in this chapter. A unique idea may be original to the individual or group even though it may not be novel to the universe. Originality should be noted and applauded at each and any phase of the problem-solving process. There is a tendency to view creative thinking activities as fillers, fluff, or special event projects. While it is true that baseball opening, the first snow, candy bars, and the like seem to be natural areas for creative thinking strategies, the built-in motivation and sense of play transfers easily to required learning in language arts, social studies, science, and math.

Instructional Grouping

Using a variety of group sizes makes good sense to keep learning interesting. And with today's children it is a necessity. Perhaps most important, the group size should be appropriate to the learning styles of the students and to the type of subject matter to be learned. Traditionally, the class-sized group of twenty to thirty students has been widely used. This type of group is useful for skill or format introductions, dissemination of basic knowledge, assignments, some field trips, and direct instruction. But it definitely has limitations. Working in small groups lends itself to skill practice, special interest discussion, certain field trips, and project preparation. Large groups are appropriate for listening to resource persons, some visuals on a topic, and introducing units or projects. Working with a partner is ideal for science experimentation, data gathering, and peer-partner assessment activities. Independent study or working alone works well for highly motivated, confident learners who are pursuing a specific goal. Mentorships provide unique experiences for students who are capable of going beyond a knowledge or experience base that is readily accessible to the teacher.

Grouping will vary from topic to topic and task to task. But on any given new skill, format, idea, or strategy, viewing the student as someone learning to walk is one way to facilitate group planning. At first, the teacher as facilitator holds on with two hands—guiding, steering, leading, and generally helping the student avoid pitfalls and wrong turns. As confidence builds, the facilitator holds only one hand while offering assurance and assistance when needed. Some students may remain at the assistance level for much of a given unit while others are ready to pass through this phase quickly or skip it altogether. Finally, the facilitator is on the sidelines, offering encouragement, praise, and an occasional reprimand as the situation requires. Most importantly, varying instructional groups helps provide flexibility and interest while fostering confidence and independence.

Timeline and Budget

All unit plans need to consider timelines and budgets. A *timeline* will help organize the unit to ensure that an adequate and justifiable amount of time will be spent on the unit as a whole as well as an equitable and rational distribution of time to the various subtopics in the unit. For example, while one could conceivably spend an entire school year on an environmental concern such as "destruction of natural habitats," establishing week-long topics such as wetlands, rain forests, old-growth forests, and the like help make the topic more manageable. A more defined unit facilitates the identification of district or grade-level objectives, skill activities, and projects that are appropriate to the interdisciplinary unit.

The *budget* is particularly relevant in relation to resources needed to teach the unit adequately and for field trips or work in learning environments other than the classroom. For example, a nature reserve may provide tours and/or resource people. If more than one grade level could benefit from a resource person's presentation, a joint program may be more cost effective. A field trip to a facility or site may also be shared by more than one grade level with each level focusing on different objectives and activities while sharing costs and providing grade-to-grade continuity.

Timelines and budgets are elements of instruction that are too often shortchanged in planning. Timelines are overlooked, taken for granted, or thought of as unnecessary. Budgets are often not worked out carefully by teachers before they ask for funds. Sometimes, if funds are not immediately available, there is a lack of search for alternatives such as cooperative funding between the students, a parent organization, or the school or district. Often teachers just assume there are no funds for taking students beyond the school area, and they don't bother to ask. Or they are afraid to ask for funds because they think they will be refused.

A school may have an established assembly budget monitored by the principal and possibly a committee. As numerous groups and individuals advertise assemblies through the mail in any given year, it may be advantageous to be a part of the decision-making committee. It is important to note that most parent–school organization budgets are established in the spring for the following school year. Often a monetary request is denied simply because it wasn't budgeted. Being aware of options, knowing curriculum needs, and being timely in making requests usually results in securing necessary funding. The teacher should work with the principal to develop a budget and ask for funds in their school or district.

Assessment Considerations

Plans and tools to carry out assessment should be in place at the onset of the unit. Assessment can be both formal and informal and should always be carried out with the idea of improving instruction both for the individual student and for instruction in general. Some written or videotaped record of a teacher's evaluation of a student's performance should always be made. It can be as informal as an observation checklist or as formal as a cognitive or performance test. For example, required activities in a given unit may include objective and essay test questions to check for understanding of content. Partner or small-group work could be monitored with a checklist that focuses on task commitment, group interaction, teamwork, and communication. Project work may need weekly checks on general progress and specific assessment of format criteria. Preparation and participation may be areas for both student and teacher to evaluate in large-group settings.

An often-neglected aspect of assessment is the evaluation of the unit design and its success with students. In the unit designs presented here, each one of the ten elements can be evaluated, revised, updated, or eliminated. This enables the teacher to pinpoint difficulties without "throwing away the entire unit." Likewise, successful activities may be highlighted, rescheduled, and possibly budgeted to be included in the following year's plan. Student and parent responses to various aspects of a unit may also be helpful. At the culmination of a unit, a written evaluation including teacher and student comments may be sent home requesting parent input and return of the evaluation to the teacher. Information from this evaluation may also be helpful when requesting funds for particular field trips, special speakers, or materials.

Ten elements to help teachers prepare for successful instruction where students have opportunities to think and solve problems were discussed here. Ways to use these elements in interdisciplinary units of instruction about historical homes, a class trip to the zoo, advertising, writing for success and employment, and the intrigue of mysteries are described in the remainder of this chapter. The first two units take the students out of the classroom to other learning areas. The next two focus on written and oral communications. And the fifth unit deals with the unique learning opportunities that surround mysteries of all kinds.

REACHING BEYOND THE CLASSROOM

It is not enough to prepare students for life beyond the classroom at some later date. The classroom is only a part of a student's daily life experience. A sense of community and connection to a larger society must be cultivated from a young age. The classroom may be thought of as the "home office" where preparations are made, basic knowledge is gained, and plans are formulated. From there, community resources become the branch offices where skills are practiced, insights gained, and information is collected. Back at the home office, data and perceptions may be compiled, analyzed, debated, and communicated. Further investigation or a new plan may result in sending the student back out to the community for answers.

Units on historical homes and a class trip to the zoo are described here. They rely on student participation in activities beyond the classroom during the school day. The discussion also illustrates ten elements of successful teaching.

There's No Place Like Home

In this unit, historical homes provide a focal point for project-based, problem-solving learning. Most communities highlight their past by establishing museums and preserving examples of period architecture. Ethnic and historical celebrations are also a part of community life. These sites and events provide unlimited opportunities for intermediate-level students to solve real problems and produce authentic products. They can use a multitude of skills while also participating in community efforts to preserve and celebrate the past.

The intermediate grades are often a period when children become more independent and less likely to share learning experiences with their families. My experience with this unit is that families with children of various ages become engaged in activities as a family project. This results in exciting intergenerational and communication-building projects. A strong sense of family fun and community pride make it one of my favorite units to teach. It is a favorite of many students, too.

Unit Overview. Students participate in a year-long interdisciplinary unit of study centered on the universal themes of change and patterns targeting the lumbering era (1839–1939) in the Chippewa Falls and Eau Claire, Wisconsin, areas. The unit addresses the idea that change is inevitable and that patterns emerge, cycle, and repeat. It also illustrates that change and patterns may be traced through the architecture, art, music, and written records of a time period.

Ideas are explored using local history, community resources, a variety of learning environments, and group and individual projects with provisions to share insights and projects with the community. Visits to two local historic homes, the Cook-Rutledge mansion in Chippewa Falls and the Schlegelmilch-McDaniels house in Eau Claire, encourage a real-life transfer of learning from a school setting to the community. Participation in Chippewa Falls's Pure Water Days and Eau Claire's Sawdust City Days festivals provide culminating activities for the unit.

This unit may be presented in a variety of ways from a two-week overview to an indepth study across two or three grade levels. Objectives, activities, and products accomplished would depend on the duration and the focus of the unit that the teacher chooses. For instance, a two-week overview or "appetizer" unit may be planned with a field trip to a local historical home as the focus. Selected house-centered objectives, activities, and products in art, language arts, social studies, and math would be explored. Some preparatory activities would be completed in the classroom prior to the field trip. Others could be initiated and completed while at the historic home, and still others as a follow-up to the trip. Interested individual students or small groups of students may also choose to pursue an independent study project as a result of this type of overview.

An "entire" historical home unit would broaden the unit focus and expand over a longer time period. It could be confined to one grade level or cut across several grade levels. All objectives, activities, and products presented here could be addressed within a school year. As the big idea of change and patterns emerge, cycling and repeating is played out throughout the year. Each month could have a different focus to provide an organizational format to make planning easier.

Since state history is a required topic in most fourth-grade curriculums across the United States, there is a natural connection to fifth- and/or sixth-grade curriculums that usually focus on American history. Teachers within grades 4–6 could coordinate and add or delineate objectives, activities, and products to provide a spiraling experience for students based on a growing knowledge and skill base and student maturity. For example, a fourth-grade teacher might present a segment of the unit in the spring. A fifth- or sixth-grade teacher could continue and/or build on that knowledge and complete a unit segment in the fall. In areas of special interest, students across grade levels may work cooperatively on particular projects as well. This type of spin-off and self-initiated learning in the form of independent study, working with a mentor, or working in small groups would be the "dessert."

Instructional Objectives. Objectives for several subject matter areas and grade levels can be met throughout this unit. Some examples are listed as follows.

Social Studies

- Identify career opportunities in the social studies fields.

- Identify individuals and their contributions to society.

- Demonstrate a knowledge and sense of history of our culture.

- Demonstrate effective citizenship skills.

- Identify, explain, and apply economic principles and concepts.

- Show relationships between and among nations, races, and cultures.

- Demonstrate an awareness of current and continuing issues and historical perspectives.

- Explain the chronological story of the development of the Chippewa Falls and Eau Claire, Wisconsin, areas.

- Give some examples of the historical development of modern economic activities in Wisconsin by following the growth of a business established in the early 1900s that is still a part of the community or state today.

Language Arts

- Write reports, notes of appreciation, business letters, descriptive paragraphs, comparison paragraphs, persuasive paragraphs, and scripts (composition).

- Use appropriate resources, take notes, organize and document sources and materials (research).
- Use various capitalization, punctuation and format rules, proper use of quotations, application of grammar usage, and spelling rules (mechanics).
- Demonstrate interviewing techniques, telephone etiquette, role playing, oral presentation skills (speaking and listening).
- Compare sources, read for detail and bias and so on, build vocabulary, and exhibit comprehension skills (reading).

Art

- Explain that art serves various functions and reflects the culture and time period in which it is produced.
- Produce artworks that are original, expressive, decorative, and functional.
- Produce artworks that are modeled after a particular culture or time period.
- Produce art works that are modeled after a particular artist or style of art.
- Explain that line, shape, color, and texture are elements of art with expressive potential.

Math

- Illustrate skills associated with computation (multiply, divide, add, subtract).
- Illustrate skills associated with measurement of angle, length, area, and time.
- Illustrate improvement in estimation skills.
- Identify descriptive patterns such as increases, decreases, and trends using a graphic representation of a set of data (table, diagram, graph).
- Explore the implication of statistics in society.
- Identify when a problem exists and devise problems of one's own.
- Represent problem situations using operations, numbers, and relations (< = >) that may or may not include the unknown.
- Make various representations of a problem and its solution.
- Recognize and use patterns to make generalizations.
- Establish subgoals for solving parts of a problem.
- Evaluate and revise solutions.

Resources. *Print* materials include novels of historical fiction, short stories, journals with daily entries, genealogical charts, public records, newspapers of the era, history textbooks and articles, and general reference materials. *Audiovisual* materials are available from Public Broadcasting System (PBS) presentations, theater productions, filmstrips, documentaries, art prints, and the computer-aided design (CAD) system.

Human resources include museum personnel, historical society members, chamber of commerce personnel, librarians, architects, antique collectors, local theater people, people involved in historical home restoration, local citizens and relatives of those who lived during this era, local and state newspaper personnel, high school students experienced in CAD systems, and historical homes docents. *Real property* resources that are available are university and public libraries, museums and their artifacts, historical markers, historical buildings and areas, and historical homes that are open to the public.

Activities. There are many and varied activities that can be matched to student needs, abilities, learning styles, different sizes of instructional groups, and other variables. Some of these in several subject matter areas are listed here.

Social Studies

- Compare the wants and needs of people that are several generations apart—for example, those of the lumbering era with those of today.
- Compare the leaders and leadership styles of the two eras.
- Parallel the local scene with the national and international scenes in regard to historic events in the lumbering era.
- Trace a family tree back to identify individuals who lived during the era.
- Identify local businesses whose roots are in the lumbering era.
- Organize a timeline that traces local, national, and international events from the targeted era through today.

- Assemble a "museum in a box" kit that focuses on one aspect of life in the era.
- Determine inventions indicative of the times and speculate why they were successful or why not.
- Host a historical home "open house."

Language Arts

- Conduct an interview with a person or relative of a person from the era.
- Determine appropriate resources, and write for specific information on the era.
- Engage in independent and guided reading of novels, short stories, and articles from and/or about the era.
- Participate in a vocabulary study of architectural terms and styles of the era.
- Write a script for a tour of a local historical home or area.
- Create an infomercial for a local historical event.
- Write a description of an item to be used in an antique furniture magazine or museum scene.
- Write and produce a skit depicting a local historical event.
- Create a brochure highlighting a local historic landmark.

Mathematics

- Compute the cost of field trips.
- Determine a budget for restoring a historical home, one room, or one aspect of restoration.
- Compare costs of restoring a historical building with building a new structure of the same kind.
- Work with a high school student using a CAD system to incorporate a variety of architectural features into a computer drawing.
- Describe a home by "walking through" its floor plan (blueprints).
- Raise money for projects.
- Communicate collected data through charts and graphs.

Art Related

- Identify artists and art works from the era, including local, national, and international representation.
- Re-create a city block to illustrate "then–now" in a mural.
- Create a "room" within the classroom or other area in the school using furnishings from the lumbering era.
- Identify architectural features and designs common to the era.
- Identify local buildings by architectural style in a style scavenger hunt.
- Compare and contrast an architect's work in various locations in the cities of Chippewa Falls or Eau Claire or other local geographical area.
- Research the fashions and costuming of an era through photographs, magazine articles, and so on.
- Illustrate "then–now" clothing ensembles.
- Show how certain fashion elements have cycled and recycled since their initial appearance in the era.
- Sketch a home from the targeted era, using a local historical home as a model.
- Plan an architectural walking tour of a historical area.
- Design a poster advertising a local festival such as Pure Water Days or Sawdust City Days.
- Create a display in store front windows, reception areas, or lobbies in buildings throughout the community depicting change in the area from the lumbering era to the present.
- Refinish a piece of antique furniture from the era.
- Design and build a float centered around a historical change theme to be displayed at a local festival.

Authentic Products. Many products such as a timeline, family tree, map and script for a walking tour or museum visit, item description, brochure, informational display, and a parade float are described in the activities just listed. The skill levels and complexity vary greatly. As discussed earlier in this chapter, identifying the knowledge base, required skills, and format familiarity are crucial to the creation of a quality project. Grouping enters in to product production as some students may work as part of a group, as a partner, or individually depending on their skill, interest level, and learning style. Products could be categorized to allow for self-selection within a category in addition to required products. Identification of an appropriate audience whether it be another class, parents at an open-house event, or the community through a window display will help students focus their attention and communication style.

Learning Environments. The activities for this unit take place in locations from the classroom, to the district, and in many different places in the community. Opportunities exist for students to participate in walking and/or bus tours of historic neighborhoods and downtown areas within the community. Visits to the Cook-Rutledge Mansion, home of a lumber baron, and the Schlegelmilch-McDaniels house, home of a working-class family, provide a view of life during the lumbering era. Making advertising posters for community festivals allows students to interact with the business community. Conducting interviews with senior citizens, and museum and business personnel encourage communication between generations. Many activities also help students to look at topics at the regional, state, national, and international levels. These provide vicarious if not completely realistic environments outside their local area.

Thinking Skills and Problem Solving. The activities in this unit provide opportunities for practicing skills in all thinking skills areas and for multistep problem solving. The topics of the unit lend themselves particularly well to the critical skills of comparing and contrasting, reliable and unreliable sources, cause and effect, sequencing and prioritizing, and point of view. Many activities encourage use of creative skills—fluency to generate a wide range of ideas, flexibility in adapting materials and ideas to a by-gone era, and elaboration on a basic idea. And, of course, there is lots of room for originality in activities and products such as assembling a "museum in a box" kit, hosting an historical home "open house," producing a skit, and designing a poster display or parade float.

The inquiry skills of observing, classifying, inferring, and predicting are widely used, as are the single-step problem solving techniques of make a model, act it out, make a drawing or figure, recognize patterns, and forming analogies. Students have opportunities to work at all levels of Bloom's cognitive taxonomy, with considerable emphasis on analysis, synthesis, and evaluation. Most students produce a real product that is the result of solving a problem. Some examples are recreating a city block in a then-and-now mural, determining a budget for restoring a historical home, producing an infomercial, and tracing a family tree.

Instructional Groups. Different grouping strategies may be employed depending on the nature of the product. For example, writing a persuasive paragraph and creating a brochure may be independent projects; refinishing a piece of antique furniture and conducting an interview, a paired project; making an artifact collection and a description of a museum piece, a small-group project; and conducting an historical home "open house," a large-group project.

Timeline and Budget. The timeline for this unit relies on the approach (one grade level, cross grade levels) and focus (overview or all encompassing) of the unit. Whichever approach is taken, blocking out activities and projects on a calendar prior to presenting the unit is beneficial. The more people involved, as in across-grade-level teaching teams, the more crucial a timeline is to success.

Visits to historical areas such as walking tours or architectural-style scavenger hunts are best planned as fall and spring events, since midwestern winter weather is a deterrent, but this would not be an issue in many parts of the country. Since displays or parade floats need to coincide with a local summer festival, plans for the theme and festival date need to be communicated in the fall to allow ample time to complete the projects. I find that students and teachers retain their enthusiasm and motivation if a unit timeline including topics, projects, and deadlines is shared at the onset of the unit and reviewed and updated as needed as the unit progresses.

Monthly newsletters to parents keep everybody informed of progress and challenges yet to come. Small group and independent projects and products are highlighted in the newsletters as well as articles about student accomplishments. These add to the students' sense of pride. Another benefit of a unit timeline is the wonderful sense of accomplishment that both teachers and students feel as yet another project is crossed off, bringing the goal closer into view.

Budgeting is not a major issue in the "There's No Place Like Home" unit. Most materials are readily available at the school or are a part of basic classroom materials. Resource people may volunteer their time and expertise, high school students may have access to computer-aided design (CAD) systems at their school, and art teachers may provide prints, fashion information, and architectural resources. Admission charges to historical homes or museums are often reduced or waived when administrators in the school and district become part of a cooperative effort. Here, students provide a reciprocal service to the site by making display item descriptions, posters, brochures, tour scripts, acting as volunteers, and the like. Transportation costs to get to the historical areas are minimal since destinations are within a fifteen-mile radius of the school. Because of the community involvement of this unit, budgeting does not pose a hindrance to its activities.

Assessment. The idea of assessment in a problem-solving, product-based, interdisciplinary approach to learning has many facets. The process strategies, specific skills, and final product as well as group cooperation, individual effort, and participation should be addressed. Assessment should be a continuous activity throughout the unit. Self-evaluation by the students should be built into the assessment process. And both formal and informal means may be helpful in describing and evaluating individual and/or group progress.

A shared timeline including activities and project deadlines provide a basis for ongoing assessment. Comprehension and knowledge of information and concepts basic to the unit are assessed in a paper-and-pencil test format. Product assessments include criteria for evaluation that are communicated prior to, during, and at the culmination of the product. The teacher weights particular criteria that are most appropriate to each product. An example of a product assessment form for a business letter is shown in Figure 4–1.

Group projects require monitoring while in progress. A weekly project progress check includes both self-evaluation and teacher evaluation components in the areas of individual preparation and participation within the group as well as progress of the group as a whole. This type of assessment helps to

FIGURE 4–1 Product Assessment Form: Business Letter

Student Name: _____

Date: _____

Criteria:	Possible Points	Earned Points
Standardized business letter format; direct, to the point, stating request, providing appropriate information, polite language	40	_____
Grammar—usage	20	_____
Mechanics—spelling	20	_____
Sentence structure	10	_____
Neatness	10	_____
Totals	100	

Student Comments:

Teacher Comments:

identify student accountability as well as strategic planning and guidance for the upcoming week. An example of a weekly group project check form is shown in Figure 4–2.

At the end of a unit or a section of a unit in a long-term study, a packet of product and assessment tools are sent home with the student to communicate his or her progress. The parents are then able to see a group of related materials complete with work samples and intermediate assessments leading to a better understanding of the student's progress. Parents are invited to comment on products, activities, topics, and the assessment. Through these parent comments I find out the extent to which the unit becomes a "family project" that extends into family discussion, planned outings, and research.

The success of "There's No Place Like Home," is, I believe, based on the real-life, in-my-own-backyard flavor of the content that relates to civic pride and community involvement. Opportunities for self-selection within interdisciplinary activities and projects allow students to pursue an interest to a level of their own choosing. I find this aspect of the unit to be very positive. Real places, real people, real projects, and real products add relevance to a multitude of required objectives and learning activities. Each student is able to participate in the problem-solving process at a very personal level. This makes the transfer of skills and processes to other learning at other times become much more likely.

It's a Jungle Out There: A Trip to the Zoo

Children and animals just naturally go together. Children's inherent curiosity and interest level provide high motivation for a project-based, problem-solving unit centered on a class trip to the zoo. The mention of "class trip" or "field trip" often conjures up images of students flitting here and there with little or no learning or transfer of skills and knowledge. These images, coupled with a high price tag has often

FIGURE 4–2   Group Project Progress Check Form

Student Name: _____

Project Title: _____

Date: _____

Directions: Please evaluate yourself in regard to this week's work in the following areas. Circle your response to each category. Write personal comments using a pencil. Your teacher will write comments using a pen.

Preparation:	Excellent	Very good	Fair	Poor
Participation:	Excellent	Very good	Fair	Poor
Progress:	Excellent	Very good	Fair	Poor

Student personal comments:

Teacher comments:

had teachers thinking twice before attempting any out-of-classroom experience.

I have found, however, that these drawbacks can be avoided by sandwiching the zoo trip in between lead-up and follow-up activities and projects. In fact, the shared experience of one day at the zoo provides the catalyst for skilled-based learning, creative and critical thinking, and opportunities for real-life problem solving like no other unit I teach. What began as an extension to a science unit on animal classification grew into an interdisciplinary problem solving unit with science, social studies, language arts, art, math, and performing arts strands. Since the zoo trip is an annual event in fifth grade, many students look forward to it for several years.

Unit Overview. Students participate in a three-month-long, interdisciplinary unit of study based on the universal themes of interdependence and social responsibility centered on the world's wildlife. This unit addresses science topics of animal classification, adaptation, and ecosystems. The language arts focus is research and communication. Math skills are used in the fund-raising aspects of the unit. World geography, law, mass media, and social change are social studies concepts. Art activities are interspersed throughout the unit with performing arts showcased in a culminating program for schoolmates and parents.

The focal point of the unit is a day-long class trip to the Minnesota Zoo in Apple Valley, Minnesota. Lead-up activities and projects that students complete prior to the trip provide the basic knowledge necessary to gain the most from the zoo visit. In addition, fund-raising activities are an important part of the lead-up portion of the unit. During the day at the zoo, a series of information-gathering activities are completed, including a small-group photography project. Once back at school, the science, language arts, and art activities are based mainly on information and perceptions the students gained at the zoo. The social studies strand of the unit begins after the trip, since it relies on student options and reactions.

The Minnesota Zoo has an animal adoption program where, for a nominal fee, people may contribute to the care and feeding of a chosen animal on a yearly basis. Information, photographs, and public recognition are provided by the zoo to the adopting "parent(s)." Being involved in this program as a class, encourages student involvement throughout the unit and fosters growth and independence at a very personal level. Each year the students determine which animal the class will adopt. Focusing on a different animal from year to year provides a freshness to the activities and projects even though the instructional objectives stay much the same.

Instructional Objectives. Objectives for several subject matter areas and grade levels can be met throughout this unit. Some examples are listed here.

Science

- Classify animals according to their characteristics.
- Explain and give examples of animal interdependence using the concept of a food chain.
- Identify and give examples of animal adaptations for survival.
- Describe the basic needs of all living things, and give examples of how different species meet those needs.
- Show evidence of similarities and differences among ecosystems.
- Identify factors that would lead to endangered or extinct status for an animal.
- Identify career opportunities to work with animals in various fields of science.

Art

- Explain that art serves various functions and reflects the culture and time period in which it is produced.
- Produce artworks that are original, expressive, decorative, and functional.
- Produce artworks that are modeled after a particular artist or style of art.
- Explain that line, shape. color, and texture are elements of art with expressive potential.

Language Arts

- Demonstrate skill in expository writing.
- Demonstrate skill in narrative writing.
- Demonstrate skill in public speaking.
- Read for information and detail.
- Build vocabulary.

- Exhibit comprehension skills.
- Use appropriate resources, take notes, organize and document sources.
- Use proper mechanics, grammar, usage, and spelling.
- Demonstrate interviewing techniques.
- Read a variety of kinds of literature.

Mathematics

- Illustrate skills associated with adding, subtracting, multiplying, and dividing.
- Illustrate improvement in estimation skills. Identify and/or illustrate descriptive patterns such as increases, decreases, and trends using a graphic representation or a set of data (table, graph).
- Represent problem situations using operations, numbers, and relations (< = >), which may or may not include the unknown.
- Recognize and use patterns to make generalizations.
- Establish subgoals for solving problems.

Social Studies

- Explain how laws are made and changed.
- Identify, explain, and apply economic principles and concepts.
- Provide examples of protest strategies.
- Demonstrate geography skills.
- Explain the role of governments (local, state, federal, international) in the decision-making process.
- Demonstrate map-reading skills.
- Identify individuals and their contributions to society.
- Explain the role of media in the decision-making process.

Resources. *Print* materials include fiction and nonfiction books with wildlife themes, wildlife and science-related magazines, children's newspapers, local and national newspaper articles, science textbooks, and general reference materials. *Audiovisual* materials are available from school, district, and public libraries, Public Broadcasting System (PBS) presentations, filmstrips, videotapes, and art prints.

Human resources include zoo personnel, department of natural resources wildlife managers, Sierra Club members, local naturalists, Audubon Society members, local government officials, wildlife rehabilitation center personnel, biologists, newspaper reporters, art teachers, nature photographers, and media center/library personnel. *Real property resources* are the Minnesota Zoo, the Zoo Mobile (traveling wildlife presentations from the Minnesota Zoo), wildlife rehabilitation centers, and nature reserves.

Activities. A class trip to the zoo that takes place part-way through the unit is the highlight of this three-month unit. Basic knowledge, focus, and directions for the trip itself and plans for specific follow-up are provided. The activities listed as follows are presented in a somewhat chronological manner to show the organization of *lead-up, zoo trip, and follow-up phases* of the unit. Optional grouping strategies are noted in parentheses.

Lead-up activities that meet objectives in several subject areas are carried out during a six-week period prior to the zoo visit. Examples are presented as follows.

Science

- Establish classification rules noting that characteristics must be constant, measurable, described, not named, identified as has or has not rather than two separate descriptions, and each level must include two or more members (grouping: large group, whole class).
- Apply classification rules to completed classification trees and analyze errors (grouping: small group, pair or trio, whole class for reports).
- Create classification characteristics charts for each class of vertebrate and invertebrate; include information on habitat, body parts, adaptations, reproduction–life cycle, food, enemies, warm- or cold-blooded, and examples of members (species) that belong to each class (grouping: independent).
- Classify members of various groups following classification rules; create a classification tree for
    - Right shoes of a class member (grouping: whole class)
    - A set of buttons (grouping: pair or trio)

- A set of school supplies (grouping: independent)
- A self-selected group of objects (grouping: independent or pair or trio)
- A set of known animals; see Figure 4-3 as an example (grouping: independent, for evaluation)

• Given a set of characteristics of an unknown animal, determine which animal class it should be included in; give rationale for the decision (grouping: pair or trio, independent).

• Attach a picture of a different animal to each student's back. The student gathers information about his or her animal by asking characteristic-based yes-or-no questions of classmates. Each student then determines what animal he or she represents (grouping: large group, small group).

Art

• Given information about food, habitat, and enemies, create an imaginary animal whose adaptations would facilitate survival; determine the class of the animal with a species name such as robin for the class bird (grouping: small group, pair or trio, independent).

FIGURE 4–3 Classification Key Activity

Problem: The problem in this activity will be to classify the set of animals listed as follows.

Directions:
1. First, observe and record the data about the animals listed on the following chart by putting a check (✓) under the correct responses.
2. Now complete the classification key by filling in the blanks with the letter that represents the animal with the characteristics indicated.

1. ANIMAL	Has legs (tell how many)	Breathes with lungs	Has a trunk	Can fly	Lays eggs	Has hoofs
Horse = H						
Whale = W						
Goldfish = G						
Penguin = P						
Dog = D						
Robin = R						
Elephant = E						
Snake = S						

Title: (fill in) _____

2. Set of Animals: __H__ __W__ __G__ __P__ __D__ __R__ __E__ __S__

   has legs   does not have legs
   _____ _____ _____ _____ _____ _____ _____ _____

   Has 4 legs   Does not have 4 legs   Breathes   Does not
                                                  with lungs   breathe
                                                                  with lungs
   _____ _____ _____   _____ _____

Has trunk Does not have trunk   Can fly   Does not fly
   _____   _____   _____   _____   Lays   Does not
                                                            eggs   lay eggs
           Has hoofs Does not have hoofs   _____   _____
              _____   _____

- Using the concepts of camouflage and disruptive coloring, make a palm-size drawing of a frog that would be undetected in the classroom; place the frog in its new environment and note how long it is able to remain hidden (grouping: independent).

- Study a variety of professional zoo and natural habitat wildlife photographs; note background, foreground, position of animal (subject), focal point, lighting, and theme (grouping: whole class, small group, pair or trio).

Language Arts

- Dissect a fish using a diagram to identify body parts and adaptations; follow the directions for the dissection carefully (grouping: pair or trio).

- Use appropriate reference material to establish habitat, classification, and geographic locations of little-known animals such as the duck-billed platypus, kiwi, booby, flamingo, Tasmanian devil (grouping: pair or trio, independent).

- Write a letter of commendation to wildlife-friendly government and business representatives and private citizens lauding their specific accomplishments (grouping: small group, pair or trio, independent).

- Keep a journal throughout the unit to record activities, projects, and reactions to the lead-up, zoo trip, and follow-through activities (grouping: independent).

- Write a persuasive letter to parents outlining reasons for the zoo trip, estimated expenses, and extra chores or projects the students are willing to undertake to earn the money needed for the trip; establish a plan for accomplishment of the chores and a date for the payment (grouping: whole-class introduction, independent project).

- Prepare a persuasive speech stating reasons for the zoo trip, student preparation, curriculum correlations, and monies requested; present the speech to the principal and/or a parent organization (grouping: small group, pair or trio, independent).

- Write a business letter to the zoo requesting information on student admission rates, special classes or exhibits available, and animal adoption programs (grouping: small group, pair or trio, independent).

- Using at least three sources, research the soon-to-be-adopted animal; write a multiparagraph expository article about the animal (grouping: independent).

- Write interview questions for the soon-to-be-adopted animal's keeper or zoo volunteer; include animal- and job-related questions (grouping: small group, pair or trio, independent).

Mathematics

- Determine field trip costs, including admission to the zoo, transportation, animal adoption, disposable cameras, and food (grouping: whole class).

- Use an oversized graph updated daily to communicate progress to the class about the amount of monies contributed for the zoo trip through parent organization donations and student contributions (grouping: small group).

- Investigate ways of cutting costs such as buying snacks in bulk prior to the trip; make recommendations to the class (grouping: small group).

Zoo-day activities that students carry out during the one-day field trip to the zoo are described as follows. They involve practice of thinking and problem-solving skills in a variety of subject areas.

Science

- Record information about plant and animal life for each of the six ecosystems re-created at the zoo; note endangered species represented in each area (grouping: independent).

- Record at least one example from each class of vertebrates and invertebrates that you (the student) had never seen or noticed before today (grouping: independent).

- Participate in the following (grouping: whole class):

  - A self-guided walking tour of the six unique zoo areas

  - A guided monorail tour of outlying areas of the zoo

  - An educational bird show

- An interactive session with animals and zoo volunteers in a structured zoo lab situation

Art

- Make detailed sketches (grouping: independent):
  - The animal the class adopted and its environment
  - The coral reef (frame a section with your hands for background; add your choice of animals from the aquarium into the reef exhibit)
  - An animal of your choice; be sure to make notes about color and texture for use in your final drawing
- Photograph three different animals of your choice; pay attention to background, foreground, lighting, focal point, and interest (grouping: three students per disposable camera).

Language Arts

- At the enclosure of the class-adopted animal, independently make notes about the animal and (grouping: independent):
  - its simulated environment
  - its specific appearance details
  - its sound and smell details
  - additional factual information about it from audiovisual resources
  - your personal reactions to it
  - things you (the student) wonder about
- Interview the adopted animal's keeper or zoo volunteer in regard to the animal and his or her job working with it (grouping: small group).
- Give an oral presentation about monies needed for the adopt-an-animal program on behalf of the class (grouping: independent).

Follow-up activities occur after the zoo trip. Several of these in various subject matter areas are described here.

Science

- Using information gathered at the zoo, make a class list of endangered animals; research causes for the endangered status of each animal; and brainstorm possible solutions to the problems (grouping: initially whole class, small group for research, returning to whole class for reports).
- Each student writes the name of his or her "never seen before the zoo trip" animals on cards; other students take turns drawing cards either describing the animal they drew or asking for information from those who can provide it (grouping: small group).

Art

- Add color and detail to sketches made at the zoo for a final product for (grouping: independent):
  - Adopted animal work will become a report cover
  - Coral reef section will be added to classmates' work to create a collage
  - The animal of each student's choice will be framed for display
- Discuss and critique composition and interest of photographs taken at the zoo (grouping: whole class).
- Using notes from zoo areas, create a mural depicting a particular ecosystem (rain forest, ocean, desert, etc.); include food sources, representative plant and animal life, and examples of animal homes (grouping: small group).
- Use a variety of media to portray realistic details of the ecosystem(s) (grouping: small group).
- Study wildlife as the subject of art by different artists using different media and styles (grouping: whole class).
- Using one of the finished sketches from the zoo trip, re-create the scene using a different artistic style (grouping: independent).
- Create a display highlighting the adopted animal; include the adoption certificate, photographs and captions, narrative and expository writing samples, and artwork (grouping: small group).

Language Arts

- Write follow-up thank you letters to the principal, parent organization, and parents; communicate the value of the zoo trip, and show appreciation for funding (grouping: whole class, small group).

- Using notes from the zoo trip, write a reaction paper focused on the adopted animal; this narrative piece should be personal in nature (grouping: independent).

- Compile a class list of "I wonder about" questions from reaction notes taken at the adopted animal's enclosure; divide the list by resource or topic; assign groups to research each set of questions and report back to the class (grouping: whole class, small group, whole class).

- Continue writing daily journal entries to focus on follow-up activities and projects (grouping: independent).

- Using photographs taken at the zoo, write two sets of captions for each photograph; one set should be informational as if writing for a magazine article; the other set should be humorous as if writing for entertainment (grouping: small group).

- Create a bibliography of animal-related folk tales; become proficient at reading or telling a story; share it with a primary-grade class (grouping: small group, pair or trio, independent).

- After reading a variety of Rudyard Kipling's "Just So" stories, model his style to write an animal "Just So" story of your own (the student's) choice; share it orally with the class (grouping: independent, whole class).

- After researching how Native Americans used animal totems to represent personal qualities and aspirations, choose an animal totem for yourself and describe its meaning for you (grouping: independent).

- With a group of interested readers, read and discuss biographies of wildlife researchers or enthusiasts (grouping: small group).

- Collect wildlife poetry; memorize at least one example for an oral presentation (grouping: small group, pair or trio, independent).

- Write a job description for an animal keeper of the adopted animal; create a job advertisement for that position (grouping: whole class, small group).

- Model Lewis and Clark as they explored the Louisiana Territory and write descriptions of animals they found en route; draw or find magazine pictures of the animals to include in your report to the U.S. government (grouping: small group, pair or trio).

Mathematics

- Calculate monthly food costs for the adopted animal using information from the zookeeper; determine factors that could cause that figure to fluctuate from month to month (grouping: whole class, small group, pair or trio).

- Estimate zoo costs for next year's class; create a proposed budget for use in securing funds for next year (grouping: small group, pair or trio).

Social Studies

- Read and discuss *The Lorax* by Dr. Seuss in regard to interdependence and social responsibility (grouping: whole class).

- Research local, state, federal, and international laws that attempt to manage wildlife; include hunting regulations, requirements for zoos and reserves, the establishment of rehabilitation centers, and exotic animals as pets (grouping: whole class).

- Identify protest strategies (such as letter writing campaign, boycott, public awareness) that are often used to benefit wildlife (grouping: whole class).

- Identify situations where protest strategies have been successful and unsuccessful; identify reasons for successes or failures (grouping: small group).

- Plan arguments and participate in debates for and against issues such as (grouping: whole class, small group):

    - "Cute" versus "ugly" animal protection

    - Economics of rain forest destruction or preservation

    - Zoo protection of endangered species

    - Keeping wild animals in captivity

    - Use of furs, feathers, and skins in fashion industry

    - Hunting and fishing regulations

- After collecting newspaper and magazine articles that focus on wildlife issues, analyze pro and con articles for fact and opinion; take a grade-level or school-wide poll to determine local sentiment on the issues; post the results as a brief summary with a graph to visually verify the description (grouping: whole class, small group, pair or trio).

- Simulate a town meeting to determine use for a large area of newly acquired government waterfront property; participants (grouping: whole class, small group) may include:

Hikers	Resort owners
Gun hunters	Cross-country skiers
Bicyclists	ATV riders
Sailboaters	Water skiers
Service-related business owners	Environmental club members
Bow hunters	Loggers
Bird watchers	Canoeists

- Determine ways to add to the economic base of rain forest areas without deforestation; investigate iguana farming, florist industry, and tourism; create a brochure highlighting your best ideas (grouping: small group, pair or trio).

Performing Arts

- Participate in a "wild things" production for schoolmates and/or parents; areas of involvement may include (grouping: independent, small group, whole class):

  - Creating sets or securing costumes and props for skits or storytelling
  - Designing a program cover for the event
  - Writing and laying out the program copy
  - Reciting wildlife poetry, narrative, or expository pieces
  - Acting in skits
  - Singing in choir
  - Narrating and introducing responsibilities

Authentic Products. Products and activities are closely linked, and many products for students to produce are described in the preceding activities section. The uniqueness of many of these activities is their medium- to long-term opportunities and a two- or more-stage process that is inherent in many of them. One three-stage example is (1) study professional zoo and nature photography, (2) plan and take one's own photographs, and (3) write factual and humorous captions for the photographs to be included in a display. Another example with five stages is (1) provide a rationale for funding, (2) determine a budget, (3) procure and acknowledge funds from a variety of sources, (4) communicate fund-raising efforts, and (5) evaluate the feasibility of the budget in order to project next year's costs.

Written and oral communication products focus on different types of writing and different types of audiences. Oral presentations to a variety of audiences—classmates, primary-grade students, administrators, parents, and community members—are interspersed throughout the unit. Diverse types of writing are required by projects. Some examples are journal entries, descriptions, captions, bibliographies, brochures, expository reports, reaction papers, interview questions, advertisements, letters, and creative descriptions. Communication products include gathering information, modeling formats, writing and revising written materials, and presenting a final product to an identified audience.

Learning Environments. Most activities for this unit took place within the school building. A one-day trip to the zoo provided the focal point for organizing the unit. During the lead-up, information-gathering part of the unit and again in the follow-up and action–response parts, resource people came to the school to share their insights and expertise.

Thinking Skills and Problem Solving. The activities and products students made in this unit provided opportunities for solving multistep problems and practicing a wide range of thinking skills. Inquiry processes of observing and classifying were the basis for many of the science-related activities. Measuring and interpreting data were the focus skills of the math activities. Language arts activities centered around communicating. Inferring and predicting were most apparent in social studies. Critical thinking skills of fact and opinion, cause and effect, point of view, analyzing arguments, and deductive and inductive reasoning were emphasized in role playing and debate in social studies. Creative thinking was encouraged throughout the unit in art activities, captions, brochures, storytelling, and creating never-seen-before animals.

Instructional Groups. Grouping strategies for this unit were determined according to the nature of the activities and products. In the activities section, grouping options for each activity were listed at the end of the description. A basic knowledge activity may involve all the sections of an entire grade level in large group instruction or all the students in a class for an initial presentation. Small groups or pair or trio groups may be used for specific information-gathering, discussion, or problem-solving projects, which are then communicated back to the larger group. Or a student with high interest or ability in a specific activity may be challenged to pursue it independently.

Timeline and Budget. The basic timeline for this three-month unit is outlined in the lead-up, at the zoo, and follow-up activities. Lead-up, information-gathering activities were carried out during the first six weeks. This was followed by the one-day field trip experience from 8 A.M. to 5 P.M. This included about three hours of travel time. The remaining six hours at the zoo were divided among self-guided walking tours of the six unique zoo areas, a 45-minute monorail tour of outlying areas, a 30-minute educational bird show, and a 30-minute reserved lab time for individual students to interact with animals and volunteers. The second six-week period was spent on follow-up activities. Here, students used the information they gained at the zoo as well as their knowledge base from lead-up activities. A social studies strand to explore social responsibility and public opinion added a new dimension to the ongoing unit. Plans and preparations for a wildlife theme program for parents and schoolmates provided a show case for the final products and a culmination to the unit.

Budgeting was an issue in this unit. Transportation, zoo admissions, animal adoption fee, and disposable camera costs needed to be considered. While budgeting and securing funds is usually a teacher role, this unit was unique because the students took much of this responsibility. Being involved in establishing a budget, soliciting and acknowledging monies, evaluating this year's trip, and planning for next year's trip provided real-life application of skills for the students. Personal involvement in goal setting and attainment of goals was a lesson in itself. I sensed more appreciation among the students for the opportunity to go on this class trip than any others we take. I believe the level of student participation and sense of purpose established in this unit gave students a sense of pride in their accomplishments.

Assessment. Since this unit had strong subject matter area strands, assessment for the most part was done concurrently within each area. Objective and essay tests were used to determine satisfaction of science objectives. Composition projects in language arts were evaluated separately using criteria-based product assessment forms. A sample of such a form for a business letter was shown in Figure 4-1. Oral presentations and art-related products were assessed using objective-based, criterion-referenced checklists. Since the unit encompassed an entire grading period in some subject matter areas, it was imperative to pursue a deliberate, ongoing system of assessment.

Assessment of the unit itself and its impact on students was accomplished through home–school communications. Each objective or essay test and project assessment was sent home for parent perusal and returned to school after being signed by a parent. At the end of the unit, a list of activities and project grades were sent home to provide a broader perspective. Students and parents made comments about challenge, insights, and opinions of particular activities as well as the whole unit. These comments helped me assess the unit and improve for it for future years.

I feel very positive about this unit. Its success is due to its appealing subject matter linked to action-oriented, curriculum-based activities and products. The three-phase structure of the unit is novel to most students who have little previous experience with setting and attaining long-term goals. The idea of writing to communicate and solve problems is also a new experience for many students. Although composition and oral presentation skills are often thought of as drudgery, I find the practice of carrying them out in a variety of styles and forms in response to real situations is well received by the students and produces excellent results. As a teacher, it is satisfying to watch students' sense of adventure, responsibility, and independence grow in tandem with their knowledge and problem-solving abilities.

COMMUNICATING WITH PEOPLE

Effective communication is a basic human goal. Whether it is between friends or family members, consumers and producers, or world leaders, giving and receiving information is a necessity. Good communicators are well aware of their purpose, choose their audience accordingly, and tailor their format and delivery to match. Becoming an effective communicator involves understanding and practicing the process in a variety of situations. The language arts-based units discussed in this section provide opportunities for students to become good communicators.

The topics presented here are advertising and written communication through letter writing. "And Now a Word from Your Sponsor..." suggests activities for students to analyze and create print and nonprint advertisements. "Sincerely Yours" asks students to apply types and purposes of letter writing to real-life situations. In both these units, students experience being both the giver and receiver of information.

"And Now a Word from Your Sponsor..."

Everywhere we turn we are bombarded with advertisements for goods and services of every kind. From television screens to cereal boxes, billboards to newspaper inserts, the message is the same: "Try it—Buy it!" The preteen and young teen population is frequently targeted by advertising campaigns. Intermediate-age students often experience managing their own money for the first time. Thus, focusing on the techniques used in advertising not only provides students with thinking and problem solving experiences, but also timely and beneficial information for their growing sense of responsibility and independence. Being able to make informed consumer choices is a lifelong skill that is best learned early.

Analyzing existing ads for technique, format, and creativity and using those ads as models for students to make their own original ads raises awareness and provides practice in the art of persuasion through advertising. These strategies may be used to support eating school lunch, entice a classmate to read a book, or to publicize a community event. The emergent consumer is an eager student. Consumer products and ad campaigns are ever-changing to provide up-to-date, readily available, and inexpensive resources. This unit is always well received by both students and their parents.

Unit Overview. Students explore print and nonprint advertising and its influence on consumers. This language arts-centered unit relies on critical thinking, careful reading, and listening with an emphasis on written and oral communication. The subject areas of social studies and art are highlighted with a lesser emphasis on economics and graphic arts. Knowledge is gained by studying examples of print and nonprint advertising and talking with representatives of the advertising business community.

Students apply their knowledge of advertising techniques by developing their own school- and community-oriented advertising campaigns. Participating in an area-wide "Design an Ad" contest and creating a school service project provides focus and incentive to the unit. The length of the unit is determined by the number of projects that individuals or small groups undertake. However, by selecting representative activities and projects, the unit may be completed over a four-week period during a regularly scheduled language arts time block.

Resources. One of the pluses of this unit is the multitude of readily available, free, or inexpensive resources. Magazines, newspapers, and advertising inserts are delivered to our doors. Telephone book "yellow pages" provide many business and service ad examples. A collection of expired posters for theater, musical, or other community events are real-life examples of layout, content, and design. Radio and television commercials may be taped for classroom use. Each year, awards are given within the advertising industry. A copy of the award-winning commercials of the year may be available through local, nationally affiliated television stations or public libraries. Students can supply empty packages from a variety of products. Transparencies can be made of particular ads to use with the whole class to illustrate specific graphic or persuasion techniques. An abundance of materials at school is of special benefit to students who do not have access to print resources at home.

Representatives of consumer research businesses, product or company representatives, ad salespersons, and producers of television, radio, and print ads are excellent people to invite into the classroom as resource persons. They are able to discuss the financial and creative aspects of advertising. Since their business is communication, they are usually able to provide a wealth of firsthand knowledge at the intermediate student's level. After this initial classroom experience, a trip to a newspaper office or television or radio station may be beneficial. With so much to become involved in at any site, keeping the focus on the advertising aspect of the business is crucial. Using a site for a specific purpose allows for repeat visits to highlight other aspects of the business at a later time.

Objectives, Activities, Products, and Assessment. Because of the nature of the advertising unit, these four elements of the successful teaching format have been combined for discussion and teacher implementation purposes. Five general advertising topics form the headings for this discussion. They are (1) persuasion strategies; (2) brand names, trademarks, slogans, and logos; (3) investigating print and nonprint advertisements; (4) analyzing advertisements; and (5) applying advertising techniques. For each topic, objectives and activities for all students along with some extensions to meet student needs and interests are presented. Curriculum products for students to develop and ways to assess them are also discussed.

Persuasion Strategies

Objectives

- Identify and categorize advertisements by the persuasion strategy used.
- Write an explanation of the strategy in paragraph form.
- (Extension) Prepare and present an oral explanation of the strategy.

Activities

- Participate in a whole-class discussion using print advertisements as examples of the following persuasion strategies:
  - Bandwagon approach—everybody's doing it
  - Emotional appeal
  - Endorsement or testimonial approach
  - Beautiful people approach; sex appeal
  - Snob appeal
  - "Good life" approach
  - Incentives—rebates, coupons, related merchandise
- With a partner or as a member of a trio, find examples of each persuasion strategy in magazines. For each example, write a paragraph explaining how it is representative of the strategy. Create a cover for your writing and organize your information in booklet form.
- (Extension) With a partner, as a member of a trio, or independently, view taped television commercials to identify examples of each persuasion strategy. Prepare an oral explanation of how each ad represents its category. Present your findings orally to the class.

The *product* from these activities is a booklet made up of a cover, examples of advertisements, and explanations in paragraph form from each pair or trio in the class. The booklet is *assessed* for accurate categorization of strategies, paragraph structure, mechanics, explanation details, neatness, and creativity.

Brand Names, Trademarks, Slogans, and Logos

Objectives

- Demonstrate an awareness of the importance of brand name, trademark, slogan, and logo to advertising a product or service.
- Write precise, easy-to-follow directions.
- Write a humorous story.
- Give an oral presentation; be aware of content, organization, voice, volume, eye contact, and style.
- Create a business card using an appropriate format.

Activities

- As a part of a small group, collect examples of slogans for the product, service, or company addressed. Devise a game where the object is to match a slogan with its product, service, or company. Create game pieces, written directions, game name, and packaging. Share the game with classmates.

The *product* is a slogan-matching game. It will be *assessed* for accuracy of information, creativity of name and packaging, neatness, and easy-to-follow and accurate directions.

- With a partner or as a member of a trio, choose one product (for example candy bars, cereal, bath soap). Brainstorm and list all the brand names you can think of or find that represent that product. (*Tip:* A walk down the aisle of a supermarket provides a wealth of information.) Create a humorous story using as many brand names as you can. In the final copy, write each brand name in bold, colored letters. Be sure the story has a title, a beginning, middle, and end. Present the story orally to the class or videotape it for later viewing.

The *product* is the humorous story created by using many brand names to describe one type of product. It will be *assessed* for basic story structure, creative use of brand names, grammar, usage, writing mechanics, and neatness. The assessment of the oral presentation of the story will be based on voice, volume, eye contact, and style.

- As a class member, collect business cards from family members, neighbors, and other sources. As a member of a small group, analyze the cards to determine what information is generally included on business cards. Graphic design, logo, trademark, and slogan should also be noted. Each student chooses one (required) or more (extension) business card project option(s) to be completed independently from the following list:
    - Create a business card for yourself and a job you now hold (such as dog walker, dish washer, garbage carry-outer).
    - Create a business card for yourself and a job you may hold in the future.
    - Create a business card for a historical figure.
    - Create a business card for a fictional character (such as Johnny Appleseed, The Big Bad Wolf, a book hero).
    - Create a new business card for the family member or neighbor whose business card you asked for and brought to school.

The *product* is a business card with real or imaginary information. It will be *assessed* for format, appropriate information, graphic design, neatness, and creativity.

Investigating Print and Nonprint Advertisements

Objectives

- Identify the target audience for print and nonprint ads.
- Be aware of the frequency of print and nonprint ads.
- Be aware of the multitude of goods and services communicated to consumers through advertising.
- Read TV schedules to plan television viewing.
- Devise a chart, and accurately record a variety of information.
- Use data to draw conclusions, establish guidelines, and make predictions.
- Use the telephone directory "yellow pages" to locate specific information.

Activities

- As a member of a small group, use a TV scheduling guide to assign each group member a half-hour of television-viewing time during a one-week period. Assigned viewing times should include programs of the following types: news, sports, prime-time drama, prime-time comedy, and animations or cartoons. Devise a chart to keep track of the number of commercials, advertisements, brand names, and the target audience for each type of program. Each member of the small group can use a chart to record information during the assigned program. At the end of the one-week period, group members share the recorded information to draw conclusions about correlations among advertising approach, target audience, product, and programming.
- From the information on the chart, determine what products would be best marketed during what types of programs.

The *products* here are (1) a chart including areas for recording brand name, target audience, a tally of commercials aired during half-hour time slots from a variety of programming categories; (2) a list of general guidelines that match product, audience, and program type; and (3) a listing of appropriate products that were best marketed under each type of program. The charts will be *assessed* for organization, clarity, and neatness. The list of guidelines should be based on information gathered. The products listings should show evidence of application of knowledge about advertising.

- As a member of a small group, each member should be assigned a magazine targeting a particular audience. Sports, fashion, nature, homemaking, gardening, music, and dogs or other pets are examples of publication topics. Devise a chart, develop guidelines, and determine a product list as described in the preceding activity, based on the print ads found in the magazines.

Products and *assessment* are the same as in the preceding activity.

- With a partner or as a member of a trio, participate in a class scavenger hunt. Given a list of goods and services, find a newspaper ad that satisfies that want or need. The first team able to find an ad for each listing or the most listings in a given time period is the winner. (*Note:* This activity may also be carried out using the yellow pages of the phone book and recording business names rather than cutting out ad examples.)

The *product* is the selected ad or business examples. *Assessment* uses a teacher-created, multiple-choice format with standard ad or yellow page examples. Students determine which ad gives the required information.

- Within the class, conduct a survey to determine the "best ad of the week." The ads chosen would be part of a "best ad of the month" contest.

- (Extension) Vary the audience for the weekly and final contests. Survey school staff, parents, primary-grade students, or preschoolers instead of classmates. Compare the results among the groups.

The *product* is an oral or written report of survey results. *Assessment* will be based on accurate collection and organization of data and communication of results.

Analyzing Advertisements

Objectives

- Use critical thinking skills to recognize and analyze the following:
  - Fact and opinion
  - Relevant and irrelevant information
  - Reliable and unreliable sources
  - Assumptions and generalizations
  - Point of view
  - Bias and stereotype
  - Missing information

- Participate in an oral discussion and be able to cite examples as well as voice opinions on a given topic.

- Write a position paper stating personal opinions about a topic, based on evidence.

Activities

- With a partner, as a member of a trio, or independently use print materials to find ads that rely on statements from "seemingly" reliable resources to sell the product or service. Determine what constitutes a reliable source and explain how using such a source is a positive selling technique. Discuss your ideas with the class.

The *product* is oral discussion and *assessment* will be based on participation, citing appropriate examples, and stating personal opinions.

- React to the following statement: "Many people believe that the tobacco industry uses advertising to woo young people into using its products." Do independent research of print materials to find evidence to substantiate or disprove this statement. Write a position paper stating your opinion based on your findings.

The *product* is a position paper stating personal opinions. The paper is *assessed* for paragraph structure, evidence for findings, grammar, usage, mechanics, and neatness.

- React to the idea that "advertising focuses on the positive aspects of a product." However, many products (such as alcohol, tobacco, high-fat food) have negative aspects as well. Find an ad for this type of product. Divide your paper in half lengthwise and head the columns "Stated" and "Not Stated." Now analyze the ad, listing the information in each column. Draw conclusions about why certain information is in the ad and why some is left out. Share your ideas in a small group or whole class discussion.

Here the *product* is oral discussion. *Assessment* is based on participation, citing appropriate examples, and drawing conclusions based on data and logical reasoning.

- Study examples of the type of ad where product endorsements are done by well-known public figures. Look for evidence of bias, stereotyping, or image building in the company's choice of a spokesperson. Create a list of goods, services, and companies that are paired with public figures you feel would be appropriate spokespeople.

- (Extension) Discuss how image building, stereotyping, and bias play a part in the choice of cover models, clothes models, and actors and actresses for TV, print, and radio commercials.

- (Extension) Discuss how a goods, service, or company spokesperson can lose his or her job if his or her personal life fails to uphold the image the company pays them to portray. Cite examples. Share personal opinions about this practice.

The *product* is a list of possible spokespeople for goods, services, or companies. *Assessment* will be based on appropriateness of choices.

Applying Advertising Techniques

Objectives

- Recognize graphics arts components of advertisements.
- Produce artworks that are original, expressive, decorative, and functional.
- Apply persuasion strategies, graphic arts components, and language skills to produce original ads such as
    - Testimonials (for example, taste tests, soap, personal products, other)
    - Local business ads (such as newspapers, supermarkets, ice cream shops)
    - Audiovisual infomercials
    - Brochures
    - Real estate ads
    - Classified ads
    - Posters
    - Public service announcements

Activities

1. With a partner, as a part of a trio, or independently, use print ads to find a variety of examples for graphic arts components such as lettering, color, border, use of white space, and logo. Meet with another small group or individual to discuss effective designs. Write a list of design and layout guidelines to share in a whole class discussion.

The *product* is a list of design and layout guidelines. *Assessment* will be based on participation, citing of appropriate examples, and stating personal opinions.

2. With a small group, plan, conduct, and analyze the results of a taste test between two brands of identical products. Solicit consumer testimonials during the test. Produce an audiovisual commercial and a print ad based on the taste test results.

3. (Extension) Using the testimonial strategy, create an audiovisual and/or print ad to encourage classmates to read a particular book.

Products from these activities include (1) a descriptive paragraph to outline details of the taste test plan, (2) an audiovideo commercial with "live" testimonials, and (3) a print ad with a quoted testimonial. *Assessment* takes several different forms. The descriptive paragraph is assessed for structure, detail, mechanics, grammar, usage, and neatness. The audiovisual commercial assessment will focus on oral presentation "salesmanship," creativity, and effective and appropriate use of the testimonial strategy. The print ad will be assessed for format, appropriate information, graphic design, effective use of the testimonial strategy, neatness, and creativity.

4. Participate in a "Design an Ad" contest by creating an original newspaper ad for a local business.

The *product* is a final copy of the original newspaper ad as requested by a local business. In class, *assessment* will be based on application of persuasion strategies, graphic arts components, language skills, neatness, and creativity. Each local business involved will assess its own entries and award the winner a cash prize. The local newspaper will print the winning ads in a special supplement to recognize each student and his or her work.

5. As a part of a small group, produce an audiovideo infomercial highlighting one of the following curriculum aspects of the school:

   - Math activities, kindergarten through grade 5
   - Computer use
   - Experimentation in science
   - The writing process
   - Physical education activities
   - Music activities
   - Art activities

6. As a part of a small group, produce an audiovideo infomercial highlighting school personnel and services provided and an audio infomercial focusing on student and parent testimonials about the school, its people, and programs.

7. (Extension) Produce a brochure that deals with the same information as the video for distribution to parents and students new to the school or to acquaint members of the community with the school.

The required *product* is a video-recorded infomercial highlighting aspects of school life. It can be used as a public relations tool with new students, kindergartners, parents, and other groups. *Assessment* will be based on accuracy of information, organization of material, oral presentation skills, and creativity.

8. As a part of a small group, study examples of travel brochures noting content, layout, use of color, lettering, and language. Determine places of interest within a two-hour drive from home. Create a travel brochure for one or more of those places for a class display.

9. (Extension) Provide a copy of the travel brochure in pen and ink or from a computer printout to be easily copied for students to take home to share with parents in planning family outings.

The *product* is a travel brochure for a local attraction. *Assessment* will be based on format, organization, accuracy of information, neatness, and creativity.

10. As a part of a small group, study examples of real estate ads noting content, layout, use of abbreviations, language, and format. Individually, model the writing style and format of the real estate ad to create an original real estate ad for two or more of the following:

    - Your home
    - A "dream" home
    - A "fixer-upper" home
    - An oceanside, riverside, or lakeside home
    - A vacation home
    - A "haunted" house
    - A country home
    - A home located in a metropolitan area

11. (Extension) Using the same procedures as described in the preceding activity for the real estate ad, create an ad or ads for selling a car, truck, or van.

12. (Extension) Put the homes "on the market" by including them in a class display. Have classmates "buy" the house that most appeals to them. Display a "sold" sign with the home ads that are "bought."

The *product* is two or more real estate ads highlighting two different categories of housing. *Assessment* will be based on the format, appropriate detail, neatness, and creativity of the ad(s).

13. As a member of a team, participate in a scavenger hunt using newspaper classified ads as the only resource. Scavenger hunt items may require a particular item, brand name, price range, color, size, or similar detail. The team able to find an ad for each item or the most items in a given time period is the winner.

The *products* are specific ads from the classified ad section of the newspaper. *Assessment* will be based on meeting the requirements of specific information stated in the ad that satisfies the scavenger hunt item listing.

14. As a part of a small group, read newspaper classified ads to determine format, content, and style. Write an original classified ad for two or more of the following:

    - Help wanted (tutoring to learn long division, pet care while on vacation, sports coaching, etc.)
    - Work wanted (tutoring, dog walking, lawn mowing, babysitting)
    - Miscellaneous merchandise (used sports equipment, books, toys, furniture)

15. Individually or as a part of a small group, write two or more ads that represent real types of goods or services that the ad writer is able and willing to provide. Display the ads by category allowing classmates to purchase the advertised goods or services (with parental permission).

The *product* will be two or more classified ads representing different categories. *Assessment* will be based on ad format, appropriate detail, neatness, and creativity.

16. View a variety of public service announcements (PSAs) with the class. Determine PSA topics that would be appropriate and beneficial to the school. As a part of a small group, write and produce a print (poster), audio (intercom or cassette tape), and audiovisual (videotape or live) public service announcement. Each type of ad should convey one aspect of the overall message. Present the PSA campaign to schoolmates. Topics may include

- Returning library books on time
- Reading every day
- Lost-and-found items
- Healthy habits
- Safety reminders (bus, bike, crossing streets and roads, etc.)
- School rules
- School pride
- Teacher–staff appreciation
- Support for school lunch

17. (Extension) Individually or as a part of a small group, check out the possibilities of upcoming contests at local radio and television stations for student-generated public service announcements. Enter the contest and prepare such a PSA.

18. (Extension) Enter a local, national, or international poster contest using the format for PSA posters. Work individually or as part of a small group according to the requirements of the contest. Choose a topic that appeals.

The *product* is a public service campaign that includes posters, audio commercials, and live or taped audiovisual commercials. *Assessment* of the poster will be based on content, graphics, neatness, and creativity. The audio and audiovisual ads will be evaluated on content, presentation, and creativity.

Learning Environments. While most of the activities for this unit take place in the school building, the topics and resources provide the students a far-reaching view of society through local and national advertising. The focus of activities included peers, adults, younger students, older students, parents, and community. Business people provided another dimension to the unit as class speakers. Class trips to view advertising businesses in action also took students beyond the classroom.

Thinking Skills and Problem Solving. The activities and products in this unit gave students a variety of chances to practice thinking skills and to solve realistic, multistep problems. Instead of the teacher stating specific guidelines, formats, strategies, graphic designs, and language skills for each aspect of advertising, students in small groups were asked to analyze and synthesize examples and information for themselves. Application of knowledge resulted in real-life products created by small groups or individuals. This emphasis on independence fostered student creativity. Advertising is a highly creative and competitive field that relies heavily on originality. Here, students were able to experience this through the variety of products they produced such as posters, real estate ads, testimonial ads, classified ads, infomercials, audio ads, audiovisual ads, brochures, and public service announcements.

Instructional Groups. Small groups were used most often in this unit. They allowed for constant and focused interaction to ensure active participation by all students. The multifaceted nature of creating ads gave group members a chance to do specific tasks that met their interests and abilities. While one member focused on graphics and layout for a particular ad, another could plan and produce the art work. A language-talented member could write the script while another could "star" in the commercial. Since many ads were produced throughout the unit, students were able to "try on" and "try out" different roles in the creative process. The target audience—classmates, schoolmates, parents, and community members—changed with the focus of the ad and the products the students made.

Timeline and Budget. The objectives of this unit may be met through activities and projects over a four to five week, 20 to 25 hour-period. Since most activities are language arts-based, a daily scheduled language arts block of time works well. Time for interaction accounts for a large part of each activity period. While group members may continue a project or discussion during free time or study hall, class interaction time is crucial to carry out activities successfully and develop quality products.

The subject matter lends itself well to any part of the school year. Once language skills, graphic arts components, ad strategies, layouts, and format are mastered, students are ready to apply them. Many poster contests seem to be offered in the spring and the local newspaper "Design an Ad" contest is traditionally published in March. Public service announcement campaigns may be launched during any and all months of the year. In the Midwest, where the winter months tend to keep students "school bound," I have found doing this unit then provides an active change of pace to the daily school routine. It is also much easier to invite speakers into the classroom than to go on field trips when the weather and road conditions are unpredictable.

Budget is not a major factor in this unit. Examples of a variety of print advertisements are readily available at little or no cost, and all students have access to radio and television at home as well as at school. Resource people volunteer their time and expertise. Field trips to the newspaper office and radio and TV stations require only the cost of transportation, which is minimal.

Assessment. Throughout the discussion of the unit, assessment suggestions are made for most activities. Although a few whole-class activities do not include an immediate assessment of knowledge or skill, transfer and application of that knowledge or skill will be apparent in subsequent activities and projects. Assessment usually takes place at the product stage rather than at the foundation-building stage. A variety of products that are based on advertising format such as brochures, posters, business ads, and PSAs are included in the unit and are assessed by format criteria as well as graphic and language components.

Participation in small-group work and whole-class discussions is also assessed. Parents are provided with copies of each major product and an assessment criteria sheet with earned points, comments, and grades. Informal assessment of some ad products was accomplished through ad displays and peer evaluation. Students who entered poster contests and the newspaper "Design an Ad" contest faced real-world assessment in the wider marketplace. During this unit, it was interesting to note that the students' peak awareness level occurred in regard to advertising in their daily lives. Here, they developed a more questioning view of print and nonprint advertising and showed evidence of critical thinking about persuasion techniques used in advertising. I believe the result was more informed and cautious young customers.

The focused small-group work and real-world application of knowledge and skills are components that lead to student success. This unit provides opportunities for each student to find his or her niche based on skill, personality, or interest. Reading, writing, art products, and performance are just some of the areas where a student can shine.

A team spirit prevails when students in a small group must define and delegate smaller tasks to accomplish the larger task of making a product. Working in a group also provides variety from working alone. In this unit, very few of the activities involved teacher direction. Instead, I presented a basic idea or technique and then allowed the students to follow through while I monitored their progress. It is often hard for me as a teacher to allow my students the freedom to arrive at their own conclusions, establish their own guidelines, and proceed as they see fit. But it is necessary to provide such an atmosphere if they are to grow in the art of thinking and problem solving.

"Sincerely Yours"

My preschool daughter remarked about her unwillingness to speak to her beloved grandmother via long distance on the telephone, "If I hear her but can't keep her, I'll be even more lonely for her!" In most situations the fleetingness of oral communication is unavoidable. In contrast, written communication provides a lasting record that can be reread to check detail, prove a point, or re-experience a pleasant idea. While many of us have bunches of cards and letters tied up in ribbon and stored in some private place, I have yet to find anyone with a series of phone bills preserved in the same manner.

The sense of caring conveyed by a written thank you or congratulatory note is well worth the time and effort it took to write it. Personal opinions and even complaints speak louder when written and shared with appropriate audiences. Letters of inquiry, introduction, and recommendation may open doors to opportunity. Even writing clear, concise memos and accurately recording homework assignments are everyday applications of writing skills. Since the telephone is by far the communication device of choice for intermediate-grade students, establishing purpose and motivation for a written communication unit is a challenge. The key, I found, is to provide variety, flexibility, and real-life applications. Once a student receives a reply as a result of a written communication, he or she is usually anxious to repeat the experience.

Unit Overview. In this language arts unit, students practice written communication skills using letters as the vehicle. The focus and format of each project varies with the purpose of the communication and its audience. The subject areas of reading and social studies along with personal interests and needs provide topics for student writing. Writing projects will be based on real-life applications. Eleven kinds of letters—complaint, persuasion or permission, opinion, commendation, advice, inquiry, introduction, recommendation, friendly letter, postcard, and memo—will be addressed. Language usage, grammar, mechanics, and punctuation will be stressed, since most writing projects will be sent to appropriate audiences in anticipation of a response.

By using a typical language arts time block, this unit may be completed in a four- to five-week period. This is based on presenting two types of letters per week. While some finished letters have been sent and await replies, others will be in the rough draft stage. Students will keep two portfolios—a showcase portfolio for letters and their replies, and a working portfolio for letters in progress. Assessment will be based on student skill, effort, and achievement.

Instructional Objectives. Some examples of language arts objectives for written communications that can be met throughout this unit are

- Apply usage, grammar, mechanics, punctuation, and spelling rules and to written communication.

- Identify and use a variety of types of written communications.

- Identify purpose and audience for a given writing project in order to focus on ideas and decide on an appropriate format.

Resources. Print, human, and real property resources are applicable to this unit. *Print* materials include a variety of reference materials such as a telephone business directory, a zip code book, and an atlas. Examples of letters to the editor and advice columns from newspapers provide format models for the student letters. *Human resources* include postal workers, public relations personnel, other students and their teachers, and other recipients of students' written communications. *Real property resources* related to information gathering from public and university libraries, museums, and other specific locations may be used according to the topics students choose. Consumable materials include two folders of two different colors for each student. Writing paper, envelopes, and postage are also required.

Activities. There are a large number of varied activities in this unit. Instruction is centered on a particular type of written communication, and projects are completed independently with a specific purpose and audience. A student's showcase portfolio will consist of at least eleven final products that represent a variety of communication projects. These types of written communications form the topics for this discussion.

Letter of Complaint

Although my experience has been that children have an innate ability for complaining, few are skilled in the process of registering a formal complaint with the expectation of satisfaction. A warm-up or prewriting activity before writing a formal complaint sets the stage and provides ideas to the students for their final project. One warm-up is to ask students to brainstorm possible endings to the statement: "Don't you just hate it when . . . ." Individual lists may be shared with small groups or the entire class to give each student a multitude of possibilities for his or her project. These lists may also be used to create individual posters for display.

The next step is to categorize these responses according to "those that could possibly be changed" and "those where change is not realistic." Diversifying the school hot lunch menu or revising a student's bedtime are examples of responses that fit the first category. Banning homework or prohibiting the President from speaking to the nation during prime television-viewing time would represent the latter category. Using the list of complaints with potential for change, students can brainstorm prospective audiences to receive their letters.

With the motivation, purpose, and audience designated, the need for an appropriate format is clear. Guidelines for writing a formal letter of complaint are established by the class. They include (1) follow a business letter style; (2) describe the specific problem of the complaint; (3) use polite, formal language; (4) state a request for satisfaction that includes a deadline; (5) outline a plan for a next-step communication if necessary; and (6) convey appreciation for consideration of the matter. Each student identifies one complaint for change from the list as the focus of his or her final project.

Once the final project is completed, it is mailed to the selected audience. A copy of the letter is kept in the student's working portfolio. If a response is received, it is shared with the class and kept in the student's showcase portfolio along with a copy of the letter of complaint. Assessment is based on the guidelines established for writing a letter of complaint and proper use of language skills.

Throughout the school year, further practice at writing a letter of complaint may be gained by reading- or social studies-related assignments. Fictional or historical characters and their problems could generate formal complaints. When students write from others' points of view, they also practice critical and creative thinking.

Letter of Persuasion or Permission

This type of letter is closely related to a letter of complaint. It follows the same general writing guidelines, but topics tend to be more personal in nature. Some examples include

- Request to a parent to attend or host a sleepover.
- Written argument for a raise in allowance.
- Appeal to a school bus driver to plan an ice cream stop on the way home from school.
- Written explanation to family members to knock before entering your room, handle your video games in a particular way, or stay out of your collection.
- Appeal to your teacher for no homework assignment over a weekend or holiday.
- Written chore plan with the purpose of raising money for a class trip or project.
- Written explanation about why a teacher should reconsider a grade on an essay or other subjective project.
- Formal request for permission to go on a class trip; this may be directed to a parent and/or a teacher.
- Appeal to students to join a club, team, or other extracurricular activity.
- Appeal to a business to carry a particular brand of merchandise.
- Request to Santa, including gift ideas and reasons why they should be given; this can also be written from another person's point of view such as from a grandfather, the principal, an art teacher, a 3-year-old, and so on.

Letter of Opinion

Because of the emotional aspect of personal opinion, topics chosen from this writing project may be universal in nature, but the writing becomes much more intense. Although a reader may be swayed to a particular viewpoint as a result of a letter of opinion, persuasion is not necessarily the focus of the project. Stating personal opinion and providing justification through examples and personal experience or conviction is the goal. In contrast to letters of complaint and persuasion, no specific action on the part of the reader is requested in a letter of opinion. Examples include

- Protest to a parent(s) about a punishment or consequence.
- Protest to a sports coach or game official about a ruling or decision.
- Statement to principal or other school authority about a policy or rule.
- Statement to a newspaper editor about a local or national issue such as cutting sports from the school budget, extending the school day or year, putting up stop lights at dangerous intersections, and so on.
- Personal testimony to schoolmates or parents to remain drug free.

Letter of Commendation

As with words of appreciation, letters of commendation are unfortunately a rarity. Being recognized for one's accomplishments or action is one of life's bright spots. Letters of commendation should be personal, but specific, and speak directly to the act or accomplishment. As a direct result of writing and sending a letter of commendation, my students have been rewarded with appreciative notes, long-distance phone calls, hugs, and kind words. November, with the Thanksgiving holiday focus, and the end of the school year are ideal times to write letters of commendation. However, students have little difficulty coming up with people or acts for writing topics at any time during the year. Topics may include

- Congratulations to a classmate on mastering a difficult skill.
- Congratulations to a sports team member for a good play.
- Appreciation to parents for preparing a favorite meal or dessert.
- Appreciation to a favorite person for special time spent together.
- "Thank you" on receipt of a gift.
- Praise to a primary student on an accomplishment.
- Congratulations to an older student who has made the honor roll; examples are babysitter, neighbor, family member, sibling of a friend.
- Acknowledgment of participation in a school program, play, music event.
- Appreciation to a former or current teacher for teaching a specific skill, gaining a particular attitude or insight, or participating in a meaningful activity.
- Fan letter to an admired public figure.
- Appreciation to a nonhuman subject such as pet, teddy bear, video game, skeletal system, library, television, or Disney World.
- Appreciation to a military veteran or active duty personnel.
- Recognition of efforts of police officers and their roles in the school such as DARE officers, safety instructors, and safety patrol mentors.
- Tributes to parents for services rendered such as tutor, taxi driver, cook, housekeeper, counselor, nurse, secretary, and so on.

Letter of Advice

Miss Manners and Ann Landers have based their careers on extending advice. Some of their published advice columns provide examples for classroom use of this type of written communication. Children's magazines usually include an advice section, too. Both real-life and imaginary situations can provide material for writing advice letters. As pseudonyms are usually substituted for real names, a sense of anonymity can be preserved. Giving advice for a specific situation is real problem solving. Most suggestions can be applied immediately, keeping interest high. Students should be encouraged to present realistic and solvable problems for this project. Leave more involved personal or family problems for the school counselor.

To provide materials and practice for the letter of advice projects, divide the class into two groups. One group will be responsible for writing about a problem, seeking advice. The other group's responsibility is to provide strategies or suggestions to solve the problem. The two groups then switch roles to provide practice from each point of view. Problems should be clearly stated and attempts to solve the problem from step to step should be communicated. Advice should be specific to the problem and provide two or more suggestions. No guarantees or promises should be stated. Video game strategies, how to pitch a fast ball, how to keep a younger sibling out of personal things, friendship pointers, and how to overcome shyness are some examples of topics students suggest for advice letters. Projects may extend beyond the classroom with students establishing drop boxes for schoolmates to deposit advice-seeking letters. It may be wise for a teacher or other staff member to look through these letters to be sure they are appropriate before distributing them to students for replies.

Reading and social studies extensions can also take the form of advice. Book or story character's roles may be taken on by students who write letters to seek or give advice that is incorporated into story detail and character traits. Historical or contemporary public figures may be used as the advice seekers or providers as well. Asking for or giving advice before the end of the story or before all knowledge is gained allows the writer to check on the accuracy of the advice later on. Following different advice may lead or have led to different outcomes.

Letter of Inquiry

Requesting information is a skill all students should master. Written requests should use a clear and concise business letter format, be specific, and use formal language. Students should be sure to include a return address, and enclosing a self-addressed, stamped envelope often prompts a response. There are many ideas and sources of topics for inquiry letters. Lists and dates of community events may be requested from the chamber of commerce. Museum and zoo public relations personnel will provide information about specific exhibits, tour prices, and hours of operations. Sports clubs will supply game dates and locations. The possibilities for topics for letters of inquiry are as many and varied as the information the students may seek. There are also books on the market whose sole purpose is to supply lists and addresses to write for free and inexpensive materials.

More structured letter of inquiry projects may also be pursued. My class became part of a Massachusetts class project where students randomly chose a U.S. city using a zip code book. They then sent a letter of explanation and a survey form to any fifth-grade teacher at any elementary school within a specified city, state, and zip code. The survey asked for information on the geography, economics, historical and/or contemporary significance, population, and climate of the area. Fashion trends, slang terms, favorite books, sports teams, and music groups were also polled. The plan of the Massachusetts class was to use the information in a geographical and cultural study of the United States.

Browsing through an atlas or gazetteer of the United States will reveal many unusual and intriguing place names. Burnt Cabins, PA; Coffee Pot Creek, OR; Sleepy Eye, MN; and Birthday Cake Peak, WY, are just a few. Letters of inquiry projects may focus on finding out how or why a place got its name. The chamber of commerce, historical society, or bureau of tourism in an area are good starting places for gathering information. Public libraries often have a section of out-of-town telephone directories that provide access to addresses.

Letter of Introduction

In more formal times, a traveler or person relocating to a new city or job would carry with him or her a letter of introduction. It would have been written by a prominent, well-respected person with the purpose of "paving the way" for a newcomer by vouching for his or her character. In resurrecting this form of writing, students have fun creating letters of introduction for their peers, family members, teachers, and themselves. The format can be used to introduce a classmate to one's self, to a next-grade teacher, a friend's parents, or a new classmate. An entire class may send letters of introduction with a student who is moving to a new school as a way to "break the ice." The key point in letters of introduction is to focus on the person's character.

Letter of Recommendation

In contrast to a letter of introduction, a letter of recommendation tends to be skill and achievement oriented. It is usually written on a request from a person seeking a particular job, position, or role. Intermediate-grade students may become familiar with writing recommendations by identifying and writing about the strengths of their classmates. Students may write letters of recommendation for classmates who aspire to be safety patrol members, team captains, bus line leaders, hall monitors, peer mediators, or committee chairpersons. Letters of recommendation written by peers may also be beneficial in securing paid positions such as babysitting, dog walking, plant tending, lawn mowing, snow shoveling, and so on. Focusing on a person's strength in relationship to the position is the key to writing recommendation letters.

Friendly Letter

A student's first experience with sending or receiving a letter was probably in the form of a friendly letter. Parents and grandparents treasure them. Friends that have moved away expect them. Everyone appreciates them. To provide practice in writing friendly letters in the intermediate grades, a new slant is necessary to boost motivation. In-school, across town, out-of-town, and out-of-state pen pals are some ways to do this.

The U.S. Post Office, recognizing the merit of the written word, has established the Wee Deliver Program. It sets up and runs a postal substation of sorts at an elementary school to handle in-school mail only. The postmaster and postal helper positions are advertised. Students apply and interview for a specific job, and workers are selected. Usually an adult (aide, parent volunteer, retired postal worker) oversees the operation, but students are responsible for sorting and delivering mail to the classrooms. Each school location has a street address. Mail is returned to the sender if it is not properly addressed. Students write to other students, teachers to students, students to teacher, brothers to sisters, and so on. Sometimes parents drop a note in the mail box with a message for their son or daughter. The program promotes the practice of letter writing by providing a system of free mail delivery on an ongoing basis.

Across-town pen pals may be secured by interested teachers joining together to form a pen pal network. Planning a face-to-face meeting of pen pals at the middle and end of the year adds interest to the project. Establishing a connection with a student from another school may help ease the transition from elementary to a larger, more formal middle school situation that is just ahead for intermediate-grade students. Across-town pen pals of another type provide a different perspective. Many nursing home residents are willing and eager to establish pen pal relationships with a young person. These intergenerational pen pals often help students gain insights and understanding of another segment of society.

Out-of-state pen pals may be secured through children's news publications. Each fall, a call usually goes out for classrooms seeking pen pals. Matching of classrooms is done randomly by grade level. It is often a requirement to exchange letters at least twice during the school year. Individual students may choose to write more frequently and continue the relationship beyond the school year. Parents or grandparents who travel for business or pleasure may also be prevailed on to be a class pen pal. A public relations consultant filled that role for my class. She shared her monthly itinerary with us and allowed lead time for the students to formulate and communicate questions (letters of inquiry) that we would like her to answer. She would send the class postcards from each location to answer our questions and also pose more questions for the students to research. We kept track of her whereabouts by moving her picture around the map and displaying her postcards at each location.

Postcards: An Abbreviated Friendly Letter

Students studying early North American exploration enjoy participating an an "Explorers Write Home" postcard writing activity. Here, each student selects an explorer, determines the intended reader, and tells of the trials, successes, and geographical route of his expedition. Factual information that must be included is home country, events, and routes and locations in North America. The picture part of the post card, address, receiver, and embellished and speculative details of the message provide opportunities for students to be creative. Classmates should be able to easily determine which explorer is writing the postcard on hearing it read aloud (minus the signature).

Memo

The message in a memo should be short, sweet, and to the point. Memos may be the verification or result of oral communication, personal thoughts, committee meetings, or other situations where timely notification of others is important. Two school applications of memo writing are recording homework assignments in an efficient, organized manner and updating small-group work. There are many home applications for memo writing, such as taking telephone messages, weekly family activity schedules, chore lists, grocery or supply lists, and television viewing and/or videotaping plans, to name just a few. Home-related memos may be written at school with family input providing the teacher has access to them for assessment purposes. Telephone message memos may be written based on classroom simulations. In all cases, assessment is based on concise, precise, and correct written communication.

Products. Each type of written communication in the "Sincerely Yours" language arts unit results in a unique product. At the conclusion of the unit, each student's showcase portfolio included at least one example of eleven types of letters: complaint, persuasion or permission, opinion, commendation, advice, inquiry, introduction, recommendation, friendly, postcard, and memo. While the eleven types of letters were required, students were allowed flexibility about subject, topic, or theme. Much practice was gained in matching writing format and style with purpose and audience. And most products were developed in response to real problems and shared with real audiences.

Learning Environments. With only the cost of postage, students communicated with people across town and across the country. They reached out to initiate written communication with peers, parents, younger students, older students, members of the business community, government officials, school administrators, neighbors, and nursing home residents. Each written response, when shared with the class, provided knowledge and expanded students' thinking. The responses of the people who were contacted through writing projects added dimension and motivation to the learning environment.

Thinking Skills and Problem Solving. The writing process of generating ideas, gathering information, writing a draft, and revising, editing, and publishing a final piece is in itself an example of multi-step problem solving. Thus, successful outcomes in this unit relied on students using appropriate problem-solving stages and strategies. Critical thinking skills of sequencing and prioritizing were practiced in all writing projects. Determining cause and effect and relevant and irrelevant information were most apparent in letters of persuasion and complaint. When students were asked to take on the role of a story character and historical or contemporary public figures, creative thinking skills were employed. Students had to be flexible in their thinking to choose purpose, audience, style, and format for their writing projects.

Instructional Groups. Grouping strategies of whole-class, small-group, and independent work were used in this unit. Whole-class grouping was effective for skill lessons, introduction of writing formats, and sharing responses to writing projects. Small groups took on the role of writing coaches. While one group member shared a written piece orally, other members were active listeners. Group members also provided feedback about word choice, clarity, proper language use, and sentence structure. The writer then decided which changes, if any, to make. Small groups remained consistent throughout the unit. This way, each member was aware of every other member's work and the progress each made. Ultimately, the final writing project was an independent task.

Timeline and Budget. The *timeline* for the unit was four to five weeks. In-school work included skill lessons, introduction of writing formats, small group reaction sessions, and whole-class group sharing. Some independent writing was accomplished within the school day, but it was my experience that some writing homework was also necessary. Since most intermediate-grade students are familiar with letter-writing format and basic composition skills, presenting the "Sincerely Yours" unit in the beginning of the school year works well. Students can apply grammar, usage, and mechanics as they are reviewed. The variety in format, flexibility of topics, and anticipation of responses add to the excitement of a new school year.

If this unit is to be taught in the fall, a *budget* and ordering of consumable materials need to be carried out in early spring of the year before. Writing paper and envelopes are standard school supply items. Students can purchase their own folders for portfolios. Postage is the most expensive item. A classroom of 25 students would require over $75 in postage if each student completes and mails eleven types of letters. Some students will choose to write more than one of a particular type of letter, raising postage costs even higher. Many school districts have bulk mailing capabilities, and it may be worthwhile to check into this possibility to keep costs lower. Classroom teachers often have a fund for special materials allocated by parent–teacher organizations. I have used this fund for half of the postage costs, with students providing the other half. In any case, by tapping a variety of sources, covering the cost of postage was not a problem.

Assessment. Each writing project that was completed during the unit is assessed separately. A criterion-referenced assessment sheet is shared with students prior to their writing and students are told it will be used to assess their final products. Criteria varied with each type of written communication. In each case, the emphasis is on the type of communication. Therefore, specific format criteria are weighted with the most possible points. An assessment form for a business letter is presented in Figure 4–1. An assessment form for a letter of complaint is shown in Figure 4–4. Throughout the writing process, small group members helped assess each other's writing by providing feedback and suggestions at the rough draft and revisions stages of the letters. As with other projects described in this chapter, parents are kept informed of student progress and achievement by sending home assessment sheets of completed projects for their comments and signatures.

Active participation and self-initiation on the part of students are for me indications of a successful unit of study. The constant connecting with the out-of-classroom world added depth and interest to what most students consider a rather mundane topic in a writing unit. All students received some responses to their letters and enjoyed sharing this information with their

FIGURE 4–4 Product Assessment Form: Letter of Complaint

Student Name: _____

Date: _____

Criteria:	Possible Points	Earned Points
Standardized business letter format: direct, to the point, providing appropriate information, polite and formal language	15	_____
Formal complaint format: specific problem described; request for satisfaction; deadline stated; next-step communications stated; appreciation conveyed	25	_____
Grammar—usage	20	_____
Mechanics—spelling	20	_____
Sentence structure	10	_____
Neatness	10	_____
Total	100	_____

Student Comments:

Teacher Comments:

---

peers. A sense of personal pride seemed to stem from the idea that someone took the time and effort to send them a response. In this way, the power and satisfaction of the written word was exemplified.

Many of the ideas for letters were initiated by the students. For example, my fifth-graders have first-grade reading partners. The older students read to younger students and listen to younger students read to them. Their relationship builds over weekly meetings throughout the year and the fifth-graders are usually quite impressed by the progress the first-graders make. They also come to realize the effort it takes to learn to read, a skill most fifth-graders take for granted. The Wee Deliver Program was used to send younger students letters of praise and encouragement.

Students also apply letter-writing skills to their out-of-school life. Parents report receiving persuasion and opinion letters about redecorating a student's bedroom, planning a family outing, changing chore responsibilities, and raising allowances. I received a letter from a school bus driver who was impressed by the written persuasion skills of one of my students who rode her bus. It seems that the student had written a letter to the bus driver requesting that on one of the last days of school she stop the bus at a local ice cream takeout store to allow students to buy a treat. The student also enclosed a sample letter that explained the plan to parents and included a permission slip they could sign. Due to one student's effective use of written communication, an entire bus load of children were rewarded!

IT'S A MYSTERY TO ME

There is something appealing, almost compelling about the intrigue and suspense of a good mystery. It is, I believe, that very sense of bafflement that urges one on to divulge an explanation or conclusion. Unraveling a mystery requires imagination, logical reasoning, deductive and inductive thinking, and critical and creative thinking paired with task commitment and knowledge. These are the very components of multistep problem solving. While one hardly has to be prodded to turn the next page or watch the next episode of a mystery, other areas of investigation in the curriculum do not afford such motivation. But, by broadening our thinking about the elements of mystery, some intermediate-level curriculum can be refocused and repackaged to create renewed interest and motivation.

The interdisciplinary unit "It's a Mystery to Me" is built on that idea. Creating cartesian graphics, tessellations, palindromes, and working with mathematical symbols present students with puzzling predicaments. Scientific phenomena of eclipse, earthquake activity, chemical change, air pressure, surface tension, and light reflection and refraction establish a sense of bewilderment. The who's who and what's what of library research projects lead students through a labyrinth of reference material as they follow clues to reach a goal.

Setting the Stage to Teach Mysteries

How story elements and language come together to create mood, purpose, and interest is a mystery to most students. Why the same happening is often perceived differently by each participant or observer challenges thinking. How does this affect court proceedings? Do many of life's mysteries provide clues that may lead to an acceptable answer? Is there a pattern or process revealed? How does one determine relevant information as opposed to irrelevant information? What about point of view, how is it used to crack a case? After experiencing a more traditional literature-based mystery unit, this unit gives students opportunities to investigate mysterious aspects of math, science, social studies, and language arts.

Unit Overview. Students participate in a three- to four-week interdisciplinary unit of study based on problem-solving strategies and creative and critical thinking skills while investigating a variety of mysteries. This unit includes a traditional literature study of the mystery genre and then broadens its focus to incorporate other curriculum areas and topics. The unit has three sections. "Sleuth Stories" is a literature sampler with a language arts base. "Order in the Court" provides social studies opportunities to examine cases and trials in an attempt to understand the idea of justice. "Intriguing Investigations" is a potpourri of patterns, processes, and phenomena in the areas of research, science, and math. Throughout the unit, creative and critical skills are identified and applied as they relate to multistep problem solving.

The "It's a Mystery to Me" unit lends itself to a variety of planning and presentation schemes. One plan that I like requires all students to participate in the "Sleuth Stories" and "Order in the Court" sections of the unit in an activity-based, teacher-directed manner. Students would then self-select activities and projects from the "Intriguing Investigations" and "Scientific Phenomena" sections based on interest or talent and work individually or in small groups. Presentation skills may be highlighted as students provide leadership for an "Intriguing Mysteries" program for peers and/or parents and others. Fifty more ideas with mysterious dimensions are also included.

Instructional Objectives. A sampling of language arts and social studies objectives that may be met throughout this unit are included here. Although science and math activities are present later in this section, I chose not to include them here since their topics and number are limited only by one's imagination. Creative and critical thinking skills and objectives provide the basis for the unit and relate to all curriculum areas.

Creative-Critical Thinking

- Demonstrate keen observation skills.
- Determine relevant from irrelevant information.
- Identify bias, stereotyping, and assumption.
- Use single-step problem-solving techniques such

as working backward, making a chart, acting it out, setting up an equation, and so on.

- Draw conclusions based on evidence.
- Analyze a situation from more than one perspective.
- Determine multiple possibilities.
- Employ inductive and deductive reasoning.

Language Arts

- Show evidence of how an author helps create a mood for the reader through the use of descriptive language.
- Identify story elements of setting, character, plot, and epilogue in a mystery pattern.
- Show evidence of a growing vocabulary.
- Give an oral presentation—being aware of voice, volume, eye contact, body language, and style.
- Write a character description.
- Read for detail and comprehension.
- Experience a variety of literature; folktale, science fiction, legend, and so on.

Social Studies

- Identify career opportunities in a variety of fields.
- Identify individuals and their contributions to society.
- Explain the constitutional rights of American citizens in regard to search and seizure, crime and punishment, and trial by a jury of one's peers.
- Demonstrate knowledge and understanding of historical events.

Resources. The resources for this unit are unique to each section. Ideally, print, audiovisual, human and real property resources should be included in each section. In planning for the "Sleuth Stories" section of the unit, the challenge is in which resources to choose as mystery stories are abundant at the intermediate reading comprehension level. So include a variety of basal series mystery selections. Many teachers retain a classroom set of basal readers each time texts are replaced to provide a resource pool for grade-level materials. Providing exposure to many mystery stories allows a basis for comparison between selections and determining characteristics unique to the mystery genre. Inexpensive sets of a chosen mystery title may be available through mail order children's book clubs as well.

School and public library collections often include multiple copies and series of grade-level books for individual or small-group reading. Students' personal libraries may also include mysteries that they are willing to share for the duration of the unit. In addition, videotaped mysteries from the movie and television industries are easily accessible (appropriateness for classroom use is a consideration, too, however). Local universities or technical colleges may have access to names of mystery writers enrolled in creative writing classes who may speak to students about their craft to provide a human focus.

The "Order in the Court" section requires a working knowledge of human rights as provided in the Constitution of the United States. A knowledge of courtroom procedure and vocabulary are also needed. Intermediate social studies textbooks and topic-based nonfiction books may help provide background information. Vocabulary used in the context of mystery fiction throughout the "Sleuth Stories" section of this unit may be beneficial, too. But the best source is probably people involved in the business of providing justice within the court system. Private investigators, police officers, detectives, lawyers, victims, witnesses, jurors, or judges can speak in general about processes and procedures using terminology associated with their jobs without addressing specific cases. A visit to an open court session is also an excellent learning experience.

Resources for the "Intriguing Investigations" section are as varied as the topics and questions students or teachers choose to pursue. In all cases, a primary source of someone who has "seen it" or "done it" provides the most enthusiasm and learner satisfaction. Secondary sources from those who have become experts in their knowledge of the topic should also be included as human resources or print and audiovisual resources. Students may take on the role of an expert as they present their investigations to others.

Collections of word games, math "tricks," science experiments, and "magic" tricks are readily available to teachers and students as they plan their presentations. Encyclopedias, atlases, and dictionaries are familiar resources to intermediate students and lead them to other useful sources for library research. By choosing mystery research questions carefully, the teacher may easily introduce less-familiar resources such as biographical dictionaries, books of quotations, and thesauruses.

Investigating Mysteries: More Than Eighty Activities and Ideas

Possibilities for solving mysteries exist throughout the curriculum as well as in everyday life. The focus here is on the process and thinking skills students apply to bring closure to a mysterious situation and the ability to communicate their findings to and with others. Activities are presented for each of the three sections—"Sleuth Stories," "Order in the Court," and "Intriguing Investigations." Activities are also suggested for "Scientific Phenomena" along with a list of "Fifty Topics for Student Investigations." The list of topics is not meant to be exhaustive, but a starting point for a teacher's own creative ideas. Many teachers look for curriculum connections where they may share their own interests, collections, and hobbies with students. This is one area where they may be able to do this.

"Sleuth Stories" Activities. Can't you just see your students acting as sleuths in the corridors of a cold and musty house on a rainy, dreary night? Try these:

- Collect examples of passages from a given work or a variety of works that help create suspense, fear, curiosity, or suspicion for the reader.
- Classify mood-enhancing passages according to story elements of setting, character, plot (action).
- Classify mood-enhancing passages according to the senses—sight, hearing, taste, touch, smell.
- Recite a chosen mood-enhancing passage, including music and sound effects.
- Write a physical description of an original mysterious character. Have a classmate create a drawing from your description.
- Create a "wanted" poster.
- Brainstorm plot ideas for each of the following categories: suspect, victim, crime, motive, alibi, evidence, and epilogue. Randomly choose an idea from each category to tell and/or write an impromptu tale of intrigue.
- Use a given mystery example to create a chart highlighting suspect–motive–evidence–alibi for each suspect presented.
- Identify and use mystery-related vocabulary in oral and written discussions: sleuth, alias, alibi, hoax, motive, circumstantial evidence, crime of passion, and so on.
- Create a graphic organizer (visual representation) of the mystery plot pattern for a given story.
- Plan and present a thirty-second commercial advertising a chosen mystery book.
- Create a character bag for a book character that class members will be familiar with. Include items such as clues to the character's identity without telling the name. Students will determine which character is represented.
- Given one item as evidence, weave a mystery incorporating that item into the plot. Compare stories with other students.

"Order in the Court" Activities. These involve students in learning about the very roots of democratic governance. Isn't this an exciting way to learn about what is too often imagined as a dry and dull subject?

- Write job descriptions for jobs and careers related to mysteries such as archeologist, private investigator, medical doctor, mystery writer, judge, mediator, researcher, and so on.
- Read biographies of people who have had a mystery-related job or career.
- Participate in role plays of mock trials. Nonthreatening examples may include trials of storybook characters such as the wolf in *The Three Pigs* for assault and harassment, or Goldilocks in *The Three Bears* for breaking and entering and vandalism. More contemporary themes may include graffiti on public property or dress codes at work, school, or public places.
- Identify and use vocabulary related to court proceedings: plaintiff, defendant, evidence, objection, exhibit, witness, and so on.
- Write a character description and justification for an "ideal jury member" for a given trial.
- Determine what qualities, experiences, or opinions would exempt a potential juror from a given trial; write from a lawyer's perspective.
- Given a brief description of an event, "tell the story" from the perspective of a variety of bystanders. Note language, body language, and sentence structure as well as information that was provided and omitted. Bystander groups may

include a mix of ages, educational levels, economic circumstances, or other factors that may carry bias, stereotype, or assumption.

- Discuss how perception of an event may carry over to courtroom–jury bias.

- Given one bag of garbage, determine as much information about the garbage producer(s) as you can. Write a character description based on your assumptions. Have more than one group write about each bag of garbage separately. Then compare character descriptions.

- Attend a public hearing or trial noting procedures, processes, and outcomes.

- Participate in conflict mediation training; conduct a peer mediation session.

- Compare and contract real-life courtroom proceedings to television accounts of the same event.

"Intriguing Investigations" Activities. Total involvement in learning is combined with more advanced academic skills in these mysteries. What fun!

- Participate in a research scavenger hunt. Ask students to find answers to fact-based questions using a variety of reference material. A general topic such as weather may be pursued or a specific item such as a color may be highlighted. In this way, the activity may be used different times during the school year to provide skill practice while maintaining student interest.

- Propose a series of fact-based questions and a limited array of resources. Ask students to determine and give justification for finding the best source to match each question.

- Given a topic, use at least five library references to write research questions for other classmates to answer.

- Participate in a "Mystery of the Week" fact-finding activity where the first student to find the answer writes the next "Mystery of the Week" question.

- Based on the classic television show *What's My Line?"* write scripts for three different character actors' answers to common questions. In all cases, be sure that each character sounds credible but that only one is truthful. Present the panel to classmates who determine through research which actors are impostors and which ones are not.

- Develop and present a play or program about various kinds of mysteries for peers and/or parents.

Scientific Phenomena Activities. The activities here show how a discipline can be a source of many intriguing phenomena. This is just a beginning.

- Find folktales from different cultures that attempt to explain the same natural phenomena. Compare and contrast the accounts.

- Write an original folktale that attempts to explain a natural phenomenon.

- Give examples of how science fiction attempts to explain the uncertainties of technology and the unknowns of the future.

- Compare and contrast the literature genres of folktale and science fiction.

- Choose a natural phenomenon such as the colors of the rainbow, solar or lunar eclipse, earthquake, or the eruption of a volcano. Find a folktale from any culture based on that idea. Find out the scientific explanation for the same idea. Now present both fictionalized and scientific accounts of the phenomena to the class, and have the students justify the differences between them.

- Produce a "magic show" where water disappears (evaporation), colors change (secondary colors), lines move (optical illusion), knives bend (refraction), and so on. Present the show to primary-grade children.

Fifty More Ideas for Mystery Investigations. Fifty ideas students can investigate as *mysteries* are listed as follows. They can be used in many of the activities just described to vary their content. Also, students can select the ideas that interest them most.

air pressure	earthquake
Amelia Earhart	ecosystems
Anasazi	eclipse
black holes	electricity
buoyance	energy
chemical change	evaporation
color spectrum	fingerprints
comets	food chains
condensation	fossils
crystals	UFOs
decomposers	Virginia Dare
digestion	volcanic activity

tornado
magnetism
optical illusion
owl pellets
palindromes
photography
photosynthesis
precipitation
reflection
refraction
respiration
sound
surface tension
tangrams
tessellations
transpiration
tropisms
tsunami
geography
gravity
inertia
sunspots

Looking at Where, What, and How Well

Mysteries lend themselves to the school environment and also offer opportunities to reach out into the community. They integrate all disciplines to enable students to select from a wide range of ideas to develop a myriad of written and other products. And these products need to be assessed appropriately according to the level and extent of the product produced.

Learning Environments. This unit may be presented totally within the confines of the school building. The library is available for research and peers and younger students are available for audiences to share the knowledge with. Resource people, especially those suggested in the "Order in the Court" section, may be invited to the school as speakers. A courtroom visit is very beneficial but not essential to the success of the unit. The variety and insights will come from the many different resources used in all three sections. As the unit takes on three different focuses, interest tends to remain high.

Authentic Products. Most products suggested in this unit fall into the categories of composition and presentation based on research and opinion. Charts, collections, and graphic organizers are produced to help students categorize materials for easy retrieval. Composition-based products include writing job descriptions, questions, wanted posters, scripts, character descriptions, mystery plots, and complete stories. Providing testimony, describing perfect jurors, sharing research findings, offering peer mediation, giving explanations, and producing magic shows are products that rely on presentation skills.

Assessment. As discussed throughout this chapter, assessment is based on criteria established for each product. Composition assessment forms such as those shown in Figures 4–1 and 4–2 are used for each type of writing. Presentation-based products are assessed according to content and presentation components. Students are aware of assessment criteria at the start of any given project. Parents are also provided copies of criteria-based assessment forms.

I attribute the success of "It's a Mystery to Me" to its appeal to the natural curiosity that students possess. Students are excited to pursue their interests because the unit provides the tools and guides them but doesn't limit investigation. As new questions, resources, and ideas are presented, new doors are opened and students are eager to find out what's behind them. The opportunity to present information to others in a unique way also adds to student motivation. Being part of mock trials and producing magic shows are also highlights for most students. Becoming more familiar with the tools and skills of research, composition, and presentation help build personal pride and confidence as well.

SUMMARY

This chapter focuses on a thematic, interdisciplinary approach to problem solving at the intermediate level. In my teaching experience, this approach encourages participation, boosts motivation, and promotes student success. The purpose of this chapter is to highlight interdisciplinary units of study that closely couple skills and content with real-world applications. Ten aspects of preparing for teaching are presented in a variety of topics. Each unit provides information and suggestions in terms of an overview of the unit, instructional objectives, resources, student activities, authentic products, learning environments, thinking skills and problem-solving opportunities, instructional groups, timeline and budget, and assessment of student achievement and the unit itself.

Five units of instruction were described in this chapter. Those on historical homes and a trip to the zoo took students out of school and into communities around them. Writing different kinds of letters and advertising strategies focused on practical written communication and analyses of persuasion strategies. The mystery unit helped students to broaden their own thinking of mysteries as literature to find and solve them in science, math, and social studies, too.

REFERENCES

Drake, S. (1993). *Planning integrated curriculum: The call to adventure.* Alexandria, VA: Association for Supervision and Curriculum Development.

Jacobs, H. (Ed.). (1989). *Interdisciplinary curriculum: Design and implementation.* Alexandria, VA: Association for Supervision and Curriculum Development.

Willis, S. (November 1992). Interdisciplinary learning: Movement to link the disciplines gains momentum. *ASCD Curriculum Update,* 2.

CHAPTER 5

Problem Solving: The Perfect Match for Middle Schoolers

Picture a classroom that is rich in stimulation with a bustle of hands-on activity; an environment that is supportive, nurturing, and psychologically safe. Creative students are eagerly learning through discovery and play. Their curiosity allows them to investigate and explore with enthusiasm. These are students full of wonder and excitement who continually question, experiment, and take risks. They discover through trial and error, use their imaginations to create and solve problems with their classmates, laugh and have fun while learning. In short, they are active participants who look forward to coming to school each day.

Did you envision a middle school classroom? On the contrary, I would venture to say that you probably pictured a typical preschool or kindergarten setting. Had I been describing a middle school classroom, I might have portrayed a more controlled, curriculum-oriented environment. Instead of involved, enthusiastic children, I might have introduced you to a number of inattentive, uninspired students who feel that school is boring. Rather than inquisitive, curious learners, I might have described disinterested students who have stopped asking questions and taking risks. Unfortunately, by the time they reach middle school, adolescents tend not to be the active, enthusiastic classroom learners they once were.

What happens to the excitement for learning that seems to naturally occur at age 4 or 5? Somehow, somewhere along the way, it seems to virtually disappear. Is it the nature of the middle school "beast" to be inactive or generally disinterested? Are they so easily distracted that it is futile to even attempt to interest them in our classrooms? Should we simply resign ourselves to the fact that they are victims of the inevitable middle school "brain drain" syndrome and are impossible to reach?

Although this may certainly seem to be the case at times, on closer examination we will find just the opposite to be true. Adolescents are indeed curious about their world, about why things are the way they are, and about how others think. They continually explore as they examine personal issues and beliefs, seek acceptance, and search for who they are. They most certainly do experiment and take risks, be it to question authority, verbalize an outlandish idea, or wear an outrageous outfit to get a reaction. They have mastered the art of "fooling around," although too often they do it with each other rather than with ideas. In short, adolescents are engaged in a process of inquiry and problem solving as they evolve from child to young adult, and they are indeed more imaginative and creative than we often give them credit for.

Why then the discrepancy between these promising characteristics and what we typically see in the middle school classroom? It is often not the student who is the problem. Rather, it's what we teach and how we teach it that can exacerbate the middle school "doldrums." If we fail to match our teaching methods and classroom activities with the characteristics of our middle school students, they will often hide behind a curriculum that bores them to death.

In this chapter we will examine why problem solving is especially appropriate for middle school students. Teacher attitudes and behaviors, environments to promote learning, and creativity will be examined as they relate to the problem solving classroom. In addition to a discussion of the Future Problem Solving Program, exemplary units will be outlined for each of the following areas: interdisciplinary options, social studies and language arts.

WHY PROBLEM SOLVING AND MIDDLE SCHOOLERS GO TOGETHER

Middle school students are at a unique stage of their lives. It is easy for those of us well past adolescence to become frustrated by many of the behaviors that typify this age group. As educators, we might respond with a get-tough approach, insisting on a tight structure and an out-of-the-book curriculum to maintain some sense of order during these years of unpredictability. However, a far more productive strategy would be to consider the unique characteristics of adolescents as positive assets that can be capitalized on to enhance their learning experiences. In doing so, we see that problem solving stands out as a logical approach for adolescents and their middle school education.

First and foremost, adolescents are an extremely *diverse* group of individuals, varying widely in their physical, conceptual, social, and emotional development. Therefore, middle school students need diverse educational experiences (Maynard, 1986). Problem solving can be the vehicle that provides a variety of approaches to the discovery of information. There is no one right way to solve a problem, and the possibilities for solutions are endless.

Adolescents are making the *transition from concrete to abstract thinking* (Dorman, Lipsitz, & Verner, 1985). Arnold (1991) suggests that we help students make this transition when we emphasize inquiry and problem finding and solving. Adolescents are also *curious and inventive* (Maynard, 1986). They need time to explore, investigate, and "stretch their minds and imaginations" (Lewis, 1990, p. 48). These students should be asking "what-if and suppose-that questions" (Task Force on Education of Young Adolescents, 1989, p. 43). Problem solving builds on students' inquisitiveness and their natural tendencies to pry and probe. It can help to keep middle school students absorbed in the complexities of life and learning, and it can stimulate an interest in knowledge and discovery.

Adolescents are also in the *process of "becoming."* They are exploring their beliefs and values to define how they fit into the scheme of things. Problem-solving strategies make use of higher-order thinking skills to critically examine real problems of the world. They can help students reason through a variety of opinions as they make personal decisions about significant issues.

Anyone who has worked with adolescents can confirm the fact that they are *controversial and love to argue*. Problem-solving activities can help students to examine the strengths and weaknesses of their arguments, scrutinize different viewpoints, and focus on interrelationships. Students can be challenged to understand the complexity of ideas by carefully examining the evidence, expressing opinions appropriately through debate, and modifying their actions via negotiation and conflict resolution.

Adolescents are beginning "their vacillating journey toward *independence*" (Toepfer, Lounsbury, Arth, & Johnston, 1986, p. 8). They value freedom and the opportunity to self-direct and assert themselves. These students need opportunities to make their own decisions (Task Force on Education of Young Adolescents, 1989, p. 36). In problem solving, students can begin to direct their own learning with the teacher as a guide. With no one right answer, students are empowered with the freedom to take risks and experiment through trial and error.

Adolescents need a *sense of structure and clear limits* (Lewis, 1990, p. 48). Problem-solving activities provide the perfect combination of freedom within structure. Students are free to explore a myriad of possibilities within a designated framework. It is also important that middle school students *feel competent*, *experience success*, and *be recognized for their efforts*. With problem-solving activities, students are more free to create. A sense of accomplishment results, as students feel they are more in control of their learning. Anything goes, so to speak; therefore, students cannot help but be successful in producing an idea or solution to a problem (Lewis, 1990, p. 48). A curriculum rich in problem-solving opportunities will provide one of the best means to success in the middle school classroom because it values the decisions that students make.

Problem solving matches the adolescent learner because it recognizes and uses the characteristics of their age group. When it is incorporated into their educational experience, middle school students take a more active role in their learning, and they stand a much better chance of internalizing the concepts we present.

THE PROBLEM-SOLVING CLASSROOM

For problem solving to be most effective, certain conditions must be present. Classroom climate plays an important part in setting the stage for successful problem solving. This is determined by the attitudes and behaviors of teachers and students as well as the classroom environment. Creativity also plays a significant role in successful problem-solving. These elements, along with specific problem solving techniques and ways to diverge within the regular curriculum will be discussed in this section.

Teacher Attitudes and Behaviors Set the Stage

The way teachers approach students and respond to their ideas can help to create classroom climates that are more conducive to effective problem solving. This involves establishing a psychologically safe environment, promoting greater tolerance and appreciation for ideas among class members, and acting as facilitator rather than director.

Creating an Atmosphere of Safety and Acceptance. "A safe environment and a high tolerance for ambiguity promote a spirit of trust and safety. Feeling safe and trusting others allow one to be more authentic, open, and honest. Openness to experience and honesty facilitate mutual respect and understanding, which in turn foster synergy and interdependence" (Buckmaster, 1994, p. 51). The implementation of activities that allow students to get to know themselves and each other better, explore values, stress the importance of similarities and differences, and examine decision-making strategies, all help to promote a more psychologically safe atmosphere. Here are some examples:

- *I Am.* Students list and share ten things they are, such as "I am a pianist," "I am a dog-lover," or "I am the oldest child in my family" (Stanford, 1977, p. 60).
- *Rank-Ordering Situations.* Students are given three choices and must rank them in order of preference. For example, "How would you like people to see you — bright, honest, or physically attractive?" (Menasha Joint School District, 1977, pp. 139–50).
- *Murder Mystery Mania.* Each student receives one or more clues to a murder mystery. Clues may only be shared orally and may not be passed from person to person. Without teacher intervention, students must discover ways to organize themselves in order to solve the mystery (Stanford & Dodds Stanford, 1969, pp. 23–31).

Too often in middle school, we feel pressure to complete certain curricula in a given amount of time. Consequently, we tend to neglect these types of activities in our regular classes. Experience has shown that when I do take the time to implement them, students gain a greater understanding and appreciation for each other, all of which helps to promote a more effective problem-solving climate.

Cultivating Tolerance and Appreciation of Ideas. Students need to feel that their ideas are valuable, and that they can express them without being ridiculed. This is sometimes easier said than done in a middle school classroom! Lack of tolerance for those who are different often abounds, and adolescents are typically quick to criticize or laugh at an idea they consider outrageous or "uncool." It isn't always easy for middle school students to take the risk to offer an off-beat suggestion or solution when they are simultaneously struggling for acceptance from their peers. Middle school teachers must therefore work even harder to create an atmosphere of safety and acceptance in their classrooms.

How can one accomplish this? First of all, a teacher's behavior helps cultivate a spirit of greater tolerance and appreciation. I make it clear from the beginning that criticism is simply unacceptable, and that I welcome "wild and crazy" ideas. I stress that even though such ideas may not seem practical at first, they may be modified into workable alternatives, or they may provide the spark to suggest another, more viable solution. To support these principles, I share stories of how seemingly outlandish ideas turned into successful ones. For example, Pringles Potato Chips were invented by making analogies to wet leaves. Likewise, I stress examples of "failures" or accidents that turned into profitable alternatives. For instance, Post-It Notes were born when a glue failed to perform as originally intended (Petroski, 1992). Through such examples, students begin to understand that any idea is of potential value.

Offering mini-opportunities for divergence on a regular basis will also help to promote openness to ideas. This involves taking one or two minutes to encourage wild solutions to problems ("How can you remove a hippo stuck in a bathtub?"), explore answers to provocative questions ("What if no one could talk?"), and make frivolous and bizarre comparisons ("How is a ferris wheel like a piano?"). Due to the unconventional nature of the problems posed, students tend to feel more comfortable about offering outlandish alternatives. Besides being great fun for students, these activities help to foster the acceptance of all ideas.

Acting as the Guide on the Side. In addition, teachers must often redefine their roles in order to create an atmosphere conducive to the communication of ideas and effective problem solving. Rather than direct and control behavior to produce specific outcomes, we must guide and assist students in the creation of many possibilities. Instead of telling students how to solve a problem, we must allow them the freedom to experiment and figure things out for themselves. We must acknowledge that there are a myriad of possibilities, not just one right answer. We must be open-minded and willing to deal with an element of uncertainty. We must facilitate, not dictate; encourage, not criticize.

A teacher's response to questions can make all the difference in the world in terms of motivating students to think and share ideas. One concept that has made a significant impact on my teaching is wait time (Pearson, 1980). Waiting for five seconds after I pose a question gives students time to better assimilate the information presented and formulate a response. In addition, it shows students that I am willing to wait for ideas other than those that are offered first. The number of hands that go up increases with the time that I wait to call on someone. The results are simply amazing!

Another way I modify my response to students is to defer to their judgment when they prefer my expertise. For example, some students, due to laziness or lack of confidence, look for a way out by asking me what approach they should take in creating an idea or solving a problem. Although I might initially view my direct assistance as more expedient, I have found that it is far better if I provide encouragement and convey my confidence in their ability to find the answer. This helps to empower students in their problem-solving efforts.

I have also discovered that when I ask leading questions or make suggestive comments, students are more apt to share ideas. For example, "What's the wildest thing you can think of here?" "Who has a crazy idea?" "Who will take a risk on this one?" "Really let your mind go!" "Remember, seemingly ridiculous ideas often turn into good ones." These prompters, along with an outrageous idea I might give to get the ball rolling, help to reinforce an atmosphere of acceptance and encourage more active, creative participation.

Environments to Promote Learning

Environmental factors that make learning realistic to students include classroom arrangement, use of school and local library resources, and the community as a laboratory for learning. The way I incorporate each of these factors into my teaching is described next.

The Physical Arrangement of the Classroom. I gave up the idea of desks long ago in favor of tables. Rows of individual desks are simply not conducive to cooperative endeavors. Using tables eliminates the hassle of constantly moving desks around in order to physically group students. Sitting together at a table also reinforces the concept of students working as a collective and synergistic team, rather than as individuals with ideas separate and apart from others. In addition to promoting more effective communication, tables allow me to circulate more freely around the room. I can move from group to group with ease to observe, assist, or trouble-shoot. Clustering students also eases my frustration of continually repeating instructions and directions. My rule is that students cannot ask me a question to clarify or re-explain unless no one at their table can provide the information. This provides yet another way for them to rely on each other for success. If it is impossible for you to obtain tables for your classroom, I would strongly suggest that you situate desks together in groups of four. Students who can face each other tend to interact in a more personal, cooperative, and productive manner, all of which enhance problem-solving efforts.

The School Library Media Center (LMC). Problem solving often extends beyond the classroom walls. For my students, the LMC usually serves as a starting point for conducting preliminary research and obtaining data about a particular topic. Finding relevant information is crucial, for it is hard to address an issue unless one knows something about it. For example, if we are investigating ways to solve problems that deal with the subject of space travel, we need to develop a certain knowledge base in order to better understand the issues involved. I typically begin by having students see what they can find using any available resource: the card catalogue, Reader's Guide, CD-ROM, Newsbank, and so forth. I also rely on one of our high school libraries for articles that are not in our LMC. Sources are cited and faxed to the librarian there, and she in turn faxes the articles to me. Of course, one's community library can be used in a similar fashion.

Experts in the Field. I have found that people who will come and speak to students are a most valuable resource. These individuals are particularly effective after some preliminary research has been done. Students then have a background of knowledge that allows them to better understand and interact with the guest speaker. Again and again, students tell me that an individual who has expertise relative to our topic has a far greater impact and makes the information they have read come alive. Questions that could not be answered by reading an article can be addressed by someone who has firsthand experience. Each speaker comes with a unique perspective, adding to a student's insight on a particular issue.

If a guest speaker cannot come to you, you might consider going to the guest speaker. I have taken my students on mini-field trips to our local university or area businesses to meet with professors and other experts in their classrooms, labs, and offices. Artifacts or experiments in progress make the topic more real for students. Interest is heightened, and knowledge is internalized.

Community Sites. Students will also do well to think of their community as a laboratory for problem solving. This may include their school, city, state, national, or global community. Each has its own variety of problems that need to be addressed, such as racism, litter, recycling, homelessness, and many more. Students are often eager to tackle real issues when they know that their solutions will actually be implemented. They can generate their own ideas for problems that need to be addressed in their communities, or they might contact local officials (superintendents, mayors, governors, etc.) for suggestions. With community service now at the forefront of educational reform for many districts, solving real problems represents a viable alternative.

Creativity Is the Key to Success

Creativity is essential to problem solving. In essence, creativity *is* problem solving, since arriving at solutions involves formulating and/or assimilating ideas. The creative behaviors of fluency, flexibility, elaboration and originality have already been discussed in Chapter 2. Torrance and Myers (1970, p. 22) also define the creative learning process as becoming "sensitive to or aware of problems, deficiencies, gaps in knowledge, missing elements, disharmonies, and so on; bringing together available information; defining the difficulty or identifying the missing element; searching for solutions, making hypotheses, and modifying and retesting them; perfecting them; and finally communicating the results." Donald Treffinger (1980) asserts that all students have some creative potential, and that we can enhance their creative behavior by providing them with opportunities in which to practice certain creative problem-solving techniques. When we equip students with specific tools (techniques) for creative thought, they will be far more successful in generating ideas to solve all sorts of problems, both in and outside of school.

Creative Techniques that Work in the Classroom

Many of the creative problem-solving methods featured in Treffinger's book (1980) have been incorporated into my classroom activities. His model for encouraging creative learning consists of three levels: Level I, divergent functions; Level II, complex thinking and feeling processes; and Level III, involvement in real challenges.

I use a number of techniques from Levels I and II to focus on open-endedness, the generation of many possibilities, and the the higher-level thinking processes of application, analysis, synthesis and evaluation (Bloom et. al 1956). These strategies are discussed next.

Warm-Up Activities. Warm-ups allow one to get the creative juices flowing. Just as athletes exercise their bodies before an event, creative thinkers must ready themselves by "stretching the mind" and opening the senses to original and imaginative thought. I frequently use warm-ups in my classroom to introduce or enhance a topic or unit. Any type of open-ended exercise that can be done in the span of a few minutes constitutes a good warm-up activity. For example, *analyzing a statement or direct quotation* such as, "You can't make an omelet without breaking eggs" or "An empty sack cannot stand up" is a stimulating way to initiate analytical thinking. I also put a daily quote on my board for students to think about. "Middle school students are all self-centered, inconsiderate, and wild," is an allegation that will certainly generate an active dialogue among adolescents. I have used this as a springboard for an analysis of stereotypes and prejudice.

"What if?" or "Just suppose" statements are also good warm-up activities. For example, in history I might ask, "What if we had lost the Revolutionary War?" In a unit on robotics I can project into the future by supposing that everyone had his or her own personal robot (Treffinger, 1980, p. 35). What would happen, both good and bad? Even mathematical concepts can be addressed: What if the concept of zero did not exist?

Open-Ended Thoughts and Feelings. Activities under this category help to encourage a variety of possible responses. For example, *statement completion* is another good way to begin a unit or examine opinions on a particular issue. When we began our study of censorship, I listed student responses that completed the statement, "Censorship is . . ." I challenged them to fill the board with as many ideas as they could, and I accepted all responses without question or discussion. Later their answers were analyzed: Why is "unfair" on the list? Which answers are facts and which are opinions? How many of you agree with the view that censorship is necessary? What do you think we need to find out about censorship?

Asking provocative questions also challenges students to problem-solve for an answer. For example, in science I might ask, "How many of our textbooks can you balance on one 3-by-5-inch index card?" After hazarding a guess or two, students are anxious to experiment and find out. If I ask, "How can you drop an egg from a height of 15 feet without breaking it?" students are stimulated to offer a variety of possibilities, which they later analyze before choosing one or two that they want to actually test out.

Brainstorming. Another Level I technique, brainstorming, allows one "to generate many ideas which may be helpful in the process of solving problems" (Treffinger, 1980, p. 40). The most important aspect of successful brainstorming is to defer judgment. Evaluation is a follow-up process, and should not occur during brainstorming. Too often we tend to argue, discuss, or analyze ideas that are proposed. None of this should take place during the actual brainstorming session. Evaluation only occurs after all ideas have been stated.

My rules for brainstorming are as follows (adapted from Treffinger, 1980, p. 40):

1. Try to get as many ideas as possible.

2. Absolutely *no* criticism.

3. All ideas are accepted, as long as they address the problem or question posed.

4. No discussion or analysis of any kind; only ideas should be stated.

5. Evaluation occurs *only* when the brainstorming session is finished.

Brainstorming can be used to address fun, light-hearted questions ("How many things can you think of that are red and would fit in a pocket?"), or it can be used to generate ideas for more thoughtful issues ("How might we promote better race relations here at our school?"). The opportunities for brainstorming are endless . . . how many ways can you think of to incorporate this technique into your curriculum?

Idea Checklists. This technique provides yet another way to generate new and creative alternatives, especially when the well of ideas appears to have run dry. I frequently use the SCAMPER checklist developed by Alex Osborn (1963). SCAMPER becomes the acronym for key words that help trigger new thoughts and ideas. What can we *s*ubstitute? *c*ombine? *a*dapt or add on? *m*agnify (make larger), minify (make smaller), or modify? *p*ut to other uses? *e*liminate? *r*everse or rearrange? Other lists can also be used to generate ideas. For instance, a list of cities could give one ideas for recreation alternatives; a list of foods could suggest places to visit on a trip around the world.

Attribute Listing. This involves close examination of the characteristics or attributes of an object. After identifying attributes, one attempts to examine them in a variety of ways in order to generate new alternatives. For example, in analyzing a school desk students could identify its attributes as (1) a flat surface; (2) legs; (3) a seat; and in some cases (4) an inside compartment. Each of these can then be considered in terms of possible variations. Wheels could be added to the legs, they could be painted wild colors, or they could be made wider with small compartments. The top could be improved if it had a built-in computer, pencil sharpener, or recessed compartment to hold pencils, cups, and so on. The seat could be modified by making it adjustable, able to recline or rotate, or by adding a cushion.

Checkerboarding. This technique is a variation of attribute listing. Here, problems with two or more variables are analyzed by looking at specific combinations of ideas. One simply makes a checkerboard of boxes, then puts one set of variables across the top and another down the side. Each box represents how the variables along the top and side combine with or affect each other. For example, Figure 5–1 examines ideas for new and unique candy bars. It answers the question "What crunchy and gooey ingredients might we combine and cover with chocolate to create a new candy bar?"

Forced Relationships. This technique allows one to stretch "thinking beyond the obvious and the ordinary. . . [and] involves several different ways for us to look at new possibilities and combinations of objects or ideas that might not otherwise occur to us" (Treffinger, 1980, p. 48). For example, I frequently use a set of idea cards. Each card contains a picture of a different object. Two cards are drawn, and students think of ways the attributes of one object might be used to improve the other. For example, a forced relationship could be made using one card with a picture of a washing machine and another with a picture of a suitcase. The attribute that a suitcase can be carried might be applied to the washing machine to formulate the idea of a lightweight, portable, mini-washing machine!

Synectics. This technique, developed primarily by William J. J. Gordon (1961), is included in Treffinger's Level II ("complex thinking and feeling processes"). It strives to make the familiar strange and make the strange familiar through the use of metaphor and analogy. Three specific methods include direct analogy, personal analogy, and compressed conflict. Direct analogy is a simple comparison. For example, how is a walk in the park like a moonbeam? or in what ways are a book and a newspaper alike? In a personal analogy, identification with something or someone is made. For instance, one imagines to actually be the

FIGURE 5–1 Checkerboard: New Candy Bar Possibilities

CRUNCHIES

GOOEYS		Rice Krispies	Peanuts	Granola	Cashews	Banana chips
	Marshmallow creme	Rice Krispies and marshmallow	Peanuts and marshmallow	Granola and marshmallow	Cashews and marshmallow	Banana chips and marshmallow
	Nougat	Rice Krispies and nougat	Peanuts and nougat	Granola and nougat	Cashews and nougat	Banana chips and nougat
	Peanut butter	Rice Krispies and peanut butter	Peanuts and peanut butter	Granola and peanut butter	Cashews and peanut butter	Banana chips and peanut butter
	Caramel	Rice Krispies and caramel	Peanuts and caramel	Granola and caramel	Cashews and caramel	Banana chips and caramel
	Taffy	Rice Krispies and taffy	Peanuts and taffy	Granola and taffy	Cashews and taffy	Banana chips and taffy

kernel of popcorn waiting to be popped, the atom in a sugar molecule, and so on. How do you feel? What do you do? Compressed conflict is essentially the formation of an oxymoron—two words that seemingly contradict each other. "Shivery hot" might be used to describe being sick with a fever. Gordon used the words "safe attack" to describe Pasteur's pursuit of an antitoxin. Synectics is an interesting way to generate a variety of unusual and unique ideas.

These techniques are tools that can enhance the creative potential that all our students possess. They are easy to implement in any subject area, and they provide a fun opportunity for students to expand their perspective of the subject at hand. When we view creativity as a skill that can be taught and developed, we open up a world of opportunity with regard to problem solving.

THE FUTURE PROBLEM SOLVING (FPS) PROGRAM

The Future Problem Solving (FPS) Program represents a comprehensive approach to dealing with futuristic issues within a given framework, and it incorporates many of the problem-solving skills and behaviors we wish to foster in our students. The FPS Program was developed in 1974 by Dr. E. Paul Torrance, an expert in the field of creativity and professor of educational psychology at the University of Georgia. Torrance's concern about the decline of creativity in America and the lack of interest about the future among young people led him to adapt the Creative Problem Solving Process of Alex Osborn and Sidney Parnes within a framework of future issues (Noller, Parnes, & Biondi, 1976). The International Office of the Future Problem Solving Program is located in Ann Arbor, Michigan, and administrative directors coordinate state-run programs throughout the country, as well as those in several other nations across the globe. Approximately 200,000 students are involved in this challenging program each year.

Specifically, the goals of the FPS Program are to (Crabbe, 1990, p. 21):

- Increase the interest of young people about the future.
- Increase students' creative thought processes.
- Help youngsters increase verbal and written communication skills.
- Assist young people to function more effectively as team members.
- Provide young people with a problem-solving model to integrate into their lives.
- Assist students to develop and improve their research skills.
- Help children improve their analytical and critical thinking skills.
- Guide students to become more self-directed and responsible people.

In FPS, five topics are identified each school year. Three of the topics are used in conjunction with practice problems completed by students participating in state programs, one is for use at a state competition (state bowl), and one is used at the international level (international conference). Each year, a list of topics significant to our future is generated by the international office. Students involved in the program throughout the world then vote on those they would most like to study, and the five most popular topics are selected.

FPS: The Six-Step Process

Students tackle one topic at a time and begin by researching background information. This may include reading books and periodicals, viewing videos and films, scheduling lectures and interviews with experts, and taking field trips. Students may also use the resource manual developed each year by the FPS Program. This book is organized by topic and includes a compilation of annotated bibliographies, vocabulary, and questions for discussion.

When the actual problem-solving process begins, students are presented with a "fuzzy situation." This is a scenario of future events relative to the topic. An example of a fuzzy for the topic of water is included in Figure 5–2. Working together in teams of four, students complete the six steps of the FPS process. A description of each step, along with examples of students' ideas, follow.

Step 1: Brainstorming Possible Problems. Students read and analyze the fuzzy situation. They consider the facts that are presented in conjunction with what they know as a result of their research. They then brainstorm all the possible problems that might have helped cause, or might occur as a result of the fuzzy

FIGURE 5-2 Fuzzy Situation

Water

"[Hiss . . . crackle] Mission Control . . . The Pegasus has landed." With those words, the first humans, led by explornaut Aldara Terrini, set their spacecraft down on Terrini-K.

The year was 2020. Sponsored by the IASA (International Aeronautics and Space Administration), the international crew quickly set out to explore the planet. In three short months, they learned that Terrini-K was about half the size of Earth, and was very similar to Earth in terms of atmosphere, gravity, and wildlife (plants and animals).

Terrini-K had three large continents and several smaller landmasses which took up about 25 percent of the planet's surface. One continent had a hot and wet climate; another had a moderate climate; and the third had a very hot and dry climate. The other 75 percent of the planet's surface was covered by oceans. In less than three months' time, the Pegasus crew had finished its explorations and let Mission Control know that Terrini-K was ready for people to begin settling there.

* * *

Now the year is 2035. Although it has only been fifteen years since the Pegasus arrived, Terrini-K has been settled and has become much like a smaller version of Earth. New people are arriving each day, and the population has grown enough to support many cities, towns, and rural areas. The people living on and moving to Terrini-K come from all areas of Earth. Many choose to live in a climate that is similar to the one they knew on Earth. Therefore, there are people living on all three of the continents: Rhandu, which is hot and dry; Maia, which is hot and wet; and Aldara, which has a more moderate climate. The majority of people have settled on Aldara.

About 95 percent of Terrini-K's water is found in the saltwater oceans. Of the 5 percent fresh water, about 70 percent is frozen in the polar ice caps; 29 percent is found in soil moisture, groundwater (water beneath Terrini-K's surface), and aquifers (underground lakes). Only 1 percent is found in surface water (streams, rivers, ponds, wetlands, lakes, and the like).

When people moved to Terrini-K, they brought with them their Earthly technologies and habits. For example, 65 percent of their yearly water usage is devoted to agriculture, 25 percent is used by industries, and 10 percent is used for public needs (drinking water, household requirements, personal cleanliness, etc.).

Hydrologists (water experts) and others on Terrini-K are beginning to worry. With its rapid growth and development, Aldara is developing many water problems. Projects such as dams and canals are affecting surface waters. The gradual depletion of aquifers has begun. Industrial and hazardous wastes are starting to come into contact with the water supplies. The cities and towns have sewage to manage. Agriculture is having an effect on the water supply.

Aldara's water resources are in trouble. The Terrinians need help. Use your problem solving skills to brainstorm potential problems the Terrinians face with their water resources. Then help them solve one of the underlying problems.

Source: The Future Problem Solving Program, Ann Arbor, Michigan, third practice problem 1986–87. Reprinted with permission.

situation. From their brainstormed list of problems, students select twenty they consider to be most important and write them so that they clearly explain what the problem is, why it is a problem, and how it relates to the fuzzy situation. For example, problems relative to the fuzzy situation on water are as follows:

a. When it rains on Terrini-K, the water may wash away pesticides and/or herbicides. It may also pick up oil or rubber that cars left on the streets. This contaminated water may seep into groundwater and contaminate it. Because we will bring our technology and habits with us, farmers are likely to use pesticides or herbicides on Terrini-K, and we will probably continue to drive cars.

b. The farmers of Rhandu may divert water because the climate there is hot and dry and their water might evaporate quickly. This can be a problem because the wildlife that may inhabit the waters that the farmers divert may be disturbed. They may have trouble finding a new place to live and may die.

c. Because of its large population, Aldara may have to resort to desalinization to get enough fresh water. Desalination costs a lot of money. This is a problem because Aldara may need the money for other purposes.

d. Since we brought our technology and habits with us to Terrini-K, many of the agricultural techniques we use there may be inefficient. Agricultural techniques often waste up to 50 percent of the water used due to evaporation, seepage, or spillage during transport.

Step 2: Identifying the Underlying Problem. From their list of brainstormed problems, students identify one significant problem they deem worthy of solving. This problem, if solved, may help to address many of the other problems brainstormed in Step 1. For example, "How might we utilize agricultural techniques more effectively on Terrini-K in 2033 and beyond, so that water resources will be conserved?" is an underlying problem relative to water as indicated by the research and the fuzzy situation.

Step 3: Brainstorming Alternate Solutions. Using their imagination and creativity, students brainstorm a variety of alternative solutions to their underlying problem. They then select their twenty best solutions, and write them elaboratively as proposals for action.

Each solution must tell *who* will implement the solution, *what* will be done, and *why or how* it helps to solve the underlying problem. The following are possible solutions to the underlying problem listed in Step 2, "How might we use agricultural techniques more effectively?"

a. Farmers will install a "rubber infill dam" in their main irrigation canals. The dam would be sealed to the canal wall with supplied rubber sealant. Moisture-testing devices with sensors would be placed every 10 feet in the soil. If the sensor detected that the soil was too dry, the dam's air pump would let out air, making the dam smaller and letting water over and into a pipe to irrigate the area. If the sensor detected that the soil was too wet, the air pump would take in air, making the dam bigger and not letting as much water through. This would conserve water by not letting it constantly flow and evaporate. This would be especially helpful on Rhandu, the hot and dry continent.

b. Architects could design and construction workers could build dome farms. The domes could be made out of a clear plastic material. These farms would conserve water because the water used for irrigation would condense on the inside of the dome, and then fall back as rain on the crops below. To stop seepage of water underground, a plastic cover would be used underneath the roots of the plants.

c. Arctic ice could be molded into the shape of donuts and shipped to the farmers of Terrini-K along with a machine to disperse them. The machine would drop one donut around each plant. In a few hours, the ice would melt and water the plants. This would conserve water because most of the water will go directly to the roots and none will be wasted. This would be a good solution for Rhandu, because the heat would easily melt the ice.

d. Farmers will use "stair-step farming." This is where a field will be dug with different layers carved into the earth (somewhat like stairs leading down into the ground). Each layer will have a different crop on it, with the top layers having drier crops like cotton, and the bottom layers having wetter crops, like rice or cranberries. Each layer will be watered, but the lower layers will also get some of the water from the top layers as it leaches down to the bottom. This can conserve water because additional water for the wetter crops will not be needed.

Step 4: Selecting Criteria. Five possible criteria are identified that will be used to evaluate solutions. The criteria will help students determine how well each solution measures up in terms of solving the underlying problem. The following are examples of relevant criteria for the underlying problem in Step 2:

a. Which solution produces the most food on Terrini-K?
b. Which solution is most economical for farmers?
c. Which solution will conserve the most water?
d. Which solution is the easiest to implement technologically?
e. Which solution will farmers be most willing to do?

Step 5: Evaluating Solutions. Students choose what they consider to be their ten most promising solutions. They then use a grid to rank-order their solutions according to how they meet each criterion. The solution that best meets the criterion receives a 10; the solution that least meets the criterion receives a 1; all other solutions fall somewhere in between. The numbers for each solution are then totaled, and the best solution is the one with the highest score. Figure 5–3 is the grid that was used by my students for the problem on water.

Step 6: Describing the Best Solution. Finally, students write up a plan for implementing their best solution. They improve on their idea by describing what will happen, who will be involved in the implementation, where and when it will occur, how it works, why it helps to solve their identified underlying problem, obstacles to be overcome, and so on. As you can see from the grid in Figure 5–3, dome farms and stair-step farming were tied. Therefore, this particular FPS

FIGURE 5–3 Water Problem Criteria and Grid

Criteria for evaluating alternative solutions

1. Which solution will produce the most food on Terrini-K?
2. Which solution will be the most economical for farmers?
3. Which solution will conserve the most water?
4. Which solution will be the easiest to implement technologically?
5. Which solution will farmers be most willing to do?

Alternative Solutions	Criteria					Total
	1	2	3	4	5	
1. Dome farms	9	10	10	2	10	41
2. Solar tanks	8	7	2	1	4	22
3. Covered trench	3	4	8	8	5	28
4. Drip irrigation	4	2	7	7	6	26
5. Stubbles	5	3	6	9	9	32
6. Rubber infill dam	7	8	5	4	7	31
7. Saucers	6	6	4	3	2	21
8. Stair-step farming	10	9	9	5	8	41
9. Ice donuts	2	1	1	10	3	17
10. Rain collector	1	5	3	6	1	16

team chose to combine those two ideas to create stair-step dome farms. One way they elaborated on the ideas stated in Step 3 was to include a system of pumps within the dome. Any excess water collected at the bottom would be pumped to layers needing more water, thus continuing to promote the recycling of water. Sensors would indicate which layers needed water and could control the pumps. This particular team actually devised a model of their idea to test its feasibility. It worked!!

Benefits of FPS

Future Problem Solving is a most effective and comprehensive problem-solving activity. Students become empowered with the knowledge they gain, and often take pride in the fact that they can and actually do communicate about significant issues of the future with their parents and other adults. They devise strategies for working through team conflicts, develop the art of negotiation and compromise, and learn how to put aside differences for the good of the team. Within the six-step process, students use their creativity to generate many possible problems and solutions. Analysis and evaluation represent higher-level thinking skills used to determine which information gathered from their research applies to the fuzzy situation, and which problems and solutions are most appropriate. Different ideas are synthesized as students work together to formulate a best solution. The decision-making process that incorporates identified criteria in a grid format is particularly effective. Students have even reported using it to make important decisions in their personal lives. Therein lies the beauty of Future Problem Solving: it becomes a lifelong skill that students can use outside of school. It is a powerful way to examine important issues and solve future problems.

Techniques to Enhance the FPS Process

As a result of my experience, I have discovered some helpful techniques and strategies that enhance the FPS process, such as the futures wheel, cross impact matrix and idea checklists. These will be discussed in this section, and a list of resources from the Future problem Solving Program will be provided.

Future's Wheel. "A future's wheel is a method of predicting positive and negative results of an event, idea or trend. [It] help[s] identify long-range and short-range effects of any topic" (McCumsey, 1984, p. 1). A future's wheel is based on cause and effect. It allows one to track a chain of events that might result from an identified situation. A selected event, central issue, or continuing trend is placed in the center circle (see Figure 5–4). First-order effects are then noted in the connecting circles. For example, if we place "students attend school at home via computer" in the center circle, some first-order effects may be that (1) kids may have fewer opportunities to socialize with their peers, (2) students may be able to progress through material at their own rates, (3) children may be more flexible in scheduling when they want to go to school, and (4) students could easily skip school if both parents work. Each first-order effect will in turn have a consequence, or second-order effect. These are then written in circles that are connected to each first order effect. For example, if students socialize less with their peers (first-order effect), they may become lonely and depressed (second-order effect). Third-order effects would be consequences of second order effects, and so on. The goal is to list both positive and negative consequences. Results can be discussed, compared and analyzed for similarities and differences.

The future's wheel is useful because it tends to point out consequences that were not initially recognized. In fact, some of the more interesting and creative ideas often surface as third- or fourth-order effects. I use the future's wheel for each topic during the year, particularly to map out related problems and solutions. For example, in studying the tropical rain forests, we were introduced to the solution of ecotourism. By placing this concept in the center circle of the future's wheel, we explored its consequences, both good and bad. I have also had students use a future's wheel to develop story lines for scenarios, futuristic stories that will be discussed later in this chapter.

Cross Impact Matrix. This technique, shown in Figure 5–5, "is a method for thinking about the future that is designed to help clarify interrelationships between issues, events, or trends. Each of the trends is entered on both horizontal and vertical positions of the matrix [checkerboard]" (McCumsey, 1984, p. 6). The purpose of the cross impact matrix is to answer the question, "How do x and y affect each other?" For example, in dealing with the topic of stress on students, we might identify the following trends: paren-

FIGURE 5–4 Futures Wheel

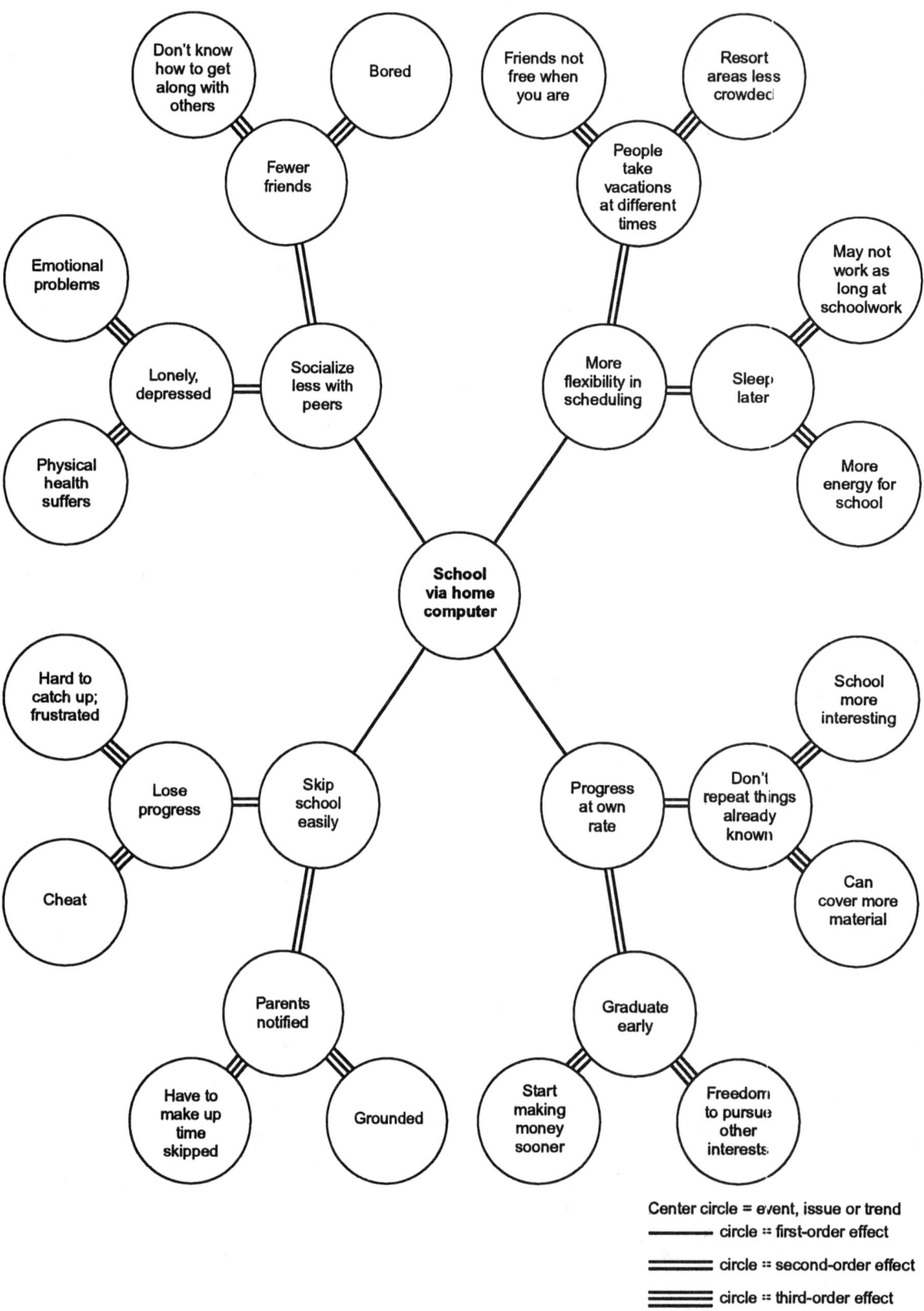

Source: Framework from J. McCumsey, *Exploring the Future*, (Carthage, IL: Good Apple, 1984), pp. 4, 5. Reprinted with permission.

FIGURE 5-5 Cross Impact Matrix

Topic: Stress on Students

Cross Impact Matrix – Today

How will this affect this? →	Parental pressure to succeed	Lack of individual attention due to large classes	Increase of violence in the schools	Eating disorders
Parental pressure to succeed		Students who fall behind may get even more pressure from parents.	Parents may be so worried about their child's safety that they may ease up on pressure to succeed.	Parents need to be educated about the causes (stress/ pressure) and signs of eating disorders so that they will reduce pressure.
Lack of individual attention due to large classes	Parents can volunteer to help in classes to facilitate greater success.		Teachers may be less willing to help those students they perceive as violent.	Students with eating disorders may be less likely to ask for help in class (due to lack of self-esteem, often a cause of the disorder).
Increase of violence in the schools	Students may be angry/ violent because of parental pressure.	Students who fall behind/fail may resort to violence to feel powerful, in control.		Poor nutrition can affect emotional well-being; could lead to violent behavior.
Eating disorders	Parents may be the cause of eating disorders.	No attention/help at school may compound the eating disorder.	Students may not be eating at school because they are too nervous about violence/being hurt or harassed.	

Source: Framework from J. McCumsey, *Exploring the Future* (Carthage, IL: Good Apple, 1984), p. 7. Reprinted with permission.

tal pressure to succeed, lack of individual attention due to large classes, the increase of violence in the schools, and eating disorders. We would then ask ourselves, "How do parental pressure to succeed and lack of individual attention due to small classes affect each other? Parental pressure to succeed and the increase of violence in schools? Parental pressure and eating disorders? All possible combinations are shown in Figure 5–5. The cross impact matrix can be used in Future Problem Solving to investigate the impact of certain problems or solutions. It provides yet another way for students to examine how one event influences another.

Idea Checklists. This strategy, mentioned earlier in this chapter, also comes in handy during the FPS process. My students learn the key verbs that each letter of the SCAMPER acronym stands for (see p. 147) and use them to generate ideas for possible solutions to identified problems. The set of categories that the program uses in evaluating a team's flexibility score may also serve as a checklist to generate new ideas. They are: business and commerce, transportation, social relationships, environment, education, technology, recreation, government and politics, ethics and religion, arts and aesthetics, physical health, psychological health, basic needs, defense, economics, law and justice, and communication. In addition to suggesting new solutions, thinking through categories helps students to avoid "tunnel vision" by forcing them to focus on other realms of possibility for dealing with issues.

Resources. I use many additional activities to promote an awareness of future events, help students to cope with change, and provide some of the tools to help them analyze and deal with the issues of the future. The Future Problem Solving Program provides a number of materials that are excellent in this respect. Selected FPS and other sources are

- Crabbe, A. B. (1983) *The Activity Book*. Laurinburg, NC: The Future Problem Solving Program.
- Crabbe, A. B. (1986). *Creating More Creative People*. Laurinburg, NC: The Future Problem Solving Program.
- Crabbe, A. B. (1988). *Creating More Creative People: Book II*. Laurinburg, NC: The Future Problem Solving Program.
- Eggers, J. R. (1981). *Will You Help Me Create the Future Today? A Guide to Making It Happen*. Buffalo, NY: D.O.K.
- Future Problem Solving Program. (1987). *Thinking ahead: Teaching for the Future*. Laurinburg, NC: The Future Problem Solving Program.
- McCumsey, J. (1984). *Exploring the future: Basic Skills and Activities for the Futuristic Thinker*. Carthage, IL: Good Apple.

Teambuilding and Teamwork

In Future Problem Solving, students work together in teams of four. Establishing teams can be tricky, especially in middle school where social relationships and rapport with peers are of primary importance to students. A strategy for grouping students and tips for developing successful teamwork skills will be discussed in this section.

Forming Teams. Through trial and error, I have devised a system for forming teams within my classroom that works well for me and my students. At the onset, I make it clear that I will be assigning teams based on the following considerations: (1) student preferences, (2) a balance of abilities, (3) FPS experience, (4) a balance of girls and boys, if possible, and (5) avoidance of personality conflicts.

To begin, students list their preferred peers, knowing that I will guarantee at least one person on their list as a teammate. In balancing abilities, I analyze intellectual talent as well as specific characteristics that help constitute a good FPS team. The ideal team would consist of one person who is a strong writer and speller; one who is highly creative; one individual with leadership abilities who can provide encouragement and direction, maintain order, and keep the peace; and one who is good at managing time and keeping team members on task. I also try to balance inexperienced students with those who have participated before, making sure that no team is composed solely of students who are new to FPS. When students list their teammate preferences, they also indicate if they (1) prefer a coed team, (2) prefer an all-girl or all-boy team, and (3) mind being the only girl or boy on a team. This helps me equalize the number of boys and girls wherever possible. Finally, I try to avoid forming a team where there are obvious personality conflicts, although learning to resolve differences is one of the skills we work on during the year. This method of forming teams has proven to be quite successful. It alleviates hurt feelings that can result when students are left to choose their own teams and blatantly eliminate one or more individuals from consideration.

Since there are three practice problems, I regroup students to form new teams for each one. This way each person gets to work with a number of other individuals throughout the year. The only exception occurs if a team's third practice problem qualifies them to attend the state bowl. In this case they will stay together as a team to prepare for and participate in this event.

When students are learning and practicing the actual FPS process, they do not always work in their teams. I constantly regroup them for daily activities that promote creativity, teamwork, and problem solving. This is often done randomly, although at times I assign groups to allow two or more individuals to work together who have not already done so. My goal is to have students experience working with all class members on many occasions during the year. Consequently, they get to know each other better, and a greater understanding and appreciation of each individual results. Hopefully, students will thus be more accepting of any classmate they are assigned to work with on a team.

Teamwork. Throughout the year, I conduct a variety of general activities to develop cooperative teamwork skills. As we examine the nature of conflict, I stress that differences of opinion are desirable and necessary. A good activity for illustrating this point is to show the optical illusion in which one sees an old lady or a young lady (or both), depending on one's perspective. This demonstrates "that two people can see the same thing, disagree, and yet both be right" (Covey, 1989, p. 27). We explore strategies for resolving disputes, such as time outs, compromise, and finding totally new alternatives when compromise cannot be reached.

Empathic listening is also presented as a way to reduce conflict. This is achieved when one listens actively to the speaker's message and rephrases both the content and the feelings. Communicating one's needs and desires in a more positive manner can also help to diminish conflict. "I messages" identify "what another person is doing, how one feels as a result, and why the other person's actions make one feel that way. For example, "I get frustrated when you keep interrupting me, because it makes me feel like what I have to say isn't important" (Buckmaster, 1994, p. 59). This works much more effectively than the comment, "Shut up! You never let me finish!"

Other activities are designed to be fun, yet emphasize the importance of teamwork. For example, in "The Chocolate Kisses Game" (Educators for Social Responsibility, 1983), "two students [are] asked to sit and grasp hands in an arm wrestling position. They [are] then told that they [will] receive one chocolate kiss every time the back of either partner's hand [touches] the table. The purpose is to demonstrate that cooperation is actually physically easier than competition, and, in this case, the activity produces immediate abundant rewards in the form of candy" (Buckmaster, 1994, p. 59).

In "Cooperative Structures" (Stanish, 1988), students work in teams and, without talking, use a bag of gumdrops and a box of toothpicks to create a structure that is free-standing, sturdy, and at least 1 foot tall. In "Scrambled Sentences" (Stanford, 1977), each student in a team receives an envelope of words. "Without talking, each student [has] to give words to and accept words from his or her teammates, so that each person in the group [can] make a sentence" (Buckmaster, 1994, p. 60). Both of these activities emphasize the importance of cooperation when working in a team. A follow-up discussion for both of these activities is necessary and valuable: Who was frustrated and why? What worked well? What didn't work? Did anyone in your group take charge and ignore the wishes of others? Did anyone hinder the group by not actively participating? What would you do differently if I had you do this activity again?

Once students are assigned to teams, I have them focus on the dynamics of their particular group. For example, as a class we list characteristics of a good FPS team. Students then individually itemize their strengths and weaknesses and later share them with their teammates. Teams then analyze their composite positive and negative attributes, discuss ways they might use their talents to overcome shortcomings, and map out specific strategies. For instance, because Janie is weak in spelling and grammar, Tony will proofread her work. Or, if too much talking or arguing is frustrating anyone, he or she will slap the table, and all talking will stop for 5 seconds.

Teamwork is a necessary skill that students will need in their adult personal and professional lives. Future Problem Solving offers middle schoolers an opportunity to contribute more positively in a group, and become more accepting and tolerant of others.

Options for Implementation

Future Problem Solving is suitable for a wide range of abilities, even though it was originally implemented with gifted students. The topics studied and the process used often stimulates students to think in new and exciting ways. The problem-solving process used in FPS is a valuable tool for all children. It allows them to analyze interesting and important information, encourages them to use their imaginations and creativity, and challenges them to make decisions about their futures. Future Problem Solving can supplement the curriculum via enrichment opportunities, or it may be directly incorporated into a number of academic areas.

Enriching the Curriculum. A teacher can use the FPS process as an enrichment activity in any subject. The program's identified topics can be used, or an issue that is familiar to students and requires no formal research can be employed (e.g., school graffiti, the food in the cafeteria, racism, or violence in the schools). One might also apply the process to a matter of importance for a particular subject area: the Vietnam War in history class, a dilemma of a character in literature, or the greenhouse effect in science. In this situation, a teacher can work with the entire class and go through the process together one step at a time.

Many schools implement Future Problem Solving as an after-school club. With this option, students often do their research on their own outside of school. Club time can then be devoted to discussing the literature, learning and applying the process, and working together as teams.

As Part of the Curriculum. The amount of reading, writing and discussing that occurs in FPS forms the basis for an emphasis in communication skills. Therefore, FPS can easily be incorporated as part of one's language arts curriculum. Because the program focuses on topics of social and scientific significance, it might also be included in a social studies and/or science class. As a seventh-grade core teacher, where students stayed with me for a two-hour time block each day for language arts and social studies, I had a perfect opportunity to incorporate Future Problem Solving. An FPS topic that focused on a social issue such as censorship could often be used to enhance curricular objectives of both subjects. I could also compact my curriculum in language arts or social studies when appropriate in order to provide more time for FPS activities.

As a language arts teacher, I also had the opportunity to teach FPS in place of seventh grade English instruction. Here students and their parents signed a statement of understanding that outlined what this class would and would not include. For both curricular options, students were selected based on their applications and teachers' recommendations. Incorporating Future Problem Solving into the curriculum on a daily basis is a comprehensive alternative that can be very successful if one has an interested teacher, along with the support of the building principal and parents.

Additional Components of the FPS Program

The Future Problem Solving Program provides additional opportunities for students in a variety of areas such as creative dramatics, scenario writing, and community problem solving. Each of these are described below.

Creative Dramatics. Teachers who use Future Problem Solving in their classrooms can incorporate creative drama in the development of presentations to sell best solutions. "The purpose of the presentations is to place the students in a position where they must actively try to convince others that their ideas are worthy of consideration" (Crabbe, 1990, p. 23). This is a most popular activity with students. Again, the art of communication within a unique format is reinforced, and it presents a fun and interesting dimension to the problem-solving experience.

At state bowl and international conference competitions, students are required to develop a three-minute presentation. They have anywhere from two hours to overnight to develop their ideas and practice. They are challenged to use their creativity in designing props, which are limited to those that can be constructed from a specified list of unusual materials (e.g., tinfoil, paper clips, a Sunday newspaper, ping-pong balls, yardsticks). Presentations are performed and judged separately from team problem solving. They are scored for the relationship of the presentation to the best solution, the degree to which it provides the audience with a complete picture of a solution that could be implemented, humaneness, appropriate use of space, communication of ideas (verbal and nonverbal), creativity, involvement of participants, and overall persuasiveness of presentation (Crabbe, 1990, p. 76).

I like to begin teaching elements of creative dramatics at the beginning the year, focusing on pantomime, expression of dialog, use of props, and improvisation. Students begin by examining emotions and how they might be portrayed without words. We move to acting out specific situations (pulling in a big fish, a day at the laundromat, and so forth), focus on body language (posture, gestures, facial expressions), and eventually use dialogue as we experiment with tone of voice and projection. As practice problems are solved, teams can apply the skills they have learned to act out their best solutions under the guidelines used at the state and international competitions. Besides developing communication skills, creative dramatics is always fun for students. It helps us focus on talents that exist beyond the academic realm and provides yet another way for middle schoolers to become more actively involved in their learning.

Scenario Writing. Scenario writing is another option of the Future Problem Solving Program. Students create a futuristic scenario of 1,500 words or less based on one of the identified topics for the year. "One of the ways for students to think futuristically is to create images of what the future may be like. The Scenario Writing component of the FPS [Program] strives to help students enlarge, enrich, and make more accurate those images of the future" (Crabbe, 1990, p. 72).

Scenarios can easily be incorporated into any creative writing experience within the language arts curriculum. A scenario, as defined by the Future Problem Solving Program is "a story that might take place as a logical outgrowth of actions or events that took place earlier. It is a prediction of the future and is written as though the future were the present. [It] is a . . . story in which one possible outcome of the future is developed through character(s) and plot" (Shewach, 1987, p. 6).

I often require that my students write one scenario during the year, particularly if I am teaching FPS as part of the language arts curriculum. Using *The Scenario Writing Guide* as a resource (Schewach, 1987), I begin by reading many examples to give students a feel for this particular type of writing. After discussing the specific characteristics of a scenario as defined by the Future Problem Solving Program, students choose one of the year's identified topics and begin by doing research to better understand the issues involved. In developing a story line, brainstorming, futures wheels (explained in a previous section), and group discussions are often used to focus on problems or solutions associated with the topic. Once students begin writing, they conference frequently with me and their peers to continually clarify and refine. As they progress, scenarios are read to the class for further feedback.

Scenarios may also be submitted for evaluation and are judged on the following elements: (1) creative imagination; (2) social and cultural influences (purposeful, humane, strong sense of values, ecological concerns, global outlook); (3) feelings and emotions (empathy, emotional reaction from the reader); (4) structure; (5) future thinking (awareness of future trends); (6) interest (exciting to read, holds the reader's attention); (7) character development; (8) mechanics; and (9) style (Crabbe, 1990, p. 73). In scenario competitions, the top three in each division are invited to attend state bowls. The three state winners in each division compete at the international level, and winners are invited to attend the international conference.

Community Problem Solving (CmPS). This option is one of the most exciting features of the FPS Program. Students use the FPS process to identify and solve a real problem that exists in their community. "A community problem may be one that exists within the school setting, the local community, the state or national community, or even the world community" (Crabbe, 1990, p. 74). Solutions are actually implemented, giving students experience in a community service project of their own design. This is FPS at work in the real world, and some of the projects that students have completed are simply amazing. A few of the CmPS activities implemented during various school years are as follows:

- Promoting awareness about medium chain acyl CoA-dehydrogenase deficiency (MCAD), a treatable genetic disease that causes infant death. Students were successful in getting House Joint Resolution 657 passed in the Virginia General Assembly, which encourages the department of health to study the feasibility of testing for MCAD.

- Improving the physical environment surrounding certain schools in Dallas, Texas, so that the students can be safe. Because of the bill they introduced and community lobbying, a few of the neighborhood liquor stores were closed down.

- Commemorating the contribution of the men in one community who gave their lives in Vietnam. This entailed the creation of a monument listing

the names of individuals from Lamar County, Texas, who died in the war.
- Preventing the sludge at a wastewater treatment plant from freezing. A solar greenhouse was built around the sludge-carrying belts of the plant. By using a wood and plastic frame, it was constructed for considerably less than the brick building the city had proposed, saving $119,500.

Community Problem Solving can be implemented in the curriculum, or it may be conducted as an after-school club. Teams are not limited to four students, and having an entire class work on a project together is appropriate. I have had experience with CmPS as a part of an eighth-grade social studies class. A group of 20 students met with me every other day to plan activities for their community project on the homeless population. On days they did not work with me, students met with their regular social studies teacher, who compacted their history curriculum to accommodate their needs. These students had applied and were selected for the class. Their project was to increase community awareness of and involvement with our city's homeless population. In addition to conducting food and necessities drives at our school, students had a two-day craft sale at a local mall to raise money for homeless shelters. Craft items sold were made by students, and $1,090 was earned. Food and necessities drives were also held at the mall grocery and drug store, and a learning display in the mall informed the public about the issues involved.

To enter the CmPS competition, a report of a team's Community Problem Solving efforts can be sent in to the state program for evaluation. This report includes the fuzzy situation that the students faced, the underlying problem that they identified, a description of their best solution(s), and their plan for implementation. State winners may be invited to attend the international conference where they have a chance to use their problem-solving skills to find solutions to an identified problem from the hosting city.

Evaluating the Program

Paying a yearly registration fee entitles teams to receive valuable suggestions from trained program evaluators. The feedback provided is designed to help teams learn how to be better communicators and problem solvers regardless of whether they enter the program on a competitive or noncompetitive level.

How FPS Work Is Evaluated. Problems and solutions are analyzed for fluency (number of relevant ideas), flexibility (number of categories of ideas), elaboration (expounding on the specifics of their ideas), originality (uniqueness of ideas), and clarity (how effectively ideas are expressed). Underlying problems are graded for completeness (inclusion of a key verb phrase, a purpose, and parameters), adequacy (importance of the problem chosen), and focus (whether the problem has been effectively narrowed). Criteria are judged as to whether they are relevant and correctly written, and the grid is checked to see if it is correctly used. The best solution is scored on its relevance to the underlying problem, effectiveness (the degree to which it solves the problem), impact (how it affects the fuzzy situation), and humaneness. Scores are also given for evidence of research, overall creative ability, and futuristic thinking. Teams receive a numerical score for each of these items, as well as extensive comments from evaluators for each step of the process. The emphasis in FPS evaluation is on encouragement. Therefore, in addition to suggestions for improvement, students are recognized and praised for their ideas. Through extensive feedback, students learn to improve their problem-solving skills.

FPS as a Competitive Option. Most states have programs that coordinate the competitive aspect of Future Problem Solving. In this case, coaches work with teams of four students in one of three divisions: junior, grades 4–6; intermediate, grades 7–9; and senior, grades 10–12. Teams receive three practice problems, each of which focuses on a different topic. When each practice problem is completed, students send their work to trained evaluators, who provide an analysis of their application of the process, use of creative problem-solving skills, and clarity of expression. Teams that score highest on the third practice problem are invited to attend their state bowl, where another problem on a fourth topic is solved. Here, one winner in each division is selected and invited to participate in the international conference, where students tackle a problem on yet another topic. This event provides an opportunity for state champions and winning teams from other participating countries (Canada, Australia, New Zealand) to meet and participate in the final competition of the year.

The FPS Program produces a number of books for teachers and coaches. These include guides for coaching and enrichment activities that focus on developing creativity and futuristic thinking. These materials, along with additional information about the program can be obtained by contacting the international office: Future Problem Solving Program, 318 West Ann Street, Ann Arbor, MI 48104-1337. Phone: (313) 998-7FPS.

INTERDISCIPLINARY UNITS GENERATE STUDENT INTEREST

There are many units that are thematic in nature; that is, they implement activities that cover a number of academic disciplines. Such units provide a common thread that we can weave through the middle school curriculum. They allow students to get a better feel for the interconnectedness of the disciplines and, as such, provide a learning experience that is more closely related to life in the real world. Two such units will be discussed in this section. One allows students to develop a new sandwich idea. The other involves the creation of a trip plan for crossing the United States.

Jam and Peas on Rye . . . Hold the Mustard!

In my teaching I have discovered that one way to my students' hearts is through their stomachs. A most successful enrichment unit is one I developed in which students create a new and unusual type of sandwich. Attributes of a sandwich are examined, variations of each attribute are brainstormed, and these ideas are used to arrive at four new sandwich possibilities. Each sandwich is then analyzed according to its popular appeal, nutrition, and cost. Students learn to apply a decision-making process to determine their best sandwich idea. Descriptions and advertisements of their sandwiches are prepared, and the unit culminates in an actual taste test. This interdisciplinary unit focuses on a variety of creative problem-solving techniques, as well as the application, analysis, synthesis, and evaluation of information in a variety of content areas.

Getting Started. To begin, my students and I work together using the creative problem-solving techniques of attribute listing and morphological analysis. Attribute listing identifies the major attributes or characteristics of an object and examines them more closely (Treffinger, 1980). Together we discuss and list the attributes of a sandwich —"holder," fillers, additives, spreads and sauces. Morphological analysis "is derived from the word *morphology,* which is the study of form and structure. Thus, in using this technique, we are attempting to solve a problem and to identify new ideas by examining very closely the form and structure of the problem. [It] helps us look at the structure of the main parts of the problem . . . in order to seek new combinations of elements and ideas" (Treffinger, 1980, p.58). Morphological analysis helps us to identify the myriad of sandwich combinations by brainstorming a list of the variations each attribute might take. For example, the sandwich holder might be whole-wheat bread, pita bread, lefsa, a tortilla, a waffle, a doughnut, a chocolate chip cookie, and so on. Likewise, spreads and sauces may consist of tobasco, mustard, yogurt, chocolate sauce, salsa, marshmallow creme, cashew butter, and many more. The possibilities for each attribute are endless! This is a time where students can be encouraged to diverge into the realm of the unusual, a most popular concept for middle schoolers.

Exploring the Possibilities. Next, by mixing and matching variations from each attribute, students are presented with virtually unlimited possibilities for new and unique sandwich combinations. "When we attempt to combine systematically all possible components . . . we are forced to consider a number of ideas or combinations that might otherwise have been discarded or overlooked" (Treffinger, 1980, p. 58). Using this strategy, students individually choose four new sandwich combinations that they personally prefer. In order to maintain some degree of sanity, a workable rule of thumb is that any sandwich combination is acceptable, as long as the student is willing to eat it. Figure 5–6 is an example of a sandwich attribute list that uses morphological analysis to illustrate two possible sandwich combinations. One consists of peanut butter, a chocolate bar and vanilla yogurt between two waffles. The second combo is avocado and radishes with Dijon mustard on an onion bagel.

Analyzing the Options. The third phase of the unit alternates class instruction with independent work as students begin to evaluate their sandwich possibilities according to four criteria:

1. *Which sandwich is the most popular?* We begin with a discussion of surveys in general. What are they used for? How are they conducted? Who

FIGURE 5–6 Sandwich Attribute List Using Morphological Analysis

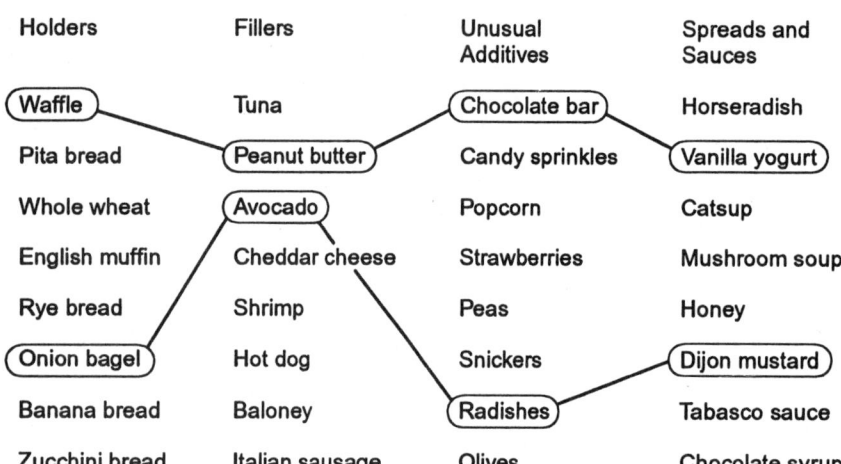

should be surveyed? Different surveys may be presented and analyzed. Students then develop their own form and conduct surveys outside of class to determine their most popular sandwich. For example, students may record the age, grade, sex, and sandwich preference of each person interviewed. Besides establishing overall popular appeal of sandwich possibilities, survey results can be examined together in the classroom in a variety of ways. For example, do any correlations exist between age and choices made? between sex and choices made? Percentages can be computed and compared. Teachers can determine just how extensively they wish to deal with analyzing the data obtained.

2. *Which sandwich is most nutritious?* A lesson on nutrition is presented. This can be structured in a variety of ways, depending on teacher preference. I like to invite a nutritionist to class to help students evaluate the nutritional value of their sandwiches. A determination can be made informally by looking at the overall representation of more nutritious ingredients, or a more formal analysis can be implemented (e.g., computing the number of calories represented by protein, carbohydrates, and fat).

3. *Which sandwich costs the least to produce?* Again, this can be done rather informally, or ingredients can actually be priced out. If price lists can be obtained from wholesalers or local supermarkets, a math lesson might be used to compute costs.

4. *Which sandwich do I like the best?* Each individual student can make a personal determination as to which sandwich combination they think they'll like best overall.

Each student, working independently, evaluates his or her sandwich possibilities according to how well they meet the criteria discussed earlier, using the decision-making grid from the Future Problem Solving Program (Crabbe, 1990). Sandwiches are ranked from 1 to 4 on each criterion with 4 given to the sandwich that best meets the criterion, 1 to the sandwich that least meets the criterion, and so on. The numbers for each sandwich are then added, and the one with the highest total is selected as the best sandwich combination. An example of a grid and the results of one student's decisions are shown in Figure 5–7.

Final Touches. After each student has selected his or her best sandwich, students help each other think of creative names for their culinary creations. Menus from local restaurants are analyzed as a class to get a "taste" for how foods are described. Then, using their creative writing skills, students work individually to create descriptions that might appear on a menu. Three examples are

- *The Flyaway Hambo*: Our chef has a special feeling for this tasty sandwich. Flavored pizza with ham add up to a striking, zesty combination when placed on a biscuit with melted Swiss cheese. A miracle with sesame seeds!

FIGURE 5–7 Sandwich Decision Grid

	Most popular	Most nutritious	Costs least	One I like best	TOTAL
The Flyaway Hambo	1	4	3	1	9
Start Spangled Banana	2	2	2	3	9
The Chessburger	4	3	4	2	13
A Dentist's Dream	3	1	1	4	9

- *A Dentist's Dream*: Try this scrumptious sandwich for dessert! This delightful treat features a hot, fresh, Danish roll covered with creamy peanut butter, smothered in hot melted chocolate, and sprinkled with candy bits and sugar. Be a pal to your sweet tooth!

- *The Chessburger*: A meal fit for a king! It checkmates your tastebuds with ground steak and fried shrimp. Gourmet popcorn and thin wafer cakes steal a pawn while fighting on your stomach. This sandwich won't end any reigns with its exquisite hollandaise sauce. Try it—it will knock your armor off!"

Next, advertising techniques are studied together as a class, and each student prepares a poster and/or a commercial to "sell" his or her sandwich. The unit culminates with a taste testing party, where posters are displayed and each student actually brings his or her best sandwich to school. Classmates taste and evaluate each other's sandwiches, a memorable activity that is often the highlight of the unit. Following the taste test, a discussion and/or vote can help to determine the overall most popular sandwich in the class.

Implementation. How one schedules the activities for "Jam and Peas on Rye..." is dependent on teacher preference, students' abilities, and other unrelated classroom activities that may take precedence. Conducted in its entirety on consecutive days, this unit takes approximately two weeks. However, teachers may also extend the unit, interspersing its activities with other classroom endeavors as they see fit.

Because "Jam and Peas on Rye..." is interdisciplinary in nature, it can be a suitable enrichment unit in a number of subject areas. Certain activities can be eliminated or extended depending on the class being taught. For example, in math or science, more emphasis can be placed on the nutritional analysis and/or the statistics behind the sandwich survey. In language arts, one could focus more on writing sandwich descriptions and on advertising. The unit may also be enriched in a number of ways to accommodate a particular subject more effectively. In social studies, one could compare sandwiches in other cultures. For example, where do sandwiches as we know them exist? What other forms of the sandwich can we find in foreign countries? The possibilities for where and how to use "Jam and Peas on Rye..." are endless. I personally have had success with it in my middle school language arts and social studies classes, as well as in fifth grade when I taught at the elementary level.

Accommodating Learning and Teaching Styles. This unit is also flexible with regard to learning and teaching styles. Large-group activities are desired at the beginning of the unit to generate a variety of sandwich ingredients. Class discussions are also interspersed to solicit ideas, present information, and reflect on what has been learned. Field trips to restaurants or advertising agencies are also possible. Small group and/or cooperative group work can be used intermittently for certain activities such as thinking of sandwich names, analyzing sandwich costs, and computing nutritional value. Students also have the opportunity to work individually throughout the project when they actually conduct the survey, complete the decision grid, and plan their advertisements. Guest speakers can also enhance the unit. Besides having a nutritionist visit my classroom, I have had a marketing professional from the Oscar Mayer Foods Corporation talk to students about food merchandising.

I have found this unit to be successful with students of all levels of ability. It is easy to simplify or extend certain activities when necessary in order to meet a variety of needs. For example, more advanced students might investigate the psychology behind advertising, write a story about a sandwich that comes to life, or contact the manager of a restaurant to see about serving one's sandwich on a trial basis. Less able students might conduct a more simplified survey, work in pairs or with a tutor to write a sandwich description, or have someone compute the cost of producing each sandwich for them. Thus, teachers are free to structure the unit as they desire, eliminating or adding activities to best suit the needs of their students.

Resources. The resources for this unit are few, and are basically ones I have developed. When brainstorming, I use large sheets of chart paper rather than the blackboard. This way one can easily stop when one class period ends and conveniently continue on another day. Students will need to neatly list the ingredients of their four sandwiches to show survey takers. Teachers and/or students may devise their own survey sheets, depending on the data they wish to obtain. Since prices fluctuate, I either obtain lists of wholesale prices from local markets, or talk directly with restaurant owners about their costs (for example, with students on a field trip). Students may draw their own decision grids, or teachers may reproduce them. The materials are simple and the format is flexible, depending on what makes sense for a particular teacher or group of students.

Evaluation. Students' work may be evaluated in a number of ways. One could put emphasis on the fact that the project is completed, noting each specific component (survey, grid, description, advertisement) successfully accomplished. I have also set deadlines for the various activities involved and awarded points based on their completion. A simple checklist can be used to record points earned as follows:

_____ Final copy of four favorite sandwiches: 10 points (Due Jan. 24)

_____ Survey completed: 25 points (Due Jan. 27)

_____ Grid: 10 points (Due Feb. 1)

_____ Sandwich description, rough draft: 10 points (Due Feb. 3)

_____ Sandwich description, final draft: 15 points (Due Feb. 7)

_____ Poster or Advertisement Script: 30 points (Due Feb. 10)

_____ TOTAL (100 points possible)

Students may evaluate each other's sandwiches via the description, advertisement, and/or taste test. Again, this is at the teacher's discretion. I do not require that each student bring in a sample of his or her sandwich for the taste test, so as not to embarrass anyone who is unable to do so. A letter home to parents about the taste test helps to explain the event and often generates support from home.

This unit represents one of the key elements to success with middle school students: freedom within a structured format. They like the fact that they are free to choose their four sandwiches, and that they may "sell" them in a way that they determine to be effective. Interest remains high throughout the unit, as students continue to analyze something that they've created. There is an element of suspense connected with the eventual discovery of the "best" sandwich. Because basically any idea is accepted, students develop a sense of pride in their concoctions. Knowing that a taste testing party is in store also keeps students motivated. Once the unit has begun, students are generally so enthusiastic, it is often hard to bring the day's activities to a close. "Jam and Peas on Rye . . ." is a most enjoyable unit; one that truly stimulates the enthusiasm and creativity of all types of students.

U.S. Trip Plan

In this interdisciplinary unit, students plan a trip within the United States. Routes are charted, daily activities are planned, and all costs are computed. In addition to learning about various U.S. cities, famous landmarks, and points of interest, students are introduced to the financial realities that would impact a trip of this kind. Because the planning involved simulates what one might encounter in the real world when organizing a vacation, students see a purpose for the assignment and interest is heightened. John Kaiser and John Sabatini of Madison, Wisconsin, developed many of the activities in this unit.

Generating Interest. This unit is implemented in our seventh social studies program during a focus on map skills and U.S. geography. To begin, I like to play an identification game with the class. I write the name of a fairly well-known location (for example, Mount Rushmore, The Grand Canyon, Disney World, Old Faithful, Los Angeles, Yellowstone National Park) on a 3-by-5-inch index card and pin one to the back of each student's shirt. When I give the signal to begin, students must try to find out who they are by asking others questions relative to their identity. The only questions allowed are those that generate a *yes* or *no* response. For example, "Am I a city?" "Am I in the western part of the United States?" "Am I a popular vacation spot?" When all students have discovered who they are, a discussion is held relative to some of the identified points of interest. Who has been to Los Angeles? What can you tell us about it? Which of these places would you like to visit and why? We then locate places on the map, classify them by regions of the United States, and/or rank-order them according to a variety of criteria (most popular, most fun to visit, farthest distance from our city, and so forth). I ask each student to come to class the next day with a list of fifteen places that they would most like to visit in the United States.

Trip Plan Prerequisites. The trip plan is briefly introduced the next day. I tell students that they will be organizing an ideal vacation within the United States, adding that money is no object. From their lists generated the day before, students work alone, in pairs, or in small groups to choose at least ten places they would most like to visit on their trip. After a review lesson on the format for a business letter, students write to one state's chamber of commerce or bureau of tourism for information on points of interest, recreational activities, lodging, and the like. During the one to two weeks it takes to receive this information, we proceed with related map activities that will enhance work on the actual trip plan. For example, using direction, scale and legends; reading charts, graphs and timetables; understanding time zones; and comparing the various regions of the United States are skills that students will need to successfully complete the project. In addition, we obtain a highway map for each student from our state's department of transportation. Lessons on how to use it are conducted, a practice packet of activities is completed, and a test is given. An instruction sheet for the unit is shown in the Appendix.

Getting Organized. Once students begin receiving information in the mail, specific details of the trip plan are outlined and discussed. In organizing their vacation, students must complete the following:

- *Cover sheet.* This includes a title, the student's name, section number, and pictures or drawings of some of the places visited.
- *Map.* Using a small outline map of the United States, students must show the city of departure and all the sites visited. These sites are connected to indicate one's basic route.
- *Daily log.* This record sheet shows the place of departure, destination, routes traveled, mileage, and approximate travel time for each day.
- *Daily costs.* This chart shows where students plan to stay each day and how much money will be spent on lodging, food and miscellaneous items (shopping, tourist attractions, supplies, and so forth).
- *Total costs.* Students use this sheet to compute total costs for the entire trip. In addition to total lodging, meal and miscellaneous expenses, a formula for determining the cost of gasoline is included.
- *Points of interest.* Students must choose up to three places that they will be visiting, to feature with a written description and picture or illustration.

Each of these activities are described in detail, and overheads of sample record sheets and points of interest are shared. Examples are also posted in the room for easy reference during the project. Record sheets and samples for logs and costs are included in the Appendix.

A discussion of travel time relative to one's chosen vehicle and type of highway (e.g., interstate versus county road) helps students focus on what is realistic in terms of their itinerary. For example, it is probably not feasible to travel 600 miles and spend eight hours at Disney World all in the same day. In their enthusiasm to plan the ideal trip, students often lose sight of such realities. Reminding them of certain limitations helps them problem-solve through their options to achieve a more sensible trip plan.

Research. In addition to information they receive in the mail, students use a variety of materials that I provide for them, such as atlases, almanacs, travel guides, and magazines (*Travel and Leisure*, *National Geographic*, and so forth). A most valuable resource is the American Automobile Association (AAA), which has provided us with U.S. road maps and a set of tourbooks for every state. The tourbooks are especially helpful in listing and pricing recreation areas, points of interest, lodgings, and restaurants. Educators who are members of AAA can contact their local office for materials.

Because students will be researching and writing about certain points of interest, I take the opportunity to provide a lesson on notetaking. I find that middle school students still rely on copying information out of books or encyclopedias. Besides pointing out that this is plagiarism, I emphasize that this method is actually far more time consuming. The following three-step notetaking strategy is most successful in encouraging students to use their own words when writing summaries and reports: (1) students read a passage and write down key words and phrases, (2) the source is removed so that students no longer see the written information, and (3) students use their key words and phrases to construct original sentences. After demonstrating the technique, I have students practice with a number of short passages shown on overheads. Having many different individuals share their summary paragraphs illustrates the variety of ways the same content can be expressed.

Once all lessons have been conducted, students have approximately two weeks of class time to complete their trip plans. We may work in the school library or the classroom, depending on the resources needed on any particular day. I continually circulate among students, providing assistance and clarifying procedures as needed on an individual basis.

Enrichment and Extension. Because students work at different rates, I like to provide enrichment opportunities for those who finish early. These include the following:

- Change the words to a popular song or write a poem or rap to tell about the highlights of your trip.

- Rank-order the places you visited according to the following criteria: (1) most historical, (2) least costly, (3) farthest distance from Madison; and (4) most fun.

- Design a travel poster or travel brochure for one of the places you visited.

- Do some research to compare and contrast the transportation costs to your farthest city (e.g., car, bus, train, plane). List the plusses and minuses of each option.

- Considering the season of the year, the length of your trip and the location of the places you will visit, make a list of all clothing and supplies you would pack to take with you on this trip.

- Research a career that pertains to the travel industry (travel agent, airline pilot, hotel or restaurant manager, etc.).

- Interview someone from a travel agency or the American Automobile Association to find out ways these organizations serve the public.

- Find out how computer technology is used in the today's travel industry.

These opportunities provide ways for students to extend their study in a variety of areas, depending on their interests and abilities. Having alternative activities available also alleviates potential problems from students who finish early and, for lack of something better to do, distract others who are still trying to complete the project.

Evaluation. I evaluate this project according to the following criteria: (1) the number of places visited; (2) the completeness and accuracy of the map and record sheets; (3) the quality of the written description of points of interest; and (4) neatness and organization. In analyzing these elements, points are awarded as follows:

- Cover sheet: 2 points
- Map: 3 points
- Number of places visited: 1 point each; 10 points maximum
- Daily log: 20 points
- Daily cost chart: 20 points
- Total cost chart: 10 points

- Points of interest: 10 points each; maximum of 30 points
- Neatness and organization: 5 points
- TOTAL: 100 possible points

Teachers can use their own scale to convert numerical scores to letter grades as they see fit. Students are informed of the grading procedure at the beginning of the project in order to help them focus their energies most appropriately. For example, students should recognize the futility in spending three class periods on a cover sheet. Instead, most of their effort should be put into completing the daily log, daily cost sheet, and points of interest.

To Group or Individualize? That Is the Question. I have implemented this unit where students complete trip plans on an individual basis, in pairs, and in small groups. All have been successful. When students collaborate in groups, work distribution becomes an issue, and specific roles may need to be assigned. For example, each student might be required to compute routes, mileage and costs for three cities and also write up two points of interest. Because evaluating a project for each individual can be quite time consuming, teachers may well opt for having three or four students work together.

Variations on the U.S. Trip Plan Theme. This unit can easily be adapted to focus on other countries. For example, Gilbert Jelinek and Paul Schoenike of Monroe, Wisconsin, have developed a similar unit where students plan a trip through Canada. They have used the Canadian Consulate General in Chicago, Illinois, as a resource for relevant materials. One might also implement a world trip plan as well. Appropriate sources of information on hotel and restaurant costs worldwide could be obtained via travel agencies or in the variety of travel guidebooks found in many bookstores and libraries.

This unit might also be modified by limiting the amount of money students may spend (daily and/or totally), the amount of time one has for the trip, modes of travel, and/or the number of total miles one may travel. Students will then need to analyze their choices and problem-solve in light of the imposed restrictions.

Another option is to include a daily twist of fate to impact decisions students must make. Cards outlining specific emergencies and windfall opportunities could be drawn each day. For example, "Flat tire," "Run out of gas," "Detour," "Dead battery," "Free admission to the tourist attraction of your choice," "shortcut saves 50 miles," and so forth, add an element of suspense and force students to modify their daily plans and expenses as they might in real life.

The U.S. trip plan has been a most successful unit in our middle school. It provides a specific structure, yet allows students flexibility in choosing places they wish to "visit." The importance of language arts skills is emphasized through letter writing, notetaking, research, and expository writing. In addition to the focus on geography and map skills, math is used to compute mileage and expenses. Students who complete enrichment opportunities use critical thinking skills in the areas of art, music, and science. Once again, freedom within structure provides the basic principle behind this project, making it most appropriate and enjoyable for adolescents.

SOCIAL STUDIES DOESN'T HAVE TO BE DEADLY

There are many opportunities within the social studies curriculum for students to use their creative and critical thinking skills. Problem solving can be the instrument that makes social studies come alive. When students have a chance to simulate, manipulate, and/or create past and future places and events, they become more involved in their learning and assimilate information much more readily.

Two social studies units will be examined in this section. The first deals with the issue of survival and allows students to apply what they have learned in an actual outdoor experience. The second works within a geographical framework whereby students create an imaginary country.

Survival of the Fittest

Our seventh-graders absolutely love the survival unit that is implemented within the social studies curriculum. Perhaps because it is a diversion from our customary focus on geography, or perhaps because it applies so practically to real life, students become enthusiastic learners. We begin the unit at the beginning of January on our return from winter break. Activities culminate with an outdoor field trip where students apply the survival techniques they have learned as they problem-solve their way around the winter woods. Knowing about the trip in advance provides yet another incentive to become more actively involved. This unit can be modified in many ways, depending upon one's location, and the materials and resources available.

Initial Investigations. We begin with a warm-up activity in which students complete the sentence, "Survival is . . . ." The class brainstorms a list of responses, which I record on chart paper. Ideas are then analyzed via discussion. I ask students why they say survival is "dangerous," "exciting," "fun," and so forth. This helps to generate further dialogue: What exactly defines a survival situation? Who has encountered such an experience? What supplies do you think are necessary in an emergency? What human characteristics help or hinder survival? Students often share a variety of survival situations that either they or someone else has experienced.

The next day we progress to a survival quiz to determine how much students already know about the topic. The quiz consists of true or false questions, such as "Snow is such an excellent insulator that it's all right to sit or even sleep directly on it," and "In cold, damp climates, wool clothing provides the best protection against the elements." The survival quiz and answer key, are reproduced in the Appendix. I like to have students work in pairs and cooperatively decide on what they believe to be the correct responses. Later, we go over the answers together as a class to clarify information and dispel common misconceptions. The quiz generates considerable discussion and storytelling, so much so that this usually takes an entire class period.

Getting the Facts. The unit continues with a number of lessons that present information on survival strategies for a variety of situations. These are carried out via videos, filmstrips, worksheets, readings, games, simulations, and so forth. The resources are many and varied, and represent a compilation of activities from many individuals. Two teachers in particular, John Sabatini and John Kaiser of Madison, Wisconsin, have worked hard to find and develop many of the materials for this unit and have generously shared them with me. Some examples are listed next. Although many of them are dated, they are itemized to give the reader a general idea of the content that can be covered. This represents a starting point from which teachers can diverge to find and create their own appropriate resources.

- *Hypothermia—Outdoor Enemy Number One* (1984). Norwood, MA: Beacon Films. This film presents information about hypothermia using two case study dramatizations. Symptoms are identified, and the proper step-by-step treatment is demonstrated.

- *Winter Survival in the Bush* (1982). Norwood, MA: Beacon Films. In this film, three real-life situations are presented to show what should and should not be done in certain winter survival emergencies. Symptoms and treatment of hypothermia, how to build a fire, how to construct a lean-to shelter, how to signal for help, and what to put in a homemade survival kit are discussed and illustrated.

- *Surviving the Cold* (1985). Santa Monica, CA: Pyramid Film and Video. Through re-enactments of three actual emergencies, the hazards of winter weather are depicted in this video. Information includes how to recognize and treat hypothermia, how to prepare your home for winter emergencies, how to prepare for travel in winter, and what to do if trapped in a blizzard.

- *Journey* (1974). Washington, DC: National Geographic Society. This film shows the challenges that a group of teenagers confront as a result of an outward-bound experience.

- *Solo* (1972). Santa Monica, CA: Pyramid Film and Video. This video illustrates three aspects of mountain climbing: sustained physical effort, adaptation to weather changes, and commitment to challenges that must be met alone.

- *Survival Sense* (1976). Portland, OR: Odyssey Productions. Four filmstrips present information on (1) how to build a fire; (2) how to build a lean-to, A-frame, wickiup, and snow trench shelter; (3) desert survival, dehydration, and how to build a solar still; and (4) food for survival in the wilderness.

- *Student Booklet: Survival* (1976). New York: Scholastic Book Services. This booklet contains a variety of survival stories including "Survive the Savage Sea," a true story about a family shipwrecked in the Pacific Ocean; "A Long Way Up," the true story of Jill Kinmont's struggle to cope and adjust after being paralyzed in a skiing accident; "I Never Had It Made," an excerpt from the autobiography of Jackie Robinson, which portrays his battle to survive insults and racial discrimination; and "Growing Up in the Barrio," a true story about how a teenage girl deals with prejudice, poverty and family problems.

- *Surviving in the Rockies* (Stanford, 1977, pp. 193–199). In this simulation, students are presented with the scenario of being stranded in a snowstorm in the Rocky Mountains after an automobile accident. They come upon a cabin that is well-stocked with camping equipment and other supplies. From a list of twenty-eight items, students must decide which they will wear or carry (not to exceed 50 pounds) for the three days they will travel to reach help.
- *Lost on the Sixth Moon of the Justinian System*. Campbell, D. (1994). Cooperative Group Problem Solving: Adventures in applied Creativity. Torrance, CA: Frank Schaffer Publications. Students simulate a forced landing on a moon 175 miles from their space station. They must rank-order fifteen items salvaged from their space ship in terms of their importance for survival.
- Lafferty, J.C. and Eady, P. M. (1974). *The Desert Survival Situation*. Detroit, MI: Experiential Learning Methods, Inc. This simulation describes a plane crash in the Sonora Desert. Students are told that they have been able to salvage fifteen items, and they must rank-order them from most to least important. This and the previous two simulations follow the same basic format: (1) students choose or rank items individually; (2) students work in small groups to compare individual rankings and reach consensus; and (3) the choice or ranking from a survival expert is shown and compared to that of students.

Other Resource Possibilities. For this unit, any activity that illustrates or practices survival techniques and strategies is appropriate. Often past and current newspaper and magazine articles that report relevant survival stories are read and discussed. For example, the James and Jennifer Stolpa story became a top news item in January 1993. Their struggle when stranded with their infant for more than a week in the snowy Nevada outback illustrates the importance of one's will to survive. Guest speakers from the American Red Cross or other organizations might also be available to give demonstrations on first-aid techniques or provide information on disaster relief. Novels that feature a variety of survival situations, such as *Julie of the Wolves* by Jean Craighead George, *Dogsong* by Gary Paulson, or *So Far from the Bamboo Grove* by Yoko Watkins can also be read and discussed. One might examine survival as a nation as it relates to war, conflict resolution, and world peace. Issues such as world hunger and dealing with the aftermath of natural disasters can also be analyzed in relation to survival. Ties to science can be made when exploring survival of the fittest in the context of evolution. The possibilities are virtually endless!

Survival Projects. During the first week of the unit, a variety of survival project opportunities are presented. Students must select one or more activities, and their project grade is determined by the overall quality of their work and the number of activities completed. This allows students the flexibility to choose a specific aspect of survival that interests them as they apply what is being learned in class. Options are provided in a variety of areas to maximize certain strengths that students may have. For example, keeping a survival log (social studies challenge activity) may interest students who enjoy a creative writing opportunity, while building a model shelter may appeal to those who prefer more of an artistic, hands-on experience. Another option is a book review of a survival story. All activities are explained in detail to the class, and more specific instructions are provided via a survival bulletin board where various worksheets are housed. Although students complete projects outside of class, two or three periods are provided for research. Project instructions and options materials also are presented in the Appendix.

One of the most beneficial projects is the survival kit. I encourage all students to make one with whatever resources they have at home to bring on the upcoming field trip. I take an entire class period to share the contents of a kit that I have put together. Discussion about the role of each object relative to survival situations is generated, along with ways to improvise for items that may not be available in individual circumstances. An enjoyable day is spent at the end of the unit when all students share their survival kits and other projects with the class. Instructions for the survival kit can be found in the Appendix.

Putting Theory Into Practice. The highlight of the unit is a half-day field trip to a near-by nature center, where students apply what they have learned. Each group of approximately ten students is accompanied by a naturalist. Equipped with survival kits and their own ingenuity, students hike to the middle of a wooded area and use the available natural resources to build a fire and make a shelter. The fact that we are working in the dead of winter certainly augments this challenge. However, I am continually amazed at the cooperative and creative efforts that always get the job done. This is problem solving at first hand! Students analyze their surroundings and decide on a plan of attack for building a shelter, based on their background information. If one idea doesn't pan out, another is tried until they are satisfied with the end result. Firebuilding in winter is never as easy as students expect, and trial and error is again the mode of operation. The naturalist serves as the true guide on the side, reinforcing concepts that are important to consider when working in the winter woods, but allowing students to experiment and learn from their own setbacks and successes. Once fires are built and shelters are completed, students feast on hot chocolate and other goodies they have brought to enjoy. This is always such a fun outing that we have a hard time getting students to leave. It is an opportunity they talk about and remember for a long time. For me, the experience continually reinforces my belief that middle school students thrive on relevant, hands-on activities where they can apply what they have learned in a creative and meaningful way. This unit fits the bill every time!

Evaluation. Three basic forms of evaluation are used in this unit: (1) performance on daily activities; (2) an analysis of students' survival projects; and (3) the results of a unit test. As indicated on the "Survival Project Instructions Sheet" in the Appendix, a project grade is determined by the number and quality of activities completed. I base my evaluation of the survival kit primarily on one's effort. Some students enthusiastically visit sporting goods and other stores for items to include in their survival kits; others cannot afford to do so and therefore should not be penalized for lack of certain items. Students receive credit toward their project grade if they bring a homemade survival kit and share it with the class, regardless of the number of items they include. Other projects are given a letter grade at my discretion, depending on the quality of work.

The survival test is an essay exam. It is designed to provide students with an opportunity to directly apply what they have learned, rather than simply memorize and repeat information. Because it focuses on Bloom's higher levels of thinking (analysis, synthesis and evaluation), it provides a way for students to address the problems and situations presented using all the information they have obtained throughout the unit.

Modifying the Unit. Although this unit is conducted during a cold and snowy winter at our school, it can easily be adapted to a variety of other situations, depending on one's location. For example, an emphasis could be placed on survival strategies for desert, mountain, or specific forest environments. Those who live in warm climates or near a desert might focus less on the symptoms and treatment of hypothermia, and more on those of dehydration.

Regardless of its primary focus, "Survival of the Fittest" provides a meaningful learning opportunity that is fun to teach. I never hear the ever-popular middle school question "Why do we have to know this?" Students seem to appreciate the acquisition of practical information that they might use in the future. The anticipation of an actual field experience maintains a high level of interest throughout the unit. Best of all, because they are genuinely interested, students experience overwhelming success.

Create a Country

Geography is the focal point of the curriculum for seventh-grade social studies in my school district. "Create a Country" is a culmination of the year's activities where students apply concepts learned to design an original nation. This unit is fairly structured in that specific elements are dictated that must be included within the project. However, students have the freedom within that structure to diverge as they desire. Important geographical skills and concepts learned throughout the year are applied in a comprehensive, yet creative way. It is adapted from activities in Rand McNally's *Exploring Geography: Using the Atlas,* 1986. This project is generally assigned just prior to the last four to six weeks of school. It consists of four required maps, a written report, and extra credit opportunities. Students may work independently, with a partner, or in small groups to complete the project, depending on teacher preference.

Geographic Considerations. I begin by providing each student with a set of instructions that we go over together (see the Appendix). I tell them that they will be designing their own country and will get to decide on its features. The following information is outlined and discussed:

- *Location and size.* Students must first decide where they want to put their country. They may put it anywhere on the planet Earth, with the exception of the poles. Although many students choose to have an island, they may also carve their country out of an existing landmass. I generally suggest that countries be from 500–1,000 miles either across or lengthwise. Lines of latitude and longitude must be drawn according to the scale they establish. Students must also specify which continent they are on or considered part of and determine their square miles, relative size, and population. I require that some type of political divisions be included within their country (states, provinces, counties, and so forth). Students enjoy creating some very clever names for their capitals and other important cities.

- *Physical geography.* Much of students' physical geography is determined by the location selected. Landforms, rivers, lakes, seas, climate (including rainfall and temperature), and vegetation are features that students must decide on and describe. These elements are also illustrated on one or more of the four required maps.

- *History and government.* This is where students can really use their creativity to tell me the origin of their country. How, when, and why did it form? Who settled the country? Wars and conflicts that occurred throughout the country's history can also be described. The type of government is specified, along with the country's past and present government leaders.

- *Economic geography.* Here students decide on their unit of currency and its U.S. equivalency. Natural resources are determined along with chief products. What the country imports and exports are also described, including a designation of the countries they exchange with and the reasons why items are traded.

- *Cultural geography.* Students have the opportunity to create some unique cultural features for their country. In this section everyday life is explained, including traditional foods eaten, languages spoken, education, religion, recreation, and so forth. Traditions and holidays are also presented. Famous places that might be visited are described as well. This is a fun section for most students. They let their imaginations go wild and create some very interesting cultural characteristics!

Mapping it Out. I encourage students to begin this project by completing the four required maps:
(1) physical and political, (2) density of population; (3) rainfall and temperature, and (4) vegetation. Students first outline their country and draw their lines of latitude and longitude. This is always one of the most difficult parts of the project. Students need to establish how far apart each degree of latitude and longitude is according to their scale, depending on where they are on the globe. For this reason, a refresher lesson on latitude and longitude is given on the first workday of the project.

I have students make one good copy of their map, which includes lines of latitude and longitude, major lakes and rivers (drawn but not labeled), scale, and the name of the country. Then I xerox four or five copies for them to use in completing the four required maps as follows:

- *Physical and political.* This map shows political boundaries and land elevation. Rivers, lakes, and oceans are labeled and colored blue. Students choose other colors to represent each level of land and create a legend. Borders are clearly designated, and all states or provinces are named. Capitals and other major cities are also labeled.

- *Density of population.* A color is chosen for each density of population designation. In deciding where different densities will occur, students are encouraged to consider the location of large cities and urban areas, physical features that people might favor, and specific regions where people would like to live (for example, near water) or not like to live (such as in a desert).

- *Rainfall and temperature.* Rainfall amounts are represented by various colors designated in a legend. Isotherms are drawn in to show summer and winter variations of average temperature. Of course, rainfall and temperature are determined by the location that has been chosen. Students need to consider what the climate is actually like in their part of the world, how the shape of the land affects climate, how mountains affect rain, and so forth.

- *Vegetation.* Varying types of vegetation will be designated by colors identified on a legend. The land, rainfall and temperature will determine the types of vegetation that will be prevalent in a particular country. Students need to consider which plants will grow in the different regions of their country.

Students are encouraged to check the atlas to find examples of areas in the world that are similar to their country. The current *Rand McNally Classroom Atlas* has been an excellent source for this project. It depicts each type of map just described for a number of countries.

Working in the Library Media Center (LMC). After our initial review lesson on latitude and longitude, we hold class in the school LMC (library media center), where students work independently on their projects. This allows for easy access to resource materials for research on specific areas or countries of the world. Even though this unit represents a culmination of information learned throughout the year, students usually need to review the characteristics of specific areas in close proximity to their created country. Specific details regarding climate, vegetation, culture, economics, and so forth provide students with a starting point from which to diverge in deciding on the features of their country. Also, because our library adjoins the production room, working here provides easy access to the copy machine, which allows me to xerox students' maps as they are completed. Teachers without such an arrangement may collect original maps as they are completed and copy them for the next day. In this case, students can work on researching, planning, or actually writing their written reports in the interim.

Final Development. For the duration of the project, students work independently as I continually circulate, monitoring progress and assisting where necessary on an individual basis. I generally allow a three- or four-week period before projects are due. This does not mean that we spend every class working on this activity. After our initial week in the library, I use my judgment as to whether additional class work time is necessary. I want to be sure that all students have a good understanding of what the project entails, and that they have made significant progress so that they can finish successfully on their own. I do expect students to work on the project outside of class. Therefore, this becomes their homework for the remaining two to three weeks before the project is due. Daily reminders and time for answering questions are provided at the beginning of each class period until the projects are collected.

A number of optional extra credit opportunities are also provided. These include creating three additional maps that feature environments (urban, farmland, and so forth), highways, and economic resources; creating a country flag and including a written description of the symbolism represented; a travel poster that features the country or one of its famous cities; and a travel brochure that describes places of interest.

Evaluation. There is no getting around it—evaluating this project is time consuming. I find that it takes approximately three to four hours to read all the projects from just one class. Students could conceivably work in pairs or groups of four, resulting in fewer overall products to grade. However, I do many other group projects during the year, and because this serves as an end-of-the-year activity, I prefer that students independently demonstrate their ability to apply some of the basic geographic concepts learned. Therefore, I simply plan ahead to allow myself ample evaluation time.

In an attempt to be as objective as possible, I use a checklist and assign points for each of the required elements. I give a copy of this checklist to students at the beginning of the project and encourage them to use it to be sure that they include all the important features. To get the full number of points, students must *describe* rather than simply list items of the feature in question. For example, in the section on physical geography, merely naming the landforms would be worth one point ("Nevar has the Isi Mountains, the Ginibex Desert, and the Lionne River"). Describing something about each one would be worth two points. Such a description might include naming the specific landform, telling where it is located, and/or adding other information that explains it in more detail. For example, "Bordering the western coast of Nevar are the Isi Mountains. These span a distance of 600 miles from north to south and feature Mount Beaumont, the highest peak at 19,864 feet. The Ginibex Desert in the north–central part of the country has an area of 2,400 square miles. No one inhabits this harsh wasteland. The Lionne River, the longest river in Nevar, winds its way through the central part of the country for 360 miles."

I compute a percentage based on the number of points a student earns and use my own scale to determine a letter grade. I also include comments for each project. This takes the form of a "comment sandwich." I begin by recognizing something positive, describe what was missing or could have been elaborated on, and conclude with another positive statement.

Students incorporate some incredibly creative ideas, and reading about each contrived country is always enjoyable. Anything and everything goes, from a dome-covered island that serves as an ecological haven and research center, to a new nation formed when Rhode Island secedes from the United States under the leadership of Rush Limbaugh! "Create a Country" provides students with the freedom to diverge and create within a geographical structure. Once again, this proves to be a perfect combination for middle school students.

THE POWER OF POSITIVE ARGUMENTATION

One of the unique characteristics of adolescents is their tendency to be controversial. After all, have you ever known a middle school student who didn't like to assert an opinion or argue with you at one time or another? But how many students know how to defend their positions logically? Our students need to learn the skills involved in presenting an argument in a rational and compelling manner. In the following approach, students are introduced to a format for examining many sides to an issue of their choice and are given the latitude to argue for or against it. In essence, they problem-solve their way through an important topic and develop an organized and convincing presentation. Once again, this activity encompasses the perfect format for the middle school student: freedom within structure.

Why Argumentation?

First of all, "students have difficulty presenting full or convincing arguments because they have little experience with well-reasoned argumentation, not surprising in a society that does much of its persuading in thirty-second sound bites" (Anderson & Hamel, 1991, p. 44). Too often when we ask students why they feel strongly about something, they respond with defensive and irrational explanations, what I like to call the "I'm right because I am, and you're not" syndrome. According to a report of the National Assessment of Educational Progress (NAEP), "on most tasks requiring eighth- or twelfth-graders to convince others or to refute an opposing position, fewer than a third of the responses were judged adequate or better" (National Council of Teachers of English, 1991, p. 33). We cannot assume that effective argumentation is something that students will naturally develop over the years. Defending one's beliefs clearly and credibly is a skill that must be learned and practiced. "We need to provide more opportunities for students to learn how to present an argument or belief in a convincing manner" (Moebius, 1991, p. 38).

Secondly, well-developed persuasive writing and speaking skills are likely to be important to our students in their personal lives outside of school. They need to be equipped with a structured way to interact respectfully with others on a variety of issues that impact them. In their workplaces and social lives, they will undoubtedly experience opportunities where the art of effective argumentation will be to their benefit.

Third, positive argumentation fosters a greater awareness of the complexity of issues (Moebius, 1991). It helps students to consider the many facets of crucial concepts and concerns, "not just a narrow 'thesis' they have arbitrarily chosen to advance" (National Council of Teachers of English, 1991, p. 33). Thus, they learn to refine their logic and develop the proof behind their ideas.

Finally, through persuasive argumentation, students become more directly and actively involved in their learning. When a school assignment revolves around issues that are dear to their hearts, students become more motivated to learn and develop their skills. They take on more active roles and become more accountable for their own learning.

I must concede that developing argumentation skills does take time. It doesn't happen in one or two lessons, especially if students research their topics and also practice their presentations. There are no shortcuts to developing the skills involved. It's up to individual teachers to decide how they will find time within the curriculum for argumentation.

Objections exist regarding the teaching of argumentation skills in middle school. One is the belief that argumentation is unsuitable for introverted, shy, or habitually disinterested students. They fear that such students will find this activity difficult and embarrassing. However, I have found just the opposite to be true. In my experience, argumentation has had a universal appeal and has stimulated enthusiastic participation from all types of students. Those who are more timid and reserved do extremely well when they work with others to form a group argument. Shy students will gain confidence the more they experience successful, enjoyable opportunities in which to present their ideas.

Another objection comes from those who say that the critical thinking skills required may prove too difficult for some students, particularly those with low ability or special needs. Again, grouping students of varying abilities can help to assure a balance of expertise. Regardless of ability, all students have opinions about issues. I have found that low-ability students are often able to provide a new perspective with an opinion, while more able students can help them refine the logic behind it. It's often a perfect combination.

Teachers may contend that it is too hard to convince adolescents of the need for well-reasoned argumentation. After all, companies in the real world constantly bombard them with fast-paced, glitzy commercials to present their points of view and sell their products. But this is even more reason to encourage critical thought. Students need to be encouraged to look beyond what is merely presented to them or what seems obvious at first. They need to know how to examine the many sides of an issue in order to make good decisions in life.

Finally, some teachers might object to the noise and commotion that can result as students plan, discuss, organize, and practice their argumentation presentations. However, you will find, as I did, that it is a productive chaos. As an added bonus, certain discipline problems often disappear because students become so involved in what they are doing.

Arguing is a way of life for most middle school students. Let's give them a structured way to state their views in a positive, logical manner. Don't argue with your students; show them the way to argue for themselves.

The Argumentation Format

The preceding section actually follows the argumentation outline presented to students. This format was developed by Lori Hamann and Loree Schultz at Cherokee Middle School in Madison, Wisconsin. The parts of the argument are as follows:

1. The argument is introduced with a *lead* to get the audience's attention, and is followed by the *claim*, a statement of one's position on the topic.
2. *Supports* present evidence for the claim. For each support a *warrant* is given, providing proof for the support.
3. Any weaknesses of your argument are made up front as a *concession*.
4. *Objections*, or arguments one might have against your claim, are stated, and a *rebuttal* is made to defend the claim against each objection.
5. The argument concludes as you *reaffirm the claim* by restating your position, and finishes with a *clincher* to leave the audience with something memorable.

Let us look at each of the five steps in more detail, using my argument as an example for clarification.

Step 1: Introducing the Argument. The introduction begins with a *lead*. The purpose of the lead is to get your audience's attention as well as introduce the topic. In language arts, I continually stress the importance of the lead. As writers and speakers, we need to "grab" our audiences to convince them that we are about to present something worth listening to. The sooner this can be done, the better, for if we neglect to get our audience's attention, our efforts to persuade others of our positions will be in vain. My lead in introducing argumentation was to ask the following: "Have you ever known a middle school student who didn't like to assert an opinion or argue with you at one time or another? But how many students know how to state their positions in a logical and convincing manner?" These are two questions most middle school teachers can identify with; hence, my hope was that you would be interested in hearing more.

The *claim* makes a statement about something that ought to be done or not done. It is a statement of opinion and tells what you personally believe. My claim was that our students need to learn the skills involved in presenting an argument in a rational and convincing manner.

Step 2: Supporting Your Position. *Supports* give as many kinds of evidence and as strong evidence as possible to prove one's claim. They answer the question "What makes you feel this way?" Possible types of evidence for supports include what the experts say, specific data (statistics, survey results, etc.), personal experience, what has happened in the past, and what is likely to happen in the future.

Each support is followed with a *warrant*, a statement that helps to prove that your support substantiates your claim. Warrants answer the question "What makes you so sure?" I gave four supports and warrants for my claim that students need to learn the skills involved in presenting an argument in a rational and convincing manner:

1. I emphasized that students have trouble presenting convincing arguments due to lack of experience (support). I stated the results of a report of the NAEP and added that effective argumentation is not a natural ability, but rather, one that must be developed by providing more opportunities (warrant).
2. I asserted that persuasive speaking skills will be important to our students in their lives outside of school (support). I cited their workplaces and social lives as environments where effective argumentation would be to their benefit (warrant).
3. I stated that positive argumentation fosters a greater awareness of the complexity of issues (support). I pointed out that students are forced to think critically, refine their logic, and develop the proof behind their ideas (warrant).
4. I argued that students become more active learners when they learn argumentation skills (support). I added that they become more involved because the activity revolves around issues that are important to them (warrant).

Step 3: Conceding Weaknesses. *Concessions* allow you to admit any weaknesses your argument might have. There may be objections to your claim that you cannot refute in rebuttal. By acknowledging these shortcomings up front, your opponents are less likely to use them against you. I conceded that developing argumentation skills can be quite time consuming, and that teachers will need to decide how and when to implement them into the existing curriculum.

Step 4: Objections and Rebuttals. *Objections* that opponents might raise to challenge your claim are now stated, and for each a *rebuttal* is given to point out the weaknesses in your opponent's objection. A rebuttal might include exposing the prejudice of the opponent's argument, presenting previously ignored information, redefining basic terms, interpreting the evidence in a new way, or quoting an authority who contradicts the opposition's authority. The four objections and their respective rebuttals presented in my argument were as follows:

1. *Objection:* Argumentation may be unsuitable for introverted, shy or habitually disinterested students. *Rebuttal:* Personal experience has shown otherwise. Shy students will gain confidence with this type of activity, especially if they work with a group of their peers.
2. *Objection:* The critical thinking skills required may prove too difficult for low-ability or special needs students. *Rebuttal:* Grouping students of varying ability can help assure a balance of expertise. At times low-ability students provide a new and interesting perspective that can be logically refined with the help of a more able peer.
3. *Objection:* Adolescents may not be convinced of the need for well-reasoned argumentation due to a society that bombards them with fast-paced commercials to present their views and sell their products. *Rebuttal:* This is even more reason to encourage critical thought. Students need to look beyond what is merely presented to them or what seems obvious at first.
4. *Objection:* There may be too much noise and commotion involved in this type of learning experience. *Rebuttal:* It is a productive "chaos," and discipline problems often decrease because students are involved in what they are doing.

Step 5: Reaffirmation. To conclude the argument, you *reaffirm your claim*. This is usually the claim rephrased. I reaffirmed my claim by saying that since arguing is a way of life for most middle school students, we should give them a structured way to state their views in a positive, logical manner. Finally, a *clincher* serves two purposes. First, it leaves the audience with something to remember. This is important because it can help to reinforce your message. Second, the clincher serves to make the presentation feel finished. My clincher was "Don't argue with your students; show them the way to argue for themselves."

Getting Started Using a Sample Argument

I have found that the most effective way to begin this unit is to actually present an argument to my students. I like to choose something that they will enjoy and can identify with. One argument that I have used successfully in my classroom follows. Each element of the argument is highlighted for emphasis.

ARGUMENT • *What's the Scoop on School Lunch?*

1. Introduction

Lead: Cheddarwurst... *Yuk!* Hot dogs... *Gag me with a spoon!!* Chicken drummies... *What is that stuff anyway?!!!* Hamburger delight... *who wants it??!!!!* Greasy corn dogs... *Who needs it??!!!!!*

Claim: I believe that our school lunches should definitely be improved!

2. Supports and Warrants

1st support: First of all, school lunches are too high in fat. *Warrant:* Many government surplus foods are used to make school lunches; foods like meat and cheese that are high in fat. Often my school lunch is simply swimming in grease!

2nd support: Secondly, school lunches are generally unappetizing. *Warrant:* They look horrible and they taste bland or flat. There's really no flavor! Yesterday I heard kids say, "What's that?" and "Yuk!" when they were served.

3rd support: Also, there's not enough variety in school lunches. *Warrant:* Do you realize that pizza is served at our school every single day? In September alone, cheeseburgers or hamburgers were served fifteen times!

4th support: Finally, most kids don't like what is offered in their school lunches. *Warrant:* Of 100 kids surveyed, 83 percent said no, when asked if they had enjoyed their lunch.

3. Concession

Now many say that schools do not have enough money to prepare better lunches. I have to admit that's true. It's always hard to get funding for education. Realistically, I don't know if we'll ever get a substantial amount of additional money, so we have to work with what we have.

4. Objections and Rebuttals

1st objection: Now those who make school lunches think that they're doing a good job; they say that school lunches are fine just the way they are. *Rebuttal:* Well, they should survey the kids. Then they could see that students don't like lunches as they are now, plus they could get suggestions for other, more popular items to try.

2nd objection: Many parents feel that school lunch is a terrific deal, and that it provides a nutritious meal for their children. *Rebuttal:* Well, I say we should invite parents to a school dinner where we serve them cheddarwurst. Let's see how *they* like it then!

3rd objection: Some kids say that they actually like school lunches! *Rebuttal:* Well, according to our survey, there are more kids who don't like them. The kids who like them now will appreciate them even more if and when school lunches improve.

4th objection: Finally, some will argue that things will never change; that there is really nothing we can do to make school lunches better. *Rebuttal:* But I say we need to lobby for action. Our voices need to be heard on this matter. Let's research the issue and present a proposal to the powers that be!

5. Conclusion

Claim reaffirmed: In conclusion, we definitely need better school lunches in this school!!!

Clincher: I'd rather fill my belly with peanut butter and jelly,
Than get my yummies from disgusting Chicken Drummies!
When it comes to school chow, we've got to improve it NOW!!

This argument is always successful with my students. The lead catches their attention right away. Therefore, they tend to listen more attentively. Because this is a subject dear to their hearts, they identify with my statements. I typically hear verbal affirmation and laughter as I reinforce their feelings through my supports and warrants. The objections are some that they are familiar with, and they like hearing a teacher rebut them. They especially enjoy the thought of inviting parents to school for a disgusting meal! The clincher is entertaining and cues them in to the fact that the argument is finished. I usually receive a round of applause!

Analyzing the Argument

Once I have finished the introductory argument, we begin a discussion: What was the premise of my presentation? What do I believe? Did you agree with me at first? Do you agree with me now? If you still disagree, do you now see the other side of the issue? Did my argument give you more to think about in terms of the basic issue?

Next, we begin to discuss the format of the argument. I usually ask students to recall how I began (lead) and what they thought of it: Did the way I began catch your attention? Why? What about the ending (clincher)? Did you know that I was finished with my presentation? The discussion continues as we analyze the structure of the argument: What did I say after I caught your attention? Did you hear me mention any objections to my position? And so forth.

After students have tried to identify the various parts of my presentation, I show them an overhead that outlines the school lunch argument. I go over each step, identifying and explaining what each entails. Because it is fresh in their minds, they can easily follow the overall structure of the argument, as well as recognize its specific elements.

Exploring the Issues

After I tell students that they will be creating their own arguments to present, we work as a class to brainstorm a list of topics and write them on chart paper. To generate ideas, the following types of questions are posed: What concerns you? What bugs you? What needs to be changed? What is being done wrong? What do you strongly believe? What are some issues that people disagree about? This activity allows students to see the variety of possibilities that exist and helps expedite their selection of a topic. The brainstorming activity, along with the presentation and discussion of my argument, is generally all we have time for in one class period. This leaves them with something to think about for the next day, when the actual planning of student arguments begins.

Planning the Arguments

I like to have my students work together in small groups of three or four to design and present an argument, especially the first time they try one. Because this activity is new to them, working in groups allows them to generate ideas more quickly and effectively. I also prefer to heterogeneously group students in order to maximize success.

Choosing a Topic. The first task for each group is to agree on a topic and claim. This is more likely to occur if you have generated a large list of possibilities the day before. Most groups can agree fairly quickly. Others will undoubtedly have trouble deciding. I continually circulate around the room to monitor progress in choosing a topic. Occasionally I will need to help a group sort through some sort of compromise in order to arrive at an issue they can agree on. Giving my students free reign in choosing their topics helps to ensure that they "buy into" the activity. I qualify this by saying that any position, or claim, is acceptable, as long as students can complete the argument successfully within the given format. At times students do choose a topic or position that I may not particularly favor. However, as they progress through the steps involved, they often recognize that their position lacks substance (that is, they cannot come up with valid supports and warrants), and they abandon it on their own. This sequence of events is far more valuable than my telling them that they simply cannot proceed with a particular point of view.

What kinds of claims are typical in the argumentations of middle school students? You will be amazed at the variety; for example,

- Hats should be allowed to be worn in school.
- Abortion should be legal.
- Too many children's toys are sexist.
- We need to do something about teen pregnancy.
- The governor's proposal to add days to the school year is a bad idea.
- There is too much racism in this school.
- The homeless need our help.

You will find that students do feel strongly about a number of issues, and they actually appreciate having the chance to prove their positions.

Mapping Out the Argument. An example of a guide and worksheet to help students map out their arguments are provided in the Appendix. Although the group collectively decides on what evidence it will use, I have every student complete the worksheet. This helps to insure that each individual becomes more actively involved in understanding the format of the argument and the specific elements the group has decided to emphasize. I tell my students to complete the body of their argument before they even think about the lead and clincher. Doing so gives students a more comprehensive look at their topic, and they are more apt to think of a better lead and clincher once they have examined the scope of their issue in detail. I like to compare it to writing a story; sometimes it is better to omit the title until the story is complete. I have seen students who never get to the actual writing of a story because they become fixated on trying to arrive at an appropriate title. Likewise, I have seen students spend an entire class period trying to think of a clever lead when they try to do so before mapping out their argument. Waiting until the basic argument is finished saves time in the long run.

I require that my students come up with four supports and warrants, as well as four objections and rebuttals. If they cannot, they must abandon the topic. Again, I constantly circulate around the room to monitor and facilitate. To assist them in thinking of supports, I have them tell me their claim, then I say, "Give me four good reasons why you think so." I help them to see that the warrant for each support will help to substantiate it; in other words, the warrant answers the question "What makes you so sure about that?" Students may need to research their topics more in order to find evidence to use as a support or warrant. It works well to spend day 2 of the unit in the classroom as groups decide on their claim and explore their ideas for the body of the argument. On days 3 and 4, time can be spent in the library researching topics. This will give students a greater understanding of all viewpoints on a particular issue and will help them to find data to substantiate their views. For example, if the claim is that students should be allowed to chew gum in school, can they find evidence that chewing sugarless gum after meals actually does help to reduce cavities? Interviews may also provide valuable insight. For instance, teachers and the principal can provide an adult perspective to the question "Why *shouldn't* students chew gum in school?" These can then become objections that students can rebut.

As students refine their arguments, I discuss the importance of words that help cue an audience to each piece of evidence they are about to present. Words like *first, second, third,* and *finally* allow for easy transitions between supports. Likewise, transitional words help to let the listener know that a new objection is about to be stated. For example, "some may maintain that . . . ," "others may say . . . ," "it could also be argued that . . . ," and "some might object to . . ." are all effective ways to preface each objection. Key words before rebuttals include *however, but, still,* and *nonetheless.*

The hardest part of the argument always seems to be the concession. Students often have difficulty admitting that there is a weakness in their position. They tend to think they have an answer for every possible objection. If students cannot think of a concession, I tell them to proceed to the objections and rebuttals. If they find an objection they cannot rebut, this becomes their concession. If not, three alternatives exist: (1) I can help them think of one; (2) they can share with another group who will try to shoot holes in their argument, thus suggesting a concession; or (3) they can omit the concession if they or I cannot think of one.

To end their argument, I encourage students to find a different way to rephrase the claim they stated at the beginning. This provides some variety and a degree of sophistication to their presentation.

Memorable Beginnings and Endings. Coming up with a lead does not usually pose a problem. Students generally create some very unique, entertaining, and sometimes outlandish ways to get their audience's attention. I encourage this, as long as it does not detract from the argument itself.

I emphasize the importance of the clincher as well. Too often when students give a presentation, they conclude by saying, "We're done," or simply shuffle off to their seats. I discuss how crucial it is to let an audience know without a doubt that the presentation is over. It makes for a more polished product and enhances the overall presentation. Students should conclude their arguments with something memorable that will stimulate the listener to reflect even more on what was presented. If students are still stuck for an idea, another group can often provide good suggestions.

Establishing a Timeframe. I usually set a deadline for when arguments must be completed. This helps to keep students on track. At the beginning of each class period, I will announce where I think students should be in the process. For example, "Yesterday you should have finished your supports and warrants. Today you should complete your objections and rebuttals." When the arguments are complete, I collect each group's worksheets and analyze them. I point out strengths, check for weaknesses in logic, indicate places where more information is needed, and make suggestions where changes need to be made. After groups work together to edit their arguments, I collect them again.

Arguments continue to be checked and refined until they represent a finished product.

I have found that implementing the entire argumentation unit takes at least two weeks. One day is spent introducing argumentation and brainstorming topics. Students use four or five class periods to research, plan, write, and refine their arguments. Finally, one week is usually needed for students to plan and rehearse the presentation of their arguments.

Presentation of Arguments

Once the arguments have been refined, students must decide exactly how they will deliver them to the class. I require that each group member participate in some way in the presentation. Students are free to decide who will present each part of the argument. They are not allowed to read from their papers, but may make and use note cards during the presentation.

Expanding the Realm of Possibilities. I encourage students to be creative in the execution of their ideas. They can create skits to accompany their arguments, use props, and include artwork or music if desired. I have many presentations on videotape from years past and show them one or two to illustrate that more can be done than simply reciting the argument. For example, one group whose claim was "We need to stop nuclear testing" depicted a courtroom with a nuclear weapon on trial. Their lead consisted of the judge demanding order in the court, declaring that nuclear weapons were now on trial, and asking what they were being charged with (plutonium!). The prosecuting attorney presented the claim, supports, and warrants to the judge. When the nuclear weapon took the stand, it presented the objections to the claim while the attorney rebutted each one. In the end, the judge reaffirmed the claim by declaring that nuclear weapons should indeed be abolished. The clincher showed what could happen if they weren't destroyed—a nuclear explosion, complete with sound effects and a giant paper mushroom "cloud."

Playing the Devil's Advocate. On the day arguments are presented, the audience listens with the intent of taking the opposing point of view. For example, if the claim is that abortion should be legal and a woman's choice, they must consider the argument as antiabortionists. At the conclusion of the argument, I ask if anyone in the audience can cite an objection that was not raised. If so, the group that presented has a chance to provide a rebuttal. Also, anyone in the audience may ask a question or identify something that needs clarification. By this time students have become experts on the issue they have chosen to argue for, and more likely than not, they are able to answer any questions and objections that are raised. We then discuss the merits of the group's presentation. I ask for comments that only pertain to the strengths of their argument and presentation. This provides each group with some final reinforcement and allows them to finish on a positive note.

Lights, Action, Camera! I videotape each argument as it is presented, and students watch themselves the next day. This is always a highlight of the unit. Since presentations were analyzed the day before, we watch purely for enjoyment this time. It is always a fun and entertaining way to culminate the unit. These videos can then be shown as examples in years to come.

Evaluating the Unit

Students' work is judged by me and their peers. Development and presentation of the argument are the two primary components that are evaluated.

Quality of the Argumentation Worksheet. Students receive a grade for their worksheets (argument in written form) after they have been revised for the final time. One grade is given for the basic argument, and each person in the group receives that grade. The criteria I use for evaluation include whether each group member has recorded the revised argument on the worksheet; completeness of ideas; logic and reasoning used in creating supports, warrants, objections, and rebuttals; and clarity. One's participation in developing the argument is also considered.

Analyzing the Presentation. The presentation is scored on a four-point scale (4 = excellent; 3 = good; 2 = average; 1 = poor) for each of the following elements: completeness (all elements of the argument present); involvement of group members (does each person take an active role?), clarity (can we hear and follow the argument?), and creativity (uniqueness of presentation).

In addition, students are graded by their peers. For each presentation, every member in the audience completes a 3-by-5-inch card with the following information: (1) a letter grade and compliment for each member of the group; and (2) a group grade and "comment sandwich" for the overall presentation. A "comment sandwich" contains three sentences: a positive statement, followed by a suggestion, concluding with another positive comment. For example, "Your presentation was easy to follow. At times it was difficult to hear what you were saying. Your lead really grabbed my attention!" This is preceded with a discussion on the purpose of evaluation: to provide specific feedback that will help the group in the future, as opposed to lambasting a person you do not particularly like. We also discuss how to be specific in writing comments. For example, "It was good" does not tell the group much at all, whereas "Your rebuttals were strong and convincing" focuses on something tangible. Students are graded on the evaluation cards they complete. A letter grade is assigned based on how well the student followed directions and provided specific, quality comments. Grading each person's evaluation cards helps to assure that their analysis will be taken seriously, and that hurtful, negative comments will not be given.

Self-Evaluation. After I have examined and graded each person's evaluation cards, I let each group see the comments made by their peers. Finally, students individually complete a "PNI" evaluation sheet where they list the *p*ositive, *n*egative and *i*nteresting aspects of the argumentation unit and give themselves grades for personal behavior and effort, along with a grade for their presentation. This allows students to reflect on their experience and also provides me with good feedback to consider when using the unit in the future.

This structured approach to argumentation is successful time and time again with all levels of students. I am always impressed with the quality of the arguments and the originality of the presentations. Adolescents are concerned about a number of issues, and this unit sanctions the expression of their beliefs. Examples of two student argumentations are included in the Appendix.

Besides having fun, students learn to present their positions in a way that will gain the respect of any adults they choose to share them with. Some students actually do present their arguments to other individuals and organizations in the community in order to initiate action they believe is necessary. They come to recognize the value of presenting thoughtful justification of their beliefs in an organized, respectful manner versus trying to demand change with no substantial reasoning. This unit empowers students with the knowledge that they can argue positively and effectively to initiate change.

SUMMARY

Adolescents stand before us on the threshhold of adulthood. By their very nature they need to actively participate in their learning and collaborate with others. They need structure and guidance, but also freedom to make independent choices, ask provocative questions, and experiment for answers. Contrary to what they might have us believe, middle school students *do* want to discover new things and are indeed willing to learn. In fact, "adolescents are ripe to be hooked. With good teaching, this is an age when kids [can] become interested and excited" in their learning (Atwell, 1987, p. 48). However, they demand meaningful and relevant involvement; they need to recognize a purpose in what we ask them to do.

Problem-solving strategies and activities provide a structure in which adolescents find the freedom to explore, analyze, evaluate, and create. Students have fun, become more actively involved, and thus more accountable for their learning. Working with peers to discover an answer or create a new idea promotes an overall cooperative spirit within the classroom. Best of all, problem solving helps to develop lifelong skills that will serve these students well as they become adults in the real world.

Problem-solving possibilities exist within every curriculum, and they can be adapted to fit any ability level or population of students. Whether it be through brief, one-shot activities interspersed throughout the curriculum or longer units of instruction, whether it be to enrich or accelerate, problem solving complements the unique characteristics of adolescents and helps to meet their particular needs. It is truly the perfect match for middle school students.

REFERENCES

Anderson, E., & Hamel, F. (1991). Teaching argument as a criteria-driven process. *English Journal*, 80(7): 43–49.

Arnold, J. (1991). Towards a middle level curriculum rich in meaning. *Middle School Journal*, 23(2): 8–12.

Atwell, N. (1987). *In the middle: Writing, reading, and learning with adolescents*. Portsmouth, NH: Boynton/Cook.

Bloom, B. S., et al. (1956). *Taxonomy of Educational Objectives: Handbook I, Cognitive Domain*. New York: McKay.

Buckmaster, L. (1994). Effects of activities that promote cooperation among seventh graders in a future problem solving class. *Elementary School Journal*, 95(1): 49–62.

Covey, S. R. (1989). *The 7 habits of highly effective people*. New York: Fireside.

Crabbe, A. (1990). *The coach's guide to the Future Problem Solving Program* (Revised). Aberdeen, NC: The Future Problem Solving Program.

Dorman, G., Lipsitz, J., & Verner, P. (1985). Improving schools for young adolescents. *Educational Leadership*, 42(6): 44–49.

Educators for Social Responsibility. (1983). *Perspectives: A teaching guide to concepts of peace*. Cambridge, MA: Educators for Social Responsibility.

Gordon, W. J. J. (1961). *Synectics*. New York: Macmillan.

Lewis, A.C. (1990). *Making it in the middle*. New York: The Edna McConnell Clark Foundation.

Maynard, G. (1986). The reality of diversity at the middle level. *The Clearing House*, 60: 21–23.

McCumsey, J. (1984). *Exploring the future: Basic skills and activities for the futuristic thinker*. Carthage, IL: Good Apple, Inc.

Menasha Joint School District 1. (1977). *Elementary developmental guidance: A curriculum for every child*. Menasha, WI: Menasha Joint School District 1.

Moebius, M. (1991). What do you believe? Persuasive speeches in eighth grade. *English Journal*, 80(7): 38–42.

National Council of Teachers of English. (1991). To take a stand: Argument and persuasion. *English Journal*, 80(7): 33.

Noller, R., Parnes, S., & Biondi, A. (1977). *Creative actionbook*. New York: Scribner's.

Osborn, A. F. (1963). *Applied imagination*. New York: Scribner's.

Pearson, C. (1980). Can you keep quiet for three seconds? *Learning Magazine*, 8(6): 40–43.

Petroski, H. (1992). Let us now praise the humble Post-It. *Wilson Quarterly*, 16: 104–110.

Shewach, D. L. (1987). *The scenario writing guide*. Laurinburg, NC: The Future Problem Solving Program.

Stanford, G., (1977). *Developing effective classroom groups: A practical guide for teachers*. New York: Hart.

Stanford, G. & Dodds Stanford, B. (1969). *Learning discussion skills through games*. New York: Citation.

Stanish, B. (1988). *The giving book: Creative classroom approaches to caring, valuing and cooperating*. Carthage, IL: Good Apple.

Task Force on Education of Young Adolescents. (1989). *Turning points: preparing American youth for the 21st century*. Washington, DC: Carnegie Council on Adolescent Development.

Toepfer, C., Lounsbury, J., Arth, A., & Johnston, H. (1986). Editorial. *The Clearing House*, 60: 6-10.

Torrance, E. P. & Myers, R. E. (1970). *Creative learning and teaching*. New York: Harper & Row.

Treffinger, D. (1980). *Encouraging creative learning for the gifted and talented: A handbook of methods and techniques*. Ventura, CA: Ventura County Superintendent of Schools Office.

CHAPTER 6

Model Problem-Solving Programs

One of the joys of visiting schools is the opportunity to talk with principals and staff and see the enthusiasm they have for their work. Staff from schools whose programs are described here also had these additional qualities:

- Teachers who enjoy working with each other, "love" to teach kids, are committed to teaching, and are willing to change to help their students.

- Principals who are "instructional leaders" and know what's going on in their school's classrooms, support the efforts of their staff, and communicate effectively with parents and community.

- School support staff who are proud of their school gladly help visitors find their way around the building and campus.

- Staff who are not afraid to be independent are willing to make changes to improve the quality of their instruction.

Diversity best describes the schools and staffs featured here. Each one approached thinking and problem solving in their curricula in different ways that met the needs of their students, communities, and states. They varied in size of school population as well as in ethnic makeup and socioeconomic circumstances. They were urban, suburban, and outer city as well as being located in different parts of the country.

A description of the unique program each school developed, along with examples of problem-solving projects that teachers and other readers can adapt to the needs of their students, schools, and communities, is the focus of the discussion. Ways schools communicated with parents and community, handled staff development, and kept their programs "alive and well" are also included.

CREATIVE PROBLEM SOLVING WITH AN INTER-DISCIPLINARY TWIST

Gulf Gate Elementary School, Sarasota County, Florida, Public Schools

Students and teachers in this pre-K–5 school are actively involved in solving real-world problems every day. Principal Catherine Kitto says," It has been particularly exciting to see students and staff solve schoolwide problems. Here, students of different ages and abilities work together to learn math, economics, and language arts concepts and processes as well as how to solve a problem—and they thoroughly enjoy doing it."

One problem that adults had failed to solve at Gulf Gate was "excess noise and lack of order in the cafeteria." This problem was turned over to a committee of students—class representatives and super leaders, the assistant principal, and a teacher. They relied on student involvement and peer pressure. Two schoolwide teams, the White Sox and Tigers, were formed, lunchroom monitors were elected from each classroom to check on clean tables and floors, and points were given for positive behaviors. Team scores were reported daily. The problem was successfully solved.

Another schoolwide problem dealt with forming a "campus post office" where staff and students interacted with resource people from the local U.S. Post Office. The Gulf Gate campus took on street names and zip codes. Students submitted job applications and were interviewed for deliveryperson positions and postmaster and learned how a post office functions. Teachers helped them learn about writing letters, addressing envelopes, costs of stamps, and services such as registered mail and express mail to meet curriculum objectives in language arts and math.

Setting Goals and Getting Started

Problem solving and higher-order, creative thinking are the heart of the school's improvement plan. They are coordinated with the state of Florida's school restructuring document, *Blueprint 2000*. Goal 3 of this document states, "Students successfully compete at the highest level nationally and internationally and are prepared to make well-reasoned, thoughtful, and healthy lifelong decisions." Standard 4 of goal 3 states, "Using creative thinking skills while performing individual and group tasks, Florida students will use creative thinking skills to generate new ideas, make the best decisions, recognize and solve problems through reasoning, interpret symbolic data, and develop efficient techniques for lifelong learning." And outcome 3 of standard 4 suggests, *"While performing individual and group tasks, students recognize that a problem exists, define the problem, investigate possible causes of the problem, identify possible solution(s), analyze, evaluate, and select the best solutions, and implement the solution(s)."*

At Gulf Gate School, the plan to reach the state's objectives took the form of a four-year project—one year in planning and preparation and three in implementation and evaluation. The group that guided this effort was the School Advisory Council. It included the principal and assistant principal, teachers from various grade levels, specialized teachers, three parents nominated by parents, two students, community members, and classified staff. Three of their early efforts were to develop a vision statement, conduct a needs assessment, and establish strategies to guide the program.

A Vision Statement. The purpose of this document was to make the broad state mandates realistic and practical for the school's 900 students and eighty staff members, including sixty-five teachers. The student population was mainly white and middle class with about thirty-five students in the English-as-a-second-language center. Their "vision" is shown next.

Vision Statement for Gulf Gate School

The parents, staff and children of Gulf Gate Elementary School join together with the Gulf Gate community to share a vision for Gulf Gate School in the year 2000 and beyond. Our vision is open and global and reflective of an underlying philosophy that all children can learn.

It is our Vision that:

- All students will become successful lifelong learners who will be able to solve real-world problems.

- The school will be a safe and healthful environment.

- Classrooms will be adaptable to a variety of instructional models and that class sizes will be appropriate to the instructional mode to allow for more individualized programs.

- The school will be equipped with state-of-the-art technology with the capability to change with continuing technological developments and an informed and educated staff to employ the technology as an integral part of the curriculum.

- The curricula will be adaptable to critical thinking skills and problem solving.

- Instructional time will be increased.

- Student learning will be assessed through a variety of means, including traditional and nontraditional techniques.

- The school will be a full-service school with an increased awareness to the needs of the children, not only as students but as members of the family and community of diverse cultures.

- The school will have the appropriate staff to meet these goals.

- Parents will be involved in their children's educational process.

- The entire school community (children, staff, parents, administration, community, school board, state and federal governments) will share the responsibility for the educational outcomes of Gulf Gate School.

- The school will become a community of learners and the staff will exemplify the learning process. There will be opportunities for staff, parents, and community members to participate in the learning process continuing to discover, create, and grow along with the students of Gulf Gate School.

Needs Assessment Results. An assessment was conducted, and its results provided some guidelines for the program. They were

- Although test results indicated that Gulf Gate students scored above the 70th percentile on basic skills in reading, language arts, and mathematics, staff were aware they needed to develop higher-order, creative-thinking skills to be successful.
- In grades 3 through 5, students exhibited difficulty using problem-solving skills in class meetings with the principals.
- Good jobs in the future will depend on people who can put knowledge to work, not simply possess it. New workers must be creative and responsible problem solvers ... high-paying, but unskilled jobs are disappearing.
- School staff believe that all students need to become successful, lifelong learners who are able to solve real-life problems.
- School staff believe students need more opportunities to organize and understand data and to make decisions where they use reasoning and creative thinking.
- In problem-solving sessions, teachers came to realize that hidden opportunities exist for students to participate in real-world problem solving; the key is to empower students through total involvement.
- Parents and community members believe all students need to become successful, lifelong learners who are able to solve real-life problems.

Strategies to Guide the Program. The staff and School Advisory Council agreed on six general strategies to initiate their higher-order thinking skills (HOTS) and problem-solving plan:

1. Teachers will participate in training in higher-order (creative) thinking skills.
2. Teachers will write action plans for real-world problems or situations.
3. Students will increase their skills in higher-order thinking by participating in real-world problems.
4. Parents and staff will search for alternative funding sources for the program.
5. Teachers will continue to participate in computer and technology training and integrate the use of technology into their action plans when appropriate; students will increase their skills set forth in the technology curriculum.
6. Students will improve their written communication skills.

For *strategy 1*, most of the action was in year 1. Tasks and activities, who was involved, a timeline to carry out the tasks, and indicators of progress were identified. A task force made up of volunteers from the staff at varied grade levels, a principal, and others carried out tasks such as listing existing resources to meet their goals; compiling a list of networks and resources with other schools and districts; designing a staff development plan in the areas of creative problem solving that would include teaching strategies, assessment, and infusing opportunities for students to practice problem solving into various subjects of the curriculum; peer coaching; attendance of teachers and staff at inservice workshops; and teachers observing staff in other schools that had implemented similar programs and sharing with others what they observed.

Action plans to involve students in real-world problems and situations, the focus of *strategy 2*, were written and reviewed. Much of this work would also occur in the first year. Other tasks to be completed included scheduling workshops to be attended by all teachers, forming peer coaching teams, and scheduling meetings to share ideas and plans and to give feedback to each other. Communication tasks included scheduling and presenting workshops that involved parents, community members, and volunteers as well as staff in techniques to teach critical thinking skills. Plans were also presented at team or full staff faculty meetings, at PTA meetings, and published for the professional library.

Strategy 3, to encourage students to increase their skills in higher-order thinking through participation in real-world problems, had goals for each year. During year 1, at least 30 percent of the students will participate in teacher-designed plans to use higher-order thinking skills in real-world problems; during year 2, at least 60 percent of students will reach these goals; and by the end of year 3, 100 percent of students who began and finished three years at the school will participate. Indicators of progress during each year may include one or more of the following:

- Portfolios by students where they describe a situation or task (problem), what actions they took to solve it, skills used, and a description of the results
- Portfolios by teachers in the same categories that students carried out, as mentioned earlier
- Checklists of problem-solving skills completed by each student
- Feedback from peer coaching among teachers
- Pre- and post- surveys of parents, students, and teachers
- Student journals
- Teacher narratives of student progress
- Sharing of successful plans at faculty meetings
- Public sharing of successful plans.

Strategy 4, the search for alternative funding sources, was crucial during the first year and also necessary during subsequent years. Activities for this strategy included forming a task force of parents and staff to search for funding sources; participate in training for writing grants, write and submit grant proposals; and actively seek funds from a variety of sources.

Strategy 5 focused on technology. Teachers needed training in computers and other technology and in ways to use them in their action plans to give the students opportunities to experience technology in the curriculum. Efforts to increase student skills in computers and technology were also addressed.

For *strategy 6* the focus was on written communication skills. This emphasis is exhibited in the large number of newsletters and written products that Gulf Gate students, starting in first grade and continuing on through grade 5, produce each year. Strategy 6 also relates directly to strategy 5. Students can use computer technology to enhance their motivation and accuracy in writing.

Staff Communicated with Parents and Community

One way the staff at Gulf Gate School communicated with parents and community about their thinking and problem-solving effort was through a monthly newsletter, *Teachers Teaching Thinking*. It was edited by Cheryl Fisher, a teacher. This communication focused on (1) how staff prepare for and keep up-to-date with the HOTS changes, (2) substantive information about HOTS, (3) strategies teachers use to infuse or integrate thinking and problem solving into various subject matter areas at various grade levels, (4) teacher behaviors to help students learn thinking and problem solving, and (5) articles about special facets of HOTS. Each of these topics are discussed next, to give the reader information about how Gulf Gate School handled the HOTS program as well as to describe the newsletter content.

Preparation for Change. One of the early articles in the newsletter described the intensive training for six key staff members in a summer institute. This was followed by 15 hours of training for thirteen teachers with Dr. Donald Treffinger, a nationally recognized expert on creative problem solving. Then all staff received a two-hour introduction to the program from the six key staff who received initial training. All staff also participated in three hours of training with Dr. Treffinger. This mix of training by their own staff and a recognized expert provided a balance that met the needs of the faculty.

Information About Higher Order Thinking and Problem Solving. The greatest amount of space in the newsletter in the first year of implementation dealt with thinking and problem solving and its application to the curriculum at Gulf Gate School. One article focused on "questioning for quality thinking." Here, Bloom's six cognitive levels—knowledge, comprehension, application, analysis, synthesis, and evaluation—were defined and classroom uses of each level were given. For example, analysis was defined as "a separation of a whole into its component parts" followed by questions such as What are the parts or features of_____? Classify_____ according to_____? or _____?

Another example was "The Thinking Web" from the *Weekly Reader*. Here, the categories of imaging, reflecting, making decisions, reasoning logically, analyzing, and solving problems were defined along with examples of the kinds of skills used and kinds of activities for each category. These were kept general so they could be applied to any age or grade level. Under "reflecting," skills included making connections, wondering, comparing and contrasting, thinking about thinking (metacognition), asking questions, and identifying what "puzzles" you as you think and solve problems. Activities for reflecting included keeping thinking logs and journals, listening carefully, observing detail, role-playing moral behavior scenarios, and writing for self and others.

Through a column titled "Inquiring Minds Want to Know," parents and community members were encouraged to find out more about thinking and problem solving. They were invited to contact members of the critical thinking team (names were listed) and to come to the school media center's professional section to read and check out some of the new books that had been purchased on the subject.

Strategies to Infuse Thinking and Problem Solving Into the Curriculum. These were illustrated in a practical manner. For example, an article titled "Remodeling a Lesson Plan: A Step-by-Step Overview" started by asking the question, "What do we do when we 'infuse' thinking into a lesson for students?" The steps are outlined next in an informal manner, speaking from a teacher's point of view (*Teachers Teaching Thinking Notebook,* from the Sarasota County Summer Critical Thinking Institute, 1993).

"Infusing" Thinking into a Lesson for Students

At its most complicated, infusing the teaching of thinking into lessons is not complicated. I will try, however, to make the explaining of how to do it as complicated as I can just so that it sounds "professional." Here goes:

Step 1: Decide on the subject matter of the lesson you are going to teach.

Step 2: Decide on the thinking skill or skills that may be appropriate for the lesson you have decided to teach.

Step 3: Analyze the lesson (that's a good thinking skill in itself!) and decide where—at what point(s) in the lesson—the thinking skill(s) can be appropriately addressed and taught or applied.

Step 4: Synthesize the thinking skill (there's another thinking skill!) into the lesson at the places decided on in step 3.

Step 5: Evaluate your lesson plan to see if your new lesson will actually allow you to teach the lesson content (subject matter) objective if you are also including the thinking skill strategies. If the answer is yes, then . . .

Step 6: Don't think about it, do it. Teach your remodeled lesson. If the answer is no, then . . .

Step 7: Question (still another thinking skill in itself!) whether the content can be treated differently to enable you to also teach thinking.

And that's about as difficult as I can make it sound.

Another article on the "ABC's of Critical Thinking" quoted a teacher, Karen Johns, from another area school that made up the ABC list as a visual reminder of types of questioning that can be added to lessons to help students develop critical thinking:

Analyze	Classify	Compare
Contrast	Deduce	Distinguish
Elaborate	Evaluate	Explain
Generate ideas	Identify causality	Identify relations
Identify patterns	Induce	Infer
Interpret	Make analogies	Make decisions
Observe	Predict	Problem-solve
Question	Relate	Restructure
Sequence	Synthesize	Verify

Teacher Behaviors to Enhance Thinking and Problem Solving. Staff would exhibit the following behaviors in the HOTS program to help students learn more easily and effectively (Sarasota County Critical Thinking Institute, 1993):

- Remember "wait time I and II." Wait after a question and after a response.
- Utilize the "think–pair–share" strategy: Allow individual thinking time, discussion with a part-

ner, and then open class discussion.

- Ask "follow-ups"—Why? Do you agree? Tell me more. Give an example.
- Withhold judgment. Respond to student answers in a nonevaluative way.
- Ask for summary of what has been discussed to promote listening.
- Survey the class. How many people agree with the author's point of view?
- Play devil's advocate. Require students to defend their reasoning against different points of view.
- Ask students to "think aloud." Describe how you arrived at your answer.
- Call on students randomly whether their hands are raised or not.
- Encourage students to develop their own questions.
- Cue student responses by saying, "There is no single correct answer for this question. I want you to consider alternatives. Let's hear some."

The newsletter, written by staff members at Gulf Gate School, was an excellent way to communicate with their parents and community members. It was also mailed to members of the administration, principals, and individuals in elementary, middle, and high schools in Sarasota County. The newsletter is available via E-mail, too.

Action Plans Bring Thinking and Problem Solving to the Students

Action plans that teachers developed to teach thinking and problem solving to students lie at the heart of the Gulf Gate program. They specified the strategies and objectives for the students, higher-order skills that are emphasized, student group sizes involved, timelines, and the curricular or noncurricular areas or objectives that are being met. Highlights of action plans for a *class store* for third-grade students and a *class newspaper* for first-grade students are described next.

Class Store for Third-Graders. Overall objectives for the class store unit of Mary Compton's students are (1) working in small groups, students will produce written critiques on various products found in a class store; and (2) these critiques will be compiled into a newsletter, *Compton's Class Consumer Newsletter,* which will be distributed to the Gulf Gate School student body and other interested people.

Topics for student hands-on participation in the first overall objective of this action plan include (1) buying at the class store; (2) evaluating a product's claim(s); (3) writing an individual report about the group activity; and (4) evaluating each student's performance in thinking and problem solving. Each topic will be described next, according to strategies and objectives, higher-order skills emphasized, size of student work group, implementation timeline, and curricular or noncurricular involvement.

Buying at the class store involves all students at the grade level. General strategies and objectives for the activities are as follows:

1. Students will earn tickets for positive behavior. These tickets will be used to buy toys at the store. Skills emphasized are evaluation and creativity; plan will be implemented by January of the school year; activity is noncurricular.

2. Students are free to choose the toy they want to purchase. Skill emphasized is evaluation, and the activity is noncurricular.

3. Students must count their tickets to see if they have enough points to buy their toy. Tickets come in denominations of 1 point, 3 points, and 5 points. Toy prices range from 10 to 350 points. Skills emphasized are application and creativity. Curricular area is math with practice in counting, addition, subtraction, multiplication, and division skills and applying math concepts.

Evaluating a product's claim(s) has two strategies and objectives. Students work in small groups, and the curricular emphasis is on reading:

1. Students will read a box or label of a given product and list the manufacturer's promises or claims for the product. Skills emphasized are comprehension and evaluation.

2. Students will judge whether the claims about the product are true or not. Skills of comprehension, compare and contrast, and evaluation are emphasized.

Each individual student wrote a report about the

group activity to meet the following strategies and objectives:

1. Explain what your group did. Comprehension skills are emphasized.
2. Evaluate what you learned by doing the activity. Evaluation is emphasized.
3. Can you apply what you learned? Application is emphasized.
4. What skills did you use to accomplish this task? Analysis and application are emphasized.

Student performances on HOTS strategies are evaluated on a 6-point scale where "1" indicated that the "purpose of the task was not accomplished because the student shows little evidence of appropriate reasoning and does not successfully communicate relevant ideas; presents extraneous information." The "6" indicated the student "fully achieves the purpose of the task, while insightfully interpreting, extending beyond the task, or raising provocative questions." These qualities are based on the student demonstrating an indepth understanding of concepts and content; communicating effective and clearly to various audiences, using dynamic and diverse means." Ratings of 2–5 fall between the two extremes. (Scale is from "Performance Standards for Student Work" from *A Sampler of Mathematics Assessment*, California Assessment Program, 1991.)

To meet the second general objective of the action plan, students organized the articles together into the Compton's *Class Consumer Newsletter*. Titles and a very brief description of five articles in one issue are presented here:

- *Nerf's Arrowstorm* described how one third-grade group tested the Arrow Storm, a new Nerf toy. They evaluated both its good and bad points. Their final evaluation was that it was a "good" toy.
- *Jet Streeks Fly* dealt with a Mattel air-powered jet, which is launched with a pump. They tried out the toy, looked at its cost and durability, and gave it a "good" rating.
- *Finding the Best Putty*. Here, one group of students compared Chemtoy's *Twin Putty* and Play School's *Nutty Putty*. They tested the advertised bounce and glow features. They decided *Twin Putty* was probably a better buy for the money, but both were good.
- *Hot Wheels Really Go Fast* indicated the results of tests of little cars that race on tracks. In addition to trying the cars out, they called Mattel, the manufacturer, and asked why some cars go faster than others. Mattel said it was related to the weight and condition of the cars. Hot Wheels got a "fun toy" rating and the price is right, $1 for each car.
- *Micro Machines New Track* described tests of a car on 7 feet of track with a super loop, ramp, and rip cord to launch the car. These tests took both practice and skill to get the car to perform properly.

Class Newspaper for First-Graders. This action plan for Marilyn Schwartz's students provided experiences in brainstorming and creative thinking skills as well as those in interviewing, researching, writing and organizing, evaluating, predicting and sequencing. Specific strategies and objectives for the newspaper unit of one to two weeks were as follows:

- Given several newspapers, the students will express and identify various sections of the newspaper.
- Students will decide what section they would like to have in their class newspaper.
- Students will decide on a name for their class newspaper.
- Students will conduct information interviews with their peers, staff, parents and community members for their articles.
- Students will write in complete sentences for their articles using prewriting, editing, and rewriting skills.
- Students will arrange the articles and pictures in an interesting manner on each page of their newspaper.
- Students will decide how many copies of their newspaper they need by making and evaluating their lists; they will send the paper to the school office to be copied; they will put the printed sheets of the paper together and distribute it to their "consumers."

They named their paper the *White Sox Hot News*. This name showed the influence of their geographical location, where the Chicago White Sox baseball team has a minor league team. Sections of their paper were devoted to sports, comics, stars, and news flashes. Topics for articles included a report by a student who imagined he was a member of the Miami Dolphins football team, a report on the class field trip to the library, the part the first-graders played in the Earth Day festivities at the school, and a trip to a nearby state park to learn about ecology and to ride on the trolley.

Each article the students wrote carried an individual or group byline. Probably the most creative part of the newspaper was the original artwork by the students. Their drawings ran the gamut from phases of the moon complete with May–June dates to cartoons and headline banners. A newspaper not only provided academic experiences for first-grade students, but also gave them a sense of pride and made them feel they were a part of the school community.

The action plans just described are only two examples. Titles of more plans are presented next. These are listed according to grade level, but most can be adapted to any age or grade level with appropriate objectives and materials. Here, students take major responsibility for planning, implementation, and evaluation. Teachers and others who assist act as facilitators.

Kindergarten: grocery store, post office, newsletter, TV news

First grade: menu planning, student-generated curriculum, adopt a real author, develop a student newspaper

Second grade: student-made books and calendars, newspaper, design of banners and stationery using the computer, students as "teachers," "adopt a block" to serve the community, plan and conduct a used book sale

Third grade: Breed and sell animals, supermarket, bank, courtyard landscaping, school stock market, paint murals on walls

Fourth grade: monitor and improve school maintenance and beautification, create, write, and perform in plays, help order science kits and organize, plan, set up a science lab, and paint a U.S. map on the blacktop (joint project with fifth-graders)

Fifth grade: student court, policies for disciplining and tardiness, school store, cross-grade-level helpers, post office, media helpers, yearbook, patrols, organize and staff a school snack shop business including investments and dividends, plan and conduct an "invention convention"

Principal Kitto sums up their experience with the program by saying that teachers are thinking and talking about how to involve students in higher-order thinking and problem solving. You'll hear them say, "Students learned so much math today and they didn't realize it. Students don't want to stop an activity." Teachers are constantly learning from successes and failures, and they are ready to make changes to improve the program. They have supported each other through peer coaching. And, student success and enthusiasm has sustained their desire for school improvement.

THINKING ABOUT THINKING AND PROBLEM SOLVING

Lincoln Elementary School, Community Unit District 205, Elmhurst, Illinois

The thinking skills and problem-solving program at Lincoln School has been in operation for eight years. It is part of a districtwide initiative to "improve student achievement through a focus on the instruction, classroom management, and communication skills that foster cognitive instruction and higher-level thinking." This district is a suburb of Chicago and serves mainly white, middle class students. Goals of the program are (1) set the climate for thinking, (2) teach explicit thinking skills, (3) structure interaction with thinking, and (4) use metacognitive processing about thinking.

These program goals led to curriculum changes in the school and district. Some of these changes are as follows:

- A mathematics program that stresses problem solving and the use of manipulatives

- A process approach to writing that emphasizes brainstorming, webbing, paired partners, and cooperative groups

- A literature-based reading program with an emphasis on whole language and integrated instruction

- A hands-on approach to science and social studies with an overall focus on interdisciplinary instruction.

Principal Billie Johnson points out that changes are both affective and cognitive. She emphasizes, "Students are more involved in and take ownership of their learning. Due to metacognition, they are more reflective learners and impulsitivity has decreased. They enjoy learning more and are self-directed, and engage in self-assessment. They interact more positively socially, extend their thinking, and look for multiple solutions. They persist in their tasks and try various problem-solving strategies when they don't immediately know an answer."

The discussion that follows focuses on four major topics. They are (1) staff development to get the program started and keep it going; (2) how the staff communicated with parents and community about the program and the changes it brought into the school; (3) two examples of interdisciplinary units of instruction the staff developed to provide many opportunities for students to use thinking skills and problem solving-strategies; and (4) ways staff, administration, students, parents, and community members keep the program alive and improving.

Supporting the Program with Staff Development

Teachers and other staff prepared for the program with a multiyear plan. Staff development was guided by the building leadership teams, who served as a resource to the staff in achieving building goals and objectives in relation to district goals. These teams provided the foundation for the program from planning to implementation, evaluation, and maintenance as an ongoing part of the district curriculum. Their "startup" plans, general mission, and thinking guidelines are discussed next.

Getting Started. The plan began with a focus on a group of teachers and administrators from each of the district's twelve schools who participated in four full-day workshops relating to instructional strategies to enhance student thinking. After the workshops, participants were expected to implement the strategies with their students and return to the next training session with examples of student work and learning that resulted from their implementation. The focus of the next workshop was the development of an action plan to continue implementation of instructional thinking strategies and the revision of the district instructional thinking goals for the following year. Also, additional volunteers were solicited for thinking skills training.

The group of initial workshop participants also served as peer coaches and presented workshops and sessions about what they had learned to staff in their buildings and to other elementary teachers in the district. The focus on thinking skills became an important link to other innovative instructional strategies such as the use of math manipulatives, drawing and graphing for problem solving, interdisciplinary and thematic instruction, and constructivist learning activities.

While the discussion here emphasizes the elementary level, thinking became an integral part of the learning process throughout the district's K–12 curriculum. It was integrated into learner goals and objectives. Some of the strategies that were stressed were open-ended questions, wait time, Bloom's cognitive taxonomy, discovery, and constructivist learning. Lincoln School Principal Billie Johnson says, "Perhaps the most important thing that happened was the creation of a 'risk-taking environment' that fosters thinking and learning."

Stating the Mission. Every program needs to write down broad objectives and commitments to guide its development. Lincoln's statement is shown next.

> ### *Lincoln School Mission Statement*
>
> We, at Lincoln School, are committed to working with parents and community to provide a nurturing learning environment which addresses intellectual, social, physical, and emotional needs of each child.
>
> Our goal is to develop skills and attitudes within the individual student which enable continuous learning and action as productive, caring, responsible members of the world community.

Thinking Guidelines. The following set of traits below reminded students, staff, and parents to be "good thinkers." They became "working guidelines" for the thinking skills program over the years, not just content for a poster.

Traits of a Good Thinker

Good thinkers know how to behave when they don't immediately know the answers to problems or questions. Good thinkers can also be observed *producing knowledge* rather than reproducing it. They know how to act on information. District 205 has selected the following characteristics of intelligent behavior to teach and observe (adapted from Costa, 1991, p. 100):

A Good Thinker

- Persists when the solution to a problem is not immediately apparent
- Reflects about ideas and/or solutions before beginning a task
- Listens to others with understanding and empathy
- Demonstrates flexibility in thinking
- Demonstrates awareness of his or her own thinking processes (metacognition)
- Checks work for accuracy and precision
- Questions and poses problems
- Draws on past knowledge and applies it to new situations
- Demonstrates precision of language and thought
- Demonstrates ingenuity, originality, and insight
- Enjoys problem-solving experiences.

Communicating with Parents and Community

The principal used her column, "From the Principal's Office," in the school's newsletter to communicate with parents and community about the goals and changes of the thinking skills and problem-solving program. Both affective and cognitive elements were emphasized—always with a focus on the students. Four of these topics are discussed here.

Information About Thinking. For a series of newsletters, the first part of the column detailed one of the traits of a thinker just listed. For example, *persistence* is related to growth in thinking and ways students keep trying to solve a problem. If one strategy doesn't work, then, they try another. One way to help children accomplish this is to ask them to express how they are thinking—metacognition. Parents and teachers as adults are reminded that children need to hear us say, "This doesn't seem to be working. I need to try another way." We all need to demonstrate perseverance to our children. The discussion also reminded readers that children make sense of their world mostly through social interaction. Watching others work through problems provides a model for their problem solving. Parents are urged to encourage their child when he or she asks for help to think of another way to try and to let the parent(s) know how it works. Allow children to try and fail and try again. This is a first step for children toward becoming self-directed learners and independent problem solvers.

Research Related to Thinking. Another area of discussion in the newsletter related to research on student characteristics and how they affected their thinking. One example is the *difference between task-focused and ability-focused learners*. Task-focused students are concerned with learning skills and abilities regardless of how they compare to their peers. They tend to exhibit adaptive patterns of learning and have more positive attitudes toward their schoolwork. Ability-focused students want to demonstrate ability and outperform others. If a task is difficult for them, they may tend to avoid it or put in little effort so they will not appear unable to solve it.

Another article lists *negative effects of competition* on both high- and low-achieving students. Research suggests and the Lincoln principal agreed that the best way to deal with competition is to experience being competent, learn the value of hard work and challenge, and build a positive attitude about one's ability to learn. Like successful athletes, successful students should measure their success on improving their own "game." Is there something really wrong when we need to make ourselves look good at someone else's expense?

Readers were also reminded that the district and school had implemented teaching and assessment strategies to create a more task-focused environment to help students become competent, independent learners. These strategies include flexible grouping, cooperative learning, portfolios, grading focused on objectives and student self-evaluation, recognition of progress and improvement, emphasizing learning for its own sake, interdisciplinary teaching, risk taking, and emphasizing higher-level thinking skills and problem solving.

Current Thoughts on Education. The newsletter also acted as a vehicle for sharing current literature and information with the parents and other readers. For example, in one issue, the principal discussed the content of an interview with Harold Stevenson, a professor at the University of Michigan and author of the book, *The Learning Gap*. The discussion centered around differences in standards and perceptions between the United States and Asia. In the United States, we tend to emphasize the importance of native ability. In Asia, this idea is seen as self-defeating because the concern is to help all children achieve. When asked, "What is the most important factor in helping children do well in mathematics," 70–80 percent of Japanese and Chinese students say "studying." In the United States, 10 percent of the students say studying is most important, but the majority say the teacher is the most important factor.

Parents of U.S. students responded that a student's college entrance exam could be predicted in about the sixth grade while Asian parents responded, "in the eleventh or twelfth grade" because only then will it be possible to see how well the student is applying him- or herself. Americans thought that tests can tell how much innate ability a student has in an area while Asians rejected that assertion.

These views reflect contrasting ideas about self-determination and consequently behaviors and attitudes toward school. The article concluded by quoting Thomas Edison's idea that "genius is 1 percent inspiration and 99 percent perspiration." Regardless of our belief in the role played by innate ability, it only makes sense that the degree to which our children work hard to learn at school and at home and take responsibility for their learning and behavior will determine their level of development and ultimately their achievements and character.

Parents as Partners in Learning. The newsletter provided an opportunity for the principal to ask parents to help the school in the learning process. After pointing out the great importance of the parents' attitudes and involvement to a student's learning in school, a quote summed up the issue: *"Smart is not something you're born with, it is something you get through hard work."* And that's why staff at Lincoln school expect your child to work hard. But the child needs to know that his or her parents expect him or her to work hard, too. Some things that can help parents bring about these attitudes include students reading at home each night, students practicing math facts at home, and students discussing ideas and observations with their parents. Students also need to limit TV-watching time and participate in enriching, diverse experiences on weekends. Students who are expected to fulfill commitments at home are better able to do so at school.

Developing and Teaching Interdisciplinary Units of Instruction

In addition to introducing thinking and problem-solving skills into every unit of instruction in the curriculum, several interdisciplinary units were developed. Two of these units—one that involved fifth-graders in learning about business and investments and another for third-graders on "discovering cities of the world"—will be described.

Hands-On Learning About Business and Investments. This exciting unit involved instruction from community members and student learning out in the community. The focus of the unit was "how to run a business and how to invest the profits." Here, an Elmhurst restaurant owner, a local banker, and a financial planner combined efforts with three fifth-grade teachers to teach elementary students.

The project began when a Lincoln substitute teacher who also worked at the Silverado Restaurant, talked with restaurant owner Jack Island about her idea of students learning to run a business from hands-on experience. Island took to the idea right away and proposed a project: *He needed to make more money at his business, but his employees didn't want to work on Sunday. So he wanted to rent his business out to an enthusiastic group of students to increase his profits.*

Island met with the fifth-grade classes and their teachers and agreed to "rent" his restaurant to them. Then the class drew up a business plan and invited an Elmhurst banker to review the plan and circulate a $200 loan petition for the students to sign. The students signed the loan, often with reluctance, because $200 seemed like a lot of money to 11-year-olds. Also, employees from the restaurant came to the school to give lessons in table setting and waiting procedures. Students decided on and designed menus for their offerings. Island commented that he had gone through graduate school with a degree in economics without ever really knowing anything about a business until he did it himself. Now the fifth-grade students were going to have this unique opportunity to "run a restaurant."

One Sunday afternoon, with their families and friends as customers, the students operated the restaurant under the supervision of Island and some of the employees. Students acted as hosts, waitpersons, and cleanup people. Teachers and others also helped By the end of afternoon, the students were very proud of their accomplishments and had made a profit of $900. Island had dealt with them as business clients rather than as kids.

Even though the students had decided to use their profits to defray the cost of a three-day, interdisciplinary outdoor education experience, they and their teachers decided to study how they might invest their profit successfully in a hypothetical situation. Again, they reached out to the community for assistance. Mr. Fettig, a financial adviser, acted as their teacher. He spent 5, one-hour sessions that were divided into "three fiscal years" to help them learn about investing.

Students were each assigned income to start with and then added income each year. Each student had a balance sheet for recording expenses and a checkbook for paying them. Fettig also prepared an assessment to find out each student's level of tolerance for risk. Questions included asking how the student might spend an extra $55 per week, while another measured the student's level of daring while riding a bicycle. Based on this assessment, students were categorized and placed in low-risk, moderate-risk, and high-risk investment groups. Each student made up an annual budget, deposited income, and wrote checks for expenses. After a lesson on savings, fixed-income expenses, and equity investment, each student decided on how much leftover money to save or invest.

Fettig discussed a chart of historical averages with expected rates of return and offered investment recommendations based on each student's risk group, but the final decision was up to the individual student. In the "first year," the equity investments went down 5 percent, but went up 20 percent in year 2. One student boasted of making $4,000 over these two years. Savings account and fixed-income investments went up 3 to 6 percent over the "three years" of their project.

Fettig was extremely enthusiastic about the project, saying, "It was great to watch the students experiment with investing." They also came up with some creative ideas. One group of students wanted to pool their resources to purchase an apartment building and all live together. Fettig saw this as a real estate limited partnership proposed by 11-year-olds. One student thought playing the lottery was a possibility and pluses and minuses of such investing were discussed. One high-risk investor had done so well in equity investments he asked about buying a house.

The fifth-grade teachers, Lee Clausen, Lyn Lang, and Kathy Marinier, were also excited about the project. They felt that making investment decisions is often confusing to adults, so it is good to expose their classes to the real world of investing and decision making. These lessons will be something the students can carry far into the future. This economics project, which incorporated language arts, math, social studies, and the use of many thinking skills will be refined and perhaps expanded for future groups of students at Lincoln and other schools in the district. Parts of this description were taken with permission from an article by Dee Longfellow Born in the *DuPage, Illinois, Business Ledger,* April, 1994, p. 18.

Discovering Cities of the World. This third-grade interdisciplinary unit began with an indepth look at the local community. During this period, the students studied map skills, learned about the importance of interdependence between various occupations in the community, and were exposed to the significant historical events of the area. Six cities, one from each settled continent, were selected for this unit. Each city was located on an important waterway for its nation. The cities were

Montreal, Canada (North America)
Manaus, Brazil (South America)
Cairo, Egypt (Africa)
Sydney, (Australia)
Venice, Italy (Europe)
Tokyo, Japan (Asia)

As the students studied each city, they also explored the culture of the nation in which the city was located. Some of the many and varied activities the students experienced, along with the country they focused on and their general category in the curriculum, are listed as follows:

Curriculum Category	*Cultural Relationship/ Country*
Customs and holidays	Tea Ceremony (Japan); Thanksgiving (Canada)
Transportation	Measurement of simulated gondola (Italy)

(Continued)

Curriculum Category	Cultural Relationship and Country
Waterways	Nile (Egypt); Amazon (Brazil); Coral Reef (Australia); St. Lawrence (Canada)
Language	Portuguese (Brazil); Kanji (Japan); French (Canada); hieroglyphics (Egypt)
Food and cooking	Rice and its uses (Japan, others)
Clothing	Kimonos (Japan)
Historical development	Egyptian Exhibit (at Field or other museum)
Art	Venetian artists and artwork (Italy)
Music	Sydney Opera House (Australia); Italian operas
Dance	History of Brazilian music and dance
Animal and plant life	Papyrus making (Egypt); Australian animals
Currency	Comparison of American and Brazilian money; also compare U.S. currency with others
Traditional stories, poetry	Haiku (Japan); fables (Italy, Japan, others)

Students practiced many thinking and learning strategies during this unit. The major skills that were emphasized are listed as follows:

Researching	Summarizing
Map using	Demonstrating
Memorizing	Organizing
Reading	Comparing and contrasting
Expository narrative, and persuasive writing	Debating Oral presenting Sequencing

As a culminating activity for the unit, students, representing each of the six cities, selected important facets of each culture to be included in a new "ideal" space colony. The students shared their ideas at a United Nations meeting and voted on and developed a rationale for which ones should be carried to the new space environment.

Third-grade teachers Susan Grote, Dena Seidenfuss, and Pat Toole felt that this unit provided a far more challenging and exciting way to teach about other cities, countries, and their cultures around the world than the traditional fare in most third-grade textbooks. The unit also provided opportunities for students with strong interest in the topics and/or special skills to further develop multiple intelligences and expand on their learning by developing projects about any of the cities and countries.

Keeping the Program Alive and Well

To keep an ongoing program dynamic and vital requires involvement and cooperation of all groups—students, staff, administration, parents, and community. Some activities that Lincoln School used to sustain their program and keep it growing and improving are listed here:

1. Encouraged staff and students to share their learning at weekly, all-school sharing time and publicly recognize accomplishments. This provides a regularly scheduled opportunity for awareness, recognition, and motivation for further learning as we build community through shared experiences.

2. Implemented "Abe Lincoln's Amazing Hat" reading program through which we, as a school community, combine our out-of-school reading time. As a reward we were introduced to various individuals in American history. Fifth-graders served in a leadership role as they computed classroom totals and reported progress to students and staff. A recent year's total outside-of-school reading was 1,453,000 minutes for 400 students.

3. Presented an all-school play in which all students, staff, and parents were invited to participate. The focus was on American history in conjunction with the supplementary reading program.

4. Expanded parent, student, and community volunteer involvement throughout the school, hopefully involving office and custodial staff as well as teachers. In order to improve the appearance

of our school, involved students in taking responsibility for "how it looks" as well as to provide hands-on, ongoing science and aesthetic experiences. A "Green Team" composed of students in Ms. Halffield's instructional learning disabilities class worked with Ms. Reinertsen, their teaching assistant, to arrange, provide, and care for plants at various places throughout the school.

5. Provided an "Opening Day of School" celebration that focused on grade-level learning goals and provided recognition and support for each other.
6. Developed a building schedule for the fine arts, physical education, and classroom teachers that maximized instructional effectiveness, interdisciplinary teaching, flexible grouping, and teaming.
7. Developed a mini-interdisciplinary unit through which parents and teachers experienced integrated instruction at the first PTA meeting of the year.
8. Developed comprehensive student portfolios as a means for staff to assess and report student progress to parents.
9. Refined and implemented a three-day, overnight "outdoor education experience" for all fifth-graders.
10. Supported the second- and third-grade teachers specifically and other grade levels as well in their effort to team and use cross-grade-level instruction and experiences where beneficial.
11. Supported the student council, faculty, and PTA in studying and planting a Lincoln School Prairie as an opportunity to study the prairie—ecologically, historically, and esthetically—to improve the school grounds and provide hands-on learning.
12. Used the Lincoln Building Leadership Team to make decisions that directly affected staff development.
13. Initiated ad hoc committees as the need arose to address concerns and make decisions that are particular to the Lincoln School community. Examples are sharing time committee, facilities committee, outdoor education committee, play committee, and social committee.

The goals and objectives of the Lincoln School program are summarized in the highlights of an article, "Creating a Culture of Thinking," by David Perkins (1993), which Principal Billie Johnson shared with her staff. It said, "Good thinking is more than skill and ability; it's a matter of commitment" and "To teach for thinking, it's not enough to teach skills and strategies. We need to create a culture that 'enculturates' students into good thinking practices" (pp. 98, 99).

START SOLVING PROBLEMS AT THE PRIMARY LEVEL

San Marcos, Texas, Independent School District

This district involves their kindergartners, first-graders, and second-graders in thinking and solving problems. The district rationale suggests that the teachers are "faced with the challenge of preparing students for what they might encounter in the future." Part of this preparation requires students to look for more than one solution, to search beyond the "right" answer, and to think divergently as well as convergently. Furthermore, the kinds of problems their students will face in the future will require differentiated thinking. We can't teach children only facts and knowledge because we don't know the questions they will need to answer at some future date. But we can provide our students with the skills needed to tackle the problems they will face.

The San Marcos district has a diverse student population—65 percent Hispanic, 10 percent black, and 25 percent Anglo. The school population of about 6,500 students is divided into elementary (K–5) and secondary (6–12) divisions. The city is located midway between Austin, the state capital, and San Antonio, a major metropolitan area of more than one million people. San Marcos is the home of Southwest Texas State University with 20,000 students and is a center for business, industry, and tourism. It is also a bedroom community for people who work in Austin and San Antonio.

The administrative strategy of the district, in order to have the problem-solving program reach as many students as possible, is to assign a general facilitator who works on each campus, to do direct teaching with the K–2 students and act as a model for the teachers in each school. The facilitator provides classroom instruction for each class, K–2, about six times each year. Other tasks of the facilitator are coordinates workshops and materials; shares resources and requests for new information with all staff; keeps records and provides enrichment for special populations of students such as gifted and talented; coordinates conferences, information, and minicourses with parents; is accountable for identification of special population students; and coordinates teacher staff development related to the program.

Elements of the Program

Objectives, instructional strategies, grouping approaches, questioning techniques, and problem solving are emphasized in the program. These are discussed next.

Objectives. Both broad and specific objectives or outcomes of the program are discussed. *General objectives* for the students, K–2, are as follows:

- The learner will be introduced to the seven skills and related tools of creative and productive thinking, one per month, in sequential order.
- The learner will build knowledge and application of each skill and its relation to the other skills as they are introduced throughout each year and expand their command of the skills from year to year.

Specific student outcomes for each skill, using curiosity as an example, are as follows:

- The learner will understand that curiosity is the ability to question and wonder about things.
- The learner will associate a "real" tool with a thinking skill for learning.
- The learner will apply the concept of curiosity through thematic, integrated learning activities.
- The learner will use curiosity in daily activities to promote and reinforce higher-level thinking skills and problem solving.

Instructional Strategies. Teachers are encouraged to provide many opportunities in all subject matter areas where students can use a variety of thinking skills. These include brainstorming (fluency) to generate many ways of doing things; sketching what they talked about following brainstorming; applying Bloom's cognitive levels, particularly within stories; and using inquiry processes such as observing, classifying, inferring, and predicting.

Grouping Methods. There are opportunities to use many approaches here. Cooperative learning groups can be used for book making; role-playing; shadow, puppet, and people plays; and creative dramatics and music. Cluster groups are appropriate for research and field trips with special interests and purposes. Learning centers work well for drafts, reading, cooking, math, science, and fine arts. And, individuals may work alone for book reports, oral interviews, and research.

Questioning Techniques. These are designed to "keep the students thinking." One excellent technique that young children handle naturally is responding to the five W's (who, what, when, where, and why) and one H (how). Teacher-led discussions should provide the students with opportunities to ask their own questions as well as give answers. When an answer is asked for, the possibility of more than one correct answer should be emphasized.

Problem Solving. The most important aspect of the program is problem solving. It allows students to apply their thinking skills and exhibit creativity. Descriptions of opportunities for young children to solve problems form the major focus of the discussions in this section.

Foundations of the Program

At the primary level, this program is based on a set of seven creative skills. While the skills are important, it is also necessary for the lessons to be interesting and challenging to motivate the young students to learn successfully. Skills and lesson components are described.

Creative Process Skills. This program introduces creative and productive thinking skills in kindergarten, develops them in first grade, and reinforces them in second. The processes of fluency, flexibility, originality, elaboration, and student's "own ideas" are five aspects of thinking. Curiosity and imagination are natural characteristics of young children that precede the creative thinking. In a teaching situation, curiosity becomes the introductory skill, and the rest follow in sequence. Evaluation, shown last in the following teaching sequence, represents a review of all of the skills. Creative process skills with representative carpenter's tools and colors are shown below.

Lesson Components. All the skill lessons for primary level students need to have attractive titles, provide for hands-on activities, have opportunities for the students to apply what they have learned, and be carefully evaluated. Details on these characteristics are discussed here:

- *Attractive titles,* illustrated here for first-graders, such as *Curious George* (Lesson 1), *Where the Wild Things Are* (Lesson 2); *Paddington Bear* (Lesson 3), *Picasso, the Green Tree Frog* (Lesson 4), *Alphabetics* (Lesson 5), *Cookie Monster's Big Surprise* (Lesson 6), *Harold and the Purple Crayon* (Lesson 7), and *A Rainbow of My Own* (Lesson 8). Lesson numbers coordinate with the teaching sequence of the creative process skills.

- Use of *hands-on* or concrete items to introduce the tool for the skill such as stuffed animals, creature characters, puppets, and giant representations

- *Applications* such as who, what, when, where, why, and how; brainstorming; creative problem-solving (CPS) procedures; and activities with the children

- *Evaluation* that is carried out by both the students and the teachers.

Kindergarten Level

Early in the school each year, the facilitator introduces the program with the first skill, curiosity, and its "tool" the "L" in the color red. The tool and its color provide a concrete symbol for young children to better relate to the abstract term *curiosity*. After the initial session, the facilitator comes back about every five to six weeks to introduce the next skill or tool. Each time, the facilitator teaches the students about a new skill and the classroom teacher observes the lesson. The teacher receives a large poster of each tool for display in the classroom, and each child gets a small version of the tool to put into his or her "tool kit." The teacher also receives a list of additional activities for the children to reinforce, extend, and apply each process skill as well as materials, patterns, and examples for classroom use.

First-Grade Level

The students are now familiar with the process skills and are ready to use them in more advanced situations. The facilitator needs to make plans to both teach the students and the classroom teacher. This includes presenting motivating and stimulating lessons. Both facilitator responsibilities and a sample lesson are described next.

Facilitator Tasks. The facilitator reviews with the students the productive thinking skills that were introduced in kindergarten the year before. She also works out tasks to expand the students' knowledge and use of the skills as follows:

- Develop a sequence for the year using the seven skills needed for creative and productive thinking. These skills will be used with an entire class in a direct teaching situation where the facilitator provides modeling for the classroom teacher.

Skill	*Tool*	*Color*	*Teaching Sequence*
Curiosity	"L"	Red	1
Imagination	Wrench	Orange	2
Own ideas	Light bulb	Yellow	3
Fluency	Saw	Green	4
Flexibility	Ax	Blue	5
Originality	Screwdriver	Indigo	6
Elaboration	Ruler	Violet	7
(Evaluation	Rainbow	All-ROY G BIV	8)

- Provide each teacher with thematic materials to reinforce, enhance, elaborate, and follow up the direct teaching of the facilitator and to continue instruction of the skill(s) until the facilitator returns the next month.
- Encourage higher-level thinking skills, creative expression, inquiry, independent learning, and application of the seven creative process skills.
- Provide differentiated materials for special populations such as gifted and talented. Materials will be at the first-grade level; be original to meet needs of the population; be thematic with hands-on application for teachers and children; be child-oriented, self-directed, and teacher directed; and include visual aids, samples of activities with appropriate directions, and evaluations for both students and teachers.

Curious George, **a Skill-Oriented Lesson.** One example of a first-grade problem is based on the book *Curious George*. This book is creatively written and stimulating to the students. Since George was a monkey, some techniques that a teacher might use here are webbing monkey characteristics, a Venn diagram relating monkeys and gorillas, and simulations that explore different environments where monkeys are found—both natural and artificial.

A lesson plan for first graders to use creative thinking tools is described next. The skill introduced here is curiosity, but lessons for each of the seven skills follow a similar format. The lesson plan specifies *materials, objectives,* ideas for *anticipatory set, procedures* the teacher carries out with the students, questions and statements for *guided practice,* activities for student *independent practice, closure,* and *evaluation.*

Second-Grade Level

If students bring the "tool kit" they received in first grade with them, they get a special rainbow sticker to put on it. If they lost their kit during the summer, they are given a new one. In the first visit, the facilitator reviews the skills, the tools that represents them, and examples of how the skill can be used. The second visit with the students starts the process of integrating the skills with different subjects, specific assignments, and problems that the student might encounter.

Applying the Skills. In creative writing, for example, the children are asked to pull out their tool kits representing the set of seven skills and lay each tool in order of the colors of the rainbow on their desks or personal spaces. Then the teacher and facilitator talk about a creative writing topic with the students and ask them what "tools" they can use. What are their "own ideas"? How about fluency? The chil-

---

CURIOUS GEORGE • *An Introduction to Creative Thinking–Grade 1*

Materials:

- *Curious George,* a book by H. A. Rey
- Stuffed monkey with a red shirt to represent Curious George
- Self-sealing plastic bags with a red, curiosity "L" tool for each student
- Large poster with red, curiosity "L" tool for the teacher
- Backpack for teacher to carry all materials

Objectives:

The learner will

- Understand that curiosity is the ability to question and wonder about things
- Associate a "real" tool such as the "L" with a thinking tool for learning
- Apply the concept of curiosity through a thematic, integrated learning activity.

Anticipatory Set:

The teacher will suggest to the students that today they will learn what it means to be curious, who can be curious, and how they can be curious. The teacher will also explain that the term *curious* means desirous of knowing or learning.

Procedures:

1. Share the "treasures" in the backpack.

2. Introduce Curious George, the stuffed monkey with a red shirt who has been hiding in the backpack.

3. Talk about George and let the children share what they know or imagine about him.

4. Read the original book about him—*Curious George* by H. A. Rey.

5. Discuss how George was curious in the story, how monkeys are generally curious, and how children are curious, too.

6. Introduce Curious George's favorite color, red, and brainstorm reasons why it is his favorite.

7. Introduce George's favorite tool for learning curiosity, the "L," and help the students associate the "L" tool with curiosity.

8. Show students what is inside their Creative Thinking Tool Kit and explain its use.

9. Give each student an "L" and have them draw their version of Curious George on the back of it.

10. Ask the students where the teacher's large poster of the "L" tool for curiosity could be posted in the room to remind them daily to be curious.

Guided Practice:

1. The teacher writes the word *curiosity* on the board.

2. Using the class poster of the "L" tool, go over the following questions:

    a. What might happen when?

    b. What would happen if we?

    c. Who do you suppose caused _____ to happen?

    d. Why do you suppose _____ is true?

    e. Imagine what _____ would be like.

    f. What questions does this raise for you?

    g. What else would you like to find out?

    h. What do you wonder about?

    i. What do you know? What don't you know?

    j. How did _____ react?

(Continued)

CURIOUS GEORGE • (Continued)

Independent Practice:

1. Students share examples orally of times they were curious.

2. Students draw and write an explanation of an example of who, what, when, where, why, or how (on paper provided).

Closure:

1. Review the creative learning skill, curiosity, and the meaning of the word *curiosity*.

2. Ask the children, "Who can be curious, and when, where, why, and how they should be curious."

3. Review and state the objectives of the lesson.

Evaluation:

Students can tell the teacher what being curious means, and give examples.

---

dren start to brainstorm a list of tools representing the skills and why they think they will be useful. The teacher or facilitator might ask, "Will we need to have many thoughts and ideas? Elaboration? Do we need detail? Why?"

When the children pull out the tools they need, they differ according to their own thoughts. But, imagination usually comes up first—and is usually their favorite tool. The teachers try to help the children see the need for several tools in their work. The more the children use these tools, the better their thinking skills develop. Teachers can ask specific questions about why they use a certain tool to check their application of the skill.

This same process can be used in art to get thoughts and ideas going before they start to draw or paint. In science, thinking about the skills and tools they will use helps students search for possible solutions that they can "try out" to solve a problem. In physical education classes when students do activities to create a form or shape with their bodies, they use the skills of imagination, own ideas, be flexible, and so on. These same strategies can be applied in all subject areas.

Marshmallow Olympics, a Problem-Solving Lesson. This activity provides opportunities for students to use many thinking skills to solve a second-grade science problem. A *rationale, objective(s), materials, procedures* and *options for the teacher to use with the students* are illustrated.

MARSHMALLOW OLYMPICS • Lesson Plan—Grade 2

Rationale: The cooperative learning groups will work together to move an object.

Objective: Supplied with a marshmallow, each group will use a variety of objects to move a marshmallow through an obstacle course as efficiently as possible.

Materials for Each Cooperative Group:

1 large marshmallow	1 straw	1 facial tissue
12-inch piece of string	1 ruler	1 teaspoon

1 toothpick   a pencil   a can with the top cut off
1 piece of 6 x 6-inch paper (individual recordkeeping sheet)

Procedures:

Review the creative thinking skills and the process for solving problems as well as the guidelines for effective cooperative groups. Here students can get out their thinking tool kits, line the tools up in order, and brainstorm which ones they would need. Then, throughout the lesson they and the teacher can refer back to the tools and the skills they represent. Students are asked to give reasons why they are using each tool and to identify the skill it represents.

1. The students meet in their cooperative groups.

2. Teachers distribute the materials listed at the beginning of the lesson to each group—sending one representative to gather materials from the supply table.

3. Thinking as engineers, each member of the group chooses two items that will help only him or her move the marshmallow.

4. Each time the marshmallow is moved, it must be moved by a different member. Each member of the group has two different items and will use each one on a rotation basis. Students explain which skills they are using.

5. For each obstacle they move successfully, they receive two points. If they drop the marshmallow, that movement is unsuccessful. (Use recording sheet for scoring.)

6. The marshmallow itself must never be touched by the student's hands.

7. Groups have twenty minutes to complete their objective.

8. The movements for the marshmallow are listed here:

   - From the supply table to the group's work area
   - Into a can
   - Out of the can and onto the work table
   - Over a 12-inch space
   - From desktop to floor
   - From floor to desktop
   - Delivered back to the supply table.

Extended Options for the Teacher to Use with the Students:

1. Write up a report as a whole class.

2. Get together with another second-grade class, and compare results.

3. Discuss the problems the children had and how they could do it differently another time.

Results of the Program

In third and fourth grades, the students continue to use the skills in increasingly more complex and abstract ways. They also add other techniques such as SCAMPER and Bloom's cognitive taxonomy (both were reviewed in Chapter 2) to their strategies to solve problems in a variety of subjects.

Judy Brown, a facilitator at the Crockett Elementary School, says, "One of our best uses of the skill tools is to solve campus problems. For example, we asked the children what they thought some of the problems at school were. They said there was 'Too much noise in the cafeteria.' Then, we used our tools to generate solutions to suggest to the principal to solve the problem." Facilitators in this district believe that using these tools are excellent ways to help young students move through the problem-solving process, generate many solutions, select the best ones, try them out, and evaluate them.

Overall, how successful is this program? Brown summarized it like this: "These tools gave the children a way to associate the skills with something concrete that they could relate to. They also helped them bridge the gap from abstract to applied learning. As children progressed through the primary grades, they were able to transfer the skills to daily work and to increase their skill development."

TECHNOLOGY PROVIDES THE BASE FOR A QUALITY COMMUNICATIONS SCHOOL

Eastern Middle School, Montgomery County, Maryland, Public Schools (MCPS)

Eastern Middle School is a magnet school in Silver Spring, Maryland, located in an urban setting adjacent to the District of Columbia. The school's population of 780 seventh- and eighth-graders includes local boundary students and magnet students from throughout the 500-square-mile system. The socioeconomic level ranges from the poorest to the wealthiest in the county. Its diverse student population is 14 percent Asian; 29 percent black; 21 percent Hispanic; 35 percent white; and about 1 percent American Indian. Fifty-eight nationalities are represented in the school population. Professional and support staff also represent major ethnic groups.

Marlene Hartzman, former principal of Eastern Middle School, says, "The **mission statement** that the staff wrote and revises every year to meet changing needs provides guidance for the program for both students and teachers." It declares:

> At Eastern, students gain and apply academic and social skills in a caring, safe, yet challenging environment where we value all people as individuals and as learners.
>
> - We learn to respect each other and develop pride in ourselves.
> - We view learning as an ongoing, exciting endeavor.
> - We learn how to succeed in a diverse and changing world.

This statement is represented by the theme of RESPECT: **R**esponsibility, **E**xcellence, **S**elf-respect, **P**erseverance, **E**nthusiasm, **C**ontrol, and **T**houghtfulness. Hartzman feels that the elements of RESPECT formed a daily "mantra" for the students and staff. Each school day began with a "thought for the day" related to one aspect of RESPECT and was broadcast to staff and students over the school's public address system. This theme was even painted on hallway walls to remind students and staff of their mission.

After staff and administrators at Eastern Middle School had written down their general mission, they needed to move from words to action. The district wanted technology to be used in every school. The district policy for middle schools suggested a team organizational structure, interdisciplinary curriculum, and attention to the learning problems of minority students and others, while still meeting the needs of gifted and talented and other fully functioning students. The state of Maryland had mandates, too. These included (1) a series of interdisciplinary assessments to be administered at grades 3, 5, 8, and 11; and (2) functional literacy tests in mathematics, reading, writing, and citizenship as a part of high school graduation requirements.

The question facing staff and administration was how to orchestrate a program that would meet the needs of Eastern students as well as the mandates. Also, staff had to be able to believe in and adequately provide the program. After considerable discussion and research, they decided to make technology the center of every aspect of their program. The discussion here explores how a team structure and technology go together, the integration of interdisciplinary curriculum and technology, and ways that technology motivates and supports a total program. Staff development to start and maintain the program and program results are also described.

Teaming Facilitates the Use of Technology

Eastern Middle School is organized on a team structure with three teams at each grade level. Each one has four teachers, a media specialist, support staff, and 100–150 students. Teachers on each team have common planning time during regular school hours to develop their instructional strategies and schedule. Students on each team are academically heterogeneous, except for the Magnet team, and include ESOL (English for Speakers of Other Languages) and special-needs students.

Students stay on the same team for their two years at the school. Curriculum is interdisciplinary on all teams and authentic projects are used for assessment and culminating activities. Mathematics teachers are not team members, so they can group and regroup students frequently. Each team has a different focus: COM-TEC (Collaborative Opportunities in Modern Technology and Effective Communication); Magnet (for highly gifted students); and ARTS (Arts Revitalizing Traditional Studies).

COM-TEC Team. Students are encouraged to develop their thinking and communication skills through interdisciplinary exploration in science, arts, and English. They have opportunities to go beyond regular instructional objectives through activities in music, photography, media production, and home economics as well as science and English. Higher-order thinking skills and communication strategies that students need to prepare for the twenty-first century are emphasized. These include a process- and product-centered approach to learning where staff hold high expectations for quality and effort from all students while differentiating instruction to accommodate varied learning levels, styles, and rates.

Students work with computers to organize and interpret data; to write, revise, and publish documents; to participate in telecommunication activities; and to participate in simulation and problem-solving activities. They also receive instruction to apply technology to communication in their science and English classes as well as in television production, photography, home economics, and music classes. They learn how to use computers and multimedia technology to publish their own documents, access and organize information, run simulations to solve problems, and link their communities, local and global, through telecommunication.

Magnet Team. Here an interdisciplinary humanities program for students from Montgomery County that are highly motivated and highly gifted and talented in writing is emphasized. The core curriculum draws together significant concepts from literature, social studies, language arts, and science. Four intensive academic courses in the program are writing, interdisciplinary world studies, foreign language immersion (as an option), and media production. In each area, computers and media technology help students expand the quality, depth, and texture of the learning process. Students are urged to develop skills for team collaboration as well as individual excellence. Many of the high-quality products that these students have created have won national and local awards in journalism, broadcasting, and film.

ARTS Team. Gifted and talented, average, and basic skills students explore academic inquiries in an arts- and technology-enhanced environment. Fine arts skills and concepts support learning in other academic disciplines—English, science, and world studies. Interdisciplinary projects allow students to go beyond the traditional class format. Blocks of time are available to students so they can work on projects and labs without interruptions of the typical seven-period day. There is an attempt to replicate the real world of work where students operate in production teams with schedules, deadlines, and areas of specialty, along with peer critiques and evaluations. Students also have access to a multimedia laboratory space to use computers, musical instruments, synthesizers, and art media to anchor, extend, and transform their learning.

Titles of several interdisciplinary arts-based units and the hands-on technology that is linked with them are summarized in the following chart:

Technology Integrates with Interdisciplinary Curriculum

The interdisciplinary curriculum of Eastern coordinates with that of the district and mandates from the Maryland State Department of Education (MSDE). There is an emphasis on teaching higher-order thinking skills using the "dimensions of learning" techniques. For example, when seventh-graders study fables in English they are at the same time studying animals and classification in science and composition in art and music. Not only will the students write fables, they will also illustrate them and compose or select music that underscores the animal's characteristics.

Effective interdisciplinary learning needs to be designed and developed carefully. The process used at Eastern Middle School is

- Arrange material topically to support the world studies, English, or science curriculum
- Provide opportunities to develop communication skills in a variety of media, incorporating writing, speaking, and visual communication
- Structure activities to promote active, hands-on learning that requires collaborative work to produce real products for real audiences and to develop and use critical thinking skills to
  - Access information from a variety of media (divergence)
  - Evaluate and select information (convergence)
  - Decide on a medium or media (convergence, synthesis)
  - Communicate ideas through writing, speaking, and visual means (synthesis)
  - Evaluate the success of the communication products (evaluation); evaluation is done by peers as well as teachers and experts.

Advantages for Students and Staff. Interdisciplinary learning makes common sense and helps students who (1) learn the content from a variety of angles, (2) achieve a higher degree of recognition and knowledge as well as an increased level of understanding, (3) develop key communication skills in an increasingly information-oriented world, (4) learn to think about and feel the importance and the tapestry

Unit Title	Technology to Support the Unit
Computer Licensing	*Macintosh* LC computer (interactive *Hypercard* stack)
Journal Writing	*Macintosh* computer with *Microsoft Works* (for word processing)
Multimedia Fables	*Macintosh* computer *Opcode* MIDI Translator (musical instrument digital interface) *Yamaha* YRP-20 portable piano or Casio CZ-5000 synthesizer *Deluxe Music Construction Set* (music composition software)
Composing the Blues	*Macintosh* computer with *Microsoft Works* (color graphics and word processing) *Deluxe Music Construction Set* (music composition software) *Opcode* MIDI Translator *Yamaha* YPR-20 portable piano or CZ-5000
Optical Illusions	*Macintosh* LC computer *Microsoft Works* with color graphics *Color Mac Cheese* with color graphics
Japan Unit	*Macintosh* LC II computer (system 7) with *Hypercard* *Video-spigot* (interface), video footage, and scanner
Multimedia Research Global Musical Practices	*Macintosh* LC computer (using System 7) *Macintosh* CD-ROM drive *Grolier's Electronic Encyclopedia* CD-ROM *Winnebago Electronic Card Catalogue* *Hyperscan* software and *Apple* scanner *Hypercard* stack development *Macintosh* LC microphone (for digital audio input) *Apple Scanner* (with *Hyperscan*)

of their learning, (5) learn to work and communicate in a group, and (6) know that their ideas and communication are taken seriously.

Staff benefits parallel those of their students and are crucial to starting and maintaining an interdisciplinary, technology-based program. In order to do this, teachers and support staff need training and support early in the process of program development. Some suggestions to facilitate teacher involvement follow:

- Put computers in staff members hands and make them accessible even before staff are formally trained.
- Provide training to staff to introduce and maintain skills, and to demonstrate the applications they will need in their teaching.
- Offer observation and consultation opportunities to staff members by sending them to into classrooms and schools where people are using technology creatively and effectively with students and staff.
- Encourage risk-taking.
- Acknowledge successes and applaud failures; consider failures to be evidence of "being on the cutting edge" and willing to take risks.

Staff Should Dare to Dream. Another suggestion to staff that want to start or expand the use of technology in their schools, is to *dream*. Many "impossible ideas" have proved possible and are in effect today at Eastern. And some of their newer dreams are "fermenting" right now. Examples are presented next.

One dream was to have a whole-eighth-grade urban studies field experience in Washington, DC, for at least a week. Here students would explore a metropolitan area from many perspectives such as planning, history, arts and architecture, by day and night, from the viewpoint of the advantaged and disadvantaged, and so on. Students could carry out activities that would benefit from the resources of many agencies and organizations that are willing to explain and share the technologies they use in their everyday operations. Then students could use the technologies they have in place at school to create products at the end of the unit.

Another dream was to develop a whole-seventh-grade unit on culture and identity that allows students to explore the various communities and cultures to which they belong. This would take students into the surrounding community of Silver Spring to investigate community needs and encourage them to create products to meet those needs, again using technology—inside and outside of the school.

A third dream involved students in a schoolwide communication enterprise such as a radio magazine show with a supporting newsletter to provide a regular forum for student products to serve the community.

And, Dr. Hartzman has a dream "in progress"—Teach students how to be ham radio operators. While doing this, they would learn a whole new set of communication skills and every student would leave school with a ham operator's license.

Assessment in the Program. Assessment of student accomplishment is carried out in accordance with the state's model for reform and accountability, the Maryland School Performance Assessment Program (MSPAP). In this model, assessment is done in grades 3, 5, 8; grade 11 will be added in the future. All tests are interdisciplinary and focus on a student's ability to solve problems. For example, a math problem might involve students working in a group to open a restaurant in their neighborhood. The problem requires students to write about the process they would use, including how they arrived at the type of restaurant they would open, its location, its pricing policies, and how much it would cost to open and maintain the restaurant. Maryland Tests of Functional Reading, Writing, Math, and Citizenship are required for high school graduation. At the school level, students' authentic projects are assessed in grade 8.

Technology Supports, Motivates, and Enhances Learning

Technology provides a strong and multifaceted support system for instruction in this school. It is used according to staff beliefs about the significance and benefits of technology in a middle school setting. These beliefs and their relationships to the school program, the learning process, and student attitudes and actions are discussed next.

Technology Is the Foundation of the School Program. Technology is involved in many ways, shapes, and forms. At Eastern, the staff finds technology to be:

- A useful tool in every facet of school life and in every discipline

- The basis, the very infrastructure, of a truly connected and collaborative school in which all school community members share in decision making

- A means toward creating an instructional program that drives the master schedule and avoids a schedule that drives the program

- An efficient instrument for assessing student needs and the effects of strategies used to meet those needs

- One of the most logical connectors when creating integrated curricula.

Technology Augments the Learning Process. In both affective and cognitive ways, technology strengthens teachers' efforts to become facilitators of student learning and empowers students to take responsibility for their own learning. It also allows students to learn and practice the skills of collaboration, decision making, problem solving, organization, and communication. It helps students keep current by putting the equipment of professionals in their hands. Many students find it easier to organize and reorganize information, synthesize their learning and construct their own meaning, and evaluate their results using a computer. Technology also promotes extension and enrichment of curricula for all levels of students.

Students Love Technology. Students and technology seem to be natural "partners." When students interact with various technologies, teachers have observed that their *attitudes and actions* seem to become more positive. They are:

- Willing to take risks and to put forth effort; for example, revision can be accomplished efficiently and is therefore possible

- Confident, and less likely to avoid a task out of frustration or fear of failure

- Focused for longer periods than usual, because they can see immediate results of their efforts and their decisions

- Responsive to the multisensory, hands-on, and experiential qualities of the equipment

- Drawn immediately to the equipment, and able to teach themselves.

- Motivated to learn unexciting but necessary skills or concepts such as writing mechanics because they see them as legitimately required to create high-quality products for the public

- Involved in instructional tasks that they perceive as relevant and interesting

- Encouraged to return to previously introduced concepts and skills.

Students and Staff Need Easy Access to Technology. For success, technology in a variety of forms needs to be readily available to both staff and students. And, at Eastern Middle School it is "at hand." All students have access to a *Macintosh* Network in the school's Media Center. This network includes several computers, *Hyperscan*, the *Patron's Automated Catalog, Grolier's Electronic Encyclopedia* (on CD-ROM), three LC computers loaded with *Hypercard*, five assorted *Macintosh* computers loaded with *Microsoft Works,* a laser disk player, a laser printer, two impact printers, *Apple* CD-ROM players, and many other items. In addition, students and staff have access to many other technologies.

In *writing and math labs*, students have many alternatives in their choice of equipment, such as (1) two computer writing labs; one equipped with 28 IIE computers and the *AppleWorks* program, one *Macintosh* LC with *Hypercard* and *Microsoft Works*, and several printers; the second has 28 IIE computers and printers; (2) one general computer lab equipped with 15 Apple IIE computers and *AppleWorks* and several printers; and (3) One Apple GS lab with 12 computers and *AppleWorks* and assorted math-related software.

Audiovisual equipment and labs give staff access to television monitors and VCRs as well as mobile video equipment, two television studios, and a photography lab. Also, each staff team has computers and printers available to them along with equipment to handle software for science, ESOL, industrial technology, and art, music, and physical education. The Apple IIE labs are scheduled all periods of every day and are used by ESOL and special education classes as well as those of regular students. The IIE labs, with twenty-eight computers each are open before school, during lunch hour, and after school and are filled most days. Lab scheduling has to be changed from time to time to meet student and staff needs.

Students need *access to labs outside of class*. During these times, they can draft and revise documents, and run simulations for problem solving in art, architecture, photography, home economics, math, and world studies. They also may compose music and graphic displays and can access or develop data bases to complete research or to organize information. Students activities also include desktop publishing, creation of *Hypercard* stacks, or the development of annotated bibliographies of books they have read. Special opportunities are also available. For example, seventh-grade English students can work with the multimedia *Hypercard* stack for *The Master Puppeteer*, a novel by Katherine Paterson, on one LC in the lab and the three LCs in the Media Center to enrich their interdisciplinary unit on Japan.

Students use more technology in workshops. English teachers use the workshop approach to encourage students to read widely and often. Here, students have choices in their book selections and opportunities to reflect on their reading. They can also work on television production and photography to develop commercials about books they recommend to other students to read. They may use the *AppleWorks* data base to develop an annotated bibliography and use video, photography, and computer multimedia technology to create the commercials. After students had produced 30- to 60-second video commercials recommending books, they looped them together and sent them with a bibliography to Eastern's media center, feeder elementary media centers, and public libraries in the community.

Opportunities to use technology effectively in every project in every interdisciplinary unit are endless. They are limited only by the curiosity and creativity of the students and staff . . . and the technology that is available to them.

Staff Development Is Crucial to Program Success

A strong staff development program is necessary to produce significant changes in curriculum, instruction, and student achievement. It should be delivered by colleagues who are currently using the approaches in their classroom; occur during regularly scheduled work hours; and have opportunities for staff to observe, discuss the underlying theory, analyze the effects, practice the approaches, and get feedback on their practice. Training should be delivered and reinforced over a significant period of time. New approaches should be be modeled by teachers who can both demonstrate them and argue persuasively and enthusiastically about their benefits for students in a rapidly changing and technologically oriented society.

Staff Involvement Is a Key Factor. Staff need to be involved in every step of staff development—planning, implementation, evaluation, and maintenance. Shared decision making was already in place as a way of operation at Eastern. All staff—teaching and support services—as well as parents were involved in all decisions affecting the school. Staff chaired all school committees such as professional development, discipline, safety, student recognition, and community involvement. Through open communication and constant feedback, they worked with parents to make policy decisions that were implemented in the school. The primary goal was that everything that happened in the school would happen by a conscientious decision-making process. Risk taking and mistakes were considered as important elements of growth. The people involved also got to know and respect each other—and they laughed a lot.

Site-Based Program Meets Staff Needs. Staff development, by design was an individualized, site-based program to enhance the professional development of each staff member. Staff worked alone or in small groups to meet yearly objectives. They also received financial support from the Parent Teacher Student Association (PTSA) to attend conferences and seminars. Staff members who accepted this support were obligated to share what they learned with parents and the rest of the staff. Everybody gained from this arrangement. When the professional development committee felt that the entire staff would benefit from particular aspects of training, the training was arranged using a metacognitive model. The intent was to model everything for the staff, then follow up with directed discussions. Staff learning was not left to chance.

To meet *individual and district needs,* this staff development plan drew dividends on investments the district has already made at Eastern. Investments included technology support for its media center, television studios, and computer writing labs as well as training and staffing opportunities already offered to staff. Site-based development can also be more cost effective than other approaches. Several staff were already involved as instructors for the department of staff development, many have presented at national or local conferences, and others have served as consultants to other schools within the district. Staff trainers already in place, served as a team of "change agents" within the school and supported similar teams in other schools.

The site-based staff development offered *flexible goals and requirements* in a variety of areas such as

1. Core training curriculum, which introduces the components of a sound interdisciplinary middle school program to promote academic achievement and self-confident learners

2. Arrangements for individual teachers to observe or receive training on a particular strategy or plan and discuss its implementation with other staff

3. Ongoing relationships between a grade-level team at Eastern and a corresponding team at another school where, over a semester or year, the teams could exchange visits to classrooms, plan curriculum, and problem-solve together to promote transfer of training

4. Exchange of similar staff positions between Eastern and another school

5. Training sessions using Eastern staff as instructors

6. Training in design and equipment acquisitions for a variety of technology labs in the media center, fine arts, media production, and writing

7. Use of the television studios and media staff at Eastern to develop, analyze, and discuss demonstration lessons and use of interactive video capability

8. Participation in a summer institute for opportunities to apply training to a diverse group of students and to provide instruction for organization skills, introduction to technology, and communication skills.

Costs needed to be reasonable for on-site staff development. Expenses included staffing arrangements to provide planning time for the group of master teachers who could act as trainers to plan and execute training and for funding a full-time staff development coordinator position. Release time for work can be funded by budgeting substitute teacher time to release teachers for staff development activities.

This model offers *professional opportunities* to all staff. First, it provides expanded professional roles for staff who have worked hard to develop innovative approaches to promote the success of all students to share their expertise with their peers at their own school and others in the district and beyond. Second, it allows district staff to spend extended periods of time observing and discussing how school success can be achieved with a highly diverse student population. Third, it takes advantage of the technology, excellent teachers, and energy already in place in the Blair School Cluster to which Eastern belongs. And, fourth, it provides a long-range training design that gives staff development an instructional focus consistent with promoting the success and achievement of all students within the Montgomery County Public Schools district.

Results of the Program

When Marlene Hartzman and current Eastern principal, John Goodloe, look back on the six years their interdisciplinary, technology-enhanced program has been in operation, they see success for students, parents, and teachers in a variety of areas.

Students. Their dramatic results included changes in behaviors, academic accomplishment, and responsibilities. Some specific changes were

1. Suspensions were reduced.

2. Grades improved, with fewer failures and less gender and racial discrepancies.

3. Student applications for the magnet school within Eastern have increased from 250 to 750 for the 100 openings each year.

4. Students have taken responsibilities around the school such as busing dishes and wiping their own tables in the cafeteria.

5. Students have had more opportunities to interact with teachers because teachers have worked around rigid bus schedules to gain contact time.

6. Students have experienced real "success" in their school work and by working together in groups have developed an appreciation for each other.

7. Instruction has become more meaningful; gifted and talented students have opportunities to stretch to their ability limits in theory and detail; special education students have gained from more opportunities to practice and apply learning.

8. Of the students from Eastern, 80 to 90 percent now complete Algebra 1 by the end of ninth grade.

9. The playing field has been leveled for minority and ESOL students; they now leave Eastern with reasonable grades and more motivated to learn; the

project focus of the curriculum gives then an opportunity to work in their areas of interest and strength to produce a tangible result of their learning

10. Student self-esteem has been bolstered; this is evident in how they carry themselves, how they approach a task, and the creativity they bring to their work.

Parents. Their involvement with the school's activities and their child's academic work have increased. Their general satisfaction about their child's schooling has soared. Overall, school has become a positive force in their lives and those of their children.

Teachers and Other Staff. Eastern has become an "adult friendly" school where teachers can focus on kids and instruction. They have no "outside" duties except "Prelude," the school's early-morning activity period. Administrators get involved in "everyday duties" of the school such as cafeteria supervision and bus duty. In addition, teachers and other staff understand their own areas of expertise with greater depth as well as learn more about the expertise of their colleagues. They learn to work and communicate in a group and think about the importance of their teaching. They know their ideas are taken seriously by the students. And, they are willing to take risks as innovators, constantly changing their approach and evaluating—therefore rejuvenating themselves.

The Eastern Middle School program has been a "success story" because technology has been integrated into every facet of its interdisciplinary learning. But, just as important is its impact to motivate and inspire students, teachers and other staff, and administrators to "want to learn" and to better understand themselves and each other.

PROBLEM-BASED LEARNING "TURNS KIDS ON"

Merwin Elementary School, West Clermont County, Ohio, Public Schools

Students in the upper intermediate grades of this school have had opportunities to solve problems related to interdisciplinary projects for many years. Mollie Niehoff, an upper-intermediate-level teacher who has spearheaded many of these efforts, says, "All students need to be able to solve problems now and in their future. Problem solving is a vital part of schooling that all kids should experience. They should learn that the more heads that work on a problem, the better the final result. Kids can learn from one another. Cooperative learning where students work on specific tasks, meet deadlines, and take on individual as well as group responsibility promotes this."

Niehoff suggests further that students can get started in problem solving as early as possible. This involves identifying the problem and developing a rationale for their decisions. Some of the best opportunities to get kids involved are in solving disputes around the school. For example, "If students have needs that the school rules do not cover, how can they express their discontent?"

This type of problem came up when Cub Scouts and Girl Scouts wanted to wear hats to match their uniforms, and several students wanted to wear hats to match their outfits on "dress-up" day. The school rules prohibited wearing hats in the school building. The students discussed the situation with their teachers and decided they would elect a team of four representatives to make an appointment with the principal to present their case. When the students met with the principal and explained their problem and rationale, he said the rule of "no hats" came from the district and he couldn't do anything about it. So the students asked their representatives to make an appointment with the superintendent to talk about their problem. Currently, the problem is "on hold," but the students are having a great experience on how democratic government functions.

Two major problem-solving projects that Niehoff has led over the years were a schoolwide effort on "consumers and producers" and an "invention convention" for upper-intermediate-level students. Both of these projects were interdisciplinary and involved parents and community members as well as school staff. They are described in detail next, with an emphasis on how students made decisions and solved problems during their hands-on learning experiences. While "working time" for both projects occurred outside of class time, curriculum objectives from several disciplines that were related to these activities were discussed in class. Brief descriptions of three other projects and ways the parents and community members were involved in all the projects are also presented.

No school or intermediate-level team of teachers would want to attempt to work on all these projects in one year. They are described here to provide teachers with a wide variety of options that feature interdisciplinary, hands-on, problem-based learning. They can adapt these ideas to their own schools or classrooms according to the needs and characteristics of their students, schools, and communities.

Experiences as Producers and Consumers

This was a schoolwide, long-term project of setting up and conducting a business. It focused on economics in the social studies curriculum but also helped students meet curriculum objectives in language arts, math, and art. It started with planning in November, was implemented over several months, and ended in May since the items the students manufactured were targeted for Mother's Day presents. Evaluation followed the sale of the products. Objectives of the project for students were to (1) experience roles as producers by acting as manufacturers, marketers, and investors; (2) solve problems related to all aspects of manufacturing, marketing, and investing; and (3) experience being consumers along with parents and community members.

Four teachers from a variety of grade levels acted as leaders. This team with student input made the following decisions for *producers*: (1) the first- and second-grade students would be manufacturers; (2) the third- and fourth-grade students would be marketers; and (3) the fifth- and sixth-grade students would be the investors and make all financial decisions. All students, along with parents and members of the community would be *consumers*.

Manufacturing. The young students had to make many decisions. First, they needed to decide what products they would produce. They followed these criteria: (1) produce products that are high enough in quality so that consumers would want to buy them, and (2) select items that were easy enough to make so young children could handle them. After considerable discussion on a wide variety of ideas, which they ranked by priority based on the preceding criteria, they and the teachers decided on four items to manufacture—*plants, napkin holders, buttons, and napkin rings.*

Before they bought anything, they needed to find out where they could get the best prices for the raw materials they needed. They decided on what they needed, such as unpotted plants, colored cellophane, felt, tongue depressors, and so on. Then a team of four students and a teacher investigated prices, including the effects of quantity buying. The report of the team was the foundation for their decisions.

They decided to purchase the plants from the school greenhouse run by the agriculture students at the high school because they gave the best quality and selection of plants at the lowest price. In addition to purchasing plants, the students needed to paint the pots, transplant the plants into the pots, and package them attractively in colored cellophane. To accomplish these tasks effectively, they needed to divide up the labor. The first-graders painted the pots. They also had to develop a method for painting from the top to the bottom of the pot, assemble their materials along a line, and find out how it functions. They also discovered what happens if someone does not do his or her part. Both first- and second-graders transplanted plants into brightly painted pots. High school agricultural students demonstrated proper potting techniques and helped them get started.

The second-graders did the packaging. They used metric measurements to estimate and measure the amount of cellophane needed for each plant. They also had to figure out how many pieces they could get from each large sheet of cellophane. This involved simple accuracy and estimation to have minimum waste and maximum efficiency. They also had to determine how they were going to close the cellophane at the top to keep it around the plant.

Both first- and second-grade students worked on their projects during recess time. Each worker was paid by the piece or product they produced. They used the same procedures of team work along an assembly line to make their other products—napkin holders, buttons with student-designed motifs, and napkin rings—as they used for the plants.

Marketing. Third- and fourth-graders use many language arts skills when they worked on advertising and publicity. Tasks included writing commercials for radio and newspaper ads as well as jingles and raps that they broadcast over the school intercom. The art teacher assisted them in making drawings and hand-lettered posters and signs. They put these up in their school and other schools in the district. About two weeks before the May sale, they displayed examples of their four products along with posters in several stores in area shopping centers. They also wrote feature stories about their products for the school newsletter and area newspapers.

Another major responsibility of marketers was to sell the finished products in the store during a two-week period in May. Considerable planning was needed to inventory and organize products on the shelves, arrange sales schedules, and assign students to sales duties. They also needed to handle and account for money. The "investors" would help them with this latter function. Marketing students were also paid for their work.

Investing. Fifth- and sixth-graders became "entrepreneurs." They had to calculate costs for each item the younger children were to produce. They had to estimate profits and possible losses. Where would they get the capital to get the project started? They decided that the fifth- and sixth-grade students would supply the capital themselves by selling shares for 50 cents each. They understood that this would involve "risk." Letters were sent to parents about this venture and a meeting was arranged with them so they could express their concerns. Parents were in favor of the idea and wanted to promote it. Parents of students who participated were asked to sign permissions forms. Many students earned money for their stocks by walking dogs or raking leaves. Others took money from their piggy banks or banks accounts. And, one group of four students ran a car wash to get capital for investment. Students who could not bring money from home were supplied two shares each from the Parent Teacher Organization (PTO) so they could be a part of the project. About 300 fifth- and sixth-graders participated. Each one received a stock certificate for shares purchased.

Before they could estimate profits and losses, students had to consider all the costs to produce an item such as raw materials, student labor, and publicity. Then, they had to determine if their items would be attractive to consumers after they added a profit of 20–25 percent. They also wanted to pay each laborer a bonus, if possible, in addition to the piecework pay. Taking all these variables into consideration, they determined their sales prices as follows: plants, 70 cents to one dollar depending on size; napkin holders, 60 cents; buttons, 60 cents; and napkin rings, 55 cents.

Consumers. When all the products were produced, they were displayed on racks which an area store had discarded. The student "store" had an inventory of 300 plants, 150 napkin holders, 200 buttons, and 400 napkin rings. Third- and fourth-graders opened the store to the public and students from 12 to 1 P.M. each day for two weeks preceding Mother's Day. It was also open for two hours in connection with a PTO meeting during this period. Upper-level-intermediate students helped third- and fourth-graders keep records of daily sales and inventory, and to make bank deposits.

The local newspaper sent reporters to interview the students about their project. They wrote a story about it focusing on the PTO sale. A radio station run by high school students in another district played a tape that the third- and fourth-graders had made to let people know about their project and sale. "Word-of-Mouth" notices from students to just about everybody they knew were great advertising, too.

Students, acting as consumers, bought products as gifts for for their mothers, grandmothers, and friends. Teachers and parents were also excellent consumers. By the end of the sales period, they had sold nearly every item. The plants were the best sellers, followed by the napkin rings.

Results and Impact. This project was a great success both cognitively and affectively. It met all its objectives and more. Students received experiences as producers in their roles as manufacturers, marketers, and investors. They learned personal and interpersonal skills to get along with each other across a wide age and grade range to "get the job done." And, they experienced the "thrill of success" when they sold their products and received recognition from their teachers, principal, and other school staff, parents, and community members as well as in the media. Financially, the project was a success, too. After bills, including a bonus to workers were paid, all profits were returned to investors. They received 75 cents back for each 50 cents they had invested.

The greatest impact of this project was the myriad of opportunities—planned by the teachers and unplanned as the work progressed—for the students to solve problems. Over and over again, they saw a need to solve a problem by going through these steps, formally or informally: (1) clarifying the problem by exploring and researching it and stating it clearly so everyone knew where they were going; (2) generating several solutions, prioritizing them, and selecting the best one(s); (3) coming up with designs to test the best solution(s) and investigating or trying it out; and (4) organizing and interpreting their results and judging them to decide whether or not the problem is solved. A unique feature of this project was to embed problems within it so that students come on them naturally as they worked along. Then the problems seem "real," not manufactured, as when they are taken from a textbook. The hands-on involvement of every student in the school in one way or another is also unusual.

Besides the multitude of cognitive problems that were described as the students carried out manufacturing, marketing, and investing, several others that were more affectively oriented also came up. Some of these, which made good whole-class and small-group discussion topics, were

- Would students be willing to give up recess time to do the manufacturing? Why? Why not?
- Who owned this project— students, teachers, others, all groups involved?
- What about the project would cause students at all age and grade levels to want to work together?

Both students and staff have an investment of time and energy in a long-term project like this one. Some students gave up their recess time to manufacture products. Others gave up recess and noon hours to help manufacture and sell the items. Teachers and other staff volunteered time before school, during recess, and after school to help the students with the many problems that arose over a six-month period. Were the results worth the effort? The high quality outcomes cited in the preceding discussion indicate it was. But a school staff would probably only want to do a project like this every two or three years. In this sequence, every student would get a chance to be a manufacturer, marketer, or investor, yet staff and students would not be overburdened. Different products could be produced each time, and other changes made to keep the event "fresh" and all participants enthusiastic.

"Invention Convention"

About 150 upper-level-intermediate students participated in this project. It started with questions in their science and social studies classes. "How did civilizations develop from nomads, to farmers, to manufacturing, to today's high-tech world?" "Who invented the zipper?" "How do we get products from washing machines, to grain combines, to television, to sophisticated satellite communication systems?" "How do people like Orville and Wilbur Wright, who owned a bicycle shop, go about inventing something like an airplane that has transformed the way we live and travel?" The result of these discussions was an "Invention Convention." It was also an alternative to a science fair, which had been held for intermediate students in previous years.

Inventions allow for the perfect integration of social studies with science, language arts, math, and visual arts. Most important, inventions always start with a problem that the students must solve. Every student that creates an invention, proceeds, consciously or unconsciously, through the stages of problem solving illustrated in Figure 2–5. The following discussion takes the reader through these stages.

Exploring Inventions. Students brainstormed to get ideas for their inventions. To do this effectively, they researched inventors and inventions. They prepared reports on individuals and companies from the areas of medicine, food, household appliances, communication devices and computers, heavy equipment, organizations such as Ford that started out on the basis of a single invention—the motor car, and so on. They also discussed how an invention might build on others that preceded it.

The students also got ideas and information by writing and calling local manufacturers such as General Electric, Dow Chemical, Allis Chalmers, and Procter & Gamble to ask them how they developed products. General Electric sent development engineers as resource people to the school. They shared a step-by-step discussion of how they developed or invented new items. They also told the students that some "inventors" worked alone and others worked on teams. Gibson Company, which produces greeting cards, sent artists and writers who shared with the students how they developed a card. The writer produces the verse first, and then the artist adds the artwork. "Invention" isn't just for making new products. Procter & Gamble, for example, told the students that it "invents" new angles or qualities to improve or renew a product like laundry soap to boost sales.

While the students were exploring ideas for invention, they also encountered patents and copyrights. They found out that inventors patent a product or process to protect it. The students also learned that the company owned a patent for a product that an individual was paid to produce. Copyrights protect products that people produce in literature, poetry, packaging, and so on. They protect them from plagiarizing or copying because people have to notify the producer and ask for permission to use any part of a patented or copyrighted product in something they are producing. Students went to the public library to see microfilms of actual patents and the steps that are necessary to get one. They also wrote for free materials on patents and copyrights.

Selecting Inventions and Making Designs for Them. After students had reviewed many "inventions," they needed to rank-order their ideas and decide what kind of product to make. When they had decided, they made an outline describing it. This description included a sketch of what their final invention would look like. They could work alone, with a partner, or as a member of a small group. They could strive for an entirely new product or improve on one that is already on the market. A form was sent home for parents to sign indicating that they knew their child would be working on an invention and that it would be an "outside of school" activity.

Implementing the Best Designs and Creating Inventions. Students were required to keep a log or diary of their decisions, reasons for them, problems they encountered and solved along the way, and progress on their invention. They discussed their invention, along with problems they were encountering with other students at school. They reported on their progress to special groups and had individual conferences with their teacher. Some students got help from parents or other resource people in the community. They were asked to indicate this kind of input in their log.

Many interesting inventions resulted from their efforts. These included a golf umbrella, toys, automatic fish feeder, mittens that toddlers couldn't lose, clothing for fashion dolls, cards for all occasions, toys, shoe laces where the plastic tip won't come off, "magic" material to absorb spills such as milk in the cafeteria, a gadget to keep an ice cream cone from dripping, a bird feeder that would keep squirrels from getting food from it, and buildings created from recycled materials.

Evaluating the Final Products. Each student invention was judged by a team of three professionals from the sciences, arts, humanities, industry and other areas, as well as university personnel, and county and city officials. Judges were assigned as appropriate to the category (e.g., arts, toys, manufactured products, environment-related products, convenience items, sports-related items) of the invention. Criteria for judging the invention included creativity, originality, amount of effort to produce it, practical value, inventor's knowledge of the invention, reasonable cost of production, and amount of outside help the student received. Each criterion was rated on a scale of 1 to 10, where 1 was low and 10 was high.

All students who participated in the convention received a ribbon, but teachers did not assign a grade to the invention. In addition, the PTO provided prizes of U.S. Savings Bonds and special ribbons for the first, second, and third highest rated inventions in each category. Local newspapers carried stories on the convention as an event and on individual inventions and "inventors."

Impact on Students and Staff. Overall, the "Invention Convention" was a big success. Even though participation was voluntary, more than 95 percent of the students that were eligible participated. Students thought making an invention was a "fun" way to solve problems. They were proud of their finished product and enjoyed the opportunity to display them for other students, parents and family, and community members. They also thought the newspaper and radio publicity about the event was great.

An invention convention, like the "producers and consumers" project, demands considerable extra effort from teachers and other staff. But it is worthwhile because students really get involved in solving problems and enjoy doing it. It also gets parents and community members involved in the work of the school. Such an event has several options. It could be expanded to several grade levels, particularly to the middle school level where students have more advanced research and manipulative skills. Or it could be a districtwide event. An "invention convention" could be held every other year so the work of coordinating and putting it on doesn't become a burden to staff and the event doesn't become too routine for students.

More Problem-Solving Projects

Three other problem-solving projects that students at Merwin Elementary have tackled over the years are cleaning up the urban environment, running the school store, and outdoor camping. Each of these projects are described briefly next.

Cleaning Up the Urban Environment. Students were studying the role of a clean environment for today and the future. One of them mentioned that there was often a lot of "junk" around the "back side" of a local strip mall. Another student suggested that cleaning up and beautifying a local strip mall might be a good project for their class. After considerable discussion, the group decided to investigate the possibilities. Several days later, they discussed the situation again and students identified two strip malls where the environment on the "back side" was contaminated.

Litter surrounded the dumpster at both malls. It included food items that could cause health hazards because they attracted animals and young children might get into them and plastic bags that small children might pull over their heads. There were also unbroken cardboard boxes that children used for sleds and sometimes slid down onto busy roadways in them. They also discovered some flammable materials and possible poisons among the piles of junk. They took pictures of the "mess" to verify their descriptions.

Their next step was to decide what to do about these situations. Here are some of their solutions: the students could volunteer to clean up the mess; they could write letters and get others to write letters to the stores and mall managers asking them to clean up the debris; or they could try to get other groups with legal clout to work on the problems. After more discussion, they decided they would like to get involved. They would first talk to the mall managers themselves and ask them to clean up their mess.

They elected four representatives to go with the teacher to discuss the problem with the manager in each mall. They would point out the environmental problems they had discovered and show them the photos they had taken. Both managers were susceptible to their efforts. At the meetings, they asked the students to come back in two to three weeks and review what the managers had done to solve the problem. Students thought this was a very good sign that they were going to clean up their environments.

Several students checked on the progress of cleanup during the two- to three-week period and took photos at the end of it. A small group of students again met with each manager. They reported that they found no food waste or hazardous materials, cartons had been cut up and tied in bundles, and plastic materials had been stuffed inside garbage bags or other containers. It was not perfect, but the dangerous materials and conditions had been taken care of. They also told the managers how happy they were that the environment had been cleaned up and that they didn't have to write letters or go to community leaders to get the job done. The managers agreed with the students!

Outdoor Camping. A five-day, Monday through Friday, camping experience in a county forest along the Ohio River provided a curriculum based on solving problems. In the forest, other trees were keeping valuable hardwoods from growing. How could the foresters change this? If the forest were used for recreation as well as lumbering, it would bring docks for boats, parking places for cars, and garbage from tourists. How would these invasions affect wildlife and homes for animals? Also, as soon as roads are cut through a forest for general transportation, people start to build summer homes on the perimeter. Students found out that effluent from septic tanks had already polluted the lake so it couldn't be used for swimming. In addition, chemicals from farms that surrounded the forest were polluting the lakes and drinking water supplies. The students also noticed that many farmers were raising tobacco. Should this be allowed or should the state buy up the land for the park so less tobacco would be raised?

Based on these problems, the students did a lot of writing. They wrote poetry and stories where they imagined what this land was like when the Indians lived there. How would Shawnee leaders such as Tecumseh and Bluejacket feel about the condition of the area today? Some wrote about how it felt to be a riverboat pirate and others about being a victim of the pirates. The students drew pictures to illustrate their stories and poems. Math was brought in by calculating how long it would take to go down the Ohio River from Pittsburgh to Cincinnati by riverboat. What provisions would they need? And so on!

School Store. This store was an outgrowth of the "producers and consumers" project described earlier in this section. It was a supply store for students to buy necessities such as pencils and pens, paper, eraser caps, rulers, compasses and protractors, folders, and so on. It was staffed by students during lunch hour and recess. At the end of the day, students took an inventory of sales and noted what sold best. They ordered their materials from catalogues, at first usually from companies that allowed 30–60 days for payments because the students had no seed money to pay cash. Once they started making profits, they discovered they could make more money by buying in larger quantities and paying cash. This enabled them to increase their business since they could offer specials to students such as "pencils at 6 for $1" instead of "20 cents each." Also, they could have sales to get rid of slow-moving merchandise at a discount price.

The expenses, inventory, and sales can be put on computer. Teachers worked with the students initially, but now the PTO has taken over the financial arrangements. Two parents work with four students during lunch hour. Students use their profits for a variety of things such as an outside bulletin board in the school yard to announce events and activities, flowers and trees to beautify the school environment, and a money gift to a school family that had suffered a catastrophe.

Parents and Community Are Vital to Success

Throughout this discussion, parents and community members have been involved in every project. They were resource people, monitors, and consumers in the business project and the school store. They acted as judges and hosts for the invention convention. They were chaperones and resource people for the camping experience. The PTO provided finances for students who didn't have funds for the business venture, and prizes for the invention convention. They buy things for the school that are not provided for in the budget. Perhaps the most important thing these parents and community members provide to the school is their enthusiasm and moral support. They are interested in the children and want them to have a positive and profitable school experience. This kind of cooperation between school and parents and community is vital to any successful venture.

The focus of this section has been on problems as they were developed over time in one school. Merwin Elementary School which has a mostly middle- class population of more than 700 students is located in a county school district adjacent to the city of Cincinnati. It is a bedroom community where people relate to many different entities. Participation in any of the projects described here helped students to reach out to their area communities and become a part of them as well as providing a myriad of opportunities to practice solving problems. Mollie Niehoff and her colleagues reflect on these projects as "Great teaching experiences that were fun and challenging. We never forget the expressions of joy and success on the faces of the students. Their interest and enthusiasm encourages us to add problem-solving projects to the curriculum whenever we can. Just the morning after the November election when voters passed a building referendum for our school, fifth-grade students were asking if they could get involved in the planning. Here we go again!"

SUMMARY

Each program described in this chapter met the goal of integrating problem solving into its curriculum. But each one used different methods to do it to meet the needs of its students, teachers, and parents.

Gulf Gate Elementary school centered their program around real-world problems. Its four-year plan also coordinated with Florida state learning guidelines. At Lincoln Elementary School, the focus was on higher-order thinking skills. The program was part of a districtwide initiative to improve student achievement and metacognitive processing. San Marcos' primary-level program was districtwide. It was built around teaching creative process skills that the students could use in all subject matter areas now and as they progressed through school. Technology was integrated into every facet of Eastern Middle School's program. Team planning and teaching facilitated its use. This program involved new learning for teachers as well as for students. Merwin Elementary School students participated in a variety of problem-oriented projects. Some were schoolwide and others focused on intermediate-level students. All of them took students out into the community to learn.

These programs were also similar in many ways. They focused often on interdisciplinary learning, allowed staff to make instructional decisions, provided training for staff before and during implementation, and involved parents and community. They all had visions of where they wanted to go and developed objectives to guide them along the way. Affective as well as cognitive results of the programs were positive. Both students and teachers felt good about what they had accomplished and they looked forward to taking part in more problem-solving experiences.

REFERENCES

Costa, A. (Ed.). (1991). *Developing minds: The search for intelligent life.* Alexandria, VA: Association for Supervision and Curriculum Development.

Perkins, D. (1993). Creating a culture of thinking. *Educational Leadership,* 51(3): 98–99.

CHAPTER 7

Effective Staff Development

Every day on television and in newspaper and magazine editorials and features, we discuss change—the information highway, the transformation of eastern Europe brought on by the collapse of the Soviet Union, and new types of work teams to increase productivity in business and industry. All these and other changes require new information, new strategies, and new roles for all personnel involved. They require time and money for "retraining" and opportunities for the personnel to "try out" their new information, strategies, and work arrangements.

Common sense suggests that provision for constant retraining should have been a part of our workplaces for many decades. After all, we have been confronting change of one kind or another ever since the Industrial Revolution of the 1840s and at an accelerated rate since World War II. Yet organizations in the United States have traditionally been slow to provide time and money for such training—very slow in comparison to those in other developed countries of the world. The United States allots about 10 hours per year per employee for retraining while western Europe allocates nearly 60 hours. And, only 10 percent of young U.S. workers receive formal company training, compared with more than 50 percent in Japan and Germany (Reich, 1994).

Provision for teachers to meet changes in their work have been even more difficult. Here, the training and retraining, usually called "inservice" or "staff development," has been almost forgotten in budgeting and operation of the schools at the national and state levels and is very mixed at the local levels. Some richer districts and those with outside support sources for special populations of students provide ten or more days of training per year, but a large majority of the districts across the country provide two to three days per year. Further, "The U.S. has no national strategy for staff development that provides depth and breadth for its 2.2 million teachers.... Staff development programs are typically one-shot affairs with scant follow-up and coaching.... While the U.S. is developing challenging and better conceived curricula and exams, there is no commensurate effort underway to improve the working conditions of teachers. Teachers still work in a structure that inhibits collaboration and professional growth" (Kirst, 1993, p. 616).

RATIONALE FOR STAFF DEVELOPMENT

Staff development has been defined in many ways and has been discussed under many labels, such as *inservice training, inservice education, professional development,* and *professional growth.* The label staff development as used in this discussion includes all these terms. Fullan suggests that "staff development is conceived broadly to include any activity or process intended to improve skills, attitudes, understanding, or performance in present or future roles" (in Joyce, 1990, p. 3). Staff development implies improvement in the staff of all teachers, not just individuals. It also connotes a need for change in the actions of teachers and administrators to better serve their students (Bierly & Berliner, 1982, p. 39).

Why Is Staff Development Important?

Since the concept of staff development seems to be controversial, we need to ask the question "Why do we need staff development anyway?" Some reasons are

- New learning—both content and process—as well as how to use and teach technologies that were not available or were not considered essential when the teachers were in college or university

- Desire of teachers to learn more and to grow intellectually as well as to be better teachers
- Needs of special populations of students such as "at risk," gifted and talented, special education, English as a second language, disaffected, and so on
- Expectations of community, parents, school board, and school, district, and state and national guidelines and mandates
- Workplace demands in today's and the twenty-first century's global society.

Stumbling Blocks to Staff Development

Staff development has a long history of frustration. It is a tale of too few successes and too many failures. What are some of these stumbling blocks, and why have so many programs failed to cause change, improve student performance, or satisfy the people involved in them?

There are many initiatives to develop more challenging and better-organized curriculums, but no real effort to improve the training or working conditions of teachers. Also, teacher preparation is usually driven by requirements of the state and independent universities rather than by current needs of students and staff.

Situations that Inhibit Effectiveness. Specific stumbling blocks have been reiterated by many authors. John Goodlad as a part of his study of schooling found the following disturbing situations in schools (Goodlad in Costa, in Collins & Mangieri, 1992, p. 169):

- Teachers are often isolated in their workplaces. They work behind closed doors and have little time in their daily schedules to meet, plan, observe, and talk with one another.
- Teachers often lack a sense of power and efficacy. They feel they are at the bottom of the hierarchy and that decisions and evaluations that affect them are made at higher levels.
- The complex, intelligent act of teaching is often reduced to formulas or a series of steps and competencies.

- Information about student achievement is for political, evaluative, or coercive purposes; it doesn't involve nor instruct the school staff member in reflecting on school improvement and evaluation.
- Educational innovations are often viewed as mere "tinkering" with the instructional program. There are so many of them, and their impact is so limited, teachers often think, "If I do nothing, this, too, shall pass." Traditional practices and politics help make conditions static rather than causing change.

Other barriers to staff innovation effectiveness are as follows (Fullan, in Joyce, 1990, p. 7):

- Lack of an adequate theory of implementation, including too little time for teachers to plan for and learn new skills and practices
- District tendencies toward faddism and quick-fix solutions
- Lack of sustained central office support and follow-through
- Attempts to manage projects from central office rather than developing school leadership
- Lack of technical assistance and other forms of intensive training
- Lack of awareness of limitations of teacher and school administrator knowledge about how to implement the project
- Turnover of teachers in each school
- Too many competing demands or overload of teacher and administrator time
- Failure to address incompatibility between project requirements and existing organizational policies and structures
- Failure to account for site-specific differences among schools
- Failure to clarify and negotiate the role relationships and partnerships involving the district and local universities.

Staff Development Has a Low Priority. Philip Schlechty suggests that "staff development has never been the primary function or even a priority goal for any of the institutions that have been the providers—not the district and not the universities" (in Shanker, in Joyce, 1990, p. 91). Staff development is often seen as being in conflict with other priority goals of school. This is based on the idea that knowledge is received by the teachers telling and learners learn by listening. Staff development often reflects a factory-like public school system where the teacher's role is to get through the curriculum, cover the materials, and show objectivity through standard practice. The individual teacher is viewed as an isolated classroom practitioner.

Staff development is also weakened by three premises that form the base for current staff development practices: (1) teaching knowledge exists mainly outside the teacher and outside the classroom; (2) the best way to teach people something is to tell it to them; and (3) the more courses and workshops teachers take, the better their teaching becomes. Yet educators realize that staff development is too important to abandon it. "The future culture of the school will be fashioned largely by how staff development systems evolve. How good schools will be as educational institutions—how humane and vital they will be as places to work—will be functions of the energy and quality of their personnel" (Joyce, 1990, p. xv). "There can be no significant improvement in administrative practice, teaching, or school programs without effective staff development" (Wood, Killian, McQuarrie, & Thompson, 1993, p. v).

How Can We Improve Staff Development?

If staff development is the key to school improvement, what can be done to improve the process? Many suggestions have been made and tried out. Three of these dealing with functions, guidelines, and conditions are discussed here.

Identify Functions. Before a program is built, its functions should be well defined. Six functions include the following (Orlich, 1989, pp. 6–7):

1. Inservice education to improve skills, implement curriculums or instructional procedures, expand knowledge of subject matter, improve instructional planning and organizing, and increase personal effectiveness

2. Organizational development to improve the building and program climate, solve problems, and increase communication among staff

3. Consultation to conduct workshops, clinics, special projects; assist with building staff development; and assist with administrative planning

4. Communication and coordination of resources to improve interbuilding and interdistrict communications, organize and provide information about resources; and provide coordination of efforts

5. Leadership training to provide suggestions for new curricula, instructional approaches, and communications about innovative approaches; identify problems and make suggestions for resolutions; research to evaluate new practices or procedures; and provide assistance with innovations

6. Evaluation to conduct or arrange for needs assessments; and evaluate resources and quality of programs, personnel, and media; evaluate staff development efforts; and organize for systematic feedback.

Follow Guidelines for Successful Learning. General trends for lifelong learning in the twenty-first century also provide a basis for staff development. These include the following (Gross, in Collins & Mangieri, 1992, pp. 135–143):

- Learn how to learn and learn throughout our lives
- Learn with our whole brains
- Learn together—in groups from the family to the problem-solving task force in businesses or professions
- Learn via multiple media, technologies, formats, and styles
- Direct our own thinking and learning
- Learn by teaching
- Change our systems of formal education to support the ideal of a learning society where future adults will acquire their own repertoire of thinking skills including techniques for solving problems.

Staff development should use an *"inside-out" model* rather than the traditional "outside-in" format. Ideas must come together in the minds and actions of our teachers if they are to come together in the minds and actions of our students (Lambert, 1988, p. 665). We have taught teachers that valid knowledge about teaching lies outside the school and "comes in" through staff development. Instead, teachers should have shared authority for the operation of the school and district, with authority based on responsibility. The teacher is responsible to contribute to the profession through the redesign of schooling to better meet the needs of all concerned, to contribute to the knowledge base of the profession, and to share in the enculturation of new teachers.

We must reduce the isolation of the teacher and create time during the day for teachers in a school to talk to each other. Teachers along with administrators and policymakers must continually redefine what is important and let go of the rest. And give teachers clerical help to carry out routine word processing, photocopying, and telephoning so they have time for professional development and improvement.

Provide Proper Conditions for Learning. Conditions such as an invitation to change, authority and flexibility, access to knowledge, and time to learn need to exist in a school and district to carry out successful staff development programs (David, 1991, pp. 12–15). Educators need both a reason and an opportunity to change. Both of these can come from a school project or grant, or an opportunity created by an external event at the local or state level.

A real invitation to change involves a shared understanding of the urgent need to change and the goals and objectives to carry it out. Granting authority implies a new concept of leadership, hierarchy, and power relationships. Flexibility results only from significant deregulation, not occasional exceptions to the rules. Knowledge must be available to the staff in what they consider a useful and accessible form. And time to learn, plan, implement, and reflect on changes must be a part of the daily schedule.

Also, successful staff development programs have four underlying assumptions (DuFour, 1991, pp. 5–11): (1) the local school and district provide the best environment or culture for school improvement, (2) school improvement means people improvement, (3) the principal plays a major role in successful school improvement, and (4) schools and the district must make a commitment to staff development programs that are purposeful and goal directed.

Needs of Teachers as Learners

Today, the American public has lost confidence in the schools. In response, some districts have increased their amount of staff development learning for teachers through noncredit and credit workshops and courses as well as through research and independent or group projects. Other factors pushing staff development are the aging teacher population, and union affiliations where staff development is written into contract agreements between the districts and the teachers. But how well has staff development been tailored to the needs and characteristics of teachers? Four of these areas are explored next.

Concrete and "Individualized" Instruction. Many teachers are almost single-mindedly focused on the subject of concrete and practical instruction, sometimes to the detriment of wanting to know why what they are learning is important. This makes it necessary for the teacher of teachers to integrate the abstract or theory within the concrete. Not only do teachers want to move quickly from the abstract to the concrete, but they also want to move from the practical to illustrations of how to teach students.

Teachers often want their learning "individualized" to their needs and learning styles—sequence, pace, interest, goals, delivery—as well as the age/grade level of students they teach. Teaching centers have helped meet this need by allowing teachers to study "what they need in their teaching" instead of requiring all teachers to attend a workshop or course on the same topic.

Time to Practice What They Learn. Practicing what they learned can take weeks to months to years. This is probably the weakest area in most staff development programs. Too often, programs are three to six hours long with little follow-up or coaching. Adapting instruction to the teachers' own classroom is very important. When a new program or innovation comes into the school or district, teachers seem to need to "reinvent the wheel" to adjust ideas and practices to their local situation. This process also helps them gain personal "ownership" of the learning.

Peer Coaching. One of the most important aspects of staff development learning is coaching in the classroom by observers who provide feedback. In looking at four kinds of staff development efforts—knowledge, modeling and demonstration, feedback and practice, and coaching— the most effective was coaching by peers, supervisors, or anyone competent in the approaches being taught. Using coaching, most teachers were able to transfer their new knowledge and skills to their own classrooms while the other three approaches helped only 10–20 percent of the teachers to make the transfer. Peer coaching is discussed in detail later in this chapter.

Teachers prefer instructors who are or were teachers. This preference relates to their desire for practical strategies and knowledge as well as to the idea that instructors from colleges and universities and consultants are too abstract in their thinking and "out-of-date" in terms of teaching today's children.

Treatment as Professionals. We too often teach teachers as if they are undergraduate college students. They are not. They are professional adults and they want to be treated as such. Some general learning characteristics to consider when teaching teachers are (Wood et al., 1993, pp. 20–24):

- Adults will commit to learning when they perceive the specified goals and objectives as realistic and important.
- Adult learning involves the ego.
- Adults need concrete, direct experiences to practice what they learn.
- Most adults learn more when they work in small groups.
- Adults want to have some control over what they learn.
- Adults are basically self-motivated.
- Adults do not automatically transfer learning from training to practice; they need opportunities and supervision to do it.

Characteristics of Successful Staff Development Programs

A synthesis of the preceding discussion, along with my own experiences as teacher, program planner, staff developer, and evaluator, suggests that successful staff development programs should have the following characteristics:

- Be visibly supported by schools and the district in terms of teacher needs, materials, follow-up, and evaluation
- Focus on student needs and meet teacher needs in relation to them
- Be systematic and continuous throughout the training process
- Appeal to teachers' professionalism as well as district and state standards
- Allow teachers to be "active" participants in their learning, not just listeners
- Involve principals and other administrators as learners
- Pay attention to the affective as well as cognitive needs of teachers
- Look at staff development on a "long-term" basis as well as short term
- Provide opportunities for teachers and others to gain personal "ownership" in the program or product they are learning or developing
- Emphasize that materials they are currently using (e.g., textbooks, software, curriculum guidelines) are a reference, not a "Bible."
- Allow teachers and others to work in teams of three to five, multigraded, if possible
- Conduct learning opportunities in sites appropriate to the learning
- Consider teacher needs in terms of their learning styles
- Produce a concrete product (e.g., curriculum guidelines, lesson plans, files)
- Consider learning in terms of needs of special populations of students
- Include specialists such as IMC or media center directors, coordinators of special populations programs, curriculum coordinators, subject matter specialists, resource teachers (computers and technology, other), principals and other administrators as well as classroom teachers as learners
- Be taught by a current or recent teacher or even better by a team of a current teachers and subject matter experts appropriate to topics to be learned.

ROLES IN STAFF DEVELOPMENT

All groups who make decisions about the education of students have a role in successful staff development. Eight role groups have been identified (Wood & Leadbeater, 1986, p. 127, and Sorenson et al., 1988, pp. 108–109): teachers, principals, administrators and other policy makers, students, parents, college and university personnel and consultants, service and community groups, and school support staff. Specific roles of each group are discussed next.

Teachers

Beginning, experienced, and specialized teachers are the most important role group in staff development. The success of the program depends on them. If they don't respond well to the program, it will not reach the students and it will fail. Thus, teachers must be involved in making decisions at all stages of staff development.

Teacher development is also important. Three levels of teacher development are—professional expertise, psychological, and career (Leithwood, in Joyce, 1990, pp. 72–79). *Professional expertise development* includes developing survival skills, becoming competent in the basic skills of instruction, expanding their instructional flexibility, and acquiring instructional expertise in the classroom. They also develop out-of-classroom skills to contribute to the growth of their colleagues' instructional expertise and participate in a broad range of educational decisions at the classroom, school, and district levels.

Psychological development includes ego, moral and conceptual development in four stages: (1) self-protective, premoral, unilateral dependence; (2) conformist, moral, and negative independence; (3) conformist, moral, and conditional dependence; and (4) autonomous, interdependent, principled, and integrated situations. *Career cycle development* starts with launching the career and moves on to stabilizing and developing a mature commitment, meeting new challenges and concerns, reaching a professional plateau, and preparing for retirement. Any group of teachers has individuals in various stages of these three levels of development.

Teachers at one or more times during the staff development process to introduce an innovation "wear many hats." They act as decision maker, adult learner, teacher of children, and instructional leader. These subroles are discussed next.

Decision Maker. During the planning stages, teachers are members of committees, visit other schools where the innovation has been implemented, and attend professional meetings to gain information and informally evaluate the appropriateness of the innovation for their school or district. Then, as a part of the group, they decide how the staff development program will be carried out in their district. They also make decisions as they perform their subroles.

Adult Learner. Teachers take this subrole during the training stage of staff development. The needs of teachers as learners was described earlier in this chapter. The guidelines that follow are also important (Leithwood, in Joyce, 1990, pp. 80–87): (1) treat the teacher as a whole person; (2) establish a school culture based on norms of technical collaboration and professional inquiry; (3) carefully diagnose the starting points for teacher development; and (4) recast routine administrative activities into powerful teacher development strategies. These guidelines meet the current perception of teaching as a "nonroutine activity that draws on a reliable body of technical knowledge conducted in collaboration with other professionals" rather than as a routine job to dispense knowledge in isolation far from other adults.

Teacher of Children. This is the traditional teacher role and probably the one teachers like best. During the implementation stage, they can apply and practice what they have learned during the training stage with their students and make appropriate adjustments in the learning. They also get support from fellow staff and administrators and feedback from peer coaches.

Instructional Leader. Good teachers don't teach like "robots" to implement what they have learned. They "see the big picture" in the curriculum and make decisions to fit learning for their age and grade level of students into it. They act as professionals by training other teachers in their school or district in their areas of expertise or presenting at professional meetings. They can also be mentors for teachers new to the district and leaders for maintenance of an innovation.

Working as a member of a group or team helps teachers gain common expectations in learning and experimenting with new practices. It also gives them a chance to share their ideas and needs and provides a forum to use their experiences, special expertise, and creativity. And it's more fun! Professional incentives or rewards in the form of money, professional concerns, opportunities to share what they have learned with others, and attendance at special meetings are helpful, too. While teachers appreciate extra pay for attendance at staff development activities, it is not enough to learn new material if professional desire is lacking.

Principals

Principals play a primary role in the staff development process from the very beginning of readiness or planning to the maintenance and institutionalization of the program. "The principal is a key figure in determining the ultimate success of any effort to develop school personnel and thus plays a major role in school improvement" (DuFour, 1991, p. 8). The principal takes four major subroles—leader, promoter of positive school climate and culture, promoter of effective staff development practices, and a "link" between teacher supervision and staff development.

Leader. The principal needs to have a "vision" of where the staff development program is going and ideas on how to get his teachers and other personnel to reach those goals. The principal needs to communicate this to staff, students, parents, and community. In addition, the principal should articulate goals, direction, and priorities for the schools and exhibit the ability to "turn people on" about a project or program.

As leader of change, the principal needs to exhibit a variety of skills. These include the following (DuFour, 1991, pp. 24–25):

- Intrapersonal skills such as knowing one's own motivation and role in change
- Assessing needs and identifying problems
- Promoting cooperative, collegial relationships
- Selecting from among alternatives and setting goals
- Dealing with resistance and determining responsibilities
- Assessing the results of change
- Institutionalizing the change so it no longer depends on the principal.

Another area of leadership suggests the principal must relate staff development plans to long-term improvement goals of the school and district. Staff development designs should be matched to anticipated outcomes as well as to participants. The principal should provide staff with access to materials and human resources, allow them enough time to bring about change, monitor their progress as they implement the desired practices, and evaluate the impact of the program on teaching and learning in the school.

Promoter of Positive School Climate and Culture. The principal can focus on three areas: predispositions, collaborative work behavior, and professional productivity (DuFour, 1991, pp. 30–31). *Predispositions* include a student-centered, improvement, and success orientation. *Collaborative work behavior* includes schoolwide agreement on common goals, continuous dialogue, shared decision making, carefully planned and coordinated action, and periodic reflection and feedback. *Professional productivity* has three dimensions—cognitive, affective and behavioral. Cognitively, staff development supports the staff having a strong knowledge base about instruction and learning principles. Affectively, the principal as leader provides opportunities for the staff to feel they are a part of a cohesive group. Behaviorally, the staff is involved and concerned and has a sense of purpose.

The principal should treat teachers as professionals by empowering them to make decisions about instruction, staff development, and other areas. Principals provide opportunities for teachers to work within established boundaries in creative and autonomous ways. Empowerment also means more responsibility for teachers, since they can't blame failure on others when they as well as the principal are part of the decision-making process.

Principals should encourage collaborative ventures. This eliminates the isolation that too often exists in teaching and lets teachers work and interact with their peers. Techniques to do this include discussions, collective problem solving, and shared decision making. Small teams of three to five people are usually the best way to achieve collaboration. These groups might be called *task forces, units, quality circles, problem-solving groups,* and so on. They might be structured by grade level or subject matter area, across several grade levels, by similar teaching assignments, or by a particular goal or idea. Team work promotes collaboration, helps build consensus, and allows for leadership potential to develop in a large number of teachers.

The principal can also form collaborative strategies with staff members. Some specific examples are (Elam, Cramer, & Brodinsky in DuFour, 1991, p. 38):

- Develop partnerships with teachers to bring about improved instruction.
- Help teachers to identify classroom problems that call for inservice training.
- Gear principal–teacher conferences toward problem-solving procedures.
- Attend inservice training sessions as partners to learn with teachers.

- Allow teachers freedom in the classroom to practice techniques learned during inservice sessions.
- Dismiss the notion that there are required ways to teach and that the principal knows what they are.
- Ask for teacher ideas in planning staff development programs.
- Make faculty meetings, at least in part, learning and self-improvement opportunities.
- Promote feelings of professional pride, and enhance self-image and self-efficacy among teachers.

The principal should encourage teachers to experiment, since one of the purposes of staff development is to persuade teachers to approach their responsibilities differently and to use new techniques and strategies. The willingness to experiment is a precondition for successful staff development.

Promoter of Effective Staff Development Practices. The principal needs to be aware that teachers have concerns about the programs regardless of their involvement and their stage of professional development. Seven stages of concern that teachers usually experience as they learn about, prepare for, and use new practices have been identified (Austin & Hall, in DuFour, 1991, pp. 66–69). These stages move from a focus on self to management associated with the task to the impact of the program. These stages, along with some ways the principal can help teachers alleviate their concerns, are discussed next.

Stage 0: Awareness concerns. "What is the innovation?" The principal should involve teachers in discussion about the innovation and share enough information to get their interest, but don't overwhelm them. Letting the teachers know that no one expects them to be knowledgeable about the innovation at this time encourages them to ask questions about it. Keep gossip and inaccurate information at a minimum.

Stage 1: Information Concerns. Teachers often say, "I need to know more about the innovation." The principal should provide clear and accurate information about the innovation and use many ways to share it—verbally, in writing, and other media. Have people who have used the innovation in other settings visit with the teachers and arrange visits to user schools. Principals can help teachers relate the innovation to their current practices and encourage them to want to learn more.

Stage 2: Personal concerns. "How will the innovation affect me?" The principal can let teachers know that concerns are natural and use personal notes and conversations to encourage and reinforce their personal adequacy. Also the principal can suggest these teachers talk to others whose personal concerns have diminished.

Stage 3: Management concerns. "How will I find time to do this?" The principal can spell out the steps and components of the innovation and provide answers that address the specific "how-to" issues that are so often at the heart of management concerns. Demonstrations of practical solutions to the logistic problems and helping teachers sequence specific activities and timelines for their accomplishments also help. The principal should focus on the immediate demands of the innovation rather than on what will or could happen in the future.

Stage 4: Consequence concerns. "How is my use of the innovation affecting kids?" The principal should arrange opportunities for teachers to visit and interact with teachers in other schools where the innovation is in use.

Stage 5: Collaboration. "I would like to discuss my findings and ideas with others." Teachers need opportunities to develop skills and to work with each other. Collaboration should be encouraged, but not forced on those who are not interested.

Stage 6: Refocusing concerns. "I have an idea for improving on the innovation." The principal should respect and encourage the interest these individuals have for "finding a better way." This could be done by channeling their ideas and energies in ways that would be productive rather than counterproductive. The principal, however, should be aware of and willing to accept the fact that these staff members may replace or significantly modify the existing innovation.

"Link" Between Staff Development and Clinical Supervision. Since effective staff development programs encourage teachers to think and talk about teaching, it is a natural combination to use reflection and discussion as a systematic part of clinical supervision. Clinical supervision (Elam, in DuFour, 1991, pp. 74–75):

- Has a primary goal to improve instruction by observing, analyzing, and ultimately changing classroom behavior
- Requires a face-to-face relationship between the teacher and the principal

- Helps the teacher to see, as objectively as possible, what is taking place in the classroom in terms of performance, not people
- Works best when the relationship between the principal and the teacher has mutual trust and collegiality
- Encourages the professional and personal autonomy of the teacher.

At the preobservation conference, the principal should encourage the teacher to do most of the talking and avoid value judgments. Observation can have a narrow or wide focus, but the principal must be objective in gathering data. In the post-observation conference, the teacher and principal discuss the observation data—with the teacher again reacting and doing much of the talking. When an innovation from staff development is integrated into the instruction program, it is an opportunity for the principal to focus on its implementation with the teacher without changing the customary pattern of two to three observations each year.

The importance of the principal's role in staff development is supported by research. (Andrews in Orlich, 1989, p. 157). Generally, elementary student achievement scores correlated directly with the principal's influence. Students of all socioeconomic backgrounds achieved at relatively high rates if their schools had effective principals. The opposite was also true for ineffective principals. Further, when effective principals took over schools with low-achieving students, student scores increased. When ineffective principals were assigned to effective schools, student achievement scores tended to decline.

The principal has the key role in staff development as well as in many other areas. Perhaps we could say, "Show me an effective principal, and I will show you an effective school—affectively and cognitively."

Administrators and Policy Makers

The administrators and policymakers role group includes superintendents or district administrators, assistant superintendents, school board members, and sometimes state department of education personnel. They need to be well informed about innovations at both the information and practical levels. This includes listening to "experts" such as practicing principals and teachers who have worked with programs along with consultants and college and university personnel who have knowledge about the innovation. Visits by members of this group to school sites where the innovation is being or has been successfully implemented are also worthwhile. If these people have a chance to interact with and ask questions of others in their same roles as well as principals and teachers, they will be better prepared to make decisions about the appropriateness of the program for their district.

Administrators and policymakers need to support programs they initiate in their district from "day 1" and through maintenance and institutionalization. Too many good programs have drifted away during the past decades because of lack of administrative and school board support. Support has to be strong enough not only to vote funds for staff development, but strong enough to survive frequent changes in personnel for superintendents and school board members.

Both written and verbal reports from the principals and teachers to members of this role group must be concise and come to them appropriate to personnel changes. Also, superintendents, assistant superintendents, and school board members need to be involved in committees and groups that function during the planning phases of staff development. They need to be observers and interact with teachers and principals during implementation, and to continue school site visits from time to time during maintenance and institutionalization. "Top–down" policy making from superintendents and school boards has been ineffective. They need to be part of a collaborative process—particularly for staff development. Student performance scores related to the innovation, teacher effectiveness and satisfaction ratings, and other relevant data on program implementation need to be reported to this role group at appropriate times.

Students

Students are the most important role group in staff development. They are the reason for staff development programs—directly to improve and broaden their performance either affectively or cognitively—or indirectly through changes in teacher performance, strategies, or attitudes to accomplish that same objective. Before an innovation is implemented, a plan to evaluate student performance should be in place. Generally, a student evaluation should contain both a cognitive component, which usually involves changes in student achievement, and an affective component, which relates to student attitudes, beliefs, behaviors, and so on.

Parents

Parents of regular students and those of special populations often have a variety of interests in the education process. Their support or opposition can "make or break" a program—particularly an innovation. They need to support the changes the innovation brings when their children talk about it or bring home schoolwork. They need to ask their children questions about how the innovation has affected their lessons and their attitudes. Parents need to be involved in the decision to plan and implement the staff development programs by serving on committees or perhaps taking part in the training sessions along with the teachers.

Parents also need to support the program as taxpayers and community members. Articles about the innovation in newsletters or newspapers and information at parent–teacher conferences about how the innovation is affecting their child and how the child has reacted to it are often effective. Parents can be the best public relations agents any school or district can have. If they feel their child is benefiting from the innovation, they are not hesitant to praise it and tell others about it. The opposite is also true if they feel a program has failed their child.

Parents can act as volunteers in the school to work with students and teachers. They can also be mentors or resource people in their areas of expertise. In many cases, principals and teachers can interact with parents during all phases of the staff development process through parent groups already in place. Again, as in the case of most role groups, involvement is the key to success.

College and University Personnel and "Expert" Consultants

Members of this group can take many roles in staff development. One role is as resource people or experts for the information-giving portion of the training program. They should be teamed with practitioners and be aware of the needs and characteristics of today's teachers to make the workshop sessions they conduct meaningful to the participants. They can also be involved in the readiness and planning phases of the program to provide, cooperatively with the principals and teachers, coaching and management for the implementation phases. They can act as evaluators and provide maintenance support after the program has been in effect.

College and university members of this role group can also act as promoters of the innovation in their role as teacher educators when they supervise student teachers. This role includes preparing the college students to work with the innovation, and observing their participation in it. Here, they also interact with cooperating teachers of the students and promote the innovations in their conversations about the student's performance.

Members of this group can coordinate general staff development groups such as leagues of schools or other groups that combine staff from several districts in a geographic area around a campus for training. Here, member districts cooperatively fund expenses for national or regional experts to come to their area. When an innovation is the focus of staff development for several districts, a national expert on the innovation could be featured during the year of readiness and planning.

Service and Community Groups

Members of this group are taxpayers who financially support the programs in the schools that they consider to be positive. They can provide support to the schools by acting as mentors, resource people for classes, and guides for field trips to business and industry, medical centers, museums, brokerage houses, laboratories, and so on. They can also act as volunteer aides to teachers and tutors for students.

People from community and service groups can support special projects. For example, a science and engineering professional group can provide financial and "expert" support for a science fair. Or a historical society can promote a heritage or genealogy event for students. Also, members of community groups can provide financial support, act as resource people, and supply transportation for out-of-town events for extracurricular activities such as *Olympics of the Mind, Math Counts, Science Olympiad,* and other similar groups. They can provide prizes and scholarships for students and make facilities that the school might lack such as computer or science laboratories or art and musical facilities available to student groups. Again, involvement is the key to support of an innovation.

School Support Staff

Members of this group include certified personnel such as counselors, psychologists, media specialists, and social workers along with clerical and custodial nonteaching personnel. While members of this group do not usually teach in the classroom, they have very personal contact with students. They need to be informed about the innovation, understand the extra effort the teachers and others are making to implement it, and support the program in contacts with students and community. People in this group are active in the community in a wide range of organizations and areas of interest. If they are knowledgeable about the innovation and its implementation, they can be positive ambassadors for the school.

Certified personnel such as curricular and psychological specialists work directly with students, often on a one-to-one or small-group basis. They need to be informed about the innovation and its implementation so they can support the work of the teachers when they work with the students. They should not be isolated from the rest of the faculty and should be involved in all phases of staff development.

Successful staff development programs require that all role groups be involved in all phases of the program. Staff development signifies change. Change is most easily brought about by leaders such as principals and superintendents involving members of all groups affected by it. A positive attitude and the idea that "I am proud of this school and its programs," permeates all staff in an effective school.

STAFF DEVELOPMENT STRUCTURES AND STRATEGIES

"Districts have spent untold dollars on outside experts expected to cure the district woes... but they have ignored the practical knowledge of their staff and shunned perhaps their greatest chance for success.... It is no longer acceptable to spend resources on staff development and say to a presenter, 'If one person gets one new idea, the day will be worth it'" (Hirsh & Ponder, 1991, pp. 45–47). "To genuinely improve teaching, we must say goodbye to quick-fix workshops and hello to staff development that provides intellectual stimulation and opportunities to develop new knowledge and skills" (Goldenberg & Gallimore, 1991, p. 69).

These quotes reflect disillusionment with past staff development practices and help set the tone for staff development in the future. They suggest that staff development efforts must come from within the staff, not be imposed with resolutions or presentations from the outside. They indicate further that staff development is a long-term process, not a one-shot presentation. It must be systematic and continuous, and involve all role groups in the school, district, and community.

Frameworks and Delivery Systems

Staff development programs need a framework on which to build. Five guidelines to integrate innovations into a program include the following (Guskey, 1990, pp. 13–14):

1. All innovative strategies in the improvement program should share common goals and premises.

2. No single innovative strategy can do everything.

3. Innovative strategies in the program should complement each other.

4. Innovative strategies need to be adapted to individual classroom and school building conditions.

5. When a well-conceived combination of innovative strategies is used, the results are likely to be greater than when a single strategy is used.

Keep Guidelines Practical. Here are some practical "tips" for successful staff development (Hirsh & Ponder, 1991, pp. 43–47):

- Seek expertise from within the staff and system before searching outside.

- Broaden the definition of inservice activities to include teachers as researchers, collegial support teams, conferences, teacher observations, mentoring, professional and personal writing, and coaching.

- Teachers in different stages of their career have special needs; new teachers need special attention.

- Principals and teachers will not take part voluntarily in meaningless inservice.

- If you wait for everybody to be ready, you may never begin the change.
- More collaboration between school practitioners and university professors will occur on practice and research in the future.
- Without appropriate follow-up, staff development will continue to lack impact.

These strategies suggest that changes in staff development will take new knowledge, new attitudes, new will, and commitment from all role groups involved. Some staff development strategies focus on individuals, others on schools, and yet others on districts, but the best programs balance their efforts across the three groups (Joyce, 1990, p. xviii; Joyce & Showers, 1988, pp. 82–83).

Get Teachers Involved. Two common strategies to deliver staff development are sources of information and teacher involvement activities (Orlich, 1989, p. 41). *Information sources* take advantage of all available technologies and resources and include classes, videotapes and films, consultant presentations, instructional television, computer-aided instruction, CD-ROM programs, extension courses, institutes, workshops, lectures, professional association meetings and training sessions, and university courses.

Teacher-involvement activities include simulations, role-playing, team teaching, internships, discussion groups, microteaching, role modeling, study groups, teacher visitations and interactions with practitioners who are using the innovation, staff meetings, paired teaching, participating at teacher centers, participating in educational laboratory projects, and sharing information they have learned with others—individuals, school staff, and district personnel.

Four factors that encouraged change in ten model schools were (Bechtol & Sorenson, 1993, pp. 356-357): (1) commitment to the school mission; (2) faculty knowledge of effective practices that were identified through education research; (3) teaming skills among the staff; and (4) a lifelong commitment by teachers and administrators to professional growth and renewal. But perhaps the most important factor was that *teachers will continue to use a new strategy only if it shows positive results with their students.* Staff development is a part of a successful school, and successful schools don't work because they follow a prescriptive staff development strategy. They work because they follow the professional judgments of their teachers and principals (Glickman, 1991, p. 6).

What Research Tells Us

Research plays an important role in staff development. Highlights of research from an analysis of 200 studies plus a review of the literature on staff development provides ten facts about the programs, along with implications for planning and developing them (Showers, Joyce, & Bennett, 1987, pp. 78–80):

1. What the teacher "thinks" about teaching determines what the teacher "does" when teaching.
2. Teachers tend to take useful information back to their classrooms from staff development training when it includes the following: presentation of theory, demonstration of a new strategy, initial practice during the sessions; and prompt feedback about their practice efforts.
3. Teachers tend to use strategies and concepts if they receive peer or expert coaching while they are trying out the new ideas in their classrooms.
4. Teachers benefit more from staff training if they are competent and have high self-esteem.
5. Flexible thinking helps teachers learn new skills and integrate them into their "tried and true" methods of teaching.
6. Individual teaching styles and value orientations tend not to affect abilities of teachers to learn from staff development.
7. Teachers need to have a basic level of knowledge or skills in a new approach or strategy before they can "buy into" it.
8. Initial enthusiasm for training is reassuring to staff development organizers and presenters but appears to have little effect on learning.
9. Location of the learning and training site and the role of the trainer—administrator, teacher, professor, and so on—has little effect on learning. The important part is that the trainer has a good design and knows how to use it.
10. Effects of training do not depend on teachers organizing and directing the program, but social cohesion and shared understandings to get teachers to try out new ideas and methods.

Other general findings indicate that the most important dimension of training and teaching is cognitive. Further, "study of attitudes toward training indicates that the greater the increase of knowledge, skills, and transfer, the more positive are teachers' attitudes toward the training" (Showers, Joyce & Bennett, 1987, p. 86). But knowledge is not enough. Teachers must practice and transfer the knowledge. And coaching helps them sustain practice and make changes in it as necessary.

Teaching and Learning Strategies

Several underlying strategies from current programs are summarized here (Strong, Silver, Hanson, Marzano, Wolfe, Dewing, & Brock, 1990, pp. 26–27). Teaching and learning are decision making processes. Therefore, curriculum should be general and focus on those ideas with the most durability. Curriculum methodology should emphasize decision making based on theory with a support system that encourages interaction between them.

Thoughtful learning leads to a curriculum that identified kinds of thinking most likely to enhance it. Methodology uses thinking in all content areas and provides a support system to incorporate thinking processes as important parts of lesson design.

Learning is tactical but teaching is strategic. In all thinking and learning, process involves content. In classroom learning, thought is either strategic or tactical. Here, both the teacher and students need a repertoire of strategic or tactical resources to attack learning problems. This leads to a curriculum that focuses on a set of strategies and tactics that model principles of successful learning theory and a methodology that encourages flexible use of many tactics and strategies. A support system that uses a variety of teaching and learning styles and choices of strategies to meet learner needs and curriculum objectives is essential.

Cooperative learning has re-emphasized that learning has a social dimension and has provided us with tools for making decisions about social roles and relationships in learning groups. Methodology should reflect and model this. The support system should include small- and large-group interaction as well as learning in pairs and individually.

Teaching and learning are artful. Teachers, like artists and writers, "wrestle indeterminate situations" into problems they can solve with the resources at hand. They produce ways of using language, numbers, pictures, and objects in order to change the thoughts and feelings of their students. Their definition of problems, learning designs for lessons or units of instruction, and responses to situations are a result of teachers' understanding of themselves, their students, and their curriculums.

Thus, the curriculum should put instruction into a problem-solving content and methodology to reflect the nature of teaching and encourage reflection on the advantages and disadvantages of various designs. The support system should encourage teachers to reflect or carry out metacognition on their own teaching and choices for defining problems and solutions.

Peer Coaching

Regardless of how much teachers know about frameworks and delivery systems, findings of research, and learning strategies, they still need something more tangible, more concrete, and more practical. The strategy of peer coaching has been very successful in meeting these needs. Many adults find learning new skills and techniques such as using the computer exciting but also frustrating. One of the most "satisfying ways people learn is by asking one another" (Brandt, 1987, p. 3).

Coaching involves illustrating, demonstrating, explaining and "give and take." It also makes learning more interesting, more fun, and more practical. Reassurance of success from a colleague when one finally "gets the learning right" is very satisfying. Coaching blends cognitive learning and affective assurance.

Teachers Like Peer Coaching. It promotes three conditions for professional growth—teacher autonomy, collaboration, and time for learning. It also makes some positive basic assumptions about teachers (Garmston, 1987, pp. 20–26):

- Technical coaching assumes that objective feedback given in a nonthreatening and supportive climate will improve teaching performance.

- Suspension of judgment will help teachers establish an open professional exchange and interaction.

- Coaching assumes that problem solving by teams of people—teachers who are responsible for instructing students—will produce improvement.

- Structuring coaching teams across grade levels or departments will help teachers become more aware of their common problems and resources.
- Coaches provide feedback by giving descriptive reports and asking judgmental questions causing teachers to analyze and evaluate their own instructional decisions.
- Teacher ownership of the program is the key to satisfaction and learning.
- Teaching strategies such as thinking skills and problem solving, cooperative learning, and writing across the curriculum provide a content for coaching.

Characteristics of Successful Coaches. What kinds of traits and behaviors do teachers who act as coaches need? These needs can be grouped under the headings of *knowledge, communication skills and priorities,* and *performance criteria* (Wildman & Niles, 1987, p. 8). At the *knowledge level*, the coach should have access to a knowledge base of successful teaching and understand ways of knowing.

In *communication skills and priorities*, coaches should help teachers reflect on research findings, base communications on what teachers already know, show good listening skills, and demonstrate a desire for teachers to adapt what they learn to their own situations. Coaches should also be patient and show confidence in teachers' knowledge and ability to learn. For *performance criteria*, coaches should measure success in terms of gradual increments of teacher performance, independence and capacity to grow, and be seen by school leaders as teacher advocates who stimulate staff to learn and improve their teaching.

Starting a Program. Some basic ideas one district used to start a peer coaching program were as follows (Chase & Wolfe, in Raney & Robbins, 1989, p. 37):

- Know what peer coaching is and what it is not. Peer coaching is a confidential arrangement between peers that includes observations and feedback in a safe environment; it is not evaluation.
- Develop a clear understanding of levels of peer coaching. Interactions between coach and teacher fall into these categories: mirroring where the coach observes but does not interpret classroom action; collaborative where the coach collects and helps analyze data; and expert where the coach gives feedback to help the teacher learn or refine skills.
- Follow three traditional steps—preconferencing; classroom observation, data collection, and data analysis; and postconferencing.
- Assess the school's culture including the school's norms, values, and beliefs that influence trust levels; administrative support; history of past change efforts; role of the teacher's union; staff experience; and school size.
- Design the program and its implementation around school characteristics.
- Look at practical elements such as budget, which will determine amounts of time for training and coaching.

Research Supports Coaching Effectiveness. Researchers found from analyses of data from many studies that coaching contributes to transfer of training in five ways. Coached teachers (Joyce & Showers, 1988, pp. 88–90):

1. Usually practiced new strategies more frequently and developed more skill in the teaching strategy than do uncoached teachers with the same knowledge and demonstration training
2. Used their newly learned strategies more appropriately than uncoached teachers in their own instructional objectives and specific models of teaching
3. Showed greater long-term retention of knowledge about the innovation and skill with the strategies related to it
4. Were more likely than uncoached ones to teach new models of teaching to their students and ensured that their students understood the purpose of the strategy and behavior to exhibit when using the new strategy
5. Exhibited clearer understanding with regard to the purposes and use of the new strategies as revealed through interviews, lesson plans, and classroom performance than did uncoached teachers.

Reasons for increased transfer related to the discussions and interactions between the coach and the teacher, opportunities for the teacher to try out innovations in a nonthreatening environment, the chance for both reinforcement and feedback, ways to correct unsuccessful situations, and more time to incorporate the innovation.

Agenda for Training Coaches. An overview of the content and sequence for seven training sessions (about 40 hours, about 6 hours per session) on peer coaching is presented here (Raney & Robbins, 1989, p. 36):

Session 1: Overview of background and research on peer coaching

Context for peer coaching—collaborative goals, in relation to school norms and culture; social and technical principles of coaching; and organizing for peer coaching

Peer coaching models

Sessions 2 and 3: Overview of observation instruments for coaching from mirroring to actual coaching, interaction analysis, time off task, drop-in observation, cognitive coaching, script-taping, checklists

Session 4: Factors influencing peer coaching relationships

A model of factors influencing teacher thinking and behavior such as teaching styles, student group sizes, educational beliefs

Session 5: Advanced skills: preconferencing, observation, postconferencing

Session 6: Tuning up communication skills such as mediational questions, probing for specifics, and identifying presuppositions

Session 7: Change theory and effective staff development practices such as learning from research, implications of peer coaching, and plans for maintenance

Regardless of differences among schools, peer coaching programs need verbal and tangible support from administrators, adequate training for coaches, trust among participants, and program flexibility to meet changing needs of staff. Peer coaching helps teachers develop collegiality and encourages them to improve instruction.

SUCCESSFUL STAFF DEVELOPMENT PROGRAMS

Staff development is the vehicle to prepare educators to meet the challenges in the changing world of the 1990s and beyond. These changes include the knowledge and technology explosion, competition for jobs and market share at a global level, shift in population demographics, the breakdown of the nuclear family, and the need for all students to achieve at high levels. Staff developers will have to say, "I trust that you can solve your own problems if given the right conditions and support," rather than teaching skills and confidence about what's right for others as they have often done in the past (Sparks, 1991, p. 2). Some guidelines for staff development are as follows:

- Address organizational development at district and school levels.

- Become more integrated with other improvement efforts such as changes in school culture, parent and community involvement, state and national efforts.

- Become more outcome oriented and make differences that show up in student performance and behavior.

- Help educators explore new development, support strategic planning processes, set courses and expectations for change; support schoolwide and district improvement efforts; and continue to provide skill training.

This approach to staff development means educators must be willing to take risks and encounter failure as they try to meet new challenges. It also means that administrators, policymakers, parents, and community must allow teachers to "fail" and correct their mistakes without "throwing the baby out with the bath water" as they have so often done in the past with new programs and innovations.

Relating Teacher Needs to Staff Development

Earlier sections of this chapter have dealt with the rationale and need for staff development, the roles of educators in staff development, and characteristics and strategies of both the providers and receivers of staff development. Taking all these facets into consideration, staff development programs must be organized into a sequence. All worthwhile programs elaborate on the tried-and-true sequence—plan, implement, and evaluate.

A Sample Sequence. One scheme that mixes sequence with strategies and teacher characteristics is proposed here (Bechtol & Sorenson, 1993, pp. 361–362):

1. Plan: "Think big, and start small; don't try to do too many new things at once."
2. Work in teams: Teaming makes changing easier by cutting the work of implementing by more than 50 percent; it's also more fun.
3. Use available resources: Beg, borrow, and steal resources from what is already available such as from special-populations programs as well as regular classroom files and those of the school and district media centers.
4. Involve all personnel in the selection of the time and place for training.
5. Follow up staff development training. Follow-up may be more important than the training itself.
6. Support teachers as they implement new strategies. Teachers have personal concerns about what the strategy means for them, their teaching, and how it affects their students.
7. Provide feedback on student learning. This is the most important step. Does use of the new strategy help students learn more?
8. Continue support and provide follow-up training as the new strategy becomes part of the school's curriculum.

Stages of Teacher Competence and Growth. It takes time for teachers to perform at a high level of competence—perhaps three or four years (Bechtol, 1984). During this time, teachers tend to go through six stages to develop professional expertise (Leithwood, in Joyce, 1990, pp. 72–76). *In stage 1*, beginning teachers develop survival skills for classroom management, gain a confident knowledge of what they teach, and learn to assess students appropriately. In *stage 2*, teachers have well-developed classroom management skills, can use several teaching models, and assess students for formative knowledge as well as achievement of most instructional goals. Expanding instructional flexibility occurs in *stage 3*. Here, management skills are automatic. They use a variety of models to keep student interest, and they assess students for both formative and summative purposes.

In *stage 4*, they acquire instructional expertise. They have integrated classroom management with instruction and are skilled at using a broad repertoire of teaching models to achieve a variety of instructional goals. They also provide for differences in student learning styles and use a variety of assessment procedures—formative and summative—on which to base instructional decisions. Contributing to the growth of colleagues' instructional expertise is *stage 5*. Here, teachers are highly competent instructors. They can reflect about their own competence and explain their instructional choices in relation to education research, beliefs, and values. They can also help colleagues to acquire instructional expertise. In *stage 6*, teachers participate in educational decisions at the individual, school, district, and perhaps state or national levels. They exercise both formal and informal leadership. They have a good understanding of how schools work and how decisions made at many levels of the educational enterprise will affect the education of their students.

Since schoolwide and districtwide staff development involves teachers at all six levels of professional development, consideration needs to be made for training as well as for selection of teacher presenters and coaches, and representation on various committees during planning, implementing, and evaluating staff development.

Overview of Models and Programs

Several traditional programs that are variations on the plan, implement, evaluate theme are discussed here (Orlich, 1989, pp. 112–127). These models can be categorized as those based on the organization, the individual, concerns, roles, and trainer.

Organization-Based Models. These focus on the school building and emphasize solving problems or learning new skills. Two models, school-based and organization-development, are described here. In the *school-based model*, the individual school becomes responsible for its own programs. It requires great personal commitment by all people employed in the building. The *organization development model* uses a series of processes and strategies to develop an organization's capacity to reach optimal performance. All members of the organization must identify, study, diagnose, and analyze the strengths, weaknesses, and potential of the organization.

Individual-Based Models. These relate to behavioral and humanistic activities. The *behavioral model* requires identifying a problem, charting baseline behaviors, introducing a contingency, charting new behaviors, and continuous evaluation. The *humanistic model* puts the teacher in the center of the training process, and each individual designs a personal agenda for growth.

Concerns-Based Model. It has seven stages and identifies change as a process that involves people both experientially and emotionally. The seven stages are (1) *awareness* (little concern about or involvement with the innovation), (2) *informational* (interested in knowing more, but not concerned about impact), (3) *personal* (uncertain about demands, but concerned about how it affects "me,") (4) *management* (concerned about logistics of implementation), (5) *consequence* (concerned about impact on students), (6) *collaboration* (interested in coordination and cooperation with others to make the innovation work), and (7) *refocusing* (interested in modifying or adapting to make the innovation more beneficial or powerful).

Role-Based Models. These can be categorized as independent study, competency based, and educator centered. In the *independent study model*, the individual or groups of individuals work with materials to meet their needs and may use a peer network and/or a workshop format for some of the training. This model has been effective for school administrators and helps job-alike individuals learn from peers. The *competency-based model* is used to develop very specific professional skills. It may use a variety of materials to carry out the training process, such as print, training and modeling, videotapes and films, and microteaching to focus on teaching behaviors or strategies such as questioning and tutoring.

The *educator-centered model* is based on three ideas: fundamental reform comes only from the teachers who implement the change; teachers are unlikely to change the way they teach just because they are told to do so; and teachers take reform seriously only when they define their own problems, determine their own needs, and voluntarily seek help.

Trainer-Based Models. These can be described in four ways: exchange, linking agent, peer coaching, and advocacy. In the *exchange model*, individuals exchange positions to get job-embedded training in terms of new insights, knowledge, or skills. In the *linking agent model*, persons act as internal change agents in their schools—working with individuals on a daily basis. The *peer coaching model*, which was discussed in detail in an earlier section of this chapter has one basic concept: a group of teachers or administrators are trained to act as coaches for their colleagues. And the *advocacy model* builds on the multiplier effect. Advocacy comes not from the program elements but from the delivery and indoctrination systems built into the presentation so that after attending a workshop, the individual teacher or other educator can advocate or teach the lower-level sessions to others.

The RPTIM Model for Staff Development

This model is named from the first letter of each of its five stages—readiness, planning, training, implementation, and maintenance. It is one of the most widely used sequences for staff development programs and incorporates many of the elements discussed in earlier sections of this chapter. The model was introduced in 1981 by Wood, Thompson, and Russell and has been used and detailed by several groups of authors and staff developers. A brief description of the model's five stages and how they are used in practice is the topic of this section (Wood, Killian, McQuarrie & Thompson, 1993; Wayne County, Michigan, Regional Education Service Agency, ca. 1993).

Readiness—Stage 1. The principal and central office personnel work with school staff members to develop a climate to support staff development. Staff members select goals and develop their commitment to implement professional behaviors and programs to achieve the goals and objectives. Program ownership develops when teachers, administrators, and parents help make decisions about the improvement goals and selection of practices and programs to reach their goals.

There are four tasks in readiness. The *first task* is to develop a supportive climate. This includes establishing a budget to provide time and staffing for staff development. The *second task* is to select a planning team or committee of eight to twelve people that includes teachers, principals, parents, and a central office representative. Community leaders and a school board member also strengthen the team. Once the team is created, members need to experience activities to develop skills, understandings, and relationships to make decisions as a group and to provide a positive school climate. Not only these team members, but all personnel in the district should have experience in team-building skills if all role groups are to work together effectively.

The *third task* is to select programs and practices. Here a procedure to present the goals and programs to the total faculty to get their support should be developed. The *fourth task* is to get support and commitment from the entire staff and other groups represented on the planning team as well as from people not on the planning team. One way to accomplish this is to have planning team members meet with a group of their peers on a regular schedule to share decisions made at the meetings.

Important elements of the readiness stage are developments of a budget for expenditures for release time for staff, materials, site visits to other schools, and consultants. Release time for staff can be provided by use of already budgeted district inservice days, paid summer work, and selective use of substitute teachers.

Designation of a facilitator or director who will guide the staff through all stages of staff development and time to do the job is essential to program success. This person needs to be a leader who "knows what to do and when, how and why to do it" (Wood et al., p. 9). The school principal and district administrator need to participate fully in all activities with the staff. District curriculum specialists should be available to help identify goals and locate promising practices and programs for site visits.

By the end of the readiness stage, the school has identified its goals and programs and most staff members should support the decisions and be ready to plan and participate in training to achieve the goals. The readiness process takes about three to six months or sometimes one year.

Planning—Stage 2. In this stage, the staff identifies what it will do during the final three stages—training, implementation, and maintenance. This stage can be divided into five tasks: (1) involving the planning team and staff in *setting up goals and objectives;* (2) *conducting a needs assessment*; (3) *identifying resources* to support long-range training; (4) *developing a five-year training plan and timeline* to implement the program; and (5) *getting staff and district approval of the written plan.* Teachers and administrators work together to complete these tasks. The planning team serves as the working group to develop and write the plan for the staff.

At the end of this stage, the school has a written plan to meet its goals over a five-year period. The inservice needs of teachers and administrators, specific training activities, a timeline for activities, and resources and support for implementation are in place. The total plan has been approved by central office personnel, and the board of education. Staff members have committed to the school's goals.

Training—Stage 3. This stage is often called *inservice.* The main objective is to provide experiences for staff to learn knowledge and skills in theory and practice to meet the objectives decided on in the planning stage. Four tasks in the training stage include (1) *selecting and designing an effective inservice program,* (2) *selecting experienced and effective trainers,* (3) *scheduling the inservice activities,* and (4) *ensuring participation by the principal and other administrators.*

By the end of the training stage, trainers have been contracted to guide the inservice training and the staff have participated in learning experiences with the principal and other staff. All have learned and demonstrated new skills and behaviors to be implemented with students. Now comes the fun!

Implementation—Stage 4. In this stage, teachers and administrators move from learning in the controlled setting of inservice training to adapting and practicing what they have learned in their daily work activities. We know from past experience over recent decades that too often teachers and administrators never implement what they have learned with their students. This, of course, leads to no significant changes in student achievement or behavior. Thus, the most important part of implementation is helping teachers realize they will probably have to make adaptations in what they learned to integrate the innovative ideas into their lessons in the classroom, their personality, and the needs of their students. In order to do this, administrators, principals, and some teachers should be prepared to provide support to staff.

Common ways to give support include trainer observation of staff members at work with students, and observations by peers, the principal or other supervisors. Teachers and others can meet with trainers to share successful implementation experiences and to seek solutions to problems they encountered. A review of videotapes of colleagues working with students during implementation is very useful. Newsletters that share successful practices and answer questions commonly raised by teachers and administrators also provide a supporting environment.

An important way to provide follow-up support is through coaching by a knowledgeable peer, administrator, supervisor, or trainer. Coaching was discussed in detail earlier in this chapter. Another important element in follow-up is communication that informs the entire staff about implementation strategies.

Reward and recognition are also important. Principals are key people to determine what kinds are possible and meaningful to staff. Some ideas include asking successful teachers to share their experiences with the rest of the faculty, sending teachers written "job well done" notes, inviting central office administrators to visit the school to observe successful practices, and asking staff members to write articles about their successes for the school, district, or community newsletter or newspaper.

By the end of the implementation stage, staff members have moved from inservice learning to practice with students. They have achieved some of their goals, and they feel comfortable with and proud of their accomplishments.

Maintenance—Stage 5. By this time, teachers and administrators are using their innovation comfortably and completely. The focus is on ensuring that the changes they have implemented continue to be practiced. Here, teachers continue to refine and extend their use of the innovation to have maximum impact on students and integrate it effectively into the curriculum.

Past experience with innovations has shown that they "die off" unless they are given regular attention. Some strategies to maintain a program include make sure that the innovation is being used regularly and appropriately; provide feedback to help teachers determine whether or not their current practices reflect the innovation; and review information from teacher self-reporting, surveys, classroom materials, teacher planning books, and collaborative research to determine how the innovation is used.

Maintenance can also be carried out using refinement, renewal, feedback, and mentoring. In *refinement*, teachers vary their use of an innovation to try to improve its effects as they work cooperatively with colleagues to integrate it into the subject matter areas. In *renewal*, teachers re-evaluate the quality of the innovation, seek ways to modify it, examine new developments in the field, and explore new goals for themselves.

Feedback from students helps teachers and others determine innovation effectiveness. This includes student written work in folders or portfolios, student self-determination in progress in various subject areas, and questionnaires where students focus on the innovation. Parent feedback from interviews about interactions with their children about the innovation; teacher reviews of lesson plans, curriculum, and student "products"; and videotaping of teachers using the innovation. Peer coaching and supervisor feedback are also part of the maintenance process.

Mentoring new staff members over time is necessary to keep the innovation going. New staff should be assigned mentors who provide an orientation to the staff development innovation and offer assistance as new teachers implement the innovation with students after training. Teachers need to establish support groups and take advantage of opportunities to attend local, regional, and national meetings and make presentations about what they are doing with the innovation. Maintenance is essential because it retains the district's investment of time, energy, and money as well as the efforts of the staff to get the innovation "up and going."

A SAMPLE STAFF DEVELOPMENT PROGRAM TO INFUSE THINKING SKILLS AND PROBLEM SOLVING INTO THE CURRICULUM

This section describes one way to develop a staff development program to incorporate the innovation of thinking skills and problem solving into the primary, intermediate, and middle school curriculum. This program is built on information that has been presented in this chapter, the practical, "how to" information of Chapters 3, 4, and 5, the background information on thinking skills and problem solving in Chapter 2, and my own experiences. The program focuses on three areas:

1. Knowledge of process in terms of (a) five thinking skills groups—inquiry processes, creative thinking, critical thinking skills, single-step problem solving techniques, and Bloom's cognitive levels—and (b) how students use these skills to solve multistep problems; and knowledge of how process is related to content, product, and environment

2. Ways to infuse thinking skills and problem solving into four basic subject matter areas—language arts, mathematics, science, and social studies

3. Use of a four-stage staff development program: planning; training sessions for teachers and other staff; implementation with students; and maintenance.

The discussion emphasizes staff development activities, committee duties and representation, general topics and detailed agendas for the program, and ways to carry out the program at each of the four stages.

Planning the Program— Stage 1

During the early part of the planning stage, called *readiness* by some authors, the staff prepared intellectually for learning new information and skills and psychologically for the changes that adopting the innovation of infusing thinking skills and problem solving into the subject matter areas would bring. They decided preparation would be best done at the building level with the principal as leader.

Introducing the Innovation. The principal started out by discussing several reasons for this change at a general faculty meeting. She emphasized that the innovation would help students meet needs in terms of academic skills in today's world, skills to succeed at higher levels of schooling in high school, college or university or technical school, and skills to find employment when they enter the workplace of a global society. Teachers and other staff got involved by working in small groups to brainstorm as many specific needs as possible. These were shared with the larger group and ranked to form a list of "five important needs."

Staff also discussed ways they felt would be most appropriate to meet these needs. Ideas included developing interdisciplinary units or "infusion" into the units of the four subject matter areas as they presently teach them. They decided on a combination of the two as appropriate to the subject matter being taught.

Advisory Committee Duties and Representatives. During teacher interactions, topics such as "How do we get time to learn more about these skills?" and "How do we decide on a specific strategy to infuse skills and problem solving into our subject matter learning?" came up. These moments gave the principal an opportunity to ask for volunteers to serve on an advisory Committee to develop a staff development plan. This committee, chaired by the principal (or a chair elected by the committee), would "keep the door open" for teachers and others to continually present their concerns. Initial tasks of this committee were:

- Getting representation from all groups of staff members, including an administrator or central office person other than the principal

- Writing statements that are clear about what outcomes are to be achieved and how to achieve them

- Making timelines for teacher inservice training and implementation

- Getting a commitment from the school board and central office to provide time during the school day or contract days for teacher inservice training.

Representation on the advisory committee included teachers, other staff, an assistant superintendent, a parent, and a board of education member. This committee determined outcomes and how to achieve them for both the teacher training and implementation stages before the inservice training sessions started.

Advisory Committee Decisions. The advisory committee decided that one year was needed for the planning, and that 60 hours of inservice training during the two-year training stage was necessary to make these changes in their curriculum. In addition, implementation would take one to two years, and maintenance two or more years.

The training stage would be the most expensive. They suggested to the central office and board of education that time for training could be obtained by (1) using four of the five inservice days already in the negotiated union contract for this project during each of two years for a total of 8 days or 48 hours; and (2) these hours could be supplemented by hiring substitutes or having volunteers for teachers on a selective basis within each building to a maximum of 6 hours per year or 12 hours total. Six hours per year could be used for site visits to other schools, building or grade-level teamwork, and special projects.

After the committee had detailed representation, specified outcomes, and agreed on a three-year timeline for planning and training, they wrote a "request for consideration" to the central office and board of education and asked for a formal reply. They indicated the chair and/or other members of their committee would be happy to answer any questions they might have and to appear at a committee or board meeting. The board advertised such a meeting to the public and asked the chair of the committee to explain the request to them in addition to giving members and the audience a written outline of the request. Several members of the board of education, parents, and community members asked questions. After a positive discussion that justified the expenditures for staff and trainer time in terms of student needs, the board of education voted to accept and support the plan of the advisory committee.

Training the Staff—Stage 2

Here, the advisory committee appointed an inservice committee of 10 people to work out the details of the training sessions over a two-year period. They would also distribute time to topics within the sixty hours, select sites for the training sessions, and identify trainers and arrange their payment schedules. Members of this committee included teachers from a variety of grade levels in the building, the principal of the building, a central office consultant or resource teacher, and one or two specialists such as media center directors, special-populations teachers or directors, or others who are involved in teaching and planning subject matter curriculum.

Identifying Timelines and General Topics for the Training Sessions. The first decision of the Inservice Committee was to indicate an urgent need for team-building skills. Teachers needed to get to know each other on a personal basis if they were going to work successfully in teams. The committee suggested that three of the sixty hours be set aside for this purpose and made this proposal to the advisory committee, which accepted their suggestion. They then decided to work out a broad, general agenda of 90-minute sessions. They used 90 minutes because they felt teachers need some kind of a break after that amount of time; two, 90-minute segments will fit into one half day or four segments into a full day; and 90 minutes allows indepth exploration of a subject without losing the attention of the participants. For purposes of efficiency, they labeled the 90-minute segments from 1 to 40. A skeletal outline of inservice sessions for the first two years is presented next.

Topics for Training Sessions—Year 1 (30 hours)

Session 1: General overview of project

Session 2: Team-building skills

Session 3: Team-building skills continued

Session 4: General overview of thinking skills and problem solving; Inquiry processes—information and practice

Session 5: Infusing inquiry processes into 1-2 units of instruction

Session 6: Creative thinking skills—information and practice

Session 7: Infusing creative thinking skills into 1–2 units of instruction

Session 8: Critical thinking skills—information and practice

Session 9: Infusing critical thinking skills into 1-2 units of instruction

Session 10: Single-step problem-solving techniques—information and practice

Session 11: Infusing single-step problem-solving techniques into 1–2 units of instruction

Session 12: Bloom's cognitive levels—information and practice; infusing Bloom's cognitive levels into 1–2 units of instruction

Session 13: Multistep problem solving and a prototype model to carry it out

Session 14: Infusing problem solving into a unit of instruction

Sessions 15–17: Infusing thinking skills and problem solving into several units of instruction in one subject matter area for elementary staff; middle school staff might work in one or two subject areas or by class subject according to their teaching assignments

Sessions 18–20: Open sessions to be used anytime during the year for site visits, small group work, other activities

Topics for Training Sessions— Year 2 (30 hours)

Sessions 21–23: Infusing thinking skills and problem solving into several more units of instruction in the first subject area

Sessions 24–26: Infusing thinking skills and problem solving into several units of instruction in second subject area at elementary level; middle school staff might continue on from sessions 21–23 or start a second subject area depending on their teaching assignment

Sessions 27–29: Continue working as in Sessions 24–26

Sessions 30–32: Infuse thinking skills and problem solving into third subject matter area at elementary level; middle school staff work appropriately

Sessions 33–35: Continue working as in Sessions 30–32

Sessions 36–38: Infuse thinking skills and problem solving into fourth subject matter area at elementary; middle school staff work appropriately

Sessions 39–40: Continue work on fourth subject area or use sessions any time during the year for special purposes.

Options Within General Topics. General topics such as those just presented can be adapted to the needs of the staff in the school and district. For example, this staff already had considerable knowledge and know-how about the inquiry processes and Bloom's cognitive taxonomy. Therefore, the knowledge and/or practice portion of these sessions was shortened or omitted. After a review of the skills, participants moved directly to infusing the skills into the curriculum for a subject area. Here the term "infusing" also includes "identifying" use of the skill or skills if they are already a part of the subject area curriculum. Teachers were urged never to throw out good activities that "work with students"—always incorporate them into the new plans.

There are also other options. Many skills in the thinking skills groups such as inferring, predicting, organized listing, and working backward can be used to solve small problems. Sometimes it is difficult to separate one thinking skill from another one. For example, synthesis (Bloom's cognitive-level skill) occurs when a student works on a product such as writing a play. But the student uses many other thinking skills besides synthesis. Since thinking is a rapid-fire operation, overlapping skills with one another and with problem solving itself often makes it difficult to pinpoint their use. Yet students need to be conscious of the characteristics of individual skills and aware of appropriate ways and situations in which to use them.

Selecting Trainers. One of the most important tasks of the advisory committee is to select trainers for the inservice sessions and other instructional and monitoring duties. Trainers should come from a variety of sources depending on the intent of the training and the expertise of the personnel. Some overall guiding principles of selection included the following:

- Teachers and other staff respond best to trainers who promote active learning; participation, not telling should be the main ways to learn.
- Staff tend to respect their peers more than experts.
- Some members of the staff who have strong interest in the topic and gain a working knowledge of the topic can become trainers at the end of the first year and beyond.
- Trainers should have experience working with teachers and children, show enthusiasm for their work, and interact well with school staff on a one-to-one and group basis.

They selected an inservice training staff that included a combination of teachers and other staff from schools already implementing thinking skills and problem solving. Personnel from nearby colleges and universities, and one consultant agency were also involved. All these people had expertise on the topic, experience working with school staffs, and experience teaching students. This combination of personnel ensured that both background knowledge and practice were adequately represented. Expert personnel handled the background information that the staff needs to understand in order to work with the topic. Teachers and other staff provided examples of how students react to the ideas and indicated the importance of background knowledge in implementing the program. School personnel who have implemented the concept with students were particularly good at answering the many questions that teachers and others asked during the inservice training sessions. Another strength of practitioners as trainers is that they can work with primary, intermediate, or middle school teachers in role-alike groups at the training sessions. They can also bring the concept closer to the participants and help them gain confidence that the innovation will work for their students in their school.

Selecting Training Sites. The location of the training sites and training times presented options to the inservice committee. There were advantages to having the site in the building in areas such as the media center, all-purpose room, or even in the cafeteria. This "in-house" site eliminated travel to another location and made having coffee and goodies—a must for inservice training sessions—convenient. Also, teachers did not have to carry their instructional materials very far. And if they forgot something, they could easily get it from their classroom or workroom.

There were also disadvantages to holding inservice training sessions in the building. There was no "change of place" to make the meeting special. Teachers and others could be torn between working on their lessons plans or other required tasks instead of concentrating on the new information and its application. Some people might not take the sessions in the building as seriously as if they were in another location. Other locations that might be used included space in other district schools, district facilities, local museums and other civic buildings, retreats, camps, or motels.

Members of the advisory committee worked out a list of possible sites—some for half-day and others for all-day meetings—and asked the staff for input on their choices at general faculty meetings or through their grade-level representatives on the inservice training committee. Feedback from these contacts guided the selection of sites—in this case, some in the building and some at other sites.

While this section has dealt mainly with training, some implementation and evaluation occur naturally during this stage. Teachers will want to try out some of the skills with their students as soon as they have learned about them, practice them in a controlled setting, and incorporate them into a unit of instruction. They will also want to try the same skills in other subject matter areas. They will evaluate the success of their efforts as soon as they try them and will want to share this information with other teachers and staff members.

Thus, in addition to the formal inservice sessions, the principal needs to provide time for teachers to get together between sessions to share their experiences and to ask for suggestions of what to do if they did not find their experiences successful. These might occur as a part of regular faculty meetings or for short periods of time before and after school, but within the teaching day. And, of course, "teacher talk" at lunch and in the teacher's lounge is always an effective way of sharing information.

Examples of Detailed Agendas. Agendas for four topics are presented here to give the reader more detail on how the training sessions are carried out. Sessions are: 2 and 3 on *team-building skills* (Bechtol & Sorenson, 1993, pp. 368–371); 8 on *critical thinking skills (information and practice)*; 13 on *multistep problem solving*; and 15–17 on *infusing thinking skills and problem solving into units of instruction* in one subject matter area at the elementary level. Elements for each session include time scheduled, objectives, trainers or presenters, outline of content to be covered, and evaluation of the session.

AGENDA • *Team-Building Skills* • Sessions 2 and 3

Time. 180 minutes

Objectives. To have teachers and other staff experience a series of activities to help them function effectively in a team situation

AGENDA • *Team-Building Skills* • *Sessions 2 and 3 (Continued)*

Trainers. A teacher or principal who has developed expertise and who has experience in leading others in team-building skills activities

Outline of Content

Getting Acquainted Activities

- "What my name means to me." where each team member gives his or her full name to the team and tell what it means to him or her
- "Paired interview" where each team member chooses another member he or she does not know very well. Then he or she asks questions and takes notes to find out as much as possible about the partner. The person being interviewed may refuse to answer a question. After 8–10 minutes, the interviewer shares information about the interviewee with the entire group. Then the two people may switch roles.

Helping Each Other

Each team member takes a turn at being the helpee while other members act as helpers. The helpee shares a real problem with the team, such as "I have trouble getting my students to work in small groups for science activities," or "I can't get my gifted students to work effectively in heterogeneous groups." Helpers help the helpee as follows:

Clarify: Helpers ask the helpee questions to explain the problem

Alternatives: Helpers give alternatives to the problem while helpee listens quietly

Application: Helpee selects the best alternative solution(s) and describes how he or she may use the plan.

Identifying Strengths

This activity comes after the team has completed several others. Now members can be asked to identify the personal strengths of other team members. One by one, each team member tapes a sheet of newsprint to the wall, puts his or her name on it, and divides it into two columns with a narrow column on the right. At the top of the left column the member writes, "Strengths Others See in Me" and at the top of the right column, "Strengths I See in Myself." After the leader has modeled this activity using a principal or someone everybody knows as an example, the members get involved.

Step 1. No one is allowed to talk while team members take turns writing the strengths of the person until it is filled or no one wants to add to the list.

Step 2: Each team member who listed a strength will look at the person and give a reason why they listed the strength.

Step 3: The person whose strengths were listed stands and validates or negates each strength, giving reasons for the decision, and checks them off in the column on the right.

Each member of the team goes through this activity.

(Continued)

240 Effective Staff Development

AGENDA • Team-Building Skills • Sessions 2 and 3 (Continued)

"We Agree"

This is probably the most important team-building skill. Its purpose is to build a team philosophy. The words "We Agree" are written on the chalkboard or newsprint. Then team members generate as many statements as they can all agree on such as "Children learn . . . ," "Thinking skills will . . . ," "Problem solving can be . . . ," "The school should . . ." Every statement must become agreeable to all team members. This necessitates much discussion so team members can explain their feelings before agreeing to it.

The importance of this activity cannot be overemphasized. Statements that are agreed on by all become part of the team's philosophy. The statements from several teams can become the school's philosophy for an innovation such as infusing thinking skills and problem solving into the subject matter areas of the curriculum.

Other team-building skills that might be included in the session are listening, developing trust, and clarifying values.

Evaluation. These activities can be evaluated on a simple five-point scale from very successful to very unsuccessful. There should also be an evaluation of the trainer's efforts and space for comments so participants can explain those parts of the sessions that were most useful to them. The tone of the evaluation should be positive and emphasize the usefulness of the content of the session to the participants.

AGENDA • Critical Thinking Skills: Information and Practice • Session 8

Time. 90 minutes

Objectives. To learn the meaning and appropriate uses of a set of ten critical thinking skills and their practical uses in a variety of subject matter areas; to identify strategies to teach these skills to students; and to practice teaching them within the team setting

Trainer(s). A teacher or other staff member or a university or college instructor or consultant who is experienced at working with teachers and other staff and who is knowledgeable about critical thinking skills and how to use them in the classroom

Outline of Content

1. "Warm-up" activity that uses a critical thinking skill, but doesn't label it as such
2. Explanation of critical thinking, a listing and explanation of twelve critical thinking skills, examples of how each skill could be used in the classroom in a variety of subject areas such as

    Fact-and-opinion skill is defined as "separating statements that can be verified (facts) from those that can not (opinion)."

    An example from a story in language arts might be "The fire started at 1:30 A.M. while three children and the mother were asleep. No one called the fire department

AGENDA • *Critical Thinking Skills: Information and Practice* • *Session 8*
(Continued)

until 1:50 A.M. when the fire was raging out of control." Which statements are fact, and which are opinion?

(Critical thinking skills are listed and discussed in Chapter 2.)

3. Practice has two parts. First, the teachers in groups of three to five people brainstorm ways they can use the various critical thinking skills with their students in a variety of subject areas. Second, one member of the group acts as the teacher and the others as students. The teacher leads the group in learning and using a critical thinking skill. This format continues until each member has acted as the teacher. The trainer moves from group to group to provide reinforcement and feedback.

Evaluation. A simple form is used for each individual to evaluate the content and practice portions of the program. These may be kept confidential or shared with the small groups or the entire group depending on the group's desires. The intent of evaluation is to improve the inservice training, not to criticize the trainers.

AGENDA • *Multistep Problem Solving: Content and Practice* • *Session 13*

Time. 90 minutes.

Objectives. To acquaint teachers and other staff with the multistep problem-solving process; to show how thinking skills from the five groups are used in problem solving; to illustrate the use of multistep problem solving in the classroom; and to involve the participants in solving a multistep problem.

Trainer(s). A teacher or other staff member, or a university or college person, or a consultant who is knowledgeable about and experienced at teaching problem solving and has taught both adults and children.

Outline of Content

1. "Warm-up" activity that involves multistep problem solving, but don't call it that. Working in a small group, have participants keep track of the steps they take without worrying about what they call them. Have each group share their procedures and rationale for doing them with the larger group. Trainer can start to formalize their steps.

2. Discuss the formal steps of multistep problem solving emphasizing the steps they took in the "warm-up" activity for examples; refer to Figure 2–5.

3. Present a formal model for multistep problem solving emphasizing that it is not a recipe, but a set of guidelines. Use the content of the "warm-up" activity to illustrate the formal steps of the model. Also refer to the worksheet in Figure 2–6 that intermediate middle-level students can use to identify each of the formal steps when they solve a multistep problem in the classroom.

4. Have teachers and others identify places in their curriculum where they can have their students practice multistep problem solving. Then, have one member of each small group practice "teaching" one of these problems with the other members acting as students. Continue this format until all members of the group have acted as a teacher. The trainer moves from group to provide reinforcement and feedback.

(Continued)

242 Effective Staff Development

AGENDA • *Multistep Problem Solving: Content and Practice* • *Session 13* (Continued)

Evaluation. Within each group, have participants discuss and rate the segments of the session as "excellent," "good," or "fair," giving reasons for their decisions. Share the outcomes with the larger group to help improve future sessions.

(Information about multistep problem solving, a model to help carry it out, a sample worksheet for students, and three examples—one in social studies, one in science, and one about an everyday occurrence—are presented in Chapter 2.)

AGENDA • *Infusing Thinking Skills and Problem Solving Into One Subject Matter Area* • *Sessions 15–17*

Time. 270 minutes. These three 90-minute modules could be held during three half-day sessions, or during a combination of a half day and a full day of training.

Objectives. To select the subject matter area to work on first, to develop a systematic way to carry out the process, and to "try out" some of their ideas to carry out the infusion process within their small group.

Trainer(s). A teacher or other staff member or university or college person who is familiar with the school's subject matter curriculum, and has experience working with teachers and students.

Outline of Content

1. The subject matter area would be selected by the group or would have been selected at a general faculty or other meeting before this session started, so teachers could bring appropriate curriculum materials to the session.

2. Teachers and others within each small group decide they will (a) identify where they are already using thinking skills and problem solving in the selected area, and (b) infuse them into the curriculum where they are not being used. (Where they do not find opportunities for students to apply thinking skills or solve problems, they search for ideas to incorporate the processes. In units such as grammar and usage, thinking skills and problem solving may not apply.)

3. Members of the group decide they will introduce a skill as follows: (a) it should be related to the type of problem they will be solving; (b) it will be formally defined and its use illustrated; and (c) the students will have a chance to practice it as soon after its introduction as possible. For example, if a mystery is selected for solving a problem, the teacher would introduce skills such as inferring, fact and opinion, relevant and irrelevant information, and induction and deduction.

4. Using the mystery as an example, the teacher guides the students in the multistep problem-solving process without naming the steps. Then, the teacher reviews with the students, the steps they took naturally and points out to them how these steps are the same as those listed in the problem solving model in Figure 2–5.

5. Now, the teacher can introduce another mystery or problem to have the students practice the problem-solving process in small groups. The teacher will circulate

AGENDA • *Infusing Thinking Skills and Problem Solving Into One Subject Matter Area* • *Sessions 15–17 (Continued)*

among the groups to provide feedback and reinforcement. (Everyday problems such as getting to school on time or deciding on where to go for a snack after a Saturday afternoon movie are often effective at this point. Students can also be introduced to the worksheet shown in Figure 2-6 to help them identify the steps.)

6. The teachers and others go through as many units of instruction as they can using the process indicated. They will not practice all the problems, but will try out those where they think students might have difficulties.

Evaluation. Since this is the first of the "working" sessions, evaluation needs to be thorough. Thus they discuss each facet of the session within their small groups and then share their ideas with the larger group. The best of the techniques used by each group are adopted and adapted by others.

The training stage has been presented here in a two-year cycle with the implication that all teachers and other staff in the school will participate since all sessions are held during working hours. This is only one option. Others include offering the training for university or college credit during a semester, a year, or in a summer session where the trainers come to the school site. The district could pay for the tuition, or other fiscal arrangements could be made with the teachers. These formats are usually carried out on a voluntary basis on the part of the teachers and other staff. The author has worked with numerous districts on these latter options and they have been very successful, but they are not appropriate for every school or district.

Implementing the Program with Students—Stage 3

This stage is the most exciting part of the program and will take about two years. Here, the new information and strategies for learning interface with students. A timeline for the trial of the first subject area of language arts—for example, three to four weeks—was agreed on, and time to share information on their trials at general faculty or other meetings was scheduled. In addition, a support system of coaching, with a peer or expert, was in place before implementation began. Other factors to be considered during this phase of the program are

- Recognition for school staff members who attempt to implement new ideas.

- A schedule for trainers from the inservice activities to visit the school to help the teachers review or refine previous learning and solve new situations that arise.

- Allocation of resources to support implementation of the program such as new instructional materials, time for planning, and additional trainer time, if needed.

- An evaluation, written and oral, to be made of the implementation near the end of the school year.

- Schedules are developed to implement the program in the four subject areas.

Again, many options exist. For example, one subject matter area could be implemented each semester or each quarter depending on the level of the teacher's assignment and inservice time allotted to preparation. Once teachers become familiar with the skills and how to infuse and teach them in the curriculum, they work rapidly. Many practical examples of using the skills to solve problems are presented in Chapters 3, 4, and 5.

Maintaining the Program—Stage 4

This stage takes two to four years once the program is implemented. It blends into a situation called *institutionalization* where the provisions of the program become part of the normal curriculum. Staff members use self-monitoring skills to maintain the new behaviors of the new program. Some characteristics of this stage are

- Systematic supervision of instruction occurs to monitor both quantity and quality of the new program behaviors.
- Staff members use self-monitoring skills to maintain the new behaviors.
- Feedback from students and parents as well as from teachers is used to monitor the program.
- Teachers and administrators share responsibility to keep the program functioning at a high level.
- Subject matter areas beyond language arts, math, science, and social studies may be added to the program.
- Provision for time and money to train new faculty members in the techniques of the program are provided and inservice training schedules are made.

How one school carried out four stages—planning, training, implementing, and maintaining— of a staff development program has been discussed here with an emphasis on the first two stages. Options for carrying out each stage were presented, and of course, many others are available according to the needs, size, and objectives of the school or district.

RESOURCES FOR STAFF DEVELOPMENT

Since staff development is a neglected area in education, good resources on the subject are often difficult to find. Current print and audiovisual resources that may be helpful to staff in various stages of staff development are listed next.

Print Materials

Cawelti, G. (Ed.). (1993). *Challenges and achievements of American education* (1993 ASCD Yearbook). Alexandria, VA: Association for Supervision and Curriculum Development.

Cutler, A., & Ruopp, F. (1993). Buying time for teachers' professional development. *Educational Leadership,* 50(6): 34–37.

Duke, D. (1993). Removing barriers to professional growth. *Phi Delta Kappan,* 74(9): 702–712.

Duke, D. (1990). Setting goals for professional development. *Educational Leadership,* 47(8): 71–75.

Elmore, R., & Fuhrman, S. (Eds.). (1994). *The governance of curriculum* (1994 ASCD Yearbook). Alexandria, VA: Association for Supervision and Curriculum Development.

Guskey, T., & Sparks, D. (1991). What to consider when evaluating staff development. *Educational Leadership,* 49(3): 73–76.

Fullan, M., & Miles, M. (1992). Getting reform right: What works and what doesn't. *Phi Delta Kappan,* 73(10): 745–752.

Glickman, C. (Ed.). (1992). *Supervision in transition* (1992 ASCD Yearbook). Alexandria, VA: Association for Supervision and Curriculum Development.

Patterson, J. (1993). *Leadership for tomorrow's schools.* Alexandria, VA: Association for Supervision and Curriculum Development.

Videotapes and Packets

Phi Delta Kappa
Center for Professional Development
P. O. Box 789
Bloomington, IN 47402-0789
Phone: 812/339-1156

This organization has produced several new videotapes. *Reinventing Our Schools* is made up of six, 30-minute videotape interviews with leading American educators. A facilitator's guide with workshop plans, background information, suggestions for follow-up activities, and resource lists accompanies each videotape. Another title is *John I. Goodlad: New Schools, New Teachers* which is a one-hour videotape with two, 30-minute segments—one on "school reform" and the other on "preparing teachers." A facilitator's guide offers plans for workshops, background information, and resources.

Association for Supervision and Curriculum Development (ASCD)
1250 N. Pitt Street
Alexandria, VA 22314-9718
Phone: 703/549-9110

ASCD has produced many video and print packages for staff development. Some of the packages relevant to this chapter are: *Opening Doors: An Introduction to Peer Coaching* which contains two videotapes (more than one hour of viewing) and a facilitator's manual; *Shared Decision Making*, a program that includes two 30-minute videotapes and a 180-page facilitator's manual; and *Adult Conflict Resolution,* which consists of one 40-minute videotape and a leader's guide with workshop outlines.

SUMMARY

Staff development for teachers and other educators is one of the most urgently needed aspects of education in the United States today. Yet it is the most difficult to achieve. The perception of the public and the press that "teachers should only teach students" is prevalent from kindergarten through college and university levels. Staff development is a term that "makes most reporters' eyes glaze over; among the more cynical, it conjures up images of parties in the guise of conferences held at exotic, sunny retreats. But staff development is hard work and perhaps in part because of its image, little money is devoted to it" (Monteagudo, 1994, p. 11).

In the Chicago Public Schools, $1.5 million of its $2.5 billion budget for 1994—less than 1 percent—is earmarked for staff development. Compare this to corporations. Motorola devotes 7 percent of its employee payroll to staff development. Do we expect teachers to learn new knowledge and strategies on their own? This view is in direct conflict with the rapid changes in knowledge, strategies, and behaviors that are demanded by a fast-moving technological and global society.

It has been the intent of this chapter to suggest practical and economical ways to conduct a meaningful staff development program. First, a rationale for staff development and roles and responsibilities in staff development were discussed. Then, successful staff development strategies and programs that have been implemented in many schools were reviewed. Finally, an example of a staff development program to infuse thinking skills and problem solving into primary, intermediate, and middle school curriculums was described.

REFERENCES

Bechtol, W. (1984). *Effective practices in the multicultural elementary classroom.* San Marcos: Southwest Texas State University.

Bechtol, W., & Sorenson, J. (1993). *Restructuring schooling for individual students.* Boston: Allyn and Bacon.

Bierly, M., & Berliner, D. (1982). The elementary school teacher as learner. *Journal of Teacher Education,* 33(6): 37–40.

Brandt, R. (1987). Overview. *Educational Leadership,* 44(5): 3.

Collins, C., & Mangieri, J. (1992). *Teaching thinking: An agenda for the 21st century.* Hillsdale, NJ: Lawrence Erlbaum.

David, J. (1991). What it takes to restructure education. *Educational Leadership,* 48(8): 11–15.

DuFour, R. (1991). *The principal as staff developer.* Bloomington, IN: National Educational Service.

Garmston, R. (1987). How administrators support peer coaching. *Educational Leadership,* 44(5): 18–26.

Glickman, C. (1991). Pretending not to know what we know. *Educational Leadership,* 48(8): 4–10

Goldenberg, C., & Gallimore, R. (1991). Changing teaching takes more than a one-shot workshop. *Educational Leadership,* 49(3): 69–72.

Guskey, T. (1990). Integrating innovations. *Educational Leadership,* 47(5): 11–15.

Hirsh, S., & Ponder, G. (1991). New plots, new heroes in staff development. *Educational Leadership,* 49(3): 43–48.

Joyce, B. (Ed.). (1990). *Changing school culture through staff development.* (1990 ASCD Yearbook). Alexandria, VA: Association for Supervision and Curriculum Development.

Joyce, B., & Showers, B. (1988). *Student achievement through staff development.* New York: Longman.

Kirst, M. (1993). Strengths and weaknesses of American education. *Phi Delta Kappan,* 74(8): 613–618.

Lambert, L. (1988). Staff development revisited. *Phi Delta Kappan,* 69(9): 665–668.

Monteagudo, L. (1994.) Retooling teachers: A lesson from industry for our schools. *Chicago Tribune* (March 9, 1994), Section 1:11.

Orlich, D. (1989). *Staff development: Enhancing human potential.* Boston: Allyn and Bacon.

Raney, R., & Robbins, P. (1989). Professional growth and support through peer coaching. *Educational Leadership,* 46(8): 35–38.

Reich, R. (1994). Are we trimming too much fat and hitting bone? New York Times News Service in *Sarasota Herald Tribune,* January 2, 1994, pp. 1, 6.

Showers, B., Joyce, B., & Bennett, B. (1987). Synthesis of research on staff development: A framework for future study and a state-of-the-art analysis. *Educational Leadership,* 45(3): 77–87.

Sorenson, J., Engelsgjerd, J., Francis, M., Miller, M., & Schuster, N. (1988). *The gifted program handbook.* Palo Alto, CA: Dale Seymour.

Sparks, D. (1991). The future of staff development. *ASCD Update,* 33(4): 2–8.

Strong, R., Silver, H., Hanson, J., Marzano, R., Wolfe, P., Dewing, T., & Brock, W. (1990). Thoughtful education: Staff development for the 1990s. *Educational Leadership,* 47(5): 25–29.

Wayne County Regional Education Service Agency. (ca. 1993). *RTPIM: Readiness, planning, training, implementation, and maintenance.* Wayne, MI: Wayne County Regional Education Service Agency.

Wildman, T., & Niles, J. (1987). Essentials of professional growth. *Educational Leadership,* 44(5): 4–10.

Wood, F., Killian, J., McQuarrie, F., & Thompson, S. (1993). *How to organize a school-based staff development program.* Alexandria, VA: Association for Supervision and Curriculum Development.

Wood, S., & Leadbeater, P. (1986). Stages of entry for target groups participating in gifted program inservice and staff development. *Gifted Child Quarterly,* 30(3): 127–130.

Appendix

This Appendix contains activities, supplementary materials, and references for teachers to use in planning, implementing, and evaluating work for students. All these materials have been referred to in the text of the book.

A Dictionary of Eighty Ideas for Creative Products   249

Resources for Teaching Thinking Skills and Problem Solving   251
    General references for teachers   251
    Resources for student activities   251
    Catalogues for thinking skills and problem-solving materials   252

Cryptoquotes   253

Enrichment Opportunities at Your Fingertips   254
    Community enrichment   254
    School enrichment   255
    Summer academic experiences   255
    Individual or small-group work at home or in school   255
    References for information on enrichment   255
    References for further exploration—catalogues and directories   258

U.S. Trip Plan   259
    Instructions   259
    Daily Log   260
    Daily costs   261
    Gas costs   262
    Total costs   262

Survival Skills   263
    Survival quiz and answer key   263
    Project instructions sheet   265
    Survival kit   266
    Survival project: social studies challenge   266
    Survival project: book review   267
    Survival project: building a model shelter   267

Create a Country   269
    Project format   269

Argumentation 270
    Guide 270
    Worksheet 271
    Example student argument 1 272
    Example student argument 2 273

A Dictionary of Eighty Ideas for Creative Products

agendas—for meetings, for class discussion for a week; key items to include are time allotments, topics, and the sequence in which events occur

autobiographies—help students relate ideas at a personal level

biographies—of local, national, and international people; develop criteria

books, booklets—plan, write on computer, illustrate, distribute, evaluate; long-term or short-term projects; all subjects; also design **book jackets** related to content

brochures—all subjects; for events, travel, meetings, programs; wide variety; write, illustrate, try out with an audience, evaluate effectiveness

bulletin boards—should include mainly student-developed materials; all subjects

calendars—can refer to present, past and future; all subjects; persons, places, things

captions—for newspaper articles, literary pieces, radio and television commercials

cartoons—situational, serial, on any topic

casts—radio or television; news or "on-the-scene" for any situation; all subjects

character sketches—of literary figures, people they know, sports figures, and so on

clues—for all kinds of situations from mysteries to how to solve a math problem

codes—secret, everyday such as zip, telephone area codes, others; use computer

collages—can be adapted to any subject; artistic as well as informative

collections—from butterflies to bottle caps and everything in between; do something with the collection beyond just collecting—classify, explain, illustrate, evaluate

conversations—from realistic between the catcher and the pitcher to real or fictional characteristics from different eras in history to a conversation with yourself

costumes—past, present, and future; all subjects

court trials—real and fictional, past, present, and future; in United States and other countries

critiques—of own or peer work; current or past, written or verbal reports, situations

dance—repeat known forms; develop new ones; combines mental and physical areas

debates—design, participate, critique; all subjects

descriptions—from paragraphs to books; all subjects, all ages

dioramas—plan, build, evaluate; all subjects

directions—write them and have others follow them for a geographical location, a game, activity, learning skills, in sports and other areas; overlaps **rules**

dramatizations—of events, situations, fiction and nonfiction; overlaps **role-playing**

drawings—of common and uncommon situations and things; varied media

editorials—take a point of view and use data to back it up; applicable everywhere

encyclopedia entries—establish guidelines for these; implement and evaluate

evaluations—criteria are an important part of these; widely applicable

explanations—relate to situations, people's actions; fact and fiction

games—include directions, pieces to play with; three-dimensional; use computer

graphs—"a graph is worth 1,000 words;" use color, texture; overlaps **charts;** computer

guides, guidebooks—to people, places, things; all subjects, limitless possibilities

headlines—write them; find unusual, "wacky" ones and rewrite them; explain faults

illustrations—math, science, artistic, kinesthetic, other

interviews—have questions to ask; ask them, summarize answers, evaluate

inventions—all kinds in all subject areas; plan, invent, evaluate

invitations—for a variety of events, situations; real and fictional, past, present, future

itineraries—for trips, field trips; real and fictional; include times, sequence, events

journal entries—all subjects, all situations

keys—study bird and insects keys; develop keys for groups of living–nonliving things

letters, memos—write on paper, computer to people you know or don't know on variety of topics; be yourself or write as a past, present, or future person or character

log entries—keep a log or "diary" on a daily basis; be yourself or someone else

logos—write them for a variety of organizations, for items to sell, causes, and so on

menus—write them for different kinds of restaurants; ethnic and American food; include unusual food items, formats, artwork, and so on; write for nonfood items

models—can be iconic, analog, symbolic; relate to a variety of subject areas

monologues, dialogues—present, past, or future characters; excellent verbals

mosaics, murals—all subjects; combines art, information, and emotion

myths—realistic or unrealistic; relate to past, present, or future

newsletters—can be about your class, school, town, an organization, hobbies, etc.

newspapers—write many kinds of stories, sections, columns—a complex project

odes—can be written to anyone or anything; past, present, future

outlines—state goals in outline form; pay attention to sequence; all subject areas

pantomimes—can tell a story or imitate in a special way; all ages, all subject areas

photographs—all subjects; combines art, science, emotion, information

plays—write, act, evaluate; use for affective as well as cognitive messages; **skits**, too

poems, rhymes—write, read, act them out on a variety of subjects; all ages

programmed instruction—for computer; write it, have others try it out; evaluate

puns—write them on a variety of topics both serious and frivolous

puppets, puppet shows—excellent for verbal skills; all subjects, ages; artistic

puzzles—at all levels of difficulty on all subjects; they intrigue, motivate, and frustrate; crossword, cryptoquip or cryptoquote, other; write, try out, evaluate; all subjects

questions, questionnaires, answers—questions are more difficult than answers; pretend you are another person living now or in another era; give answers, ask others to formulate the question(s) to go with them; all subjects

recipes—write them not only for food, but for any situation or event; present, past, future; pay attention to quantity, order of items, directions for processing

reports—all subjects; organization, clarity, language, preciseness are important

research projects—allow for a wide variety of interests; plan, implement, evaluate

simulations—good group activities; useful for information, emotion, "how to do it"

slogans—write for a variety of things, places, situations

songs—combine poetry, storytelling, music of all types; past, present, future

stories—can feature people, places, things; any era, any age can write or tell them; can represent fact or fiction; unlimited possibilities

surveys—involve student interaction with peers, adults; any subject

tales—can be based on fact or fiction; can represent past, present, future; all ages

telegrams—every word counts, brevity emphasized; all subjects, personal, business

testimonials—relate to all subjects; can involve information or emotion, both

timelines—involve sequencing, past, present, future; relationship of events

tongue twisters—involve a special use of language; fun, motivating

travelogues, trips—can combine brochures, itineraries, descriptions; all subjects

videotapes—excellent combination of visual and audio; nearly all subjects; combines many other products within this one

weather predictions—write, present, evaluate; base predictions on data

Resources for Teaching Thinking Skills and Problem Solving

General References for Teachers

Beyer, B. (1988). *Developing a thinking skills program.* Boston: Allyn and Bacon.

Charles, R., & Lester, F. (1982). *Teaching problem solving: What, why & how.* Palo Alto, CA: Dale Seymour.

Collins, C., & Mangieri, J. (Eds.). (1992). *Teaching thinking: An agenda for the 21st century.* Hillsdale, NJ: Lawrence Erlbaum.

Costa, A. (Ed.). (1985). *Developing minds: A reference book for teaching thinking.* Alexandria, VA: Association for Supervision and Curriculum Development.

Davis, G. (1992). *Creativity is forever.* Dubuque, IA: Kendall-Hunt.

Davis, G. (1990). *The good person book: Creative teaching of values and moral thinking.* East Aurora, NY: D.O.K.

Eberle, B. (1984). *Help! In solving problems creatively at home and school.* Carthage, IL: Good Apple.

Isaksen, S., Dorval, K., & Treffinger, D. (1994). *Creative approaches to problem solving.* Dubuque, IA: Kendall/Hunt.

Krulik, S., & Rudnick, J. (1993). *Reasoning and problem solving: A handbook for elementary school teachers.* Boston: Allyn and Bacon.

Krulik, S., & Rudnick, J. (1988). *Problem solving: A handbook for teachers, grades 6–12.* Boston: Allyn and Bacon.

Kruse, J. (1989). *Resources for teaching thinking: A catalog.* Philadelphia: Research for Better Schools.

Lazear, D. (1991). *Seven ways of teaching: The artistry of teaching with multiple intelligences.* Palatine, IL: Skylight.

Marzano, R., Brandt, R., Hughes, S., Jones, B. F., Presseisen, B., Rankin, S., & Suhor, C. (1988). *Dimensions of thinking: A framework for curriculum and instruction.* Alexandria, VA: Association for Supervision and Curriculum Development.

Mayer, R. (1992). *Thinking, problem solving, cognition.* New York: W. H. Freeman.

Perrone, V. (Ed.). (1991). *Expanding student assessment.* Alexandria, VA: Association for Supervision and Curriculum Development.

Resnick, L., & Klopfer, L. (Eds.). (1989). *Toward the thinking curriculum: Current cognitive research.* Alexandria, VA: Association for Supervision and Curriculum Development.

Schurr, S. (1992). *The ABC's of evaluation: 26 alternative ways to assess student progress.* Columbus, OH: National Middle School Association.

Teaching for thinking. (1992). Reston, VA: National Association for Secondary School Principals.

Treffinger, D., Hohn, R., & Feldhusen, J. (1989). *Reach each you teach II: A handbook for teachers.* East Aurora, NY: D.O.K.

Wakefield, J. (1992). *Creative thinking: Problem solving skills and the arts orientation.* Norwood, NJ: Ablex.

Resources for Student Activities

Bartch, M., & Mallett, J. (1986). *Math motivators: Grades 1–3: Math motivators: Grades 4–6.* Glenview, IL: Scott Foresman.

Bellanca, J., & Robin Fogarty. (1986). *Catch them thinking: A handbook of classroom strategies.* Palatine, IL: Skylight.

Beyer, B. (1991). *Teaching thinking skills: A handbook for elementary school teachers.* Boston: Allyn and Bacon.

Beyer, B. (1991). *Teaching thinking skills: A handbook for secondary school teachers.* Boston: Allyn and Bacon.

Brown, L. (1990). *Think book: Visually-oriented problem-solving activities.* Nashville, TN: Incentive Publications.

Caney, S. (1985). *Invention book.* New York: Workman.

Chapin, L. (1990). *Leaping into literature: A guide to enhance your primary literature program.* Carthage, IL: Good Apple.

Claggett, F., & Brown, J. (1992). *Drawing your own conclusions.* Portsmouth, NH: Heinemann.

Cropley, A. (1992). *More ways than one: Fostering creativity.* Norwood, NJ: Ablex.

De Bruin, J. (1986). *Creative, hands-on science experiences.* Carthage, IL: Good Apple.

Eberle, B. (1985). *Warm-up to creativity: Word games to kindle divergent thinking.* Carthage, IL: Good Apple.

Feldhusen, J., & Treffinger, D. (1985). *Creative thinking and problem solving in gifted education.* Dubuque, IA: Kendall/Hunt.

Flack, J. (1990). *Mystery and detection: Thinking and problem solving with the sleuths.* Englewood, CO: Libraries Unlimited.

Flack, J. (1989). *Inventing, inventions, & inventors.* Englewood, CO: Libraries Unlimited.

Fleming, G. (1991). *Keys to creative writing: Activities to unlock imagination in the classroom.* Boston: Allyn and Bacon.

Fogarty, R. (1990). *Keep them thinking—Level II: A handbook of model lessons.* Palatine, IL: Skylight.

Frank, M. (1990). *202 science investigations: Exciting adventures in earth, life, and physical sciences.* Nashville, TN: Incentive Publications.

Kruse, J. (1988). *Classroom activities in thinking skills.* Philadelphia, PA: Research for Better Schools.

Nelson, L., & Lorbeer, G. (1985). *Science activities for elementary children.* Dubuque, IA: Wm. C. Brown.

Prizzi, E., & Hoffman, J. (1989). *Re: thinking: Lessons for critical and creative thinking skills.* Belmont, CA: Fearon.

Prutzman, P. (1988). *The friendly classroom for a small planet: A handbook on creative approaches to living and problem solving for children.* Philadelphia, PA: New Society Publishers.

Rasmussen, G. (1988). *Nifty fifty.* Stanwood, WA: Tin Man.

Sobel, M., & Maletsky, E. (1988). *Teaching mathematics; A sourcebook of aids, activities and strategies.* Englewood Cliffs, NJ: Prentice-Hall.

Spivak, D., & Blond, G. (1991). *Inventions and extensions: High-interest, creative thinking activities.* Nashville, TN: Incentive Publications.

Stanish, B. (1988). *Lessons from the hearthstone traveler.* Carthage, IL: Good Apple.

Stanish, B. (1990). *Mindanderings: Creative classroom approaches to thinking, writing and problem solving.* Carthage, IL: Good Apple.

Tiedt, I., Carlson, J., Howard, B., & Watanabe, K. (1989). *Teaching thinking in K–12 classrooms: Ideas, activities, and resources.* Boston: Allyn and Bacon.

Valentine, C. (1983). *Challenge boxes: 50 projects in creative thinking.* Palo Alto, CA: Dale Seymour.

Winebrenner, S. (1992). *Teaching gifted kids in the regular classroom.* Minneapolis, MN: Free Spirit.

Catalogues for Thinking Skills and Problem-Solving Materials

Computer Curriculum Corporation (Computer courseware in higher-order thinking, many subject matter areas, and investigation through interactive multimedia)
1287 Lawrence Station Road
Sunnyvale, CA 94089; (800) 227-8324

Creative Learning Press, Inc.
P.O. Box 320
Mansfield Center, CT 06250; no phone number listed

Creative Publications: K–12 Mathematics, Language Arts and Science
5040 West 111th Street
Oak Lawn, IL 60453; (800) 624-0822

Critical Thinking Press & Software K–12 (formerly *Midwest Publications*)
P.O. Box 448
Pacific Grove, CA 93950; (800) 458-4849

Dale Seymour Publications: K–8 Educational Materials
P.O. Box 10888
Palto Alto, CA 94303-0879; (800) 872-1100

Good Apple
1204 Buchanan St., P.O. Box 299
Carthage, IL 62321-0299; (800) 435-7234

Interact-Elementary Simulations
P.O. Box 997
Lakeside, CA 92040; (800) 359-0961

Teacher Ideas Press
Department S
P.O. Box 6633
Englewood, CO 80155-6633; (800) 237-6124

Thinking Works
P.O. Box 468
St. Augustine, FL 32085-0468; (800) 633-3742

Tom Snyder Productions . . . Educational Technology Catalog
80 Coolidge Hill Road
Watertown, MA 021712-2817; (800) 342-0236

Trillium Press
First Avenue
Unionville, NY 10988; (914) 726-4444

Zephyr Press
3316 N. Chapel Avenue
P.O. Box 66006-A
Tucson, AZ 85728-6006; (520) 322-5090

Cryptoquotes*

Directions

One letter is substituted for another as in the example below. The name of the author or source follows the quote.

Example: JEDW XTM ADXTRQD JEDW JEKMN JEDW XTM.—ZKVIKS

Answer: They can because they think they can.—Virgil

Quotes

Copy these onto another sheet of paper before you work them.

1. NPFTDI TI YFP RPJVPFS TFIRTJZSTYF ZFM FTFPSH-FTFP RPJVPFS RPJIRTJZSTYF.—SXYEZI Z. PMTIYF

2. WHEO NP ABD JXPA PDINXYP ABNVM NV ABD RXIHU. N REP WHEONVM RBDV N NVSDVADU ABD EZYE-HYVM, EVU N EJ PANHH WHEONVM.—KETZYDP TXYPADEY

3. ANNX HZSP MLDN VZ VQN KSFKQGFN LFU HZS DLFFZV KNN VQN KQLUZB.—QNONF ANOONP

4. LVSVM OWN CBB NAEE NCTCMMCQ QIZN PCW DZL FC NCFZP.—NICTZG HVBBVMGCL

5. TKZ VRQ JOTQ GRWC NRWVQCG NTV IR URC GRW; TKZ JOTQ GRW NTV IR URC GRWC NRWVQCG.—MROV U. ZXVVXIG

6. YKAF KD EIDG Q TVLY VA WCFPPKFD, TIG GCFPF LKYY TF HKGD!—FGZQ TVZTFWB

7. KDU BATIPKSZK KDBZO BG ZIK KI GKIT XRUGKBIZBZO.—SQFUPK UBZGKUBZ

Answers

1. Genius is 1 percent inspiration and 99 percent perspiration.—Thomas A. Edison

2. Play is the most serious thing in the world; I was playing when I invented the aqua-lung, and I am still playing.—Jacques Cousteau

3. Keep your face to the sunshine, and you cannot see the shadow.—Helen Keller

4. Never put off till tomorrow what you can do today.—Thomas Jefferson

5. Ask not what your country can do for you; ask what you can do for your country.—John F. Kennedy

6. Life is just a bowl of cherries, but there will be pits.—Erma Bombeck

7. The important thing is not to stop questioning.—Albert Einstein.

---

* These crypotoquotes were coded by Nathaniel Daw, Boulder, CO. Printed here with permission.

Enrichment Opportunities at Your Fingertips*

The ideas that "learning is a lifelong pursuit" and "learning can be and is fun" should be introduced to all students beginning in elementary school. Preschool play certainly includes many forms of learning, and to think that this type of learning stops when a formal education begins is truly a misconception. Indeed, "play with learning included" should continue throughout life. However, as children grow older, "playing" takes on different names. It can be membership in clubs and organizations, or games, or a hike through the woods. It can be learning new information or knowledge, and/or learning and refining new skills. All these are lifelong enrichment opportunities.

As educators and parents, we need to act as facilitators in providing enrichment opportunities for children. We can expose these young minds to many different kinds of stimuli: physical, mental, or a combination of both; and encourage both depth and breadth as well as variety. Enrichment can stimulate creativity, problem solving, and leadership, intellectual, and artistic abilities—or any wonderful combination! The interest of children will certainly vary depending on their age; physical, intellectual, and emotional maturity; gender; circle of friends; and probably time of day, week, month, and year. Enrichment opportunities will have to be adapted to these changing interests.

Often special activities in the schools are called "enrichment." True enrichment can only occur, though, when it is *appropriate* for any given student as well as in an area of interest. This means that the activity should offer a high level of challenge based on the student's ability. Similar to any school curriculum, if a student does not have the background skills and knowledge, the student may not benefit from the enrichment experience nor would it be viewed by the student as fun or interesting. A caution is necessary at this point: skill level and ability level need to be evaluated separately. Chess, for an example, is a game that takes much concentration and thought, but it also requires strategy skills that must be learned and practiced. This is an unsatisfying game for novices with no guidance or help.

Likewise, if a student has already succeeded in the enrichment experience and cannot improve or advance any more, the activity may or may not be viewed as fun or interesting. But it certainly would not be viewed as a challenge nor would it stimulate further learning. These activities certainly have their place, for we all like to continue to do things we do well. This is where adults can be the guide to entice the student into new areas of learning, challenge, and fun.

*Developed by Nancy Schuster, Educational Consultant, Wisconsin Center for Academically Talented Youth.

Enrichment activities never replace appropriate school curriculum for any student . . . the remedial, average, or accelerated learner!

This appendix provides ideas for pursuing enrichment activities that would work for students, K–12. This is a "brainstorm" list with some references to help you and your students find many ideas that may be of interest. Goals for enrichment are many, but certainly may include both short-term and long-term satisfaction. A skill or activity may be found that can be a meaningful part of the rest of a person's life!

The following categories for activities are community enrichment, school enrichment, summer academic experiences, individual or small group work, references on enrichment, and catalogues and directories. Many of the sources are annotated. Addresses, phone numbers, and contact people are listed for the reader's convenience wherever applicable.

Community Enrichment

The following list of resources can be found at least in part in most areas, both urban and rural. Once you begin to make inquiries in your community, you will most likely be able to add to this list. Many of these institutions and organizations also hold periodic workshops and classes on areas of interest for people of all ages.

Museums
Parks
YMCAs, YWCAs
Libraries
Universities and colleges
Technical colleges
Girl Scouts and Boy Scouts
4-H
Church groups
Other specialty clubs
    Chess
    Computers
    Crafts

Contests and opportunities are run by other local organizations as well. You can then contact them directly to inquire about their opportunities for youth. Your chamber of commerce will have a list of local service organizations. Some examples are

    Optimist International Oratorical Contest for children under 16 is annually run by local Optimist Clubs.
    Rotary Foreign Exchange brings students from all over the world to local communities and sponsors local students to live abroad.

School Enrichment

Your school may already have some of these activities. Often the obvious areas for enrichment are overlooked. Flexibility and creativity by educators and parents can continue to provide stimulating activities for students, often at low costs. (See the references following this listing for more ideas and contact information on the "*" items.)

    Academic Decathlon*
    American Express Geography Competition*
    Citizen Bee*
    Drama and play groups
    Forensics and debate
    Future Problem Solving*
    Invent America*
    Junior Great Books*
    Mathcounts*
    Mock Trial Tournaments*
    Music groups—jazz bands, swing choirs, ensembles, music competitions and contests
    National Geography Olympiad*
    Odyssey of the Mind*
    Science Olympiad*
    Sports—major school sports (both as spectator and participant), but also "scratch" games, open gym, and intramural. Noncompetitive sports should also be encouraged in the school such as bike riding, hiking, swimming, golf, ice and roller skating
    Student council
    Yearbook and school newspaper
    Young Astronaut Program*

Summer Academic Experiences

Many school districts, community organizations, technical colleges, and universities offer summer classes for students to stimulate interest in unique subjects and introduce them to new subjects and careers they may want to explore. A summer opportunity provides the setting for students to meet others with similar interests and abilities, thus increasing self-esteem as well as learning. Usually these classes are more "hands on" in nature. The experiential approach tends to excite the students and give them a taste for subjects they may study in depth at a later age. Some common subjects for classes are chemistry, rocketry, telescopes and astronomy, dinosaurs, different aspects of computers (e.g., Lego-Logo), storytelling and short-story writing, exploring your past (genealogy, history), exploring your community, and conversational foreign languages.

There are many directories listing other programs around the nation that offer summer academic enrichment and accelerative programming. Your library can be a good source to help you find programs. There are also some directories listed at the end of this appendix. Two examples of summer programming are

Science Summer Institute
University of Wisconsin-Eau Claire
Eau Claire, WI 54702-4004
715/836-5843
FAX: 715/836-6043

> A two-week summer residential *enrichment* program for high-potential students, ages 12–16, to explore one of twelve areas of science, such as astronomy, chemistry, physics, biology, HyperCard on the MacIntosh, supercomputer applications, aviation science, experimental psychology, veterinary medicine, environmental geology, action electronics, and advanced digital electronics.

WCATY Summer Program
Wisconsin Center for Academically Talented Youth
2909 Landmark Place
Madison, WI 53713
608/271-1617
FAX: 608/271-8080

> A three-week summer residential *accelerative* academic program for high-potential students, grades 7–10, that allows most students to complete the equivalent of one year of high school course work in such subjects as literature, writing, Japanese, geometry, self-paced mathematics, social studies, and computers.

Individual or Small-Group Work at Home or in School

An interesting (and enriching) activity for students might be to do their own research to find something that is of interest. This could be done in small groups, alone, or with an adult partner. Thumbing through the *Encyclopedia of Associations* in itself is very enlightening. One is amazed at the number and variety of existing groups—probably some in your own neighborhood!

Reminder: Most organizations and groups are formed in the true spirit of the description given. However, it is imperative that there be adult guidance and facilitation when exploring a new opportunity to assure a safe, healthy, and productive experience.

References for Information on Enrichment

Here are some ideas of books, guides, clubs, contests, career explorations and competitions to get started in providing ways of enrichment for your students. These resources offer opportunities for students of all levels of academic ability, but can particularly help to stimulate the gifted and talented students with challenge. Learning is truly an adventure ... enjoy the trek!

Academic Decathlon
P.O. Box 5169
Cerritos, CA 90703-5169
310/809-4995
FAX: 310/809-4441

> Teams of high school juniors and seniors composed of A, B, and C average students compete in ten content areas. Different themes are introduced each year.

American Express Geography Competition
800/395-GLOBE (ask for Atlas Map)
P.O. Box 672227
Marietta, GA 30067-9077

> Here is an opportunity for students across the nation, grades 6–12, to solve an authentic task using critical thinking, geography, and writing skills and submit the project for competition. Award money of $100,000 is distributed to winners.

The Citizen Bee
Bert Cieslak, Director-Educational Outreach
Close Up Foundation
44 Canal Center Plaza
Alexandria, VA 22314
703/706-3300

> This academic competition for high school students is based on American political and cultural history, government, geography, economics, and current events.

Computer Pals Across the World
C. Richard Turnbull
20902 Church Lake Dr.
Sumner, WA 20902
206/862-1240
internet:vwarner@equinox.unr.edu

> Join an international writing project that matches classrooms/groups in different countries to exchange ideas and information. (grade 5)

Daughters of the American Revolution History Essay Contest

> Information regarding this history essay contest for students in grades 5–8 are sent to public and parochial school principals each year. The deadline for submission of the essay based on the yearly theme is January 1.

Future Problem Solving Program
318 W. Ann St.
Ann Arbor, MI 48104
313/998-7377

> This competition challenges teams of students to write solutions to complex scientific and social problems of the future throughout the school year. Critiques and judging are held at state, national, and international levels, for grades 4–12. Problem-solving methods can be taught to entire classrooms.

International Society of Worldwide Stamp Collectors
Carol Cervenka, Secretary-Treasurer
Rt 1, Box 69A
Caddo Mills, TX 75135
903/527-3957

> Here is a group that promotes and encourages philately for all levels of interest. They offer assistance to young collectors, and, through the ISWSC Youth Stamp Program, provide worldwide stamps free-of-charge to interested youth groups. Services for sales, exchanges, identification, and translation are offered.

Invent America!
United States Patent Model Foundation
1505 Powhatan St.
Alexandria, VA 22314
703/684-1836

> For those with imagination, join an invention competition designed to spark the development of creativity and higher-level thinking skills. This national education program is for elementary school students.

JETS, Inc. (Junior Engineering Technical Society)
1420 King Street, Suite 405
Alexandria, VA 22314-2794
703/548-0769 or 703/836-4875

> This organization coordinates precollege engineering career guidance, sponsors competitions, and publishes *JETS Report* newsletter.

Junior Achievement
One Education Way
Colorado Springs, CO 80906
719/540-8000

> The business community works with students, grades K–12, to help students understand the business community of today, economics, and the free enterprise system.

Junior Great Books
The Great Books Foundation
35 E. Wacker Dr.
Chicago, IL 60601
800/222-5870
312/332-5870
FAX: 312/407-0334

> This program promotes discussion and understanding of stories and books through group discussion for grades K–12.

Mathcounts Foundation
Camy Griffin, Executive Director
National Society of Professional Engineers
1420 King St.
Alexandria, VA 22314
703/684-2828
E mail: 74603.3273@Compuserve.com

> Seventh- and eighth-grade students can compete in regional, state and national competitions each spring. It is a challenge for students to excel in math! Schools can also incorporate the materials into the regular curriculum for all students to benefit. Principals and math departments receive materials each year.

Mock Trial Tournament
Contact your State Bar of Lawyers or

Dee Runaas	Philip Newton
State Bar of Wisconsin	State Bar of Georgia
402 W. Wilson St.	50 Hurt Plaza 800
Madison, WI 53703	Atlanta, GA 30303
800/728-7788 or	800/334-6865
608/257-3838	

> For teams of students, grades 9–12, this competition is designed to develop and test critical thinking and public speaking skills while exposing students to the atmosphere of a real-life trial situation.

National Geographic Society
Educational Services Division
1145 17th St., N.W.
Washington, DC 20036
800/368-2728
202/857-7378

> Sponsors the National Geography Bee and has other information for teachers, described in a catalogue.

National Olympiads
P.O. Box 5477
Hauppauge, NY 11788-0121
516/265-4792

> Continental Mathematics League
> Current Events League (National Social Studies Olympiad)
> National Geography Olympiad
> National Language Arts Olympiad
> National Science Olympiad
> National Social Studies Olympiad

> Designed for elementary through high school students, teams compete in the desired curriculum area at their home school site. All of the Olympiads provide challenges in problem solving and analytical reasoning.

National "Written & Illustrated by . . ." Awards Contest for Students
Landmark Editions, Inc.
P.O. Box 4469
1402 Kansas Ave.
Kansas City, MO 64127
816/241-4919

> Here is an opportunity to compete in having a book published that was both written and illustrated by the same student (ages 6–19). For instructions and an application form, send a self-addressed, stamped envelope.

Odyssey of the Mind
OM Association
P.O. Box 547
Glassboro, NJ 08028
609/881-1603
FAX: 609/881-3596

> Teams in grades K–12 compete in long-term, hands-on problem solving and spontaneous problem solving. Students are judged on their originality, creativity, presentation style, and the success of their product. Other OM Enrichment Programs during the summer are also available.

Teen Association of Model Railroaders (TAMR)
c/o John Reichel
1800 E. 38th St.
Oakland, CA 94602-1720
510/482-8760

> This organization is for students interested in model railroading. They help teens plan, build and operate model railroads; promote fellowship; and conduct modeling and photography contests at an annual convention.

Westinghouse Science Talent Search
1719 N Street, N.W.
Washington, DC 20036
202/785-2255

> This is a scholarship competition for students in the last year of secondary school. Each student must submit a written report on an independent research project.

Young Astronaut Council
1308 19th St., N.W.
Washington, DC 20036
202/682-1984

> A national educational program for preschool, elementary, and junior high school students, it is designed to promote the study of science, mathemat-

ics, and related subjects. There is an electronic mail system and chapters can participate in essay, art, math, and science competitions, both locally and nationally.

Young Entomologists Society, Inc.
1915 Peggy Place
Lansing, MI 48910-2553
517/887-0499

The group promotes trading of insects and information, sponsors essays and competitions, offers educational materials, and produces a magazine.

Younger Scholars Program
Younger Scholars Guidelines
Room 316, Division of Fellowships and Seminars
National Endowment for the Humanities
1100 Pennsylvania Ave., N.W.
Washington, DC 20506
202/786-0463

Through this program, high school students can receive nine weeks of support of full-time work on independent projects in literature, history and other fields of the humanities.

References for Further Exploration, Catalogues and Directories

Some general publications are listed here that can help you find other possibilities for enrichment and challenge. Many of these publications may be at your local library, or your library may be able to obtain them for you as a reference. Also, check with your state department of education for any documents it may publish that describe summer opportunities for students. You will soon find that once you begin exploring, many potential opportunities will emerge. Keep your mind open and flexible in the quest for new adventure!

Advisory List of International Educational Travel and Exchange Programs, Council on Standards for International Educational Travel, 1906 Association Dr., Reston, VA 22091, 703/860-5317.

Directory of American Youth Organizations, Judith B. Erickson, Free Spirit Publishing, 1994, Minneapolis, MN 55401.

Directory of Student Science Training Programs for High Ability Pre-College Students, Science Service, 1719 N Street, N.W., Washington, DC 20036.

Educational Opportunity Guide, Talent Identification Program, Duke University, Box 40077, Durham, NC 27706-0077.

Educational Program Guide, Center for Talent Development, Northwestern University, 617 Dartmouth Place, Evanston, IL 60208-4175.

Encyclopedia of Associations, 29th Edition, Peggy Kneffel Daniels and Carol A. Schwartz, Editors, Gale Research, 1994, Detroit, MI 48226-4094.

Guide to Accredited Camps, the American Camping Association, Martinsville, IN 46151. Phone: 800/428-CAMP.

Guide to Summer Camps and Summer Schools, Porter Sargent Publishers, 11 Beacon St., Boston, MA 02108.

U.S. Trip Plan

Instructions

The basic idea of the trip plan is for you to plan a vacation that you would like to take within the United States. It can be a vacation planned for your family, yourself, or a vacation with friends. Once you have decided on the places you would like to visit, you will develop a plan to cover your routes, transportation, mileage, and expenses. The requirements for the trip plan are as follows:

- *Cover Sheet.* This should include a title, your name, your section number, and pictures or drawings of some of the places you plan to visit.
- *Map.* Using a small outline map of the United States, show the city of departure and all the cities and towns you plan to visit. Connect them to indicate your basic route of travel.
- *Places visited.* Part of your grade will be determined by the number of places you visit. You must visit ten places in order to receive full credit.
- *Daily log.* This record sheet will show your place of departure and destination, the routes traveled, mileage, and your approximate travel time for each day.
- *Daily cost chart.* This chart will show much you plan to spend each day on lodging, food and miscellaneous items.
- *Total cost chart.* This will help you compute the total cost of your trip, including what you will spend for fuel.
- *Points of interest.* You will choose three of the places you visit to feature with a written description and a picture or illustration.

Samples of all charts and a point of interest are posted on the bulletin board. Be sure to refer to them for clarification. Additional daily log sheets and daily cost charts can also be found in their respective folders on the bulletin board.

Your grade for this project will be determined by (1) the number of places visited, (2) the completeness and accuracy of your map and record sheets, (3) the quality of your written descriptions for points of interest, and (4) neatness and organization. Points will be awarded in analyzing the preceding elements as follows:

Cover sheet: 2 points
Map: 3 points
Number of places visited: 1 point each; 10 points maximum
Daily log: 20 points
Daily cost chart: 20 points
Total cost chart: 10 points
Points of interest: 10 points each; 30 points maximum
Neatness and organization: 5 points
TOTAL POSSIBLE POINTS: 100

Source: Adapted from materials developed by John Kaiser & John Sabatini, Hamilton Middle School, Madison, Wisconsin. Reprinted with permission.

Daily Log

Day	Place of Departure and Destination	Routes and Directions Traveled	Mileage	Travel Time

Sample Daily Log

Day	Place of Departure and Destination	Routes and Directions Traveled	Mileage	Travel Time
1	Madison, WI, to Chicago, IL	I-90, SE	150 mi.	2 1/2 hr.
2–3	Stay in Chicago	—	—	—
4	Chicago, IL, to St. Louis, MO	I-55, SW	300 mi.	5 hr.
5	Stay in St. Louis	—	—	—
6	St. Louis, MO, to Kansas City, MO	I-70, W	245 mi.	4 1/2 hr.
7	Kansas City, MO, to Denver, CO	I-70, W	616 mi.	11 hr.
8–10	Stay in Denver	—	—	—
11	Denver, CO, to Medicine Bow, WY	I-25, N I-80, NW Rte. 30, NW	200 mi.	4 hr.
12	Medicine Bow, WY to Salt Lake City, UT	Rt. 287, SW I-80, SW	350 mi.	6 hr.

NOTE: To allow for more room to record information, the daily log should be printed across the length of the paper.

Source: Adapted from materials developed by John Kaiser & John Sabatini, Madison, Wisconsin. Reprinted with permission.

Daily Costs

Day	Lodging		Meals		Miscellaneous	
	Name of Motel or Campground	Fee	Place & Cost	Total Cost	Item & Cost	Total Cost

Sample Daily Costs

Day	Lodging		Meals		Miscellaneous	
	Name of Motel or Campground	Fee	Place & Cost	Total Cost	Item & Cost	Total Cost
1	Palmer House (2 rooms)	$180	B-McDonald's ($15) L-hotel café ($30) D-Trader Vics ($150)	$195	Theater ($100) Snacks ($10)	$110
2	Palmer House (2 rooms)	$180	B-Wendy's ($20) L-Field's ($25) D-Benihana's ($180)	$225	Shopping ($500) Souvenirs ($35) Car rental ($75)	$610
3	Palmer House (2 rooms)	$180	B-hotel café ($35) L-museum ($30) D-hotel ($120)	$185	Museums ($15) Souvenirs ($25) Bus tickets ($10)	$50
4	Hilton (2 rooms)	$200	B-hotel ($25) L-Bergman's ($40) D-McDonald's ($30)	$95	Snacks ($15) Map ($2) Movie ($15)	$32
5	Hilton (2 rooms)	$200	B-hotel ($30) L-Carson's ($50) D-Top of Hilton ($230)	$310	Arch tickets ($25) Shopping ($200)	$225
6	Day's End	$90	B-McDonald's ($25) L-Mall food court ($20) D-The Ritz ($115)	$160	Umbrellas ($45) Puzzle books ($20) Video games ($50)	$115

NOTE: To allow for more room to record information, the daily log should be printed across the length of the paper.

Source: Adapted from materials developed by John Kaiser & John Sabatini, Madison, Wisconsin. Reprinted with permission.

How to Calculate Gas Costs

1. Estimate the miles per gallon your vehicle will use. For example,

   - Corvette—20 miles per gallon
   - Compact car—40 miles per gallon
   - Motor home—6 miles per gallon
   - Motorcycle—70 miles per gallon
   - Large van—18 miles per gallon
   - Truck with camper top—12 miles per gallon
   - Camper van—12 miles per gallon

2. Compute the total number of miles you travel in your vehicle.
3. Divide the total miles driven by the miles per gallon to see how many gallons of gas you will need.
4. Multiply the number of gallons you will use by the cost of one gallon of gas to find your total cost for gas.

Example

1. Compact car = 40 miles per gallon
2. Total number of miles traveled = 2,000
3. 2000 ÷ 40 = 50 gallons of gas needed
4. 50 × $1.50 per gallon = $75 total cost for gas

Total Costs

Total Lodging Expenses	$ _____
Total Meal Expenses	$ _____
Total Miscellaneous Expenses	$ _____

Gasoline Expenses (*see* How to Calculate Gas Costs)

　Type of vehicle _____

　Miles per gallon _____

　Cost of gas per gallon $ _____

　Total mileage _____

　Total mileage divided

　　by miles per gallon = _____ gallons

　Gallons used multiplied

　　by price per gallon = Total Gasoline Expenses　　$ _____

Total Trip Expenses　　$ _____

Source: Adapted from materials developed by John Kaiser & John Sabatini Hamilton Middle School, Madison, Wisconsin. Reprinted with permission.

Survival Skills

Survival Quiz and Answer Key*

Below are 35 questions. Knowing the answer to these questions could some day be the difference between a good time or a miserable time, or the difference between life and death. If you score a perfect 35, you will make the All American Survival Team. If you score in the thirties, you may consider yourself an expert. Twenty correct means you are an average outdoors person. If you score less than 15, you'd better stay behind and do the cooking!

1. **In any season, the main dangers when lost in the woods are dying of thirst or starvation.** FALSE. Exposure can kill you far more quickly. A person in good condition to begin with can, under favorable conditions, last up to about a week without water, a month or more without food, but no more than a few hours in severe weather unless he takes positive precautions against it.

2. **Smooth rocks from a nearby stream are fine for building a fireplace.** FALSE. Entrapped moisture often causes stream rocks to burst and splinter dangerously.

3. **It's all right, as long as the weather is clear, to camp in a ravine or stream bed.** FALSE. A sudden storm far from you could wash you out even though the immediate weather, offering no warning, continued fair.

4. **In cold, damp climates, wool clothing provides the best protection against the elements.** TRUE. Wool affords far better protection than other materials.

5. **In the desert, if you keep your head and body covered during the day, you'll survive longer on less water.** TRUE. If you can, wear long trousers and shirts with the sleeves rolled down. Keep them loose and flapping to stay cooler.

7. **Snow is such an excellent insulator that it's all right to sit or even sleep directly on it.** FALSE. Snow is then too prone to melt, and wet clothing, susceptible to freezing and so difficult to dry in cold weather, is one of the major dangers in snow country under survival conditions. Use even as slight a substance as a thin sheet of plastic, or perhaps a strip of bark between the body and snow.

8. **Dry cattails, available autumns and winters, as well as spring in many localities, make good tinder.** TRUE. So does a handful of extremely dry evergreen needles, especially if they have been rubbed and broken together. So will a part of a tree that has dry-rotted and can be powdered.

9. **If your feet are cold, put on your hat.** TRUE. Because the head has such an abundant blood supply, and because it is the only part of the body where this flow is not reduced in frigid weather to conserve warmth for the vital organs, it is the major radiator for excess body heat. If you want to shunt this heat down to your feet, you must make certain it is not lost through the head.

10. **Three closely fitting pairs of good woolen socis are warmer than two loose fitted pairs.** FALSE. Aside from the fact that the feet's already poor circulation is further impeded by such a tight fit, the resulting compression of the wool fibers cuts down on the insulative dead-air spaces.

11. **A good way to dry damp clothing is to take it into your sleeping bag at night.** FALSE. A great part of the dissipated moisture is eventually absorbed by the bedding itself, both increasing its weight and decreasing its warmth.

12. **There are many occasions when sitting out an emergency is preferable to trying to make it out on your own.** VERY TRUE. You may in fact worsen your situation by trying to make it out. You may become lost or disoriented and/or be more likely to suffer from hypothermia in the cold or heat exhaustion in the summer.

13. **The general rule for survival when water is not available or is in short supply is to eat nothing.** TRUE. Even fish juices contain a high amount of protein, to the point that more water is required to digest them than is derived from the juices.

14. **If you are unaccustomed to desert travel, a rule of thumb is to multiply your estimate of distance by three.** TRUE. Otherwise both the clear dry air and the absence of land features are apt to make underestimation likely.

15. **Water can be boiled directly in vessels made of bark or leaves.** TRUE, although such containers will burn above water level unless they are kept moist or the fire is held low.

16. **Anyone caught in a snowslide has a good chance of surviving it.** TRUE. Especially if you can keep on top of the swirling, billowing, sweeping avalanche. One way to accomplish this is by swimming. The backstroke, particularly effective if you can manage it, has saved many lives in such emergencies.

17. **The sound of birds chirping in a semiarid brush country often means that water is at hand.** TRUE. And in dry deserts, flocks of birds will often circle near a water hole. Places where animals have scratched

or where flies are hovering indicate recent surface water and are good places to dig.

18. **Never fall asleep outdoors in subzero temperatures, or you're likely never to awaken.** FALSE. The best thing to do on an extremely frosty night, unless of course you can build fire and shelter, is to find as protected a spot as you can, curl up on something dry, even though it be nothing better than evergreen boughs, and go to sleep. When you get too cold, you'll arouse, stir around just enough to get warm, and then go back to sleep if you can, or at least relax again. The weaker one becomes by keeping going, the less he or she will be able to resist the environment.

19. **A police whistle is a good survival tool.** TRUE. Some camping mothers tie whistles around the necks of their youngsters, who are instructed to blow them if they ever find themselves strayed or otherwise in trouble. All in all, a whistle can be useful for juvenile and adult alike for attracting attention, keeping a group together, transmitting messages, and for other uses when it will serve better than a shout.

20. **Any survival kit should include writing paper and at least a pencil.** TRUE. When you quit a survival camp, you should leave behind, for possible would-be rescuers, a written record of who you are, where you have been, and in which direction you are headed.

21. **You can't find your bearings at night after the sun has gone down.** FALSE. In the Northern Hemisphere, you can locate the North Star by sighting along the two stars on the lowest side of the Big Dipper. The North Star can also be found by drawing an imaginary line from the center star of the constellation Cassiopeia (made up of five stars) and the innermost of the two stars on the handle of the Big Dipper; the North Star will be about midway between them. In the Southern Hemisphere, you can find south by sighting along the long axis of the Southern Cross.

22. **To avoid being struck by lightning, the best thing to do is to stand under a tree.** FALSE. To avoid being struck by lightning, you should stay away from the highest point in the area. Try to find a low valley or a cave, but don't stand next to a tree, especially if it's the only tree in a field or meadow. Don't stand out in the open so that you are the highest point in the area, and remember not to touch anything metallic.

23. **Three of anything—three sounds or three articles arranged in a row—is a universally recognized distress signal.** TRUE. Three gunshots or whistle blasts, or a trail of three stones on the ground may lead rescuers to you. Presumably this is a variation of the traditional SOS signal—three dots, three dashes, three dots.

24. **If you are lost, you can find your way by following a stream.** TRUE. Following a stream is usually a good bet. As soon as you realize you are lost, you should stop, sit down, relax, and try to remember landmarks that you have passed. Then climb a tree or a hill and look for some of these landmarks; see if you can figure out where you are. The most important thing to remember is not to panic; you probably are not very far from civilization.

25. **You have a better chance of finding food near a body of water.** TRUE. Fish are difficult to catch with makeshift equipment (or even with good fishing equipment), but frogs, snails, crabs, clams, shrimp, crayfish, salamanders, turtles, and insects are easier to snare.

26. **Since some plants are poisonous, it's best never to eat any when you're in the wilderness.** FALSE. Plants are a good source of food if you know which ones to avoid. There are 300,000 species of plants in the world, of which 120,000 are edible. Learn to recognize poison ivy, poison oak, and poison sumac. If you're really desperate and you're in doubt as to whether a particular plant is edible, try a small amount and wait several hours. Then try a little more and wait for at least five or six hours. If there are no ill effects, the plant is probably OK. This method should only be used when there are no other food sources available.

27. **Salt water may not taste very good, but you can drink it if you have no other water.** FALSE. Never drink salt water. Because its salt concentration is so high, body fluids must be drawn off to eliminate it. This will eventually cause the kidneys to cease functioning.

28. **You can become sunburned or dehydrated even in the winter.** TRUE. Snow reflects sunlight even on cloudy days, and you can become dehydrated at any time if you don't drink enough water. The average adult needs about two quarts a day.

29. **It is possible to die of the cold at temperatures in the forties.** TRUE. The effects of cold are multiplied by wind chill, especially when one is in the rain or is wearing wet clothing.

30. **If you think you may be frostbitten, you should rub snow on the affected parts.** FALSE. Never apply snow to a frostbitten area. Try to warm the affected part by immersing in lukewarm water or by holding a warm hand on it, but do not rub the affected part.

31. **Most cases of snow blindness recover within 18 hours without medical treatment.** TRUE. Incidentally, the symptoms of so-called snow blindness, when you're not actually blind even if only temporarily, are redness, burning, watery or sandy-feeling eyes, the halo one ordinarily sees when looking at lights, and poor vision.

32. **If you are lost in the tropics, it will be all right to sleep on the ground.** FALSE. Never sleep on the ground, perhaps populated with ants, scorpions, leeches, spiders and other such critters. A reasonable bed can be contrived by covering a pile of brush with layers of palm fronds or other broad leaves.

33. **If you are bitten by a poisonous snake, the best method of treatment is making a cut in the skin over each fang mark and sucking out the poison.** TRUE. Commercial snakebite kits are sold for this purpose, or you can use a pocket knife and suck out the poison with your mouth. You should also apply pressure (but not a tourniquet) on the limb at a point two to four inches closer to the heart than the bite. If possible, immobilize the affected part; moving it will spread the poison. For more information on what to do in the event of a snakebite, contact your local chapter of the American Red Cross.

34. **One should never eat insects because they carry disease.** FALSE. Insects are a good source of protein. However, some of them do contain disease-causing parasites, so cook all insects before you eat them.

35. **A cold person trying to survive can keep warmer by buttoning something such as evergreen tips, dry leaves, or thick dry moss inside their shirt.** TRUE. Convective insulation depends not on the material used, but on the thickness of the dead air.

*This quiz has been a part of the survival skills materials developed by John Kaiser and John Sabatini for many years. They and other teachers have changed its content from time to time. Original source of quiz is unknown.

Project Instructions Sheet

Name _____

Project Due Date _____

Choose one or more projects from the following list. Your grade will be determined by the number of projects you complete and the quality of your work. The following will be used as a guideline to determine your grade:

A = 2 projects of excellent quality plus survival kit
B = 2 projects of good quality plus survival kit
C = 1 project of satisfactory quality plus survival kit
D = 1 project of poor quality, no survival kit
F = Survival kit only; no project

See the "Survival Kit" instruction sheet

Project Choices. Detailed instructions for these options can be found on the survival bulletin board.

1. Keep a survival log for a minimum of 5 days. Be sure to carefully follow all instructions on the sheet entitled "Social Studies Challenge."

2. Read a survival novel and complete a book review sheet. See the list of recommended survival books for ideas. You may also read a survival novel that is not on the list. The book review sheet can be found on the survival bulletin board.

3. Make a booklet that contains the drawings of 10 wildflowers that would be useful for you to identify in a survival situation. Include details of leaf and flower. Tell what habitat the plant prefers. Tell why identification would be useful.

4. Make a booklet that contains the drawings of 10 trees and/or shrubs that would be useful for you to identify in a survival situation. On the drawings include details about leaf and bark, as well as any particularly helpful identifying characteristics. Describe the habitat and tell why identification would be useful.

5. Make a booklet on survival. Include information such as how to build a fire, how to build a shelter, how to build a signal fire, how to find or trap food, first aid tips, etc. Include some illustrations.

The following projects may be used only as a second choice toward a B or A. If you have an alternative project idea, you must have it approved by your teacher.

6. Build a scaled-down model of a lean-to, A-frame and/or wickiup shelter and display it. See the instruction sheet entitled "Building a Model Shelter."

7. Give a 5-minute presentation of an actual survival situation that was personal or one a friend experienced. Emphasize the actions taken to survive.

8. Give a 5-minute presentation of a skill that you have that relates to survival (hiking, first aid, etc.).

9. Make a survival comic book. This should be a teaching comic book, and your story line should focus on a survival situation and the techniques used to survive.

10. Write a children's story that incorporates lessons on survival. Read it to a younger child and write a paragraph about your experience. Note the child's opinion or the story and what he or she learned.

Source: Adapted from materials developed by John Kaiser & John Sabatini, Hamilton Middle School, Madison, Wisconsin. Reprinted with permission.

Survival Kit

Your survival kit should be designed to help you acquire the necessities of life during an emergency by providing **instant internal warmth, instant body protection,** and **instant energy.** When making your kit, look for things around the house that would help you achieve these three qualities. Although you would normally want to include them, the following items should **not** be brought to school in your survival kit, even though they are mentioned: matches, razor blades, or pocket knife. These and similar items are considered to be dangerous, as they could be used as weapons or to destroy property. Bringing them to school could result in expulsion. Therefore, leave them out of your survival kit until you have your kit back at home after the unit is over.

Instant Internal Warmth. The inner body must be at or near optimum temperature (98.6°F) for living cells to produce the energy to sustain life. The following items should be included:

- *Can*—an empty coffee can with a plastic lid works best. It can serve as the container for your other survival items. Seal the lid with several wraps of electrical tape. This metal can can be emptied and used to heat water over the fire.

- *Candle*—a large candle will help kindle a fire or heat small cans of water.

- *Matches*—strike anywhere matches work best and would be used to light the candle or start a fire. Put them in a plastic self-sealing bag or a waterproof tin, or waterproof the matches yourself by coating the tips in wax.

Instant Body Protection. Keeping dry will help you retain the vital topical air layer around your body and lessen the transfer of warm air with cold air. Staying dry also helps to conserve your limited energy supply. Include the following items for this purpose:

- *Leaf bag(s)*—a 7-bushel size fits a 6-foot man. Cut a hole in the sealed end for a face or head opening. Cover the head if possible.

- *Garbage bag(s)*—the 30-gallon size works well. Pull them up over your legs and tuck them in your pockets to protect yourself from wind and rain. These bags can also be used for shade from the sun.

Instant Energy. Sugar is what the muscles use to produce heat to keep the body at the nearly constant 98.6°F. You will have a given amount of energy at the time of your emergency. It can be conserved to last a long time, or it can be used up very quickly—the choice is yours alone.

- *Sugar*—6 to 12 sugar cubes will give instant energy needed to move muscles for heat protection. Wrap them in plastic. You might also include candy bars and/or some other high-energy snack (trail mix, granola bars, etc.). Nonperishable items will last longest.

If you cannot obtain a coffee can with lid for your survival kit, virtually any type of container will do. For example, students have used shoe boxes, plastic ice cream containers, cookie tins, small backpacks, and the like. In this case, since the container cannot be used over a fire, consider placing an empty soup or vegetable can inside your survival kit to heat water.

Here are some other items that will add to your survival kit. Include as many as you can:

Band Aids/first aid dressings	Bandanna (for a sling)
Bouillon cubes	Salt packets for flavoring
Nylon fish line and hooks	Cord or rope
	Needles and thread
	Tea bags
Small mirror for signaling	Pencil and paper
	Flint and steel
Space blanket	Quarter(s) for phone
Antiseptic	Whistle
Wire	Hand warmers
Deck of cards	

Include any other items you feel would come in handy in a survival situation. You don't need to go out and buy things for your kit unless you choose to do so. Most students assemble excellent survival kits by using what they have on hand around the house. Use your survival expertise and your creativity!

Source: Adapted from materials developed by John Kaiser & John Sabatini, Hamilton Middle School, Madison, Wisconsin. Reprinted with permission.

Survival Project: Social Studies Challenge

Many times we take our survival for granted. We assume that our basic needs for survival (food, shelter and clothing) will be met. Our lifestyle, complete with homes, supermarkets and cars, demands little effort from us to survive. But what if you were put in an situation where you would have to use your knowledge of that environment and your resourcefulness to survive? Could you do it? This assignment is designed to see if you can. For this project you will write a creative story whereby for some reason you have been stranded in an uninhabited area of the world. Your story should be a day-by-day account of your experiences in trying to survive. You must include the following:

1. **Tell how you became stranded.**
   Was it a plane crash, mountain-climbing accident, or shipwreck? Did you become lost somehow on a hiking trip? Any other incident that has caused you to be put in a survival situation is also acceptable.

2. **Tell where you are stranded.**
   Remember, it must be an **uninhabited** part of the world. Some suggestions include Siberia; the North or South Pole; Greenland; any desert or dry area such as the Sahara, Kalahari, Gobi, or Mohave; any of the seas or oceans; a jungle area along the Amazon; or the tropical rain forest of Africa.

3. **Assume you only have following 3 possessions:**
   - A pocket knife
   - A book of matches
   - 3 gallons of water.

4. **Describe the surrounding landscape or terrain.**
   To tell the story accurately, you should find a good source of information on the place you are going to be stranded. *This means you will have to identify the climate, landforms, vegetation, animals, and* **natural resources** *of the area.* Be sure to include the natural features of your chosen area.
   - **Identify and describe 3 specific plants and 3 specific animals found there.**

5. **Tell how you meet the basic needs of food, shelter and clothing.**
   The food you eat, the shelter you construct and the clothing you wear must come from the environment in which you have been isolated.
   - **Identify the materials you use for your shelter and describe how you build it.**
   - **Describe the source and methods of gathering food and water.**
   - **Describe ways in which you improvise using the available resources.**

6. **Describe the mental aspects of survival.**
   For example, you might tell how you deal with panic, boredom, thoughts of family, lack of food, or hope for rescue.

7. **Describe efforts to aid in your rescue.**
   What do you do to enhance the possibility of being rescued? Do you build a signal fire? Use a whistle? Signal with a mirror? Etc.

8. **Add some illustrations to your log.**
   For example, you might include maps and/or drawings of wildlife, vegetation, your shelter, etc.

9. **The length of your survival log should be 5–8 days.**
   Use your imagination in your account of your experience. **Describe** not only what you see, but what actions you take to survive. Be sure to tell if you do survive!

10. **Your survival log should have a cover sheet with the title, your name, and the date.**

Source: John Kaiser & John Sabatini, Hamilton Middle School, Madison, Wisconsin. Reprinted with permission.

Survival Project: Book Review

Title of Novel: _____

Author: _____

Number of Pages: _____

1. Describe the cause(s) of the survival situation.

2. What are some of the personal traits or characteristics that helped the victim(s) survive? List the trait. Then describe an incident in the book that illustrates how each characteristic enhanced an individual's survival. List at least three traits and examples.

3. What personal traits interferred with a character's chances for survival? List at least two traits and tell how each hindered survival with a specific example from the book.

4. How did the character(s) improvise with the resources at hand in order to survive? Give at least two examples.

5. Describe what the character(s) did to increase the chances of their rescue.

6. Had you been in the same survival situation, what would you have done differently and why?

7. Give your overall opinion of this book. Justify your response by telling why you feel as you do.

Source: John Kaiser & John Sabatini, Hamilton Middle School, Madison, Wisconsin. Reprinted with permission.

Survival Project: Building a Model Shelter

1. Select the type of shelter to be made. Research to find out the following:
   - Materials used
   - Methods of construction
   - Appropriate places for this type of shelter
   - The advantages of this type of shelter

2. Construct the model on a base made of plywood or other study material. Paint or decorate the base to simulate an outdoor scene. If possible, show the various stages of construction.

3. On the base, include a notecard or piece of paper that (a) explains the materials required and (b) outlines the steps to take in making the shelter.

4. Present the model to the class. In your presentation tell us the type of shelter, materials you used in making the model, materials you would use if actually constructing the shelter, the procedure for constructing it, and situations in which this shelter would be appropriate.

Source: John Kaiser & John Sabatini, Hamilton Middle School, Madison, Wisconsin. Reprinted with permission.

Create a Country

Project Format

Cover Sheet. This must include (1) the name of your country, (2) your name, (3) the date, and (4) your class period. You may also include drawings related to your country, but that is optional.

Written Report of Your Country. Your report will be a written description of all the features of your country. Your paper should be organized in the order described below. Each section should be labeled and should ***explain*** (**not merely list) the items indicated.** Use the checklist to help make sure you include all of the required elements.

1. *Location/size:* Introduce your country by telling its name, the continent it is on or a part of, its latitude and longitude, bordering countries, square miles, relative size, population, capital and other important cities.

2. *Physical geography:* Name and describe your landforms, major rivers, lakes and seas, climate, and vegetation.

3. *History/government:* Explain how your country came to be, who settled it, significant wars or conflicts, your type of government, your country's leaders, etc.

4. *Economic geography:* Tell about everyday life in your country. Identify language(s) spoken, traditional foods, recreational activities, the education system, and major religion(s). Describe the traditions and holidays that exist. Tell about some of the famous places that your country is noted for.

Maps. The specific requirements for each map are attached. Each map must have a *title,* a *key,* and a *scale.*

Required Maps

1. Physical or political
2. Density of population
3. Rainfall and temperature
4. Vegetation

Your atlas features a variety of these types of maps. Use them as a guide for creating yours. When you make one map with your lines of latitude and longitude drawn and labeled, the teacher will make copies for you to use for your other maps.

Optional Maps for Extra Credit

1. Environments
2. Highways
3. Economic
4. Other (your choice)

See your teacher for instructions should you decide to do an extra credit map.

Other Extra Credit Options

1. Design a flag for your country with a written description of what it stands for.
2. Design a travel brochure for your country.
3. Design a travel poster for your country.

Argumentation

Guide

Lead: Get your audience's attention and introduce your topic.

Claim: Make a claim that something ought to be done or not done.

Supports: Give as many kinds of evidence and as strong evidence as possible to "prove" your claim. Possible types of evidence include

- What has happened in the past
- What is likely to happen in the future
- What the experts say
- Specific data (statistics, survey results, etc.)
- Personal experience

Add details to your supports to make your argument as convincing as possible.

Warrants: Show *how* your support proves your claim. For instance,

- *Claim:* Students should be able to chew gum in school
- *Support:* Chewing sugarless gum after lunch can actually help reduce cavities.
- *Warrant:* Research has shown that chewing sugarless gum after meals when you can't brush helps reduce the plaque that leads to tooth decay.

Concessions: If your argument has a weakness, admit it. Then the opposition can't use it against you.

Objection(s): Point out objections to your argument that opponents might raise.

Rebuttals: A rebuttal might include

- Denying the ideas behind the objection
- Previously ignored information
- Redefining basic terms
- Interpreting the evidence in a new way
- Quoting an authority who contradicts the opposition's authority
- Exposing the prejudice of the opponent's argument

Reaffirm Claim: Restate your claim in a different way.

Clincher: Leave the audience with something to remember. Make the presentation feel finished.

Source: L. Hamann & L. Schultz, *Argumentation Guide* (Madison, WI: Global Process Communication). Reprinted with permission.

Worksheet

Introduction

Lead (introduce the topic and get the audience's attention)

Claim (state your position on the topic)

_____

Body

1st Support: (give evidence for your claim; why do you feel this way?)
Warrant: (give proof for your support; what makes you so sure?)

_____

2nd Support:
Warrant:

_____

3rd Support:
Warrant:

_____

4th Support:
Warrant:

_____

Concessions: (admit the weaknesses of your argument)

_____

Objections: (give the arguments against your claim)	*Rebuttals:* (defend your claim against each objection)

_____

_____

_____

_____

Conclusion

Reaffirm Claim: (restate your claim)

Clincher: (leave the audience with something memorable)

Source: Adapted from L. Hamann & L. Schultz, *Language Arts Workshops Forms Manual,* (Madison, WI: Global Process Communication). Reprinted with permission.

Example Student Argument 1

Lead: "Barbie and the Rockers" tape plays.

Claim: Too many toys promote stereotypical ideas among children.

1st Support: First of all, Barbie is one of the most popular among sexist toys.

Warrant: She makes young girls feel unattractive because they lack such features as slim waists, curvacious figures, and blonde hair, thus lowering their self-esteem.

2nd Support: Secondly, Ken and He-man are the male versions of Barbie.

Warrant: They create an image of the "perfect man" as being muscular and nearly invincible. Most boys do not meet those stereotypes and may become emotionally scarred because of this.

3rd Support: Also, we might point out that Little Tyke and other kitchen toys may add to the idea that cooking and cleaning are women's work.

Warrant: The reason we feel this way is because most, if not all of the advertisements show little girls cooking away. They do sometimes have boys in the commercials, but the boys are generally eating, not cooking.

4th Support: Lastly, look at Ninja Turtles. The TV show and figurines help to create and develop the image of women being helpless without men.

Warrant: For instance, have you ever noticed how April O'Neill tries to help in saving the city, but almost always manages to become a prisoner of the enemy? Then the all male turtles appear to save April and New York City from destruction. Basically, they are suggesting that a woman can try, but not succeed in a difficult situation.

Concession: We admit that these statements are not necessarily reasons to abandon the products. However, we do feel a change is in order.

1st Objection: Now, if you were a parent, you might point out that these toys are all the rage, and that denying this pleasure to your children would be too difficult.

Rebuttal: But perhaps to contradict the possible negative effects of these toys, a discussion about positive self-image with your children would help.

2nd Objection: Many of you might say you have played with these toys for years yourself, yet you have not felt any negative effects.

Rebuttal: But possibly, in your subconscious, or at least in our society's general mind-sets, these toys *do* add to certain stereotypical beliefs.

3rd Objection: Manufacturers may be angered and call these views radical and illogical because they might lose valuable profits they could be making from the sale of these toys.

Rebuttal: But what these companies don't realize is that they could be making even more profits off the sale of positively influential merchandise.

4th Objection: Finally, some may argue that these toys are positive role models; that they represent feminity and beauty among girls, and toughness and masculinity among boys.

Rebuttal: But these are untrue, sexist views and do not allow people to be themselves.

Claim Reaffirmed: In general, we feel many toys on the market add to the stereotypical views of our society and wrongly influence young children.

Clincher: So say bye bye to Barbie (throw her in the garbage can). Play music again and fade out.

Example Student Argument 2

Lead: Tropical music plays in the background. Students have their backs to the audience. They say in unison, "The rain forest." Then they turn one by one, showing a sign and saying the word that's printed on it: THE TROPICAL RAIN FOREST. Music fades out.

Claim: We need to preserve the rain forests of the world.

1st Support: First of all, there may be undiscovered medical cures within the tropical rain forests.

Warrant: Many cures that we have now have come from the rain forest. If we cut the forests down, we may never discover possible cures for other serious illnesses, such as AIDS.

2nd Support: Secondly, the massive group of trees in the rain forests provide an abundant supply of oxygen.

Warrant: It's been scientifically proven that trees take in carbon dioxide and give off oxygen for us to breathe. Without this oxygen, we may suffer in ways we can't even imagine.

3rd Support: Also, many unique species of animals that live in the rain forest will not be able to survive if we don't do something soon to stop the destruction.

Warrant: Most of the world's species of animals live in the rain forests of the world. If we ruin their habitat, the animals will not be able to survive in the harsh conditions and will become extinct.

4th Support: Finally, we need the trees of the tropical rain forest because they act as a giant sponge for rain.

Warrant: If we cut down the trees, the rain water will hit the ground directly with more force, causing severe erosion and flooding.

Concession: We admit that there is a great demand for farmland to grow food and raise cattle. By cutting down the rain forest, land becomes easily accessible to those who are trying to survive there.

1st Objection: Now some people argue that indigenous peoples of the rain forests need to cut down areas so that they can farm in order to earn money to escape poverty.

Rebuttal: But these people can earn money by harvesting things in the rain forest, such as nuts for Ben and Jerry's Rain Forest Crunch. When they have an alternative way to earn money, they will not need to resort to slash and burn techniques to grow crops.

2nd Objection: Some may say that the cost of saving the tropical rain forests is too high, and that we simply can't afford to be concerned.

Rebuttal: But how can we afford not to do something to stop the destruction? We could simply spend a little less money on defense and a little more money on the environment.

3rd Objection: Others point out that it takes a lot of time and effort to get involved in helping the organizations that work to save the tropical rain forests.

Rebuttal: But we feel that it is a worthwhile cause, and it really doesn't take much time to write a check to support agencies like World Wildlife Fund, Greenpeace, and The Nature Conservancy. It would be worth the time for students to organize fundraising events to buy an acre of rain forest for future preservation.

4th Objection: Finally, some may argue that as the population increases in these countries, more rain forest land is needed for housing and urban development.

Rebuttal: However, family planning to decrease the numbers of offspring in these nations could help to solve this problem.

Claim Reaffirmed: As we stated before, the rain forest is a unique and precious biome that needs to be preserved.

Clincher: Fade in music and all say: "The rain forests, the tropical rain forests. Help stop the destruction!"

Author Index

Abarbanel, S., 59
Akers, J., 55
Albrecht, K., 28
Anderson, E., 173
Arnold, J., 143
Arth, A., 143
Ashworth, S., 45
Association for Supervision and Curriculum Development, 3
Atwell, N., 181

Beamon, G., 50, 51
Bechtol, W., 7, 15, 16, 19, 20, 26, 28, 31, 33, 34, 35, 40, 43, 45, 46, 47, 48, 227, 231, 238
Bell, T., 4
Bennett, B., 227, 228
Berliner, D., 216
Betts, F., 49
Beyer, B., 5, 19, 26, 30
Bierly, M., 216
Biondi, A., 149
Bitter, G., 5, 7, 9, 10
Bloom, B., 31, 146
Brandt, R., 14, 19, 228
Brock, W., 228
Bruno, A., 48
Buckmaster, L., 144, 157
Bush, G., 4
Butler, K., 45

Carpenter, T., 62
Charles, R., 2, 5, 6, 8
Clarke, J., 28
Clinton, B., 5
Collins, C., 217, 218
Costa, A., 5, 23, 191
Covey, S., 157
Crabbe, A., 149, 158, 159, 162
Curry, L., 47

David, J., 219

Davis, G., 23, 32
Daw, N., 253
Dewing, T., 228
Dodds-Stanford, B., 144
Dorman, G., 143
Dorricott, D., 48
Dorval, K., 23
Doyle, D., 49
Drake, S., 101
DuFour, R., 219, 222, 223
Dunn, K., 47
Dunn, R., 47, 48

Eastman, S., 32
Eberle, R., 25
Edmund, N., 48
Educators for Social Responsibility, 157
Edwards, N., 5, 7, 9, 10
Engelsgjerd, J., 15, 19

Fennema, E., 62
Francis, M., 15, 19
Frayer, D., 18
Frederick, W., 18

Gallimore, R., 226
Gardiner, B., 48
Garger, S., 47
Garmston, R., 228
Glickman, C., 227
Goldenberg, C., 226
Golub, L., 18
Gordon, W., 148
Guild, P., 47
Guilford, J., 40
Guskey, T., 226

Hamann, L., 270, 271
Hamel, F., 173
Hancock, V., 49
Haney, R., 16, 17, 20, 34

Hanson, J., 228
Harris, C., 17
Harris, M., 17
Hatfield, M., 5, 7, 9, 10
Hiatt, D., 3
Hirsh, S., 226
Hollingsworth, H., 32
Hughes, S., 19
Hunt, D., 47

Isaksen, S., 23, 24

Jacobs, H., 101
Johnston, H., 143
Jones, B., 19
Joyce, B., 47, 216, 217, 218, 227, 228, 229, 231

Kaiser, J., 259, 260, 261, 262, 265, 267, 268
Keefe, J., 47
Killian, J., 218, 232
Kirst, M., 216
Klein, R., 23
Krulik, S., 5, 9

Lambert, L., 218
Leadbeater, P., 220
Lester, F., 2, 5, 6, 8
Lewis, A., 143
Lindquist, M., 5, 7, 28
Lipman, M., 26
Lipsitz, J., 143
Lounsbury, J., 143
Lyman, F., 50

McCumsey, J., 153, 154, 155
McQuarrie, F., 218, 232
McTighe, J., 50
Maker, C., 7, 14, 41
Mangieri, J., 217, 218
Marzano, R., 19, 41, 52, 228

Maynard, G., 143
Mecklenburger, J., 49
Menasha Joint School District, 144
Miller, M., 15, 19
Moebius, M., 173
Monteagudo, L., 245
Mosston, M., 45
Myers, R., 146
Myers, S., 41

Nardi, A., 34
National Commission on Excellence in Education, 4
National Council of Teachers of English, 173
Nelson, N., 18
Nicol, C., 5, 53
Niles, J., 229
Noller, R., 149

Orlich, D., 218, 224, 231
O'Neil, J., 3, 4
Osborn, A., 147

Parnes, S., 149
Pearson, C., 145
Peck, K., 48
Perkins, D., 2, 195
Peterson, P., 62
Petroski, H., 144
Ponder, G., 226

Presseisen, B., 19

Raney, R., 229, 230
Rankin, S., 19
Reich, R., 2, 216
Renzulli, J., 16
Reys, R., 5, 7, 28
Rimm, S., 32
Robbins, P., 229, 230
Rudnick, J., 5, 9

Sabatini, J., 259, 260, 261, 262, 265, 267, 268
Schiever, S., 6, 7
Schnitzer, S., 53
Schultz, L., 270, 271
Schuster, N., 15, 19, 254
Shewach, D., 159
Showers, B., 227, 228, 229
Silver, H., 228
Sorenson, J., 7, 15, 16, 17, 18, 19, 20, 26, 28, 31, 32, 33, 34, 35, 40, 41, 42, 43, 45, 46, 47, 48, 220, 227, 231, 238
Sparks, D., 230
Sprague, M., 40, 41
Stager, R., 34
Stanford, G., 144, 157
Stanish, B., 157
Sternberg, R., 23, 30
Strong, R., 228

Suhor, C., 19
Suydam, M., 5, 7, 28
Szetela, W., 5, 53

Task Force on Education of Young Adolescents, 143
Taylor, A., 44
Thompson, S., 218, 232
Toepfer, C., 143
Torrance, E. P., 23, 146, 149
Treffinger, D., 23, 34, 146, 147, 148, 161

Vavrus, L., 80, 81
Verner, P., 143
Voelker, A., 18

Wales, C., 34
Wayne County, Michigan, Regional Education Service Agency, 232
Wiggins, G., 52
Wildman, T., 229
Willis, S., 3, 40, 52, 102
Wisconsin Department of Public Instruction, 20
Wolfe, P., 228
Wood, F., 218, 220, 232
Wood, S., 220
Wooten, P., 7
Worsham, A., 51

Subject Index

A Nation at Risk, 4, 5

Bloom's cognitive levels, 31–32 *(see also* Process)

Content, 14–19
  concepts, 16–19
    analyzing, 17, 19
    forming, 16–17
    teaching, 17–19
  definition, 14–15
  facts, 16, 17
  organizing, 16
  principles, 16, 17
  relationships among components, 17
  selecting, 15–16
  theories, 16, 17
Convergent thinking, 23 *(see also* Creative thinking; Problem solving*)*
Creative thinking, 23–26, 249–250 *(see also* Process*)*
  convergent thinking, 23
  dictionary of 80 activities for, 249–250
  divergent thinking, 23
  processes, 23–26
  Scamper technique, 25–26, 147
Critical thinking, 26–28, 240–241 *(see also* Process*)*
  skills, 26–28
  staff development agenda for, 240–241
Curriculum, 13–50 *(see also* Content; Environment; Intermediate-level learning; Middle-level learning; Model programs; Primary-level learning; Process; Product*)*
  content, 14–19

definitions, dimensions, relationships, 14–15
elements of, 13–14
environment, 43–50
process, 19–39
product, 39–43

Dictionary of 80 ideas for student products, 249–250
Divergent thinking, 23 *(see also* Creative thinking; Problem solving)

Eastern Middle School, Montgomery County, Maryland, 202–209
  assessment of the program, 205
  interdisciplinary arts-based unit, 203–204
  mission statement for, 202
  results of the program, 208–209
  staff development, 207–208
    site-based format, 207–208
    staff involvement, 207
  team organization, 203–204
    ARTS Team, 203–204
    Collaborative Opportunities in Modern Technology and Effective Communication (COM-TEC) Team, 203
    Magnet Team for gifted and talented students, 203
  technology, 203–207
    access to by students and staff, 206–207
    advantages for students and staff, 204–205
    facilitates staff teaming and creativity, 203–205
    facilitates student learning, 206
    foundations for the program, 205–206

    loved by students, 206
    supports, motivates and enhances learning, 205–207
Educational change, 3–5
  A Nation at Risk, 4–5
  Goals 2000 Educate America Act, 3, 4
  influences on, 3–5
  national goals for, 4
  reforms for, 5
Enrichment opportunities, 254–258
  community, 254
  references for information on, 255–258
  school, 255
  summer academic experiences, 255
Environment, 43–50 *(see also* Learning styles; Teaching styles; Technology)
  definitions, 4
  human resources, 44–45
  learning styles for students, 47–48
  physical sites, 43–44
  student characteristics, 48
  teaching styles, 45–45
  technology, 48–50

Future Problem Solving Program (FPS), 149–161 *(see also* Middle-level learning)

Goals 2000 Educate America Act, 3, 4
Gulf Gate Elementary School, Sarasota County, Florida, 182–189
  actions plans (units of instruction) for students, 187–189
  class newspaper for first graders, 188–189
  class store for third graders, 187–189

(Cont.)

278 Subject Index

Gulf Gate Elementary School *(Cont.)*
  ideas and titles for grades, K–5, 189
  communicating with parents and community, 185–187
  information about thinking and problem solving, 185–186
  infusion strategies, 186
  teacher behaviors for, 186–187
  setting goals and getting started, 183–185
    needs assessment, 184
    strategies to guide the program, 184–185
    vision statement, 183–184
  staff development for change, 185

Inquiry processes, 20–23 *(see also* Problem solving; Process)
  activities relating to, 20–23
  hierarchical arrangement of, 20
Inservice *(see* Staff development)
Interdisciplinary learning, 84–100, 101–120, 136–140, 161–167, 187–189, 192–194, 204–205, 210–213 *(see also* Intermediate-level learning; Middle-level learning; Model Programs; Primary-level learning; Staff development; Units of instruction)
  integrates with technology, 204–205
  planning for, 102–106
  students relate to, 101–102
  units of instruction for, 84–100, 106–120, 136–140, 161–167, 187–189, 192–194, 210–213, 259–262
    business and investments (intermediate), 192–193
    cities of the world (primary), 193–194
    class newspaper (primary), 188–189
    class store (primary), 187–188
    consumers and producers (intermediate), 210–212
    dinosaurs (primary), 84–100
    historical homes (intermediate), 106–112
    inventions (intermediate), 212–213
    making a more creative sandwich (middle), 161–164
    mysteries (intermediate), 136–140

    trip to the zoo (intermediate), 112–120
    U.S. trip plan (middle), 164–167, 259–262
Intermediate-level learning, 36–37, 101–141, 192–193, 210–213 *(see also* Model programs; Units of instruction)
  communicating with people, 120–136
    advertising techniques, 121–128
    writing 11 kinds of letters, 128–136
  elements of successful teaching, 102–106
    activities for students, 103
    assessment, 106
    environments, 104
    grouping, 105
    objectives, 102–103
    products, 103
    resources, 103
    thinking skills and problem solving, 104
    timeline and budget, 106
    unit overview, 102–103
  interdisciplinary focus, 101–102
  mysteries: a detailed unit of instruction, 136–140
    assessment, 140
    investigating, more than 80 activities and ideas, 138–140
    setting the stage for teaching, 136–138
  reaching beyond the classroom, 106–120
    historical homes, 106–112
    trip to the zoo, 112–120
  units of instruction, 36–37, 106–140, 192–193, 210–213
    advertising techniques, 121–128
    business and investments, 192–193
    consumers and producers, 210–212
    egg or water balloon in a bottle, 36–37
    historical homes, 106–112
    inventions, 212–213
    mysteries, 136–140
    trip to the zoo, 112–120
    writing 11 kinds of letters, 128–136

Learning *(see* Content; Curriculum; Environment; Intermediate-level learning; Middle-level

learning; Primary-level learning; Process; Product)
Learning styles, 47–48 *(see also* Environment)
  definitions, 47
  matching with teaching styles, 47–48
  overview of, 47
  research and programs, 47
Lincoln Elementary School, Elmhurst, Illinois, 189–195
  communicating with parents and community, 191–192
  current thoughts on education, 192
  information about thinking, 191
  parents as learning partners, 192
  research on thinking, 191
  curriculum changes, 189–190
  goals for the program, 189
  interdisciplinary units of instruction, 192–194
    business and investments for fifth graders, 192–193
    cities of the world for third graders, 193–194
  maintaining the program, 194–195
  staff development, 190–191
    getting started, 190
    stating the mission, 190
    thinking guidelines for, 190–191

Merwin Elementary School, West Clermont County, Ohio, 209–215
  inventions, an upper intermediate-level unit, 212–213
    evaluating final products, 213
    exploring inventions, 212–213
    impact on students and staff, 213
    selecting and producing inventions, 213
  parents and community involvement, 215
  producers and consumers, a school-wide project, 210–212
    consumers, 211
    investing, 211
    manufacturing, 210
    marketing, 210–211
    results, 211–212
  projects, 213–215
    cleaning up the urban environment, 213–214
    outdoor camping, 214
    school store, 214–215

Subject Index 279

Middle-level learning, 37–39, 142–181, 203–204, 259–273
(*see also* Interdisciplinary learning; Model programs; Units of instruction)
  characteristics of adolescent learners, 142–143
  creative techniques that work, 146–149
    attribute listing, 147–148
    brainstorming, 147
    checkerboarding, 148
    forced relationships, 148
    idea checklists, 147
    open-ended thoughts and feelings, 147
    synectics, 148–149
    warm-ups, 146–147
  environments for, 145–146
  Future Problem Solving Program (FPS), 149–161
    additional components, 158–160
    benefits of the program, 153
    evaluation methods, 160–161
    options for implementation, 158
    overview of, 149
    six-step process, 149–153
    techniques for enhancing, 153–156
    teambuilding and teamwork, 156–157
  interdisciplinary units of instruction, 161–167, 259–262
    making a more creative sandwich, 161–164
    U.S. trip plan, 164–167, 259–262
  learning and teaching styles, 163–164
  positive argumentation, an unusual unit of instruction, 173–180, 270–273
    analyzing the argument, 177
    argumentation format, 174–175
    evaluating the arguments, 180
    examples of arguments, 272–273
    exploring the issues, 177
    getting started using a sample argument, 175–177
    guide form and worksheet, 270–271
    introduction to, 173–174
    planning the arguments, 177–179
    presenting the arguments, 179–180
  rationale for, 142–143
  social studies units of instruction, 167–173, 263–269
  teacher attitudes and behaviors for, 144–145
  units of instruction, 37–39, 161–180, 203–204, 259–273
    arts-based/technology units, 203–204
    creating a country (social studies), 170–173, 269
    making a more creative sandwich (interdisciplinary), 161–164
    positive argumentation (language arts), 173–180, 270–273
    survival of the fittest (social studies), 167–170, 263–268
    too much trash, 37–39
    U.S. trip plan (interdisciplinary), 164–167, 259–262
Model programs (*see* Eastern Middle School; Gulf Gate Elementary School; Lincoln Elementary School; Merwin Elementary School; San Marcos Independent School District)
Models, 14, 17, 19, 33, 232–234 (*see also* Problem solving; RPTIM model)
  multi-step problem solving, 33
  relationships among content components, 17
  relationships among curriculum elements, 14
  RPTIM, 232–234
  steps in concept analysis, 19

Parents and community, 185–187, 191–192, 209, 215, 225 (*see also* Model programs; Staff development)
Peer coaching, 228–230
  agenda for training coaches, 230
  characteristics of successful coaches, 229
  research support for, 229–230
  starting a program for, 229
  teachers attitudes toward, 228–229
Primary-level learning, 57–100, 187–189, 193–194, 197–201
(*see also* Model programs)
  assessment methods, 79–84
    paper-and-pencil tests, 81–82
    peer teaching, 80
    performance tests, 82–83
    projects, 83–84
    student journals, 79–80
    student portfolios, 80–81
    teacher observation, 79
  characteristics of a problem-solving classroom, 57–60
  dinosaurs: an interdisciplinary unit of instruction, 84–100
    a classroom dig, 90–91
    background for, 84–86
    debate activities, 97–98
    extension activities, 99–100
    extinction theories, 95–96
    introduction to, 86–88
    learning stations for, 91–94
    meanings of dinosaur names, 94–95
    researching, 88–90
    working in a dinosaur museum, 98–99
  planning for problem solving, 62–70
    building a new unit (math), 65–68
    revising a successful unit (science), 62–65
    using party planning as a learning opportunity, 68–70
  rationale for, 58
  strategies for success, 59–60
    help students enjoy success, 60
    let students know it is OK to feel anxious, 59
    make problem solving a student-teacher effort, 60
    model metacognition for students, 60
    spend enough time on problems, 59
  units of instruction, 62–79, 84–100, 187–189, 193–194, 197–201
    blowing bubbles, 76–79
    building a new math unit, 65–68
    cities of the world, 193–194
    class newspaper, 188–189
    class store, 187–188
    creative process lessons, 197–201
    dinosaurs, 84–100
    experimenting, 75–76
    grouping things together, 72–75
    inference and deduction, 71–72
    party planning, 68–70
    revising a science unit, 62–65
  ways to integrate problem solving into the classroom, 60–62
    consider student learning styles, 60–61
    group students in many ways, 61
    master basic content, 61–62
    organize curriculum for interdisciplinary teaching, 61

Principal's roles and responsibilities, 222–224 (*see also* Model programs; Staff development)
  as leader, 222
  as "link" between staff development and clinical supervision, 223–224
  as promoter of effective staff development practices, 223
  as promoter of social climate and culture, 222–223
Problems, 5–7 (*see also* Problem solving; Process)
  definitions, 5
  types of, 6–7
    knowns and unknowns as a base, 6–7
    operations as a base, 6
    other bases, 7
Problem solving, 1–11, 28–30, 32–39, 50–55, 240–243, 251–258 (*see also* Process; Thinking skills)
  assessment strategies for, 50–53
    alternative, 52–53
    teacher questions and responses, 50–51
    traditional, 51–52
  characteristics of successful solvers, 9–10
  definitions, 5–6
  enrichment opportunities for, 253–258
  guidelines for, 9–10, 32–34
  influences on, 3–5, 7
  multistep, 32–39, 241–243
    background for, 32–34
    examples of, 34–39
    model for, 33
    staff development agendas for, 241–243
    student worksheet for, 35
  need for, 1–3
  overview of, 10–11
  recommendations for teaching, 3
  resources for teaching, 53–55, 251–252
    kinds of, 53–55
    sources of, 55, 251–252
  single-step techniques for, 28–30
  stumbling blocks to, 8–9
  teaching strategies for, 10, 50–51
  thinking skills for, 19–32
Process, 19–39 (*see also* Problem Solving; Thinking Skills)
  Bloom's cognitive levels, 31–32
    activities related to, 32
    definitions and examples, 31–32

creative thinking processes, 23–26, 249–250
  activities to illustrate, 25
  definitions, 23
  dictionary of 80 student activities for, 249–250
  elaboration, 24–25
  flexibility, 24
  fluency, 23–24
  originality, 25
critical thinking skills, 26–28
  analyzing arguments, 27
  comparing and contrasting, 26
  distinguishing between fact and opinion, 26
  distinguishing between relevant and irrelevant information, 27
  distinguishing between reliable and unreliable sources, 27
  identifying bias and stereotype, 27
  identifying cause and effect, 27
  identifying induction and deduction, 27–28
  recognizing assumptions and generalizations, 27
  recognizing consistent and inconsistent reasoning, 27
  recognizing point of view, 27
  sequencing and prioritizing, 27
inquiry processes, 20–23
  classifying, 21
  communicating, 21–22
  experimenting, 22
  formulating models, 22–23
  formulating questions and hypotheses, 22
  inferring, 21
  interpreting data, 22
  making operational definitions, 22
  measuring, 21
  observing, 20–21
  predicting, 21
multistep problem solving, 5–6, 32–39, 234–244, 241–243, 251–252
  definitions of, 5–6
  guidelines for, 32–34
  model for, 33
  problems to illustrate uses of the model, 34–39
  resources for, 251–252
  staff development agendas for, 241–243
  strategies to infuse it into the curriculum, 234–244

student worksheet for, 35
single-step problem solving techniques, 28–30
  acting it out, 30
  forming analogies, 30
  guessing and testing, 29–30
  making a drawing or figure, 30
  making a model, 30
  making a table or graph, 30
  organizing lists, 29
  recognizing patterns, 29
  simplifying and reducing, 28–29
  working backward, 28
Products, 39–43
  audiences for, 42
  definitions, 39
  dictionary of 80 creative ideas for, 249–250
  enrichment activities related to, 254–258
  evaluation of, 42–43
  rationale for, 40
  real problems for, 40–42
    competitions, 42
    meaningful knowledge, 41–42
    general categories, 42
    "W" questions, 41

San Marcos, Texas, Independent School District, 195–202
  elements of the program, 196
  first-grade level instruction, 197–200
    Curious George, a skill-oriented lesson, 198–200
    facilitator tasks, 197–198
  foundations of the program, 196–197
    creative process skills, 196–197
    lesson components, 197
  kindergarten-level instruction, 197
  results of the program, 202
  second-grade level instruction, 198, 200–201
    applying the skills, 198, 200
    Marshmallow Olympics, a problem-solving lesson, 200–201
Scamper technique, 25–26, 147
Single-step problem solving techniques, 28–30 (*see also* Process)
Staff development, 216–246 (*see also* Model programs; Peer coaching; Principal's roles and responsibilities; RPTIM model; Teacher's roles and responsibilities)

characteristics of successful
        programs, 220
    programs and models, 230–234
        relating teacher needs to, 230–231
        RPTIM model, 232–234
        sequence for, 231
        typical models of, 231–232
    rationale for, 216–220
    resources for, 244–245
    roles in, 220–226
        administrators and policy
            makers, 224
        college and university personnel,
            225
        parents, 225
        principals, 222–224
        school support staff, 226
        service and community groups,
            225
        students, 224–225
        teachers, 221
    RPTIM model, 232–234
        implementation, 233–234
        maintenance, 234
        planning, 233
        readiness, 232–233
        training, 233
    sample program to infuse thinking
        and problem solving into the
        curriculum, 234–244
        advisory committee for, 235–236
        agendas for, 238–243
        goals for, 235
        implementing the program, 243
        maintaining the program, 243–244
        planning the program, 235–236
        selecting trainers and training
            sites, 237–238
        timelines and topics for training
            sessions, 236–237
        training the staff, 236–243
    stages of concern, 223
    structures and strategies, 226–230
        frameworks and delivery
            systems for, 226–227
        peer coaching, 228–230
        research base for, 227–228
        teaching and learning, 228
    stumbling blocks to, 217–218
    teacher's needs as learners,
        219–220
    ways to improve, 218–219

Teacher's roles and responsibilities,
    221, 230–231 (*see also* Staff
    development)
    as adult learner, 221, 230–231
    as decision maker, 221
    as instructional leader, 221
    as teacher of children, 221
    development levels of, 221
    professional growth stages of, 231
Teaching styles, 45–46, 47–48 (*see
    also* Environment)
    assessment of, 46
    definition, 46
    kinds of, 45–46
    matching with student learning
        styles, 47–48
    relationship to learning variables,
        46
Team building skills, 238–240 (*see
    also* Staff development)
    arriving at agreement (We Agree),
        240
    getting acquainted, 239
    helping each other, 239
    identifying strengths, 239
Technology, 48–50, 204–207 (*see
    also* Eastern Middle School;
    Environment)
    advanced, 49
    advantages for students and staff,
        204–207
    commonly available, 48–49
    definition, 48
    integrated with the school curriculum,
        204–205
    reasons for use in schools, 48
    reluctance to use in schools, 49–50
Thinking skills, 19–32 (*see also*
    Process)
    Bloom's cognitive levels, 31–32
    creative thinking, 23–26
    critical thinking, 26–28
    inquiry processes, 20–23
    listing of, 15
    relationships among, 19–20
    single-step problem-solving
        techniques, 28–30

Units of instruction, 36–39, 62–79,
    84–100, 106–140, 161–180,
    187–189, 192–194, 197–201,
    203–204, 210–213, 259–273
    (*see also* Intermediate-level
    learning; Interdisciplinary
    learning; Middle-level
    learning; Model programs;
    Primary-level learning;
    Problem Solving)
    intermediate-level, 36–37, 106–140,
        192–193, 210–213

    *And, now a word from your
        sponsor* (advertising),
        121–128
    Business and investments,
        192–193
    Egg or water balloon in a bottle
        (science), 36–37
    *Experiences as producers and
        consumers*, 210–212
    Invention convention, 212–213
    *It's a jungle out there: A trip to
        the zoo*, 112–120
    It's a mystery to me (mysteries),
        136–140
    Sincerely yours (writing 11 kinds
        of letters), 128–136
    There's no place like home
        (historical homes), 106–112
    middle-level, 37–39, 161–180,
        203–204, 259–273
        arts-based/technology units,
            203–204
        Creating a country, 170–173,
            269
        Jam and peas on rye . . . (creative sandwiches), 161–164
        Survival of the fittest, 167–170,
            263–268
        The power of positive argumentation, 173–180, 270–273
        Too much trash, 37–39
        U.S. trip plan, 164–167, 259–262
    primary-level, 62–79, 84–100,
        187–189, 193–194, 197–201
        *Blowing bubbles: Beyond fun and
            games*, 76–79
        building a new math unit, 65–68
        Class newspaper for first graders,
            188–189
        Class store for third graders,
            187–188
        Creative process lessons K–2,
            197–201
        Discovering cities of the world,
            193–194
        *Discovering dinosaurs; An
            interdisciplinary unit*, 84–100
        *Focusing on inference and
            deduction*, 71–72
        Grouping things together, 72–75
        Learning how to experiment,
            75–76
        Party planning, 68–70
        revising a successful science unit,
            62–65